What people are saying about The Innovation Race

'an inspirational and unconventional look at innovation'
'easy to read, accurate, provocative and entertaining'
'a fresh insightful tool ... you will be educated and entertained by compelling stories'
'thoughtful and engaging'
'essential for the human race'
'every executive should own a copy of this book'

Every company in the world is now struggling to define themselves for a future they have yet to imagine. They all know they have to innovate to survive; the best appreciate that innovation is what gives their businesses relevance and drive. But few know how to get there from here. Culture, of course, is key, but what kind of culture? That's what this book sets out to explore and define. No question in business today is more urgent. So read this book before it's too late.

—**Margaret Heffernan**, author of bestsellers
Willful Blindness and *Beyond Measure*, BBC TV producer,
CEO & entrepreneur, *Huffington Post* blogger

The Grants have done it again with another inspirational and unconventional look at innovation. Not a re-hash of worn-out stories about the companies that we all believe are 'innovative' but a fresh look at innovation. This book will turn your idea of innovation and competition upside down and on its head. Be prepared for a great ride!

—**Dr Roger Firestien**, Senior Faculty,
International Center for Studies in Creativity—
State University of New York Buffalo and
author of *Leading on the Creative Edge* and
Why Didn't I Think of That!

The Grants have nailed it! This book is not only easy to read, accurate, provocative and entertaining but most importantly about people. Creativity—and especially innovation—are only sustainable and authentic with the right mindsets and outlook. Andrew and Gaia have authored a definitive guide to ensure that any reader takes action.

—**Richard Gerver**, UK Business Speaker of the Year,
broadcaster, and author of bestseller *Change: Learn to Love It,
Learn to Lead It* and *Simplicity: An Uncomplicated Guide to Success*

This excellent new book on transformative innovation brings together the Grants' long time focus on creativity and their extensive experience in working with global teams and organisations. Easy to read, with many diverse and insightful reflections and anecdotes that reinforce the 'why' and the 'how to' in developing purposeful innovation. Highly recommended.

—**Subhas DeGamia**, Former CEO India and Executive Director International Banking, ANZ

This book is a must read for whoever has wondered what 'innovation' really means, and what organisations can do about it.

—**Dr Eric Knight**, Sydney University Business School Faculty innovation specialist and author of *Reframe: How to solve the world's trickiest problems* and *Why we argue about climate change?*

The Grants have provided a fresh and insightful tool that not only explains innovation in a unique way but also helps the reader understand how to apply this to gain competitive advantage in today's business world. You will be educated and entertained by compelling stories about organisations that both failed and succeeded to understand the importance of innovation in their market. Every executive should own a copy of this book!

—**Sam Lasseter-Moore**, Sales Director New Zealand, Salesforce.com

The Innovation Race vividly describes the growing importance of innovation to economic performance, and more importantly, provides a comprehensive guide to how to foster innovation in any organization. This thoughtful and engaging book needs to be read by every leader committed to making their organization, and the world, better through creative action.

—**Dr William Wurtz**, Chairman and Managing Partner at Wurtz and Company, Past President American Creativity Association

This wonderful book is brought to life through the same latest thinking, in-depth research and tactics on innovation that Andrew and Gaia apply to everything they do. They wrap the book in the metaphor of flying around the world, examining the differences in innovation and leveraging the comparisons to explain key lessons. Too many people use the word 'innovation' too loosely, but not after you have read this book.

—**Robin Speculand**, CEO of Bridges Business Consultancy Int and author of *Beyond Strategy: The Leader's Role in Successful Implementation* and *Bricks to Bridges: Make Your Strategy Come Alive*

It is difficult to condense my view into a few sentences that will do justice to this book, but, I will try. Many people talk about the importance of innovation, the causes of no longer having it, where we lost it and the imperative of regaining it in order to be successful in today's business world. This book gives us important and clear information on how to actually do it including understanding the barriers that will get in the way. An excellent tool.

—**Mike Braggins**, Regional Manager Marketing Communications and Learning Asia Pacific, FujiXerox

The Innovation Race is essential for the Human Race. It provides guidelines for improving an organisation's ability to translate novel ideas into new products and services. This is done with a human-centered approach that applies what is known about personal development and growth toward developing a culture of innovation. Whether at the scale of a family, a company, a country, or the whole world, the insights provided in *The Innovation Race* provide a roadmap to sustainable growth.

—**Gino Yu**, Associate Professor School of Design, Hong Kong Polytechnic University

The world over, nations are caught-up in 'the innovation race'. All need help and help that is grounded in reality and experience. This book locates practical help within sound principles, offering numerous examples of both success and failure. The authors put the case squarely and robustly. This is a must-read.

—**Dr Kirpal Singh**, Professor at Singapore Management University and author of *Thinking Hats and Coloured Turbans: Creativity Across Cultures*

The Grants are masterful story tellers and have compiled a rich and diverse set of tools, explained through colourful examples, to stimulate those looking to develop sustainable innovation methods.

—**Derek Laney**, Head of Product Marketing Asia Pacific, Salesforce.com

An engrossing journey that gathers insights from the fields of economics, anthropology, ethics and psychology. It also examines when we shouldn't innovate and challenges us to ask what innovation is for.

—**Peter Martin**, Economics Editor, *The Age*

THE INNOVATION RACE

Compliments of

CHIEF EXECUTIVES
—— GUILD ——

Sanctuary   *Mastery*   *Legacy*

www.CEOGuild.org

Lovely to meet you Sydney!
All the best with
your innovation
journey!
Gaia.

First published in 2016 by John Wiley & Sons Australia, Ltd
42 McDougall St, Milton Qld 4064
Office also in Melbourne

Typeset in 11/13 pt Bembo Std

© Tirian Pty Ltd 2016

The moral rights of the authors have been asserted

National Library of Australia Cataloguing-in-Publication data:

Creator:	Grant, Gaia, author.
Title:	The innovation race : how to change a culture to change the game/Gaia Grant, Andrew Grant.
ISBN:	9780730328995 (pbk)
	9780730329015 (ebook)
Notes:	Includes index.
Subjects:	Technological innovations.
	Organizational change.
	Creative ability in business.
	Creative thinking.
	Critical thinking.
	Employee motivation.
	Success in business.
Other Creators/	
Contributors:	Grant, Andrew, author.
Dewey Number:	658.406

Cover design by Wiley
Cover image © iDesign/Shutterstock
Part and chapter opener plane image: © Butterfly Hunter/Shutterstock

Printed in Singapore by C.O.S. Printers Pte Ltd

10 9 8 7 6 5 4 3 2 1

Disclaimer

THE INNOVATION RACE

HOW TO *CHANGE* A CULTURE
TO *CHANGE* THE GAME

ANDREW GRANT | GAIA GRANT

WILEY

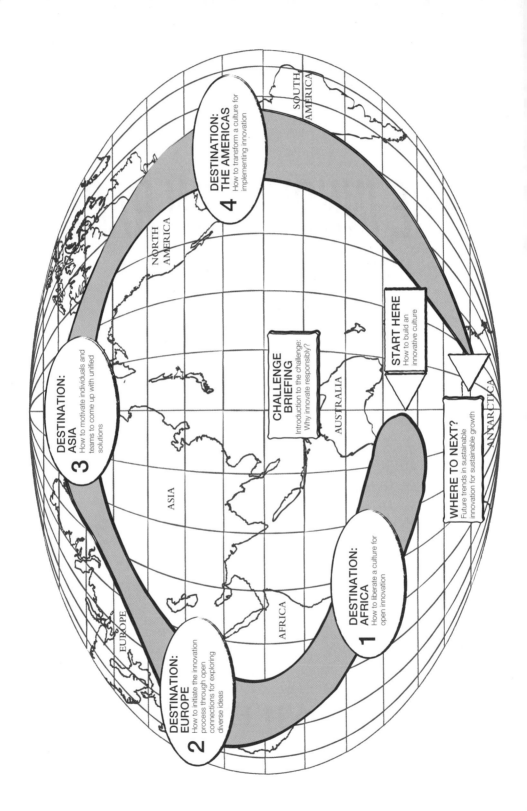

CHALLENGE BRIEFING
Introduction to the challenge: Why innovate responsibly?

START HERE
How to build an innovative culture

WHERE TO NEXT?
Future trends in sustainable innovation for sustainable growth

DESTINATION: AFRICA
1 How to liberate a culture for open innovation

DESTINATION: EUROPE
2 How to initiate the innovation process through open connections for exploring diverse ideas

DESTINATION: ASIA
3 How to motivate individuals and teams to come up with unified solutions

DESTINATION: THE AMERICAS
4 How to transform a culture for implementing innovation

NORTH AMERICA

SOUTH AMERICA

ASIA

EUROPE

AFRICA

AUSTRALIA

ANTARCTICA

CONTENTS AT A GLANCE

CONTENTS

Chapter 6: Initiate 139

How to initiate the innovation process through open
connections for exploring diverse ideas

Destination: Europe (Paradox Challenge: Focus vs Openness)

Chapter 7: Motivate 183

How to motivate individuals and teams to come up
with unified solutions

Destination: Asia (Paradox Challenge: Individualism vs Group Engagement)

Chapter 8: Transform 223

How to transform a culture for implementing innovation

Destination: The Americas (Paradox Challenge: Stability vs Flexibility)

ABOUT THE AUTHORS

Andrew and Gaia Grant are best-selling international authors and the founders and Directors of Tirian International Consultancy. They are a dynamic husband and wife team who have worked together for more than thirty years, initially working in the field of education and working for not-for-profit organisations, before moving on to include corporate work to top Fortune 500 companies for the last twenty years. Andrew and Gaia now focus on bringing organisational culture transformation in a wide variety of contexts—from indigenous communities through to corporate CEOs—to support authentic innovation and growth in all sectors and at all levels.

In the corporate sector Andrew and Gaia have worked with market leaders to assist with creating a sustainable innovation culture for purpose-driven innovation in a variety of regions around the world, including Allianz, Barclays, Citibank, Colgate Palmolive, Disney, Dyson, Estee Lauder, FedEx, Four Seasons Hotels and Resorts, Fuji Xerox, Johnson & Johnson, Mercedes Benz, Nestle, PwC, UBS, Salesforce, Singtel, and Visa.

Their work with not-for-profit development organisations has included assisting with creating a health curriculum designed to reach over 25 million people in India and worldwide (HEPI), drug education for tribal groups in the north Indian tribal area of Nagaland and on the Thai Burmese border (BWA), development in an orphanage in El Salvador (BWA), health education in Sumba Indonesia (Sumba Foundation), and teaching transformational education techniques in the Philippines (The Central Philippines University). They also work with Amnesty International, and with Chilout in advocating to get children out of immigration detention centres.

Andrew and Gaia travelled extensively and worked from a base in Asia for almost fifteen years, and their business continues to operate globally. Currently based in Sydney, Gaia oversees Tirian's international business and works with Sydney University (as a guest lecturer at the Business School, while completing research towards a PhD on creating an innovation culture for sustainability), while Andrew focuses on keynote presenting and executive facilitating. Gaia has previously completed an MSc in Creative Thinking and Grad Dip in Change Leadership (from the State University of New York Buffalo), along with BA Dip Ed and BD (hons), while Andrew has a Dip Tch, BEd.

The Grants have designed and produced more than thirty unique interactive licensed workshops, simulation games, keynotes and resources, including an investigative simulation game based on their first international bestselling book on the topic: *Who Killed Creativity?...And How Can We Get It Back?: 7 essential strategies for making yourself, your team and your organisation more innovative.* Gaia has also authored *A Patch of Paradise* (Random House, 2002) and *The Rhythm of Life* (Transworld, 1998).

Often requested as keynote presenters and facilitators for international conferences, Andrew and Gaia have delivered feature keynotes at a number of specialist events including TEDx (Hong Kong), World Presidents Organisation (YPO) Global Edge CEO Conference (Australia), The World Innovation Conference (France), HR Summit and WorkTech conferences  (Singapore), the Leadership Bootcamp (Middle East), and the American Creativity Association (USA).

In the media, Andrew and Gaia have featured in a number of different international publications, broadcasts including the Harvard Business Review, BBC, Reuters, ABC TV, Fast Company and the Wall St Journal.

For client endorsements and videos:
http://www.whokilledcreativity.com/authors/andrew-grant/
http://www.whokilledcreativity.com/authors/gaia-grant/
http://www.whokilledcreativity.com/endorsements/intro-endorsements/

For more information and resources including about the seminars, workshops, keynotes, articles, blogs, surveys, videos and downloadable tools contact us at info@tirian.com or visit:
Websites: www.the-innovation-race.com, www.whokilledcreativity.com, www.tirian.com
YouTube channel: www.youtube.com/channel/
UCUlq3aSEzDsHDLzkdiKoDMQ
Facebook: www.facebook.com/whokilledcreativity
Twitter: @andrewlgrant/@gaiagranttirian

ACKNOWLEDGEMENTS

We would like to express our heartfelt appreciation to all the people who have contributed in so many different ways to the process of putting this book together and getting it over the line. We have included a few details about these special people so you can appreciate the unique diversity of backgrounds and ideas that they bring with them that have contributed to the wealth of perspectives in the book.

Our wholehearted thanks, firstly, to the thought leaders who gave us their time to share their perspectives on innovation, including: Adam Bryant (*New York Times* editor and columnist (USA)), Wade Davis (*National Geographic* resident anthropologist (Canada)), Professor Patrick Dodson (Aboriginal Elder and Senator (Australia)), Christopher Norton (President Global Product and Operations at Four Seasons Hotels and Resorts (France)), Claudio Viggiani (Director of Social Responsibility at ABIHPEC (Brazil)), Scott Anthony (*Harvard Business Review* contributor), Sam Keen (*Psychology Today* editor and philosopher (USA)), Ram Raghavan (General Manager Latin America Innovation Centre at Colgate Palmolive (Mexico)), Margaret Heffernan (Chief Executive, TV Producer and entrepreneur (UK)).

Other fascinating people we have appreciated being able to interview to gain more depth into topics we have explored have included: Rick McPhee (TV Series Producer (Australia)), Mohammad Ali Baqiri (law student and former asylum seeker (Afghanistan)), Adrian Belic (Academy Award nominated and Sundance award winning filmmaker (USA)), David Tai (Founder and Chairman Cloud Valley Group and previous IBM Director (China)), Aya Dowidar (Executive Director at Scoreplus Human Resources Consultancy (Egypt)), Ananta Malhotra (Customer Satisfaction and Process Manager Schneider Electric (Malaysia)) and Vijay Kumar Singh (Commercial Manager IT Business Schneider Electric (Singapore)), Matt McFadyen, the late Peter Malcolm and Helen Jomoa (polar adventurers (Australia and the UK)), Jornina (Joy) Sebastian (Senior Vice President Shared Services Transcom (Philippines)), Faridodin (Fredi) Lajvardi (educator (USA)), Masoud Al-Maskary (Owner and CEO Ajyal HR Solutions & Services (Oman)), Edgardo O. Madrilejo (Chief Risk Officer Bank of the Philippine Islands (Philippines)), and Grant Henderson (air traffic controller (Australia)).

(Note that full interviews with some of these people and other thought leaders can be found at www.the-innovation-race.com).

Many thanks also to the extremely kind friends and associates who waded through the rough early draft versions of the text and helped to provide invaluable feedback, including: Jane Harvey (corporate creative arts specialist (USA)), Dr Lloyd Irwin (Tirian partner and executive leadership specialist (Australia)), Maegan Baker (entrepreneurship specialist (Canada)), Toni Hassan (specialist in journalism, international development and the arts (Australia)), Rumman Ahmad (entrepreneur and founder of KLIC conference (Sri Lanka)), Paulina Larocca (corporate innovation executive (Australia)), Celia Pillai (executive strategy consultant and creativity and innovation specialist (India)), Prue Robson (creativity and change management specialist (Australia)), Carol Fusek (corporate logistics specialist (Singapore), Kate Bettes (arts student (England)), Liz Yeo (community organization CEO (Australia)), and Paul McKey (innovation consultant (Australia)).

A note of sincere appreciation too to those who read the final manuscript and provided us with their enthusiastic feedback for the endorsements, to: Peter Martin (Economics Editor, *The Age* (Australia)) Dr Roger Firestien (State University of New York Buffalo (USA)), Richard Gerver (award winning speaker and broadcaster (UK)), Subhas DeGamia (Former CEO India and Executive Director International Banking ANZ), Dr Eric Knight (Sydney University Business School Senior Faculty innovation specialist (Australia)), Sam Lasseter-Moore (Sales Director New Zealand Salesforce. com (New Zealand)), Dr William Wurtz (Past President American Creativity Association (USA)), Robin Speculand (CEO Bridges Business Consultancy Int (Singapore)), Mike Braggins (Corporate Executive FujiXerox AsiaPacific (Singapore)), Gino Yu, (Associate Professor School of Design Hong Kong Polytechnic University (Hong Kong)), and Dr Kirpal Singh (Professor at Singapore Management University (Singapore)), and Derek Laney (Head of Product Marketing Salesforce.com Asia Pacific (Australia)).

Of course producing a book requires a lot of strategic and practical guidance at the conceptual and publishing stages, so a big thank you to the great team at Wiley in Australia for their support through the lengthy process, particularly to: Senior Commissioning Editor Lucy Raymond for her always insightful guidance, to Project Editor Chris Shorten for his tolerant and astute direction, and to our incredibly perceptive and patient content editor Jem Bates.

Finally, as always, we also need to acknowledge the continued love and support of our two wonderful children Zoe and Kallen, who have had to put up with the intense process of mum and dad working together and co-authoring books together over so many years!

Preface

INTO THE SHARK TANK

We travel quite extensively, and when we meet new people we are almost always first asked: Where are you from? This question usually helps them make a quick assessment of who we are based on general cultural traits.

Until recently we always answered proudly that we are from Australia, but this response now commonly evokes a fearful reaction: 'Aargh! Sharks!' (As daily ocean swimmers we were never especially worried about sharks—until the recent media exposure.) Sometimes the people we meet also raise anxious questions about the deadly spiders, snakes and crocodiles that Australia has become infamous for.

Since *Crocodile Dundee* and Steve Irwin put Australia on the map with their dangerous animal wrestling antics, our country has become notorious for its 'deadly predators'. Perhaps it is no surprise that such venomous and sometimes fierce animals have survived in our harsh environment, yet we find it ironic that people are so afraid of creatures they are unlikely ever to encounter.

It's true that sharks can be savage, but in reality you are more likely to be hit by lightning (the odds are one in 3000) or injured by a falling toilet seat (one in 10 000) than killed by a shark (one in 3.7 million). There are also more shark attacks off American beaches than in Australian waters. Australia has little experience of war or terrorism on its home soil and is ranked in the top 10 safest and most peaceful countries to live in, yet it is commonly perceived as an unusually dangerous country to visit or live in. These *perceptions* of reality, mostly based on narrowly focused media stories and movies aiming to shock and entertain, can be so much more compelling than reality itself.

The feeling of terror that can be induced by the *idea* of a shark attack might help you understand the perceptions of the contemporary innovation environment. As one shark attack victim described his ordeal, 'It's the fear of being eaten alive, and having no control over it.'[i]

The emotionally charged shark theme was exploited by the reality TV show *Shark Tank*, a title with particular resonance in the Australian context. In this show budding entrepreneurs pitch their innovative new product to a panel of successful high-profile businesspeople: the sharks. The result is a suspenseful, gut-wrenching ride as the contestants struggle to survive the ferocious 'attack'. The ideas pitched range widely, from home delivery catering through portable washing machines to automated toilets. One we have seen was for a surfboard with a shark repellent device attached; perhaps it is only a matter of time before someone designs a toilet safety device to reduce toilet seat malfunction injuries! Contestants range from young mums to high-tech geeks. As they prepare to make their pitch, each contestant must walk down a long, dark corridor past an equally long fish tank containing — you guessed it — sharks.

When they present their idea to the panel, the camera switches between the varying expressions of the business gurus and their nail-biting victims. Following the pitch, each panellist delivers their personal, sometimes brutal judgement on the idea and declares whether they are prepared to invest in it. Years of commitment and perseverance can, in that moment, be either dramatically vindicated or utterly crushed. Finally the contestant is filmed walking back down that corridor of sharks to be interviewed for the last time. It is at that point that it is possible to consider the impact of the event from the contestant's perspective, to feel the competitive drive for innovation through one individual's personal experience.

Shark Tank adopts a much more aggressive approach than past 'inventors' shows, in which judges were generally polite and encouraging, but it may reflect more realistically just how ruthless the field has become. Today the business environment is harsh and competitive. It's do or die, the survival of the fittest, the cleverest idea, the best marketing approach, the biggest investment opportunity, finding that slight competitive edge in an already flooded market. Most readers will already be aware of the realities of entering a race like this, and of the sobering statistic that 90 per cent of startups fail.[ii] The drive to innovate seems to have become a mad cut-throat dash towards an apparently unachievable goal.

On our journeys we have asked a broad range of people what they think the popular phrase 'the innovation race' has come to mean: including psychologists and philosophers, anthropologists and academics, indigenous elders and business executives, poets and politicians, scientists and social workers. As we have listened to these varied opinions, we have realised that when you break it down, the three words in this phrase are all significant. First, 'the' can imply there is only one approach to innovation. Secondly, the concept of 'innovation' is itself often bandied around without a clear understanding of what it means. And lastly, there is the assumption that innovation is a 'race'. But is innovation always a 'race'? Does it need to be a race? We use this popular phrase 'the innovation race' to set up a discussion for how this concept has shaped contemporary views of innovation, but the ambiguities inherent in this expression soon become clear. It might be only as you progress through to the end of the book that you will realise how important it is to deal with the contradictions and challenges that this phrase evokes.

To be equipped to navigate the potentially perilous innovation race successfully, we believe it is necessary to change *perceptions* about innovation by challenging the common metaphor. Prolific author and *Harvard Business Review* contributor Scott Anthony has told us that he is concerned that the concept of the innovation race is too closely connected to the idea of the rat race, and the notion that we are moving faster but are still ultimately standing still in 'a race that can never be won.' Philosopher, professor, author and past *Psychology Today* editor Sam Keen has shared with us that he believes 'the weapons race and the nuclear race are symptoms of what can go wrong when we assume innovation is just about unbridled competitive rivalry.' When we asked *National Geographic* resident anthropologist and award winning author, photographer and filmmaker Wade Davis about his thoughts on the concept of 'the innovation race', he asked us to emphasise his beautiful and incredibly powerful words from *Wayfinders* that, 'Our economic models are projections and arrows when they should be circles. To define perpetual growth on a finite planet as the sole measure of economic well-being,' he has challenged, 'is to engage in a form of slow collective suicide.'

It will also be important to dive beneath the surface to look at the deeper factors involved — in particular the cultural change needed to create a climate that supports *sustainable* and *less-competitive* innovation. 'Innovation is more of a relay race than a marathon,' says corporate executive Claudio Viggiani, now Director of Social Responsibility at ABIHPEC in Brazil. 'The important thing is that a GROUP of contributors, one relaying on the others is able to hand-off the baton at the right moment so the ideas can "progress" smoothly until they become applicable realities. This concept encompasses collaboration work and common objectives.' *New York Times* science editor, columnist and author Adam Bryant shared with us his 'two cents worth' that, 'The companies that will win the innovation race will have the most effective cultures – a workplace where the shared ethos and strategies for teamwork are clear.' Sam Keen also went on to explain to us the deeper commitment he believes we need to make to get past the potentially destructive common competitive concepts, saying, 'The most creative innovations are not beating someone else or being number one, but learning what the world is asking of you and creating in that arena. We have to create from our values.'

In this book we will take you on a whirlwind global ride that will lift you out of your comfort zone and the 'viewer's armchair', and will help you to start looking for these deeper values and seeing things from different perspectives.

We want to show that to survive in the current 'innovation race' a passive armchair position is actually not an option. We will also challenge you to think about the implications, and some useful practical applications, at each stage of the journey so you can become more engaged in the process that we are all, knowingly or unknowingly, a part of.

The innovation challenge

So what is the main conceptual premise of this book? We aim to explore the contemporary concept of 'the innovation race'—to find out who 'wins', who 'loses', who gets 'eliminated' by the standard rules of the game and why—while also challenging this metaphor to see if it provides the best basis for sustainable growth and development that benefits all. We will then explore some potential alternatives as we progress through the book.

Research has revealed that when organisations innovate there is typically a tension between the need for open discovery of new ideas for growth (*exploration)* and maintaining and developing existing systems for stability (*exploitation)*. This tension leads to a paradox that can either frustrate or fuel the innovation process, depending on how the potential conflict is dealt with.[iii] We plan to unpack some of the key factors underlying this tension to reveal how they can be better managed for long-term innovation success.[iv]

In Part I, we introduce some important concepts we have developed as foundations for the book to prepare you for the journey:

- **Innovation with purpose:** We start with the concepts of *purpose-driven* and *sustainable innovation*—that is, how to innovate with a clear purpose in mind for better connection, more authenticity and long-term viability for the organisation, society and the planet.
- **Innovation for real growth:** Once these needs are effectively balanced we believe it is possible to achieve *transformational innovation*—that is, innovation that effectively manages the tension between exploration and exploitation and uses this dynamic energy to drive authentic growth on all levels for all people.
- **Innovation applications:** These innovation principles can then be applied effectively by aligning the right mode of innovation with the right culture change at the right time through *situational innovation*.

In this section we will also discuss how to develop the right mindset to prepare for the innovation process, and how to understand and incorporate the different elements of the innovation process to launch on the journey.

In Part II we look at four key paradoxical pairings related to the *exploration/exploitation* tension that have been identified as needing to be resolved at each stage of the innovation process (the successful management of these paradoxes ensures the culture for innovation is *purpose-driven*):

1. **Control (*exploitation*) vs Freedom (*exploration*)[v]:** For creating a solid, long-term foundation for innovation through questioning assumptions, exploring ambiguities and sparking curiosity and imagination
2. **Focus (*exploitation*) vs Openness (*exploration*)[vi]:** For enabling ideation and supporting productive new ideas
3. **Individualism (*exploitation*) vs Group Engagement (*exploration*)[vii]:** For pulling together diverse individual ideas and integrating them into united solutions
4. **Stability (*exploitation*) vs Flexibility (*exploration*)[viii]:** For testing and prototyping potential solutions and working through to implementation

At each of these stages we will be challenging you to consider some new *stretch concepts,* which are designed to stretch you beyond standard ways of thinking about innovation through synthesising the paradoxes. So at the first stage, rather than choosing control *or* freedom, for example, we recommend considering the stretch concept of *guided freedom.* This concept incorporates the need for both direction *and* empowerment simultaneously. Learning to continually balance the tensions of these paradoxes effectively can help create a sustainable culture that supports innovation over the long term.

Who should read this book?

This book is aimed at leaders interested in building up a contemporary global perspective on innovation, as well as those seeking practical ideas on how to create an organisational culture that best supports innovation. We have been conscious of the need to balance pertinent deeper principles and practical applications. We present ideas that are both strategic and 'hands on'—a critical combination, we believe, for effective leaders.

We are confident there will be important takeaways for the realists and pragmatics as well as the idealists and altruists among our readers. Leaders today need to synthesise these critical opposed yet complementary skillsets: they need the practical skills to deal with immediate threats and maintain the status quo, but they also need to be visionary enough to rethink the future and conceive of better ways of doing things for long-term survival.

What are some immediate takeaways for the realists and pragmatists? These include tools for surviving the current innovation challenges by building a solid culture of innovation, and this means identifying the roadblocks and detours as well as the fast-forward strategies needed to stay relevant. For the idealists and altruists, the longer-term implications include strategies for sustainable transformational innovation through deeper culture change. All this means challenging the typical assumption that innovation is about designing bigger, sleeker and faster products and services, and exploring instead how it can bring about creative culture change for all of society.

Enjoy the journey!

PART I

PREPARATION FOR THE GLOBAL REALITY RACE

Destination: Australia

In Part I you will be introduced to the key principle of transformational innovation—innovation that is purpose-driven, sustainable and situational, and based on real needs.

Key challenges addressed:

- *How to prepare for the purpose-driven innovation process (chapter 1).*
- *How to learn to see issues from multiple perspectives (chapter 2).*
- *How to develop a deep understanding of real innovation needs through authentic empathy (chapter 3).*
- *How to balance the paradoxes of purpose at each stage of the innovation journey (chapter 4).*

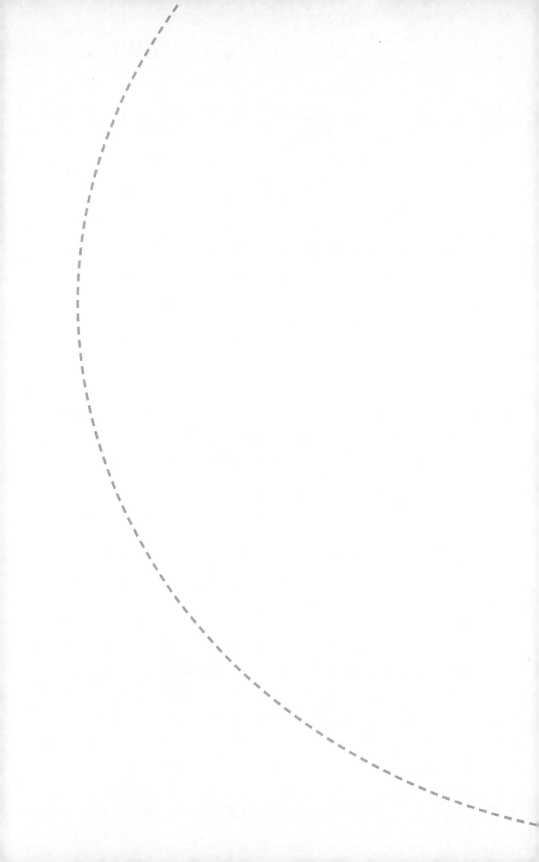

1

THE AMAZING INNOVATION RACE

Who wins, who loses, who gets eliminated—
and why we need to change the game

Welcome to the global reality race. In this chapter we start the adventure by questioning the typical assumptions about innovation and proposing the need for a new paradigm that will propel us forward into the future.

This chapter will help you to:

- *examine the concept of the 'innovation race' and the impact on individuals and organisations*
- *identify how strategic your innovation focus is*
- *explore the need for a clear sense of purpose and connected process in innovation*
- *consider the benefits of proactive and sustainable innovation*
- *appreciate the importance of purpose-driven innovation for greater social responsibility and environmental sustainability*
- *understand the elements of transformational innovation.*

Key challenge: How to prepare for the purpose-driven innovation process

Back in 1985, when hairstyles were boofy and TV was serious business, a television camera zoomed in on a veteran Australian journalist as he stood in the middle of the brutally hot North Australian desert. On one side of him stood a team of highly trained SAS soldiers (an elite military special operations force) in full combat gear. On the other side was a group of traditionally (lightly) dressed Australian Aboriginals. The challenge was for the two teams to race against each other to a set destination. TV cameras would follow each team every step of the way, the winners demonstrating their superior survival skills in the punishing conditions. *The Hunting Party* was being billed as a major TV event and expectations were high.[1] It would be one of the first 'reality TV' programs ever produced.

The contrast between the two groups was striking. The disparity in their clothing stood out, as did the fact that the SAS were significantly larger and more muscular. The soldiers were highly trained, exuded confidence and determination, and could draw on the latest technologies. The Indigenous Australians, on the other hand, had survived the desert conditions for thousands of years (we now know it has been 40000 years or more) and were quite capable of looking after themselves in the inhospitable outback. They had what you might call the home town advantage.

The temperature in the Northern Australian bush can soar to 50 degrees Celsius, hot enough to fry an egg on a sun-baked stone. The second-driest continent in the world (after its southern neighbour Antarctica), almost 50 per cent of Australia receives less than 25 centimetres of rainfall a year. Desert consumes 44 per cent of the land mass, covering 2.3 million square kilometres. This vast, arid wilderness presents one of the most isolated and difficult environments on earth for flora and fauna, especially humans. Exposure to such high temperatures can threaten vital organs such as the brain and the kidneys and ultimately cause the body simply to shut down. So for most of us it is not only dangerous to be out there alone but can easily become downright deadly.

We can look back to our own potentially life-threatening personal experience with the Australian desert. In our younger years, when we were relatively naïve about the dangers, we had decided to take the ultimate road trip challenge and traverse the country in our old Holden Commodore station wagon. We planned on completing the 4000 km crossing in just three days. We thought we were ready for the challenge, but nothing can prepare you for the vast stretches of road with no more than a scattering of stones and scrubby bushes pockmarking the otherwise flat and featureless *Mad Max*–like wasteland from horizon to horizon. The Nullarbor Plain — from the Latin *nullus* (no) *arbor* (trees) — is a huge stretch of arid desert that sweeps for more than 1100 km at its widest point and covers an area of 200000 square kilometres. We imagined being stuck out there with no help in sight, and when the air conditioning broke down we thought we might die there. If we kept the windows closed it was like being trapped in a rapid bake oven. But putting the windows down was worse: then it was like being entombed in a fan-forced rapid bake oven.

After a little experimenting, we came up with the idea of hanging a wet towel over the open window. This cooled the wind a little as it passed through the towel, and provided some relief from the constant heat and dust. It took about 10 minutes for the towel to dry out completely, so we had to keep replenishing our water supply and constantly rehydrating the towel, but as a makeshift solution it was not bad. In a small way, we had overcome a survival challenge that allowed us to press on with the journey. The experience gave us a new appreciation of what it could mean to survive in this extreme environment.

Technology vs tradition

In stark contrast to our own paltry challenge, the Aboriginal people had survived this environment for tens of thousands of years with only the most basic technology. Yet the SAS-trained men had all the benefits of modern technological and scientific advances, so they also had clear advantages.

When the race began, the SAS were quickly off and running. On the other side, the Indigenous Australians started ambling along calmly, apparently unconcerned by any pressure to win. The theme music was pumping and the foot cameras were positioned in the centre of the group, set rolling to appear as if they were being swept along for the ride at a cracking pace. Yet there was no real race. The Aboriginal team were clearly not interested in the competitive aspect of the challenge. Was it going to become a hare-and-tortoise scenario, we wondered, or an easy win for the SAS? The camera crews struggled to bring out the drama, but post production would have had meagre pickings to work from when trying to pull a dramatic story from the footage.

After a great deal of build-up and advertising, it seemed there was to be no real story. Only a short time into the race, having not wandered far from the start line, the Aboriginal group found a watering hole (a billabong) they liked and decided to stop right there. They had reached a good position and had no incentive to go further. They simply could not see the *purpose* of a race for the sake of a race. Their actions actually changed the whole game, and the event that could have been an original *Amazing Race* was over barely before it had begun. The show flashed across our TV screens, soon to be forgotten, but the lessons have stayed with us ever since.

When you think about it, this outcome has profound implications for the ways we think about progress and innovation. We were all initially glued to our screens in the hope of witnessing a decisive showdown between the state-of-the-art, tech-savvy, trained and tooled-up model on one side and the practical wisdom and experience built up over many generations on the other. The same provocative tension lies behind the concept of what we call 'the innovation race'. We have come to assume that progress through innovation is a race, and that the most technologically advanced will 'win', but is that necessarily the best or only way to survive and progress?

In our everyday environments we all face harsh challenges as we try to reach targets and meet objectives. Many of us are drawn insatiably to the latest technological fix, convinced that it will give us the competitive advantage. Some of us will also recognise the value of learning from the generations who have gone before us. The two don't need to be mutually exclusive. Perhaps we need to start to look deeper into the concept of the innovation race to find the right balance.

Perhaps we need to start thinking about who is best equipped to survive—not just in technological terms, but more importantly in terms of knowledge and wisdom. We also need to think about where we're going, and the purpose of the journey.

Before digging deeper into these questions, let's further consider this concept of a race.

Addicted to adrenaline

Most of us love to watch a race. We love to see winners, losers, the eliminations. We like to observe others as they go through the highs and lows of a hard-fought competition. The designers of *The Hunting Party* and of many reality TV shows since have relied heavily on this innate competitive drive. Both the contestants and the viewers are motivated by the idea of winning, getting across the finish line first. Ultimately some will be successful and others will fail, according to the unquestioned assumptions behind these shows.

Arguably the concept of the 'innovation race' has similar foundations. Many people and organisations and systems view the world as a competitive race, with innovation being the key factor in helping us to accelerate forward. Those keen to 'advance' and 'get ahead' can be prone to the competitive drive, but does this competitiveness come at a cost?

A competitive focus requires additional mental resources that can impact decision making and opportunities for cooperation, and 'drain the brain'.[2] The factors that have been found to fuel competitive arousal are all prominent elements in modern society: head-to-head rivalry, time pressure and a bright spotlight to illuminate the competition.[3] The 'desire to win' is heightened when these factors collide, as they do in reality TV game shows. The emotional volatility in decision making can in turn lead to compelling TV viewing. When we feel and enjoy this pressure to compete vicariously from the safety of our armchairs, we feed this inherent need to compete without being impacted by the consequences.

There is nothing essentially good or evil about the concept of competition in itself, and it can have both benefits and costs. Competition can be a motivating drive to assist with achieving goals, particularly when it is internally focused on improving oneself, yet it can also become a destructive force if not managed effectively. The line can be crossed when there is unchecked competition for the sake of beating others (something we will discuss more in Part II). It will therefore be important to consider the different types of competition and potential outcomes as we consider the implications of the race to innovate.

A modern dictionary definition of competition usually refers to outperforming others and/or 'winning', but the origins of the word are actually quite different. The word itself, from the Latin *competere,* originally meant 'to strive together *(com)* to seek *(petere)* some common interest'—that is, to achieve a *mutually beneficial outcome.* Perhaps this is a first clue to how we can start to shift our focus.

In this book we will take you on a virtual race around the world, looking at different cultures, organisations and individuals in order to gain more clues on how this race to compete through innovation has fostered or impeded human progress, and how we might better navigate these challenges. It has taken us 30 years of travel, from remote tribal villages through to the executive offices of large multinationals, to try to get a feel for where we are going and why. In our travels we've encountered cultures that appear to have been left behind in the race and others that appear to be way out in front. At historical sites we've explored the remnants of ancient civilisations that in their time appeared to be race leaders, at least for a while. Think of how the Egyptian, Greek, Aztec and Roman empires expanded in leaps and bounds, becoming the invincible 'winners' of their age, before eventually being reduced to ruins. At the other extreme are the cultures, such as the Aboriginal Australians, who until relatively recently have maintained a stable hunter-gatherer, semi-nomadic way of life isolated from the rest of the world and its competitive impulses.

The initial question that confronted us as we travelled was: *How* have some countries and cultures managed to 'get ahead'? But the further we travelled and the more research we did, the more evident it became that the race would never be a simple 'two-pony' competitive run to a specified finish. So the defining question started to change to: *Why* is it that some societies, cultures and organisations seem to have raced ahead (at least technologically) while others appear to have been 'left behind', *and what does that mean?* Which led to deeper questions, such as: What is this race? Should we be in a race at all? And if so, what should we race against? Instead of racing against each other, couldn't we strive to overcome climate change challenges or worldwide poverty together? We also began to wonder if there has been a defined start and will there be a clear finish to this race, what the rules are, who calls the shots ... and ultimately whether this is the best way to measure successful progress.

This cognitive ambiguity is something you will need to learn to maintain as you read through the book. History has demonstrated again and again how those who harness *technological* innovation often race ahead *technologically* and those who don't can find themselves left behind or even 'eliminated'. In many such innovation races a win for one culture or organisation has come at the expense of others. Innovation has appeared to be a key factor in both the success and the demise of so many organisations and cultures, so can we adjust the terms of the race in a way that promotes the greater good?

Why do we need to innovate responsibly?

We believe strongly that these questions are worth pursuing, because innovation matters. A lot. Creative thinking is recognised as an essential work and life skill, and innovation is an essential business and development strategy. Creative thinking and innovation are critical for the survival not just of businesses but of the planet.

Creative thinking, for starters, has been found to be related to a number of important life factors, including: more flexibility, better problem solving skills, better relationships, more optimism, higher achievement, higher retention in education programs, higher self-esteem, and less stress.[4] Creativity and innovation are clearly currently popular topics as people come to realise the value of investing in them. Many people who recognise the importance of creative thinking actively focus on building their critical and creative thinking skills through programs such as Lumosity (with some 35 million users), and more than 100 000 books on creativity and innovation have been listed on Amazon.com.

At the organisation level, Bain and Company have found that the top companies in 450 companies surveyed on measures of innovation had better employee engagement, better productivity (up to 50 per cent more), and better decision-making effectiveness.[5] Bain's specific assessment of corporate decision-making effectiveness showed that those in the top quartile were better (in terms of speed, effort involved, quality and yield) at both making and executing decisions. Better decision making, in turn, impacted strategy, project selection and organisational alignment. A survey of 1500 CEOs by IBM (that covered 60 countries and more than 33 different industries) has also revealed that CEOs believe creative thinking is *the* most important leadership quality needed for the future, and innovation is a critical organizational capability.[6] In fact 81 per cent of the CEOs surveyed rated innovation as a 'crucial capability'.

Organisations have been found to thrive when they are innovative, and growth typically follows.[7] Companies that focus on innovation usually do well financially. The top 25 per cent of the most innovative companies grow more than twice as fast as the others (13 per cent growth compared with 5 per cent growth). When compounded over five years, this amounts to almost three times growth.

Companies that focus on purpose and sustainability also outperform control groups on a number of different financial measures over time – according to one study by almost 70%.[8] In another study, a clear and well-communicated corporate purpose was found to improve financial performance by 17%.[9] So imagine the potential when you combine a focus on innovation *with* purpose and sustainability. Economists estimate that 50 to 80 per cent of economic growth comes from innovation and new knowledge, and that innovation can be an important factor in dealing *with* social and global challenges.[10] 'Great companies work to make money, of course, but in their choices of how to do so … they invest in the future while being aware of the need to build people and society,' says Rosabeth Moss Kanter, Harvard Business School professor and director of the Harvard Advanced Leadership Initiative.[11]

Most businesses now include the term 'innovation' in their values or mission statement (or both) as they recognize the strategic value of remaining relevant and fresh. Innovation undoubtedly assists with survival in the race, new knowledge and ideas contributing to the ability to find and deal with challenges. Where positive values and principles are used to guide the innovation strategy, and where a constructive culture is created to support *sustainable* innovation, organisations are able to achieve the ultimate goal of both purpose *and* profit.[12]

The big question here is not whether creative thinking and innovation are important, as they clearly are; it is whether we are innovating in the best way and for the best reasons. Are we innovating to find the best solutions for dealing with the world's greatest challenges, or are we innovating for the sake of innovating? In the chapters that follow we will show that innovating with purpose towards a positive outcome, rather than simply for the sake of it, makes a huge difference in outcome on many levels, right down to sustained performance.

Let's now take a step back and re-evaluate what we are doing and why we are doing it, to ensure we have the best possible strategy going forward.

Keeping pace with the race

Remember Aesop's Fables, and in particular the story of the tortoise and the hare, which we mentioned in relation to *The Hunting Party*? In the best-known version of this story a slow-moving tortoise challenges a hare to a race after being constantly ridiculed by him. The expectation is of course that the hare will win easily. The twist in the tale is that the overconfident hare convinces himself he is so far ahead he can afford to take a nap, and while he sleeps the tortoise overtakes him and crosses the finish line first.

Most people assume this is a cautionary tale against hubris or about the dangers of a focus on speed, with the motto 'slow and steady wins the race'. Perhaps it's also a source for the popular contemporary saying 'if you snooze you lose'. Both lessons are worth reflecting on in this context. Speed can be important as you need to remain vigilant and in tune with the fast-changing economic and social environment to be ready to face the challenges, but strategic focus is just as important — if not more.

Let's start with thinking about the pace of the 'innovation race'. Innovation has been studied extensively since economist and political scientist Joseph Schumpeter first suggested its critical role for business in the 1930s.[13] One thing that has become apparent over those years of study is that the innovation imperative in the technology sector is rapidly increasing, as the figure 'Accelerating pace of technological innovation' reveals. This graph seems to indicate that need to innovate now more than ever, and we will need to continue to innovate faster and faster in order to survive — hence the common understanding of innovation as a race.

Accelerating pace of technological innovation

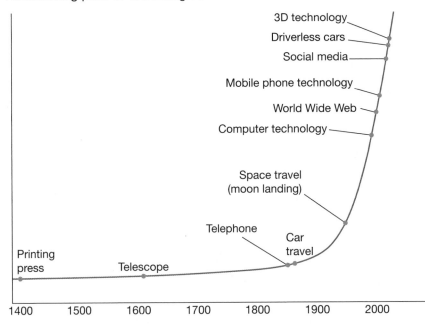

As an interesting side note, some anecdotal research has found that the biggest cities have the fastest pace of life and rely on the fastest rates of innovation, which it appears is reflected by the speed people walk in that city.[14] It seems that the average walking pace has increased by up to 30 per cent over the past few decades, as is especially evident in some of the cities that are innovating the fastest. For example, people have been found to walk the fastest (18 metres in 10.55 seconds) in Singapore, which often rates as the fastest innovating city in the world according to standard innovation measures. Perhaps we're feeling that sense of urgency so strongly that we're unconsciously picking up our own pace to try to keep up!

One of the challenges is that western economic systems are typically built on the imperative of economic growth and rapid progress. The treadmill has an automatic speed-up setting that can't be changed, because capitalism requires constantly evolving systems and structures to support it. Physicist Geoffrey West and his colleagues have identified some interesting principles from physics that help to explain this economic phenomenon.[15] For example, they have found that the open cycles of growth that characterise capitalism demand exponential rates of innovation merely to stay afloat and avoid collapse. West compares it to a clock ticking ever faster, which demands ever faster rates of innovation simply to keep up.

Disruptors and breakthroughs

Let's consider what 'the innovation race' has led to in the technology sector, where the realities are harsh. Only one out of the top five tech companies in 1995, companies that were established at the time of the introduction of the internet (the 'hares', if you like), remain in the technological innovation race today.[16] What's more, 14 of the world's 15 most valuable technology brands have disappeared during the two decades since 1995.[17] With the notable exception of Apple, all have been rendered obsolete by more agile competitors. Many of the top companies researched in Tom Peters' and Robert H. Waterman's book *In Search of Excellence* (1982) and in Jim Collins' book *Good to Great* (2001) have not lasted the distance. Good companies can fail easily when confronted by market and technological change — even the kinds of companies that are known for their ability to innovate and execute.[18] There is no permanent immunity in real business life, and it's easy to lose the lead.

When we had the opportunity to work with a number of properties in the award-winning Four Seasons hotel group, a VP from the company (whose previous property had won the best hotel award three years in a row under his management) shared with us that 'getting to number one was easy compared with maintaining that position.' Take the problem of 'premium position captivity' as an example. This expression refers to the way a company can be held back from the quick and nimble responses of competitors. 'A company that solidly occupies a premium market position remains insulated longer than its competitors against evolution in the external environment. It has less reason to doubt its business model, which has historically provided a competitive advantage, and once it perceives the crisis, it changes too little too late.'[19] A study of Fortune 100 and Global 100 companies between 1955 and 2006 found that almost 90 per cent went through a stall phase at some stage, and fewer than half of those were able to recover sufficiently. Few of the companies that stalled for more than 10 years recovered at all.[20]

Survival in the competitive technological innovation race, it has been found, often depends on radical breakthrough innovations rather than slow evolutionary adaptations. This is apparent in the figure 'Typical trajectory of breakthrough vs. incremental innovations'. And these disruptive innovations are changing the game. Unexpected rapid innovations are like wild cards thrown into the mix that catch everyone off guard. The clear message for today seems to be that you must be proactive and anticipate future trends to generate better, faster solutions, or risk being relegated to the back of the pack or even eliminated.

Typical trajectory of breakthrough vs. incremental innovations

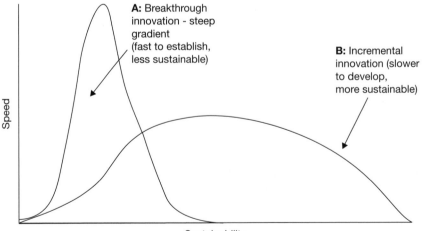

A: Breakthrough innovation - steep gradient (fast to establish, less sustainable)

B: Incremental innovation (slower to develop, more sustainable)

Speed

Sustainability

In a Formula One race, if someone brings out a significantly new car, the benchmark is moved, the bar drastically raised.[21] The switch to mid-engine cars by Australian Jack Brabham in the 1960s, for example, led to a complete revolution to this type of car. In the late 1960s the introduction of aerofoils led to the dramatic recognition of the potential of aerodynamic downforce to increase cornering speeds, which again led to a new revolution. Throughout history countless technological transitions have dramatically impacted rates of development and established new benchmarks. Think about the switch from horse and buggy to motorcar, from typewriter to computer, from snail mail to email.

Disruptive and breakthrough innovations have emerged as a way of dealing with gaps, yet these forms of rapid innovation can be risky. Sometimes they are like a game of snakes and ladders: when you land in the wrong place you can find yourself sliding back to square one, having to start all over again. Discover a significant new innovation, on the other hand, and you can leap ahead of the competition and scale a fast-track ladder to the top in one swift move. This race generates both great opportunities and great risks, fast winners and losers.

Disruptive innovations, as defined by Harvard Business School innovation expert Clayton Christensen, enable nimble smaller players to leverage simple and inexpensive ideas and products at the bottom of the market in order to compete against the big players and established products.[22] This can help lead to more equality in innovation. Breakthrough innovation also involves a 'paradigm shift' to push the boundaries of science and technology in order to keep up with the rapid pace of change, which naturally brings risk and uncertainty.[23] Both of these types of innovation allow for a faster pace of progress and pave the way for 'changing the rules of the game', but there is still a long way to go.

Playing snakes and ladders: evolution or revolution?

The free-to-air and cable TV channels, for example, spent so much time competing against each other that they didn't even see their new competitors coming. By the time the streaming companies (following the Netflix model) hit the market the customer was begging for these sorts of flexible solutions, and the TV channels were left struggling, often reduced to back-to-back reality TV and sports programs.

Traditionally companies within industries have focused on competing against each other through sustained incremental innovation and haven't had to worry about anything outside their own particular world. This system can work as long as deep change is not needed. Disruptive innovation often emerges when an outsider enters a market and defies the established system. Entrant companies have been able to trial radically new ideas and methods by importing them from different industries and applying them in a new situation.

The sharing economy, which existed well before Uber and Airbnb popularised the concept, has become an increasingly popular means of ensuring everyone has access to the best ideas. Uber has been successful because the incumbent taxi system was inefficient, and possibly taxi companies didn't innovate because they thought they had a monopoly. Taxis ended up being viewed as expensive, inefficient, lacking a customer-friendly focus and, in some countries, blatantly overcharging. Endless phone queues and slow payments contributed to creating an environment in which customers would have done anything to find a better way to travel.

What these established companies failed to see was that customers will go ahead and innovate, with or without their approval, according to their needs. But rather than looking at Uber itself, it is important to consider the conditions that led to the innovation. It's the principle behind the innovative model of efficiency, rather than the company Uber itself, that should be considered. It is interesting to note that the concept of ride sharing has taken off most in countries where the taxi system is least efficient or most corrupt. Some of the few cities where taxis are not threatened by ride sharing, such as Singapore and Tokyo, already had an efficient and user-friendly system and managed to remain strong competitors. Interviews we've had with drivers in these cities have revealed that a taxi app (Grab) already existed that streamlined the customer experience, and the taxi companies have focused on raising their standard rather than playing the blame game and falling further behind.

This reminds us of a clever quote we have referred to many times in our workshops to help increase awareness of the need to identify the real needs behind development: Bill Gates has said, 'Banking is necessary, banks are not.' When you think about it, this simple but profound statement opens up a multitude of possibilities. The idea could be applied in any industry. In relation to transport, we might say that mobility (transport) is necessary, but cars as we know them today are not. In hospitality, accommodation is necessary, hotels as we know them today are not. Or how about, 'Communication is necessary, telcos as we know them today are not'?

(Think of how pro-democracy protesters in Hong Kong switched to using Bluetooth apps such as FireChat to communicate, completely bypassing the telcos and therefore avoiding government scrutiny.) Disruptive innovation is a wild card that leaves the concept of the 'innovation race' wide open: new rules and new players creating new opportunities.

The challenge is that, just as we need to move beyond the slower but more sustainable incremental innovations that help us to survive, eventually we are going to have to go beyond the sometimes haphazard breakthrough and disruptive innovations that are helping us to get ahead in the game. We need to progress to what we call *transformational innovation*: innovation that is fast enough to keep up with the rapid pace of change, yet is also meaningful and sustainable from a social, environmental and commercial perspective.

The first step in finding a purpose behind innovation is to start to think about how we can manage the race to ensure innovation is not only commercially viable but also sustainable on all levels for the long-term survival of all.

Transformational innovation: beyond exploration and exploitation

The connection between keeping up with the pace of change through speed *and* ensuring long-term sustainability through strategic focus has never been clearer. This is recognised by researchers as a key paradox in innovation. As stated earlier, typically there is a tension between the 'exploitation' functions of the organisation (maintaining current systems and processes) and the 'exploration' functions (prospecting for new concepts). 'Exploitation' in this context usually refers to innovating in small, incremental steps and is the more sustainable approach. 'Exploration' refers to creative thinking and breakthrough innovations and is the more fast-paced approach.[24]

Typically organisations will choose to focus on one *or* other approach, yet their future survival will depend on embracing the best elements of *both* approaches concurrently. This book will explore how that can be done most effectively. Certainly large organisations today are learning to separate innovation functions to cater for both needs, with the more established divisions focusing on the slower, incremental innovations, while leaner, startup-style divisions are set up to focus on radical innovations. Leaders recognise the need for this dual focus, and the importance of continuing to explore how this can be done most effectively, perhaps through taking it a step further and *synthesising* these functions. Our concept of transformational innovation (see figure overleaf) aims to help bridge that gap.

Transformational innovation

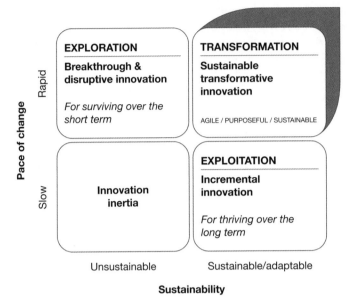

The *innovation inertia* quadrant in this figure refers to the situation where innovation fails both to keep up with the pace of change and at the same time to meet the sustainability criteria. Most organisations will at times drift into this mode, but they will have little chance of survival if they remain there too long. In the *transformation* quadrant, on the other hand, organisational leaders have their fingers on the pulse and are responding accordingly. They remain flexible and adaptable while at the same time ensuring their decisions are based on sustainable *principles* and *purpose* that will also lead to greater social responsibility and more environmental sustainability.

If left to their own devices, most organisations will move towards their preferred dominant tendency. Typically, new startups will thrive on the exploration of new ideas, while larger, more established companies will have become settled into maintaining and adjusting existing ideas and resources. Managing both positions simultaneously will bring the greatest success over the long run.

Balancing apparently competing and contradictory needs will be quite a stretch for many organisations, but if we don't start to think differently about innovation and take that leap, we risk the future of our organisations and social structures—and even, at the extreme, the very survival of the planet.

Bridging the innovation purpose gap

When our air-conditioner failed in the Australian outback our survival instinct led us to a small innovation. This incident had a significant implication for our thinking about the *purpose* of innovation and of the innovation race. Without realising it we had in fact created a simple water cooling system. Portable water-cooled units based on this concept have been produced as an alternative to air conditioning for many years. They are cheaper and therefore more accessible to poorer communities, and they are also more environmentally friendly (using 75 per cent less power than a conventional air-conditioner), which helps to solve a few challenges.

As the rapid growth in air conditioning threatens to exacerbate global warming (according to one estimate we could be using up to one trillion kilowatt-hours of electricity for air conditioning annually worldwide), developing low-energy alternatives for dealing with warm temperatures will become essential. Wind towers (being developed in Dubai), air pumped from underground tunnels (as used in India), water evaporation techniques (under development in Kuwait) and other solar-powered passive cooling projects are now emerging as viable options.

According to Darwin's famous 'survival of the fittest' evolutionary theory, innovation will most often arise from emerging needs. Yet today it has typically become something much more complicated than simply innovation for survival. Innovating beyond simple needs has become essential for commercial success. The shift from innovation based on *needs* to innovation based on *desires* has led to a significant change in the ways we innovate.

> The shift from innovation based on *needs* to innovation based on *desires* has led to a significant change in the ways we innovate.

The most commercially successful companies are now those that push the boundaries in innovation, imagining and realising ideas that would never have occurred to most people, and thereby creating a new desire. Although products and services created in this way may be commercially successful, think about how they could actually be failing to meet the deeper needs, leading to what we will call an 'innovation purpose gap'.

A classic historical example of how desire can become an overriding passion and what impact it can have is the 'cargo cults' of the late 1800s and early 1900s, which demonstrated early dramatic shifts to consumerism in traditional societies. When industrial nations came into contact with certain tribal societies, particularly in remote areas of the Pacific, the local people began to rely on and desire the new manufactured goods rich nations brought with them. Some of these objects, which they had never known or needed before, suddenly became highly coveted. In some cases this desire became so strong that a whole religion was built around the objects, with the planes, landing strips and radio equipment that brought the goods being reconstructed from local materials and worshipped as a magical source of the desired objects. 'Commodity fetishism', first identified by Marx back in 1867, persists in different forms today,[25] but a common theme is that out of context these objects were or are often totally useless.

Steve Jobs was a master at anticipating consumer appetites. Jobs, once described as 'the hippy high priest of consumer capitalism', had a genius for creating desires consumers didn't know they had, then successfully producing fabulous new products to satiate those desires.[26] What generally separated his approach to commodities from those idealised by the cargo cults is that he was able to develop products that were extraordinarily functional and useful to customers. Jobs created devices that not only looked great but that people came to rely on … and then to consider essential for them to survive. Imagine the contestants in the TV game show *The Amazing Race* hauling around a mountain of electronic devices (phones, radios, cameras, calculators, computers and so on), rather than a single slim, multi purpose mobile device that can suck data down from an imaginary cloud — that's how profound this shift became.

Henry Ford famously said, 'If I had asked people what they wanted, they would have said faster horses'. People often simply don't see the possibilities before a visionary creative innovator imagines and realises them. We need this sort of imaginative thinking to help identify and solve problems we can't always see — that is what thinking outside the box is all about. Mario D'Amico, formerly Chief Marketing Officer of Cirque du Soleil, has noted research showing that external restrictions often kill creativity. Where companies thrive on focused innovation, placing too much emphasis on what they traditionally think customers want can destroy a company's ability to be different. The most successful companies are successful because they push boundaries and do the unexpected.[27] This is the vital role imagination plays in the innovative process.

These days, rather than necessity being the mother of invention, invention has become the mother of necessity.[28] It's inventions that create blue ocean opportunities and become new fast-forward cards, enabling companies to progress to a premium position at the front of 'the race'. Yet there is a line that is often crossed between creating a useful, purposeful benefit and wasting resources on a relatively useless, excessive investment.

Here is the key contradiction, as identified by Clayton Christensen in his landmark book *The Innovator's Dilemma*: 'When the best firms succeeded, they did so because they listened responsively to their customers and invested aggressively in the technology, products, and manufacturing capabilities that satisfied their customers' next-generation needs. But, paradoxically, when the best firms subsequently failed, it was for the same reasons—they listened responsively to their customers and invested aggressively in the technology, products, and manufacturing capabilities that satisfied their customers' next-generation needs. This is one of the innovator's dilemmas: Blindly following the maxim that good managers should keep close to their customers can sometimes be a fatal mistake.'[29]

Customers like to have a lot of choice, yet this can easily go too far. It's certainly nice to be able to choose from a range of different types of milk, but should we need to walk down whole supermarket aisles of milk to find the perfect option? Consumer watchdog group Choice has identified more than 80 different brands and types of milk on the Australian market.[30] Milk is essentially a natural product that comes more or less straight from the cow! Does this excessive choice fulfil a genuine need? Is this where innovation is taking us?

Psychologists recognise that we need to determine the line between the benefits of choice and excessive alternatives.[31] Too much choice, they believe, paradoxically leads to paralysis rather than liberation and creates a dangerous escalation of expectations. When we habitually compare what we get with what we expect, we often end up less satisfied than we would be if we had fewer options to choose from. Too much choice has also been linked to depression. As people's expectations increase, new desires go unsatisfied. Some choice is definitely nice, but it doesn't follow that a great deal more choice is helpful or necessary.[32]

The dark side of desire

Once we start to look behind the scenes of the creation of a new product, the image may quickly lose some of its brightness. Sleek and sexy products too often have a darker side. Many of the big IT companies, for example, have been identified as imposing harsh or unsafe factory conditions on their workers, employing child labour or failing to meet basic environmental standards. It has even been said that Steve Jobs' genius was partly due to his ability to 'elevate his products above ethical or environmental considerations in the minds of consumers'.[33]

Of 56 IT companies surveyed by one organisation, none had completely traced the production of their raw materials, which could include tin from Indonesia or cobalt from the Democratic Republic of Congo, both of which have been linked with child labour and dangerous mining conditions.[34] An earlier report by the same organisation had found that only 9 per cent of companies in the fashion industry had traced their suppliers to the raw materials supply chain level.[35] So if we believe it's important to act responsibly in the 'innovation race', we need to ask: At what cost have we been satisfying our own desires at the expense of integrity and sustainability? Our unprecedented access to information today means we can't claim ignorance.

Looking at the impact on the developing world. While technology is undoubtedly improving the lives of many people around the world, it becomes a problem when it is prioritised over more basic needs. Unfortunately ownership of TVs and mobile phones often seems to take precedence over more basic survival needs. One study found that almost 60 per cent of people living in Asia were subsisting on less than $2 a day, but the majority of them owned their own mobile phone.[36] A United Nations report has found that more people around the world now have mobile phones than have access to a flush toilet![37]

Perhaps it needs to be asked: Are we being driven to invent and consume at all costs, rather than according to genuine need or to serve a greater purpose? Increasing expectations based on growing aspirations are raising the bar higher and higher, faster and faster.

Do we really need purple ketchup or Crystal Pepsi? It may have reached the point, as the former CIO of Google and co-founder of ZestFinance Douglas Merrill has suggested, where we are 'innovating for innovation's sake', rather than to meet any real need.[38] This devotion to innovation has been described as a religion.[39] 'And what is *innovative*?' asked communications specialist Falguni Bhuta in 'Beyond Innovation for Innovation's Sake' on *The Holmes Report*. 'Is it innovative for innovation's sake or is it something that makes a difference to people's lives, their work?' If there are no objectives for the innovation, she says, organisations can end up spending a lot of money and not necessarily adding value.[40]

> Perhaps it needs to be asked: Are we being driven to invent and consume at all costs, rather than according to genuine need or to serve a greater purpose?

By thinking about how innovation takes place, about the *why* and *what for* of innovation, we started to develop the concept of transformational innovation. Transformational innovation is about changing the innovation culture to support sustainable and purpose-driven innovation over the long term. As we will discuss in chapter 6, incorporating into innovation a sense of purpose beyond just 'winning' offers major long-term benefits.

A recurring theme in this book relates back to the message from *The Hunting Party*: the Aboriginal team didn't compete in the TV race because they could not see any purpose in participating in it. Innovating for the sake of it can be seen as trying to grab the lead without purpose. Such an approach can so easily end up with a pyrrhic victory (that is, a victory that inflicts such a devastating toll on the victor that the costs negate any potential gain).

Sustainable innovation can come only from a strategic culture change that supports innovation at all levels. When there are deliberate systems and structures in place to support innovation, and when all people are inspired by deeper values and equipped to support the innovation process, change can be effective and rapid, and can be sustained over the long term. Innovation should not be an isolated, random event limited to the creation of new ideas and products. But as a part of a greater purpose and process, it can be transformational.

Changing the culture to change the game

We have had the privilege of working with a number of companies that have been aiming to bring this sense of purpose back into their organisation, and ultimately into the way they innovate. Through our targeted innovation workshops a major food company in Europe explored ideas around more sustainable food preparation solutions for developing countries. In California's Silicon Valley IT companies have increased community commitment and engagement. A tech company developed exoskeletons to help paralysed people to walk again. An innovation centre in Latin America has made a commitment to improving dental hygiene education in developing countries. A large consulting company in Asia has adopted a comprehensive corporate social responsibility program based on local community needs. We have spent time supporting a global pharmaceutical company in the US, Europe and Asia, and have heard first-hand about their desire to make health a priority in developing countries by making important medicines less expensive and more accessible. They are working towards the lofty goal of eradicating malaria.

On the other side, we have also been disturbed by our encounters with organisations that clearly favour profit over purpose, and fail to think through the implications of their innovations. We think of the soft drink company trying to find innovative ways to sell more of their sugary product into schools (to the obvious detriment of the children's nutrition). Or the tobacco company trying to work out how to get around strict government advertising restrictions to sell more of their deadly products.

In each of these cases we have been able to identify a deeper culture driving innovation decisions and actions, a culture that, on the one hand, actively engages and inspires employees to think about how they can contribute to improving the way we all live, and, on the other, revolves around the desire to make a profit at almost any cost. Of course every business needs to make a profit to survive as a commercial enterprise, but innovative thinking can make it possible to combine purpose *and* profit. Colgate Palmolive, for example, is a highly successful company with the most penetrating brand in the world (Colgate toothpaste), but it is also ranked in the top five ethical companies in the world.

In Part II we will delve deeper into when organisations innovate to achieve a higher purpose and when they are driven purely by profit and control—and the impact this has on employees internally, as well as on organisational performance in the long-term 'innovation race'. 3M, recently named the most ethical company for the second year in a row, stated: 'The commitment of our people to the highest ethical standard and to doing business the right way promotes trust with our customers and in the quality of our products. Furthermore, it gives us confidence to grow our business anywhere in the world.'[41] 3M credited their win to the collective action of their global workforce, from the top down. The company demonstrates how ethical practice and innovative leadership of collaborative teams can generate consistent business success. In the following chapters we will unpack these ideas and show how critical they are for innovation.

We will continue to address the need for sustainability on a number of levels: the cultural and economic sustainability of the organisation necessary for its long-term viability, along with the long-term sustainability of our planet. Once there is both sustainable development *and* exploratory growth there is a solid foundation for transformational innovation.

Roadblocks and fast-forward advantages

Imagine a new reality TV show, based on *The Amazing Race*, called 'The Amazing *Innovation* Race'. This program would be designed to make it possible for viewers to travel virtually to a range of different locations around the world in order to learn about the impact of innovation. Viewers would also learn about the cultures and history of the locations they visit. Now imagine you have already been signed up as a participant!

Let's take this idea to the next level. As you set off, you discover that this version of the race is not about trying to *accumulate* the most or getting *the furthest ahead the fastest* as an individual or organisation. (Think of how many traditional games, such as Monopoly or Risk or Speed, centre on accumulation.) Instead, it is about trying to create the greatest *shared benefit* for all. How might that change your perspective on the race? We have pointed out that there are already competitors out there that are breaking the rules through the power of the *shared economy* and *collaborative consumption*, such as organisations that enable owners to rent out something when they are not using it. Well-known pioneers of this approach include Uber, Airbnb and SnapGoods (which focuses on high-end household items such as cameras). We will delve further into how these sorts of changes in approach to innovation will ultimately equalise the opportunities and change the game.

As in *The Amazing Race*, the reality show we are drawing some tongue-in-cheek parallels with, in the current competitive race there are winners and losers, eliminations and opportunities, pit stops and detours. We will see how some countries and cultures — and in parallel how some organisations — have been able to seize the 'fast-forward' advantage, while others have faced daunting 'roadblocks'. We will be looking out for 'route markers and information', the clues that will help us work out the way ahead for our generation as we navigate into the future.

To take it to another level again, think about the countries around the world participating in this race, some with the resources to acquire all the latest gear and the latest training, and others that seem to be heavily disadvantaged. Countries with a technological, economic and knowledge advantage can be expected to speed ahead on this current trajectory while others are left behind at the start line or struggle to stay in the race, or perhaps even choose to ignore or dismiss the very concept of the race (as did the Aboriginal team in *The Hunting Party*). The contextual device of an imaginary reality TV race adds another dimension to this study by highlighting in the rawest form some of the motivations and emotions that drive us to want to achieve.

To assist in dealing with both immediate challenges and future directions, this book will develop two parallel themes:

- **How to survive the current race:** Tools (for the realists!) to help your organisation keep up in the current innovation race and avoid elimination, and potentially even get ahead — in other words, ensure survival in the short term.

- **How to change the game:** Transformation strategies (for the idealists!) will help you build a culture that supports *transformational innovation,* looking at the bigger picture from a more philosophical perspective and through redefining the race—in other words, ensure innovation and progress are sustainable over the long term.

By digging back into the archives of history we can get a feel for how different approaches have played out in the past and learn from the outcomes. We can then use this learning to check the current indicators and get a feel for what might happen in the future.

In the end, the transformative question will be: 'What can we learn from one another to build a culture that can ensure a sustainable future for us all?' This is the central challenge we will be exploring throughout the book.

Purpose-Driven Innovation (PDI)

The principles explored in the chapters that follow should help today's organisations build their own cultures to support what we call purpose-driven innovation (PDI) strategies, which lead to transformational innovation. These are developments that actually help to improve individuals' lives, advance society and protect the earth. We believe innovation should not be viewed in isolation from its context, that positive, purpose-driven innovation derives from and in turn creates positive intentions (mindsets) and cultures (environments). As Tim Brown, CEO and President of innovation and design firm IDEO, has argued, only businesses that have a clear 'reason for being', or purpose, will be innovative and truly sustainable in the future.[42]

The PDI culture change model we propose can be summed up in the following equation:

$$\text{Purpose-driven innovation} = \text{PURPOSE} \times \text{PROCESS}$$

The rest of Part I explores the *process* of innovation, while Part II examines the *purpose.* We would point out here that we consider creative thinking and innovation to be two parts of the same process. Although many companies today attest to the importance of innovation (which is typically declared as a core value and included in company mission statements), very few seem to recognise the link to creative thinking. Note we are not referring to artistic creativity here, but rather to a thinking capability focused on practical solutions. That is, we believe you can't build a culture of innovation without first developing individual creative skills and capabilities that can lead to original and valuable ideas. Conversely, you can't support the development of individual creativity without ensuring there are opportunities for following fresh ideas through to implementation.

For purpose-driven innovation, certain important prerequisites will ensure a meaningful outcome. The figure 'Purpose-Driven Innovation' gives an overview of the different elements of the *process* and shows how the *purpose* can provide a strong foundation for developing a culture to support the process.

Purpose-Driven Innovation (PDI)[43]

PURPOSE | The cultural values and principles that support innovation

In the next two chapters we will explore the important prerequisites of the process in more detail, notably the ability to see multiple perspectives and to develop empathy. In chapter 4 we will look at the components and interconnections of the whole process, from imagination through to implementation. In particular, we will review the tension between creativity and knowledge generation on one side and innovation implementation and knowledge synthesis on the other, as well as how dealing with this tension can effectively fuel innovation. In Part II we will also explore how it is possible to build a purpose-driven organisational culture that supports the process. For each of the phases of culture development we will visit different locations around the globe to find both stories of inspiration and cautionary tales. And we will use these journeys as opportunities to explore principles that can assist with transformational change.

Back to the future

An even more interesting version of the 'tortoise and the hare' tale brings a unique slant to the well-known fable. In his 'True History of the Tortoise and the Hare' (1915), the Irish writer Lord Dunsany has the hare realise the stupidity of the challenge and refuse to participate in the race, whereupon the tortoise is declared the winner.[44] But the story doesn't end there. Soon afterwards there is a forest fire, and the tortoise, now recognised as the fastest animal, is sent to warn the other animals of the danger. You can probably guess how that turns out.

Let's now return to *The Hunting Party*. To remind you of the setting, in 1985 the early Australian reality TV show set up a contest in which a crack SAS army team with all the latest equipment and survival training was pitted in a cross-country race against a team of local Aboriginals. In the event, the Indigenous team chose to abandon the race. Like the hare in Dunsany's version of the fable, they just could not see the purpose of the race, so they chose to opt out. Yet have the technologically advanced competitors in the race assumed they are the superior winners? What do they think has been won? And what are the potential consequences of that assumption?

We discussed this issue with Professor Patrick Dodson (former chairman of the Council for Aboriginal Reconciliation and winner of the Sydney Peace Prize), an Aboriginal elder and Senator who has long played an active role in Indigenous affairs. We met with Professor Dodson at the same time as *National Geographic*'s Wade Davis, and we could see the deep respect this internationally recognised anthropologist had for the Australian leader. When we asked Dodson where he felt the Australian Aboriginal people stood in the international innovation race, his bemused expression made it clear that the whole concept was madness to him.

Dodson explained that the Aboriginal people have traditionally been more concerned about living in harmony with their environment than trying to change it. Life for his people, he told us, is about maintaining harmony. The Aboriginal people care about protecting and maintaining what they have been given. All their rituals and rites are related to preservation rather than progress.

For countless generations the Indigenous people of Australia were isolated from Europeans and much of the rest of the world, but then quite suddenly they were dragged into the 'modern world', with no option to opt out. In the years following the arrival of explorer Captain Cook and his crew in 1770 there was no escape. For more than 40 000 years the Aboriginal people had set their own narrative, determined their own fate and sustainably managed the land, yet they were barely able to make it to the foreign-imposed start line. The new players on the scene brought with them alien ideas and practices, technological superiority, violent weapons of control and virulent diseases, which between them all but wiped out the Indigenous people.

> The Australian Aboriginal people have traditionally been more concerned about living in harmony with their environment than trying to change it.

26

Today the 'innovation race' is ruthless. It can be as aggressive as our perceptions of the Australian shark; as harsh as the Australian desert. Survival is not assured. The challengers are also no longer playing out in separate, unconnected communities, lands and continents. Indigenous groups that may have been content with their traditional way of life, and may have preferred to be innovative in areas other than technology, have been drawn involuntarily into the global race. Somewhere along the line it became one big, interconnected, inescapable contest, televised live around the world, uncensored and in full colour. As we have been emphasising, we might like to think we can merely sit back and watch it all happen, but in reality we can no longer remain passive viewers.

All of humankind has been signed up for future episodes of the race. Some will come unwillingly and unprepared, and will end up being helpless pawns facing an unknown fate. Others will prepare themselves to be actively engaged and empowered players. As we will explore at the end of the book, some will even learn how to move past being players, to rise up to become disruptive innovators (producers), to influence the rules, and perhaps to make the race fairer and more sustainable for all—in other words, to change the game.

The first task in preparing for the innovation challenge ahead, however, will be determining how to spark the curiosity and imagination that feed the innovation process. This is the starting point for transformational innovation, for innovation that is designed to bring about real change. We have started to explore one different cultural perspective to gain some initial insights into the idea of purpose-driven innovation; now it will be helpful to go further afield to explore multiple cultural perspectives. Being exposed to different ways of thinking and different cultural perspectives can significantly enrich innovation. Yet, as we will discover in the next chapter, there can be challenging psychological blocks to overcome along the way.

PRODUCTION NOTES

Getting off the couch—the need for active participation

TV was originally a one-way medium. Passive viewers looked into a box to see a 'world' that had been framed by others. Reality TV (preceded by similarly interactive game shows) *enabled* viewers, giving them the feeling of being participants. By voting they could sometimes change the course of the show, and they could have fun predicting winners and losers through discussions with family and friends. They could even pretend to be contestants, while remaining in the safe environment and comfort of their own home.

In the 'innovation race' there are those who will feel they can only be passive observers, watching helplessly as innovation passes them by. We hope to show that it is possible to move from passive observer to active participant. More than that, we want to show that whether you like the idea or not is no longer relevant, because the 'innovation race' has now become a global phenomenon, and sitting it out as a passive viewer is not an option. The question is no longer *whether* to join the race, but rather how to think about the race we are all part of, and how to potentially change that race.

INNOVATION TRANSFORMATION CHECKLIST

- ☐ How strategic is your organisation's innovation process?
- ☐ Does your organisation suffer from innovation inertia?
- ☐ Are your organisation's innovations proactive or reactive?
- ☐ Has your organisation been able to get beyond haphazard innovations?
- ☐ Do you identify an authentic reason for new innovations: the *why* and the *what for*?
- ☐ Are your organisation's innovations and innovation processes sustainable?
- ☐ Do your innovation programs have a clear PROCESS built on a sound PURPOSE—are they purpose-driven?
- ☐ Are your organisation's innovations transformational: do they keep up with the pace of change AND are they designed for the long term survival of both the organisation and the planet?
- ☐ Have you considered your organisation's current position in and approach to the 'race'?

2

SHIFTING PERSPECTIVES

The value of diverse perspectives on creative
thinking and innovation[1]

> 'We do not see things as they are; we see things as we are.'
>
> Anonymous

*In this chapter we spend some time exploring different cultural perspectives on creativity
and innovation in order to enrich understanding and appreciation. The first stage of
preparation for the purpose-driven innovation process is a mindset check. This chapter
will help you to:*

- *challenge current perspectives*
- *open up to seeing multiple new perspectives in order to gain new insights*
- *appreciate how new perspectives can spark curiosity and imagination, which in turn
  trigger ideation*
- *understand how diverse cultural perspectives can, in particular, provide fresh new
  insights and lead to new ideas.*

Key challenge: How to learn to see issues from multiple perspectives.

You have no doubt seen images of the archetypal Buddhist monk, but have
you ever thought about what it takes to become a monk? Such a commitment
cannot be taken lightly. It involves a great deal of self-denial and service,
periods of monastic isolation, no means of self-support and a vow of chastity.
Not many people would be prepared to make these sacrifices, especially if
they enjoy a position of privilege. Would you?

Buddhist ideas are popular worldwide, particularly the desire to reconnect with a deeper spirituality in our increasingly busy lives, yet commitment to the priesthood is declining. As the modern 'religion' of consumerism increases its hold, not many people are prepared to make the considerable sacrifices needed to really embrace the principles of frugality and abstinence.

In Thailand alone, the number of monks and novices relative to the general population has halved over the past three decades, with more young Thais preferring to worship at shopping malls than temples. The assistant secretary of the Supreme Patriarch of Thailand, the head of the country's order of Buddhist monks, summarised the dilemma well when he said, 'People today love high speed things. We didn't have instant noodles in the past but now people love them…We have to make [Buddhism] easy and digestible like instant noodles'.[2] It's easy to see how deeper meaning and purpose can become victims of the insatiable race to innovate.

A famous member of the Ming royal house in seventeenth-century China chose to leave behind his life of luxury to become a Buddhist monk. Life in the royal house was comfortable, and there were no concessions to modernity and no quick short-cuts in Buddhist practice then, so what motivated this now-famous man, Shitao (1642–1707), to make such a radical change? His conversion was triggered by a dramatic series of events, which we will return to soon, but before we discuss the greater purpose that he was pursuing at the time, let's explore how this event impacted Shitao's life. This offers an insight into the first stage of the innovation process: preparing for the creative awareness needed for transformational innovation.

After becoming a monk Shitao decided to manifest his devotion through art. He became a prolific painter, travelling extensively throughout China in order to learn and to share his ideas. Inspired by his exposure to very different places and peoples, his art became equally diverse. Rather than imitating the old masters, as was the fashion at the time, Shitao used these traditions and his own experiences as a springboard for exploring new ideas. He developed as a uniquely creative artist and became one of the most influential scholar-painters of his time.

Three centuries later one of Shitao's landscape paintings became the most valuable Chinese painting ever offered at a Christie's auction, valued at more than $15.5 million. This simple black-and-white ink-and-brush composition depicting mountains, rivers and streams captured the hearts of art lovers and critics around the world.

How did Shitao's work become so sought after? What was his secret? He adopted a technique that traditional Chinese painters are renowned for but that he used particularly effectively. Through his travels he had learned to experience life from multiple perspectives, which made him perhaps uniquely qualified as an artist to capture different viewpoints on the world using a method known as 'shifting perspectives'. This involves depicting the subject from many angles at the same time, which might sound like a strange concept to those who have not grown up with it.[3]

Unlike most western painters at the time, who tended to stick to a single, static focal point, Chinese artists were traditionally masters of synthesising different perspectives, allowing the artist to zoom out to give the viewer a broad aerial overview before zooming back in to highlight the finest details. In this way mountaintops and the underside of the leaves of trees could be encompassed in a single landscape. The artist incorporated multiple points of view and the viewer was invited to move around the scene on different levels.[4]

In these paintings viewers are invited to take a journey with the visual storyteller: to soar above the treetops, wander along mountain paths, sail down rivers. Such an experience begs a personal response, but these painters go even deeper. By painting through their 'heart's mind' rather than from direct observation, using a principle called 'spirit resonance', they also connect emotionally with the viewer. As a Buddhist (and later Taoist) monk, Shitao had a deep spiritual connection with his work, and he was able to convey and share that spirituality with others.

The value of shifting perspectives

Geniuses have been found to be what has become known as 'multi-perceptive': that is, they are usually able to see several different perspectives at once. Creative genius, in fact, stretches this ability so far as to make it possible to see perspectives that no one has seen before. Albert Einstein's theory of relativity synthesised different perspectives, and Leonardo da Vinci believed that no one was truly knowledgeable unless they were able to hold at least three different perspectives.

Pablo Picasso and George Braque started a revolution in the western art world by embracing multiple perspectives in their work.[5] By 1910 Europe had witnessed more technological progress over the preceding four decades than it had in the previous four centuries. This new art was a twentieth-century response to a world changing at unprecedented speed. Photography was replacing painting as a form of realistic documentation, so art could expand to embrace 'a new way of seeing' this brave new world.

Braque and Picasso experimented with 'analytical cubism', analysing a subject from many different viewpoints then reconstructing the different images using a geometric framework. Cubism in France inspired new forms elsewhere: Futurism in Italy, Expressionism in Germany, Vorticism in England, and Suprematism and Constructivism in Russia. Paul Gauguin drew inspiration from African art, using an expressive style to explore another perspective for viewing humanity.

Ken Wilber, a prolific writer on transpersonal psychology, has exemplified this integration of different perspectives in his life's work. Ken was an exceedingly bright student who went on to study maths and science, but in his early twenties he discovered Buddhism and became strongly influenced by Buddhist principles. This was in the late 1960s, the era of psychedelic experimentation, but rather than getting caught up in the hippie drug culture Wilber chose to expand his thinking through exploring alternative forms of consciousness. Although he didn't become a Buddhist monk, he read the literature, including the *Tao Te Ching,* and started to commit to meditating for hours on end each day. This juxtaposition of science and spirituality gave him some unique philosophical perspectives.

Wilber is perhaps best known for his Integral Theory, a model that demonstrated the synthesis of all human knowledge and experience. He believed, 'Any single perspective is likely to be partial, limited, perhaps even distorted, and only by taking multiple perspectives and multiple contexts can the knowledge quest be fully advanced.'[6] Wilber used the term *aperspectival,* meaning that no one perspective has priority or superiority, and he believed that it is only through taking an aperspectival approach that we can gain a holistic or integral view.

Innovation starts with creativity, and creativity is activated by broad exposure to different experiences and ideas. The first key to Shitao's connection was his ability to see and interpret *multiple perspectives.* The Buddhist philosophy of emptiness as a starting position, then his extensive travels and his openness to learning—all enabled him to draw from diverse sources of inspiration. As you will see from the 'Purpose-Driven Innovation' model we will be guiding you through, the innovation process needs to start with this activation of creativity through broad exposure to multiple perspectives. We have already touched on a fundamental difference in perspectives between Aboriginal and white Australians exposed in the ill-fated 1985 TV show *The Hunting Party.* In a multicultural society developing multiple perspectives is not just helpful for extending thinking, but essential for building inclusiveness and ensuring mutual growth.

Multiple perspectives also help to trigger empathy, which we will discuss further in the next chapter. Together these can then lead to the sort of divergent thinking and openness that encourages curiosity, imagination and ideation and helps stimulate novel ideas.

The ability to see from multiple perspectives and, as a next step, to interpret from different cultural viewpoints, is an important stepping stone to initiating purpose-driven innovation, as illustrated. We experience and see things very differently depending on our own cultural perspective, so being exposed to different cultural perspectives is a great way of broadening our thinking and thereby enhancing our creative thinking capacity.

The importance of broad exposure to multiple perspectives in the purpose-driven innovation process

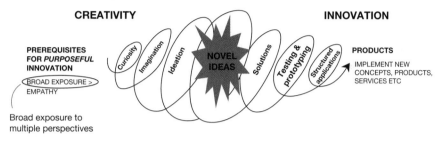

The rewards of experiencing events from different individual perspectives is one factor that has made reality TV shows so successful (we'll return to this in the Production Notes at the end of this chapter). In reality TV shows the producers and directors set up the scene so the audience can view a situation from different perspectives. Much of the action is seen from an outsider's objective perspective, as if you are looking at it from a balcony above (a Neuro Linguistic Programming concept). The cameras then zoom in to give viewers more intimate insights. The contestants' various personal perspectives are revealed through private interviews. Cameras are hidden in different positions (or in different rooms in the house in shows such as *The Bachelor* and *Big Brother*). The audience's perspective is revealed through the results of polls in which they participate.

In a sense, the TV producers and directors have captured the ancient Chinese concept of 'shifting perspectives' and given it a modern twist.

Psychological blocks and enablers

What happens when we are unable to see more than one perspective at a time? How does that impact our ability to think creatively?

Most artists see the world quite differently from non-artists. For example, when groups of artists and non-artists are filmed while viewing a series of pictures to see what their eyes focus on, artists have been found to scan the whole picture, including the 'empty' spaces (such as an apparently empty vista of sea).[7] Non-artists, on the other hand, typically focus on objects and people. This study and others that have been done in the area indicate that artists are able to break down what they see into the abstract elements, while non-artists tend to see what they expect to see as complete, archetypal images.

Most of us seem to have this psychological block of 'concept blindness' when we view the world. We see the world as a composite of what we would expect to see, rather than appraising the individual components independently. This can lead to stereotyping: we can quickly jump to judgemental conclusions, so we need to be aware of this tendency when considering the ways we view different cultures.

Another form of psychological blindness narrows our perception down so that we miss seeing what's at the periphery. Many readers will be familiar with the Invisible Gorilla video. In this video two teams, one wearing white clothing and the other in black, are playing basketball. The viewer is asked to count the number of passes made by members of the white team, and most people who watch this video for the first time are pleased with themselves if they get the number correct. The catch is that while your attention is focused on counting the passes, you typically miss seeing a gorilla as it walks right through the middle of the game. When the scene is replayed, the gorilla becomes obvious and you wonder how you could have missed it.

When you are asked to focus on counting the number of passes, a 'closed' system is introduced. Your brain targets the specific area you are being directed to and shuts out everything else to assist with better processing. Since our attention focus is literally only the size of our fingernail, by focusing your attention on one area you miss the complete picture. This is known as *inattentional blindness*. When given the closed instruction 'Count the number of passes ...', roughly 50 per cent of viewers who see the video fail to notice the gorilla. If, on the other hand, they are given the open instruction 'Tell me what you see ...',[8] most viewers see the gorilla.

Magic tricks work this way, with the illusionist misdirecting our attention while he or she manipulates the situation to make something appear to be magic. Our attention can also be constantly focused in our daily lives so we typically see what we expect to see, or what we are instructed to see (for example, by clever advertisers), or what we have always seen, which can leave us closed to new ideas and new ways of thinking. We need to learn the skill of broadening our attention to be able to take in multiple perspectives in order to prepare ourselves for the innovation process.

Culture to culture — creative insights from different cultural perspectives

'Multiperceptual' artists such as Shitao address these potential psychological blocks and open up our creative thinking. They have helped us to see what an incredibly rich, diverse and colourful place our world is.

There is a huge amount of diversity around the globe that we can learn to identify and value. The United Nations lists 196 countries, around 2000 ethnic-natural groups and 5000 distinct peoples.[9] By being exposed to different cultures we can more readily appreciate multiple perspectives. Such broad exposure makes it possible to collect and synthesise apparently opposing ideas (paradoxes) into a vibrant tapestry of interwoven concepts that can help us to better understand and utilise creativity and innovation.

> All cultures are different in terms of the expression and application of creativity. We believe it is possible to collect and synthesise ideas into a vibrant tapestry of interwoven concepts that can create a foundation for future understanding and development.

So where can we look around the world to find the greatest sources of creative inspiration? All cultures are undoubtedly creative, and inventive ingenuity knows no borders. (Did you know, for example, that the earliest evidence of pigments used in painting, found in Zambia, is at least 350000 years old? That ice cream was a royal treat in China more than 2000 years ago? That the windmill was used for grinding corn and irrigating crops in Iran in 634? Or that bowling was devised in Egypt in 332 BC?) Overall, though, there are significant differences in the *rates* and *types* of creativity and innovation between different cultures.

Creativogenic cultures, or cultures that enhance creativity, have four major factors in common[10], and it is these areas we will be exploring through the upcoming journey chapters:

1. a foundation of freedom (chapter 5)
2. openness, access and exposure to varied stimuli and resources—diversity and tolerance of different ideas (chapter 6)
3. engagement through targeted interaction (chapter 7)
4. flexibility for transformation, through an emphasis on becoming, rather than just being (chapter 8).

Urban studies theorist Richard Florida has also determined the major factors that can contribute to the development of a 'creative class' in a society, which leads to concentrated innovative regions.[11] Innovation doesn't just happen. 'The key factor of the global economy,' says Florida, 'is no longer goods, services, or flows of capital, but the competition for people'. He identifies talent, tolerance and technology as key factors. It's difficult to compete unless you have a good team, so it will be necessary to attract this 'creative class' and develop these competencies to survive. Since creative people cluster together, because they want to be with other creative people, once you start this process the culture will develop. In today's global economy, Florida says, 'The places that attract and retain this talent will win, and those that don't will lose. Even if each of these countries increases its share of the global talent pool by 5 or 10 percent, when you add the numbers up, the cumulative effect is substantial.'

From a starting point of having people who are intellectually and creatively talented, there will need to be 'tolerance' (the sort of acceptance of diversity already discussed in relation to 'openness'). The third factor Florida identifies, technology, is today considered to be a key measure of innovation as we have discussed. Many innovation measures today reveal geographical 'hotspots' for innovation, usually assessed by the number of patent applications for new inventions. On this one measure the western world generally streaks ahead of other cultures, as the following 'Mapping innovation around the world' bubble map shows.

Mapping innovation around the world

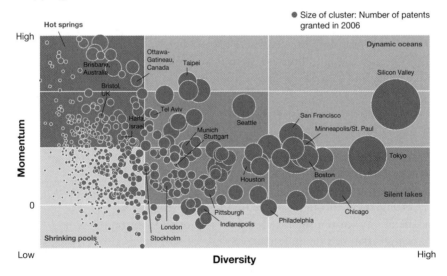

Source: 'Where will the world's primary centers of innovation be?', What Matters: Ten questions that will shape our future. Copyright © 2009 McKinsey & Company. All rights reserved. Reprinted by permission.

It's important to note here, though, that these results do not reveal the inherent creativity and inventiveness of all cultures as the map focusses only on patents. Aboriginal Australians, for example, have had a complex kinship system that traditionally stretched across the country, connecting all the people of the land socially in meaningful and useful ways, and that sort of creative organisation cannot be measured by patent registrations! So these measures need to be approached warily, but they nonetheless reveal dramatic differences between cultures that have had the resources to race ahead technologically, and those whose expressions of innovation have been subtler and less obvious to outsiders.

Why are we so different? Genetics or geography

So where do these dramatic differences come from? Differences in cultural development can emerge from our different contexts or frames of reference, which are often related to geography.

Think, for example, of how different the perceptions and needs of someone living in the desert will be compared with someone living in the jungle or the city. While the desert dweller foraging for food learns to extract nourishment from every meagre source in order to survive, the jungle inhabitant (and urban jungle inhabitant) will often enjoy an abundance of resources, but may need to focus on the potential dangers lurking behind every apparent opportunity.

Geography also plays a major part in determining how fast a culture will innovate technologically. Isolating geographic features that form natural barriers between groups of people, such as mountains and oceans, limit the sharing of ideas and concomitant openness to innovation. It makes sense that if our environments are different, we will have access to different resources.

Scientist and author Jared Diamond believes that differences in rates of development between societies through the ages owe much to environmental variances. Historically the populations living in the fertile lands stretching from the Nile Valley in the west to the Tigris/Euphrates (in modern Iraq) in the east had better access to arable land, plants and animals suited to farming and domestication. This in turn helped support larger, more permanent communities and faster technological advances through their access to more resources and economy of scale, and the growth of cities and trade.[12]

Interestingly, cultural information and innovation appears to have flowed more smoothly between distant populations across continents on an east–west axis, which has typically provided easier accessibility.[13] Where there are these sorts of adjacent connections innovations can exponentially build on each other. Science author Steven Johnson recounts how glass, for example, emerged from a series of different developments, each building on the last.[14]

The ability to heat substances in a furnace led to glass making and grinding. Eye glasses led to more reading, which in turn led to a greater accumulation of scientific knowledge, culminating in the development of fibre optics used to create the World Wide Web, which has allowed for exponentially faster communication and innovation. We will explore this concept of 'adjacent possibilities' further in chapter 6 when we introduce the strategy of 'targeted openness'.

Isolated cultures were not less creative or innovative. If they weren't able to get the first piece of the puzzle in place, however, there was sometimes no similar development path for isolated cultures to take. So *technological innovation* developed in different places at different paces.

Some other clues to differences — politics and power

Religion and politics are taboo subjects in some social situations. Both have been found to have had a significant impact on innovation. In some cultures religious beliefs are more or less fatalistic, with human destiny decided by the god(s) alone; others promote hard work and sacrifice as the only path to a better world[15] (as we will explore further in chapter 8 when we introduce the concept of *enabled optimism*). During the Ming Dynasty in China, for example, the changing political environment and the values associated with it were generally not conducive to a spirit of innovation.[16] A rejection of competition and consumerism, and a mistrust of science, contributed to a dearth of innovation in China at this time, although these conditions were ironically instrumental in shaping the works of artists such as Shitao.

A political dimension has been added to this discussion with the argument that nations develop differently in response to the relative inclusiveness of economic and political institutions.[17] Like twin studies that aim to ensure genetic factors are kept consistent so variations in other factors can be explored, economists have examined 'border cities' in different countries to study development comparatively. Such border cities may have similar geography but very different rates of development and prosperity. One powerful example is the difference between North and South Korea, which both developed differently after their imposed

> Religion and politics are taboo subjects in some social situations. Both have been found to have had a significant impact on innovation.

division 60 years ago. The neighbouring cities of Nogales in Mexico and Nogales in Arizona are similarly compared.

Democratic and pluralistic states, according to these studies, lead to open creative development. In autocracies, on the other hand, there are no incentives to innovate and there is a fear of the potential power of creative destruction (we explore this concept further in chapters 5 when we introduce the strategy of *guided freedom*). While business might try to avoid stepping into the controversial territories of politics and religion, the same mindset that shapes our views on religion and politics can also be reflected in business, and this can impact innovation.

There are also interesting economic foundations for the differences between countries and cultures. Different forms of capitalism can, for example, produce different forms of innovation[18]. The sort of risk-taking on new ideas and the rapid implementation needed for radical innovation are more possible in large, tightly coupled organisations with diverse workforces that emerge in more fluid market settings. Incremental innovation is, on the other hand, more possible where there is developed skill and the greater sense of security that comes with organisations in coordinated market economies.

Cultures that rely on *group-based* coordination and collaboration, such as Japan and South Korea, typically innovate incrementally. In Japan, for example, important business networks are built on the principle of *keiretsu*, which is families of companies with strong interconnections cutting across sectors, often with one major company at the centre. American companies, on the other hand, have more fluid market settings that allow for more radical breakthrough innovations.

What if we go back even further? An Israeli professor has studied the deeper question of why humans as a species have innovated and developed ahead of other animal species.[19] In exploring this question two major factors have been identified: our ability to be flexible (an important aspect of creative thinking) combined with our ability to collaborate in large numbers. Bees, for example, can collaborate in large numbers, maintaining colonies of up to 80 000 bees, each with its specialist role and tasks, but they are apparently unable to be flexible. (This might help explain the bee crisis that hit North America and Europe starting in the 1990s, in which whole hives of bees disappeared overnight—a phenomenon attributed to 'colony collapse disorder'.) Chimpanzees, on the other hand, can be very flexible but do not cooperate in large numbers. Collaboration and flexibility are two of the major principles for innovation that we explore in Part II—in chapters 7 and 8 respectively.

Jared Diamond believes it is critically important to understand why certain countries and cultures have become disproportionately powerful, and why some have innovated and developed far more than others—not in order to judge or grade them or to claim our own superiority, but for mutual understanding, and to consider what lessons we can draw from the past to apply usefully to the future. Diamond writes, 'I do not assume that industrialized states are "better" than hunter-gatherer tribes, or that the abandonment of the hunter-gatherer lifestyle for iron-based statehood represents "progress," or that it has led to an increase in human happiness.' Such understanding can certainly provide interesting insights into the different approaches to the current innovation race.

Comparing apples and rambutans

When one of America's most recognised anthropologists, Ruth Benedict, was appointed to research Japanese culture during World War II, she quickly identified some major differences.[20] The idea was that by understanding the cultural differences between Japan and America, the Americans could learn how to understand and cooperate with the Japanese better. Benedict went on to refer to the contrasting cultures as 'East' and 'West', and the terms have stuck ever since. The identification of this typical dichotomy has no doubt both hindered and helped our understandings of different cultures—hindered if we allow it to become a form of stereotyping, helped if we use it as a basis for understanding and respect.

The concepts of 'East' and 'West' as starkly contrasting terms now seem to be firmly established. Yet are there really such clear differences between the Asian and Islamic worlds, on the one hand, and Europe, European settler cultures and Latin America on the other, as these terms suggest? (We should note also that large parts of the world, for instance Africa, seem to have been left out of this simple division altogether.) Traditionally some general contrasts have been made between the philosophical foundations of the East (which has a long history of collectivism and cultural unity, as emphasised in the Buddhist and Taoist traditions) and the West (which stresses principles of individualism and democratic rights that to some degree stem from Christian beliefs). Such comparisons need to use very broad brush strokes, and must be used only for learning rather than for judging, but they can be helpful in identifying the different routes innovation has taken in different cultural contexts around the world. These differences have undoubtedly impacted rates and types of innovation in different cultures.

The Buddhist philosophy, for example, emphasises emptying the mind, freeing oneself of possessions and slowing down, while the western capitalist approach encourages accumulation, the active pursuit of worldly ambition and speeding up. Many in the West busily fill their minds with knowledge, their houses and their lives with things, and their time with activities. Whereas in the East creativity comes from a state of 'emptiness and openness', in the West it stems from the accumulation of information and ideas. Whereas in the East there is an emphasis on 'living in the now', in the West there is a desire to rapidly innovate towards a better future.

Edward de Bono talks about how in our constant state of busyness people no longer find the time for reflection—to think about new ideas and to 'incubate' them—which can greatly impact our ability to innovate. We are often asked by companies to help increase innovation for their busy employees through a short seminar of a few hours. In reality this process needs time—and a culture change to support it. It can be difficult to make a difference in these brief intervals squeezed in between important deadlines.

The traditional eastern view of an object is often completely different from the western view. According to the classic Taoist philosophical text the *Tao Te Ching*, empty spaces are significant. The empty space in a clay pot makes it useful as a vessel. Japanese maps work on the spaces between roads rather than by identifying the roads themselves.[21] Ask someone in the West for an address and they will refer to the street; ask someone in Japan and they will refer to the block number—the streets are simply unnamed spaces between the blocks. (Houses are also numbered in the order in which they are built, rather than physical sequential order!)

Westerners have feared empty spaces (*horror vacui*) since at least medieval times. Borders and gaps in manuscripts and artworks were commonly filled with intricate and detailed scrollwork. The edges of medieval maps, depicting a world yet unknown, were lavishly decorated with mythological creatures that were thought to inhabit these mysterious lands and oceans. Even today many in the West fear empty spaces in their lives, which might explain why we seek to avoid having too much time on our hands by keeping busy, and why we spend so much time socialising, even (through social media) when physically alone. Our time is full, our calendar is full, our life is full. We 'mind the gap' so much there are often no openings left!

> According to the classic Taoist philosophical text the *Tao Te Ching*, empty spaces are significant. The empty space in a clay pot makes it useful as a vessel; the empty space between the spokes in a wheel makes it a wheel. Westerners have feared empty spaces (*horror vacui*) since at least medieval times.

There appear to be some other interesting cultural differences when it comes to creativity and innovation.[22] Germans and some Chinese[23] may be more process oriented, for example, while Japanese tend to be more committed to follow-through. Research in Hong Kong has found that westerners view creativity primarily as depending on the individual attributes of a creative person, whereas Chinese people view creativity primarily in terms of a person's social influence. In Scandinavia creativity is related to an individual attitude providing a way of dealing with life's challenges; in the US there is a greater focus on ideation, while the Chinese emphasise the consolidation of ideas. These (certainly oversimplified) general principles offer useful perspectives on the innovation process as a whole; all are different, but all have value.

Different cultural areas of focus in the innovation process

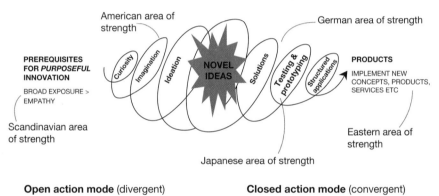

Open action mode (divergent)   **Closed action mode** (convergent)

Let's focus a little on Japan in particular, since Tokyo stands out as an exception on the innovation bubble map we included earlier in the chapter. While Japan scores very highly on innovation measures (remember, these measures are usually based on the number of patents produced), with 39 Japanese companies in the 2014 Top 100 Global Innovators List, compared with 35 US companies,[24] the cultural approach does not seem to support the typical western views of innovation. A number of companies have expressed a frustration at the levels of bureaucracy that can seem to slow down innovation. The distribution of exoskeletons that can help paraplegics to walk has been held up in Japan as a result of such challenges. 'We boast the No. 1 skill in robotics, but how we can actually use the skills is where we are behind the rest of the world,' a Japanese robot maker has said.[25]

The reason Japan has done so well is that rather than focusing on ideation, the Japanese play to their great strengths in iteration and the sorts of gradual improvements that can lead to innovative results. As a culture there is a strong commitment to, and perseverance in seeing through, the innovation process over the long term. The marketing head of a Fortune 500 company (originally from the US and currently based in Japan) has observed that while the Japanese might not be bubbling with ideas, they are a high-commitment society. With any potential change there can be a great deal of deliberation and an apparently restrictive bureaucracy, but when a commitment is made to a new idea or change everyone will get on board and stick with it. So although there may be fewer ideas coming through and the process of conversation to an innovation can be slow, those ideas are more likely to make it to the finish line. Interestingly, the Japanese seem to have a similar perception of themselves when it comes to innovation, as they tend not to rank themselves highly on creativity scores.[26]

Imagine if an organisation were able to take the best of each culture and integrate those elements into the innovation process: you would see that ideation and commitment to follow through in innovation are both important (look back to the double-sided model of the innovation process). Effective innovation needs both elements.

These are just some examples of how different cultures produce very different outcomes in relation to innovation. Let's now explore some of the philosophies behind these differences.

Linear vs circular thinking

Shitao's Buddhist philosophy had a profound impact on the way he thought and painted. Buddhist teaching represents life as a wheel, in contrast to the linear western understanding, which represents life as a straight line with a definitive start and end. We recognised the depth of this philosophy in Bhutan, where we reflected on the power of the numerous prayer wheels. The Buddhist ideal is closed synthesis, while the western ideal is open exploration.

The Judeo-Christian creation story from the Book of Genesis clearly demonstrates how western thought has been shaped to think of creativity and innovation as having a finite beginning and end, with a focus on the tangible products created. This leads to some interesting potential cultural differences. Westerners tend to privilege the idea of cosmic creation and the concept of linear movement toward a new point. They love the idea of a dramatic breakthrough, a futuristic innovation that seems to come out of the blue, but that points to new advances that will allow them to leapfrog ahead of the competition. Modern western culture also tends to emphasise the end product created as the focus of innovation. Bam! How did this inventor come up with that fabulous new IT system? Voila! There it is on the display stand, the beautiful, peerless new iPhone.

Contrast this with the eastern perspective, which focuses more heavily on the process of producing ideas and the authenticity of the discovery process, rather than on the output of creative products. Here the creative process is typically 'cyclic, nonlinear and enlightenment oriented'. [27] It involves connecting to a larger reality, reconfiguring or rediscovering existing elements. For example, in Hinduism creativity can express traditional truths in a new way, and in classical Chinese visual art a well-known topic can be reinterpreted in a new way.[28]

Rather than breaking completely from tradition, the eastern view tends to favour incremental changes.[29] These innovations may not be obvious to the western eye, but they are nevertheless significant innovations in the East. The Chinese also focus on achieving success through performing repetitive rituals, which will increase their good luck, rather than through hard work to reach a defined outcome, as emphasised in the West.[30]

Again, these broad-stroke images support some interesting differences between 'open' (western) and 'closed' (eastern) approaches. One is about *exploration* and breakthroughs, the other is about *exploitation* and incremental iterations of known ideas. One focuses on the importance of the initial ideation and end-product implementation, the other focuses on the importance of the cyclical process itself. As we have been discussing, there are always multiple angles and complexities that need to be considered. Nothing is straightforward 'black' or 'white'. As introduced in the first chapter, *transformational innovation* will synthesise different perspectives and utilise that potential tension to fuel innovation.

Hollywood and the westernisation of innovation

Can you guess the most recognised symbol in the world? It's not a religious symbol, or a cultural emblem with deep value, but a symbol that looms over many street corners and shopping centres in cities and towns in 62 per cent of countries around the world. Have you guessed it? It's the McDonald's logo! Along with Coca-Cola, Colgate and a few other dominant international brands, simple logos like this have successfully infiltrated the most distant corners of the earth, and the implications are significant. Why? Firstly, because these symbols are all American. That is tremendously noteworthy in itself. Secondly, because these are all symbols of consumerism.

Just as in art our perceptions can be limited by our psychological blocks, by our tendency to take shortcuts and see what we expect to see rather than what is really there, these symbols can become so powerful that they can limit our ability to think more openly by shaping our expectations. If most people around the world are being exposed to these western symbols, they may be influenced and limited by the values they represent.

A quick history review reveals a lot about how the concepts of creativity and innovation emerged and how they have been shaped through a distinctly western cultural perspective. *Create* comes from the Latin word *creare* (to make or grow). The first known use of the word *creativity* was by a Polish poet in the seventeenth century. It cropped up again in 1875 in a description of Shakespeare's poetry. Only after the Second World War was the usage of the word creativity common enough in English for it to be included in an English dictionary.[31]

The word *innovation* was first used in Europe as an extension of invention and with reference to renewing contracts. It implied small, incremental revisions rather than dramatic breakthroughs. In seventeenth-century Europe, riven by war and a divided Church, change was often widely feared. For both the Roman and the Reformed Church, innovation was abhorred as an individualistic pursuit that threatened their control, and to be called an innovator was actually a great insult. Puritan Henry Burton accused those who wanted to see the Church change of being 'innovators', and then in an ironic twist he himself was accused of being an innovator and sentenced to life imprisonment before having his ears amputated.

Innovation had become the hero by 1939, when Schumpeter was linking it to economics and entrepreneurship, first introducing the term into the western capitalist business context.[32]

Current interpretations of creativity and innovation generally conform to the American usage. The idea that everyone can be creative, and that everyone can be trained to become more creative, may be a distinctly western ideal. There are certainly cultures that even today do not have equivalent words for creativity or innovation. A survey of 28 languages in Africa found that 27 of them had no word directly comparable to *creativity* (the exception being Arabic).[33] In Africa the concept is more often associated with a pervasive way of life rather than a distinct, separate quality. In a study of the same African region more than two-thirds of the people surveyed described themselves as involved in creative activities in their daily life.[34] Poland, on the other hand, has several words for creativity (one word, for example, for everyday creativity and another for eminent creativity).[35] There is a clear challenge from the outset when attempting to compare cultural perspectives on creativity when a number of cultures do not explicitly recognise the concept.

The more significant the role a concept plays in your culture, the more it will be recognised in your language. It's commonly shared that the Inuit have more than 50 different words for 'snow' while the Sami have as many as 1000 words for 'reindeer'.[36] So perhaps while the defined concept of creativity is a priority in some cultures, in others it is more subtly integrated into what they do rather than explicitly discussed.

So the focus on developing creativity is an individualistic interpretation that doesn't necessarily fit well in other cultures. We mentioned that, since Schumpeter, innovation has been closely related to entrepreneurship and expansion, which are clearly linked to western capitalist ideology. Back in 1580 French Renaissance philosopher Michel de Montaigne observed that 'strangeness and novelty... generally give things value',[37] implying a link between creativity and capitalism.[38]

Many Americans are persuaded that their society is more open to creativity and innovation than others,[39] and America has successfully marketed its concept of creativity to the world. Young people in Asian countries are increasingly embracing American values over traditional eastern values. In Hong Kong, mainland China and Singapore the majority of young people surveyed in a research study were found to value individualism and imagination over community and communalism. A study of five companies in Japan has challenged the traditional assumption that group-mindedness and a bottom-up approach are essential determinants of creativity these days.[40]

A number of assumptions made about the concept of innovation are also being challenged. Firstly, there is the assumption that innovation is related to product development and technical invention, as already discussed. This has meant that when compared against other cultures, the West will always appear to be more advanced. While we may talk about the role of creativity in all cultures, innovation tends to be associated almost exclusively with the 'advanced' western cultures, and yet, as already discussed, creativity and innovation are intricately linked.

> Jugaad innovation is a fascinating creative concept directed towards reducing the complexity and cost of goods to make them more affordable ... It is all about learning to be creative to survive.

An innovation may not be scalable or designed for commercial purposes yet it can still be significant. Jugaad innovation is a fascinating creative concept directed towards reducing the complexity and cost of goods to make them more affordable, especially in poor communities in Asian countries such as India. It is all about learning to be creative to survive.[41] This idea of ad-hoc innovation and flexibility born of necessity has even been applied to space technology.[42] In this context innovation is not simply about self-actualisation or individual development or product or technical development; it is a form of creative thinking that ensures individuals and communities can deal with challenges.

The inevitable shift towards a global village

The global cultural milieu is changing rapidly. We are becoming ever more closely interconnected through advanced technology and communications and this is impacting the ways we innovate. As journalist and author Thomas Friedman has said, 'When the world is flat, you can innovate without having to emigrate.'[43] Cultures are changing dramatically, and the differences in experiences and perspectives on creativity and innovation are decreasing rapidly. With increasing globalisation people with very different backgrounds and viewpoints are gradually coming together in one big melting pot. Yet think about what would happen if we lost all these unique cultural perspectives!

All countries and cultures around the world are now pretty much interconnected, and we are all participating in the same race. We're all in it together. As we discussed in the previous chapter, this is happening whether we like it or not and whether we choose to participate in it or not. The reality is that the western perspective of the race is currently dominating, and we need to understand how this will impact our mutual future.

Back in the 1960s Marshall McLuhan first imagined the world as a global village, where physical distance is defeated by technology — an international society within which different cultural ideas and principles are increasingly shared and shaped by new relationships across countries and cultures. Of course the internet is the very embodiment of this prediction. The internet itself ironically originally emerged from US military research, as did many other technological inventions. In this case, the military was interested in connecting industry, the government and academia for strategic purposes. (It's sad to reflect on how so much money and focus has gone into preparing for war rather than living successfully in times of peace, but that's a whole different discussion ...)

We now have an 'electronic superhighway' reaching around the world, and this is impacting our experience of creativity across the globe.[44] There is a double bind inherent in this. On one level, the broader exposure to ideas will bring greater variety and creativity. Indeed these rapid changes in themselves demand more creative and innovative responses. On the other hand, the cross-pollination of ideas resulting from closer contact, more international

> The broader exposure to ideas will bring greater variety and creativity. Indeed these rapid changes in themselves demand more creative and innovative responses.

educational opportunities and global media exposure can lead to greater homogenisation, heavily influenced by the dominance of western individualism and consumerism.

The paradox is that while we are getting closer in many ways, in other ways the distance is growing. Some theorists now talk about a growing distance between countries in cultural, administrative, geographic and economic areas.[45] We are all so close yet so far apart. There is a way to go to bridge these gaps and find ways to *respect* and *connect* with one another without losing the unique traditional identity that makes each culture special.

Starting to see things differently

We have talked about the Ming Dynasty artist Shitao and how his life experiences and ability to render multiple perspectives allowed him to make much deeper connections—to paint from his 'heart's mind' through the principle of 'spirit resonance'—and brought incredible emotional and spiritual power to his art. This leads us into the next important principle for purpose-driven innovation.

We mentioned that the western painting tradition generally aimed at faithful, if sometimes static, depiction of the subject. Chinese art, by contrast, tended to emphasise movement and the dynamic changes of life. Rather than painting from direct observation, as the western artist was inclined to do, the Chinese artist would take time to walk in the woods and wander among ancient trees, or spend time in the mountains to absorb their majesty, before returning to the studio to paint from the 'mind's eye'. Not simply a detached observer, the artist would embed his personal feelings and emotions into the image created through 'spirit resonance'.

Shitao was working during a period of great social upheaval. As a member of the Ming royal house during the Manchurian invasion, he narrowly escaped death, quite by chance. This traumatic experience led directly to his decision to become a Buddhist monk and shaped his growth as an artist in close connection with his emotions. The contrast with his peers can be seen in the story of the 'Four Monks of Late Ming'.

According to the story, each of these four artists had converted to Buddhism and cut themselves off from the earthly world. Each of them, however, had very different experiences through this period and subsequently reflected their different experiences through their art. Where, at one extreme, Ba Da

Shan Ren produced works that seemed detached and aloof, Shitao drew from his religious passion to infuse incredible warmth and humanity into his paintings. This brought a timeless richness and creative intensity to his paintings that can still be marvelled at today. Most importantly, Shitao's paintings drew viewers in at an emotional level, triggering *empathy*.

Shitao's paintings used white space for dramatic effect and invited the viewer to think and imagine for themselves. They demonstrated the kind of empathy that can only have come from broad exposure and experience.

A Zen koan (a paradoxical story), attributed to a conversation between Zen Master Ryutan (760–840) and the scholar Tokusan[46], crops up quite frequently in contemporary western contexts. In the story the visiting scholar asked the Zen Master to teach him about Zen, but then immediately launched into a doctrinal monologue. The Zen Master listened patiently, then picked up a teapot and began filling the scholar's cup. After the cup was filled and the tea flowed onto the floor the scholar exclaimed that the cup could hold no more. The Zen Master replied, 'You are like this cup. You are full of ideas about Buddha's Way. You come and ask for teaching, but your cup is full; I can't put anything in. Before I can teach you, you'll have to empty your cup.'

An 'empty' mind is valued in Buddhism because it enables new thinking. According to Buddhist teaching, we usually gain new knowledge by first unconsciously linking it to something we already know. This often helps us to learn, but for creative thinking and receiving new knowledge it is not useful: we need to be able to start with a fresh mind.

You would think from what we have discussed in this chapter that travel would broaden the mind. Yet it will only do so if the mind is first *open* to new ideas and to learning. We are constantly amazed at how many people travel without actually experiencing other cultures. When Australian 'yobbos' travel abroad they continue to see and experience everything through their own narrow cultural filters. They travel on their national airline, and continue to drink Australian beer in Australian-owned pubs while watching Australian football, and they expect standards to match those from home. Though they may visit other cultures, they do not open themselves up to learning from them. They are 'tourists', outsiders looking in, rather than 'travellers', who aim to connect with and learn from the cultures they visit in order to see *from* other perspectives.

The ability to see things from different angles, to draw others in while at the same time entering their worlds, provides a formidable foundation for establishing the awareness, curiosity, imagination, and ultimately the empathy, that make an essential starting point for purpose-driven innovation. How do we become 'travellers' in life rather than 'tourists'? The answer will be tackled in the next chapter, when we look at the vital ingredients needed for making the real connections that will best prepare us for the 'innovation race'.

PRODUCTION NOTES

The 'reality' of reality TV

Dana Gould, comedian and writer for *The Simpsons*, captures the innate irony of 'reality' TV when he says[47]: 'You will never experience less reality than when you are watching a reality show. You're watching people who aren't actors put into situations created by people who aren't writers ... And you are passively observing this, watching an amateur production of nothing. It's like a photo of a drawing of a hologram.'

Reality TV is not 'real' at all, as much as it is portrayed that way. Everything the viewer sees is what the producer wants them to see: It is an artificial version of reality. Since the early days the genre has evolved into a highly manipulated version of reality, with scenes carefully framed and outcomes carefully crafted and edited in such a way that they no longer reflect the reality they were designed to reflect. Storylines are preconceived, cast members are coached, and scenes are staged specifically for the cameras. In the 1950s an Austrian philosopher observed that TV was distorting our perspectives of reality by making objects usually at great distance appear closer (for example, glaciers, exotic animals, politics), while making objects close to us become distant (for example, pets, neighbours, co-workers). Imagine how reality has become distorted by reality shows!

We need to be aware of how our perspectives can be manipulated, to ensure we can step back from these artificially created viewpoints and start to explore alternative perspectives. Through emptying the mind and developing an openness to new ideas, particularly from different cultures, we can start to develop the sort of fresh new thinking that is needed for purpose-driven innovation.

PERSPECTIVES CHECKLIST

- ☐ Are you able to use 'shifting perspectives', looking at a subject from many angles at the same time?
- ☐ Are you able to incorporate multiple points of view when solving problems?
- ☐ Are you aware of the different cultural perspectives you can draw on for the innovation process?
- ☐ Do you deliberately look for alternative viewpoints to your own?
- ☐ Do you approach the innovation process with an 'empty' or 'open' mind?
- ☐ Is the principle of 'shifting perspectives' embedded in your organisation?

3

ARE YOU A TOURIST OR TRAVELLER?

How cultural awareness can encourage empathy and
increase the potential for purpose-driven innovation

*The second part of the preparation process for purpose-driven innovation takes us
deeper — from simply being able to see multiple perspectives, to being able to experience
them through authentic empathy. This provides the best way to ensure innovations are the
most relevant, useful and sustainable.*

This chapter will help you to:

- *put yourself in someone else's place in order to see what they see and feel what
  they feel*
- *move from detachment to connection with the innovation process*
- *learn how to become a 'traveller' (able to actively connect with and learn from other
  people and cultures) rather than a 'tourist' (who merely observes another culture as
  if from the outside).*
- *build a more empathetic and authentic organisational culture*

*Key challenge: How to develop a deep understanding of real innovation needs through
authentic empathy.*

How far would you go to try to see from someone else's position and
'put yourself in someone else's shoes' in order to learn more about their
perspective? A few years ago a group of Australian celebrities did this to the
extreme by journeying to some of the most dangerous corners of the world
in a televised social experiment. This was an attempt to capture people's
emotions as they travelled the reverse journey that refugees often have to

take in their search for a safe haven, in this case from Australia back to the frightening war zones from which these people have fled.

Most reality TV shows are highly engineered and designed to take people to their limits in order to bring out the worst in them, which usually translates into high ratings. They are heavily scripted, contrived, and edited so that they no longer represent reality. When we spoke to the producer of this particular reality TV show, Rick McPhee, he explained that in this show the team had done something quite different: they had designed a 'constructed documentary' and, as he said, 'Put the participants in challenging situations, but then sat back and filmed the circumstances and events along the way.' The situations themselves were challenging enough that they readily brought out the deepest emotions. Nobody knew what the process might entail and what the outcome might be, so it was a highly risky venture on many fronts. The final result was very powerful.

The program was called *Go Back to Where You Came From*, taking its title from a common taunt that people the world over use to express their dislike or fear of 'foreign intruders'. It's a title that alludes to the fact that we can quickly pass judgment on a situation. The problem is that through this sort of mindset we can jump to simplistic conclusions and close off the opportunity to find creative solutions.

The power of a show like this is that it allowed participants and viewers to experience the multiple challenges faced by people in this predicament, through entering into the lives of others. This process allowed people to develop *authentic* empathy—the critical first step for purpose-driven innovation. Empathy allows us to see and feel multiple perspectives, and it enables us to identify the complexity of the problems people face. The result is that we are more easily able to identify a variety of creative solutions beyond the standard simple responses. Think about, for example, how many people have made judgments about refugees and never even met one, let alone heard their story or entered into their world—seen what they've seen and felt what they've felt?

Rick explained how the first episode of the show was a particularly ambitious undertaking that stretched everyone to the limit. Rick had himself accompanied the celebrities as they were filmed completing a dangerous journey in a rickety old Indonesian fishing boat across the Indian ocean, before visiting Indonesia and Malaysia (interim destinations with immigration processing centres), and flying on to war zones in countries like Afghanistan, the Democratic Republic of Congo, Iraq and Somalia. The celebrities slept and ate on the floor with refugees, and they heard their powerful stories as they spoke in tears about their desire to save their children at all costs. The participants were taken so close to the danger that they were shot at in Syria near the front line, they narrowly missed a deadly plane crash in the Democratic Republic of Congo, and they witnessed a sickening brutal midnight police raid in Malaysia.

The celebrities were not acting the part; the whole team actually made the complete perilous journey themselves. There were no stunt doubles filling in for the risky scenes, no make-up vans nearby ready to clean them up and pamper them off set, and no helicopters on standby to whisk them out of harm's way. All participants had their wallets, passports and mobile phones taken away from them and all external communications cut off for the 25 days they were involved in the project. They were to feel what it is like to be out of touch with loved ones, to be without possessions and disempowered. This was reality TV in its most literal form, a deeply visceral immersive encounter with the harsher side of life that greatly affected the contestants. It was a show that was designed as an authentic learning experience rather than pure entertainment.

Much to Rick's surprise the show was a great hit. It became the number one trending topic on Twitter worldwide the first night it was broadcast. Viewers were shocked to be literally taken so close to such a powerful issue. One of the first intelligent and educational reality TV projects we have seen, this show marked a shift in the genre. Rick and his team had taken an interesting new concept, the idea of taking people into a confronting social situation to challenge their comfort levels and prejudices and preconceptions, and had given it a new twist. A few English reality shows had sown the seeds of this idea — shows such as *Famous, Rich and Homeless,* which put celebrities on the streets of London to sleep rough, or *Blood, Sweat and Luxuries,* which took rich bratty children to meet the kids working in sweat shops producing their iPhones, or to diamond mines in Africa to experience the harsh conditions. Rick saw how powerful these programs were, and his idea was to develop this concept through the journey theme.

Just 10 years before this program went to air 48 refugees from Iraq had died in Australian waters when their boat was smashed against the treacherous rocks off Christmas Island and sank, their deaths dramatically captured on live TV news. From the comfort of our lounge rooms we watched in horror as the old fishing boat crammed with desperate people was pummelled by the large surf, while rescuers on the scene could do little to help. Events like this polarised the Australian public—some feeling deep compassion for the plight of the refugees, others becoming even more determined to 'stop the boats' and keep the problem out of sight and out of mind, and to 'protect' Australian shores from new waves of immigrants. (It's interesting to note that few with this mindset recognised the irony that apart from the Indigenous Aboriginal people *all* Australians are immigrants! Had the Eora people of Botany Bay been able to 'stop the boats' and prevent Captain Cook from landing, our nation's history might have unfolded quite differently ...) Over the years, and increasingly in recent times, such stories have been repeated around the globe, with countless thousands dying in their desperate quest to escape war and want and find a new life.

It's time to use problems such as these to develop creative thinking, and to find innovative new solutions to similar burgeoning problems.

Seeing from the heart's mind

Go Back to Where You Came From dramatically changed the outlook and opinions of both participants and viewers. Reality TV producers aim to get emotional buy-in from their audience, and this series was exceptionally successful in this regard. We know of many people (including our own daughter, who went on to champion the cause) whose empathy for refugees and asylum seekers grew after being touched by their personal stories as told on this show. And it was a great antidote to prejudice and racism. Here reality TV became a medium for education and transformation by using empathy as a powerful educational tool, which was itself an innovation.

Exposure to these sorts of confronting cultural experiences can help people to see the world through their 'heart's mind'. This enables people to develop the sort of deep empathy that opens us up to creative possibilities. In this way it is possible to became a 'traveller' (open to learning from different experiences) rather than a 'tourist' (for whom exposure can lead to judgement or indifference).

Fortunately we don't have to endure a traumatic experience personally, as did the artist Shitao (chapter 2) or even the courageous participants in *Go Back to Where You Came From*, in order to develop our capacity to see multiple perspectives and connect more deeply with other people. But to really ignite our creativity and innovation we do need to be prepared to open up to new learning opportunities. As illustrated, broad perspectives and experiences are the foundation for empathy, which in turn is a launchpad for the innovation process.

The importance of empathy in purpose-driven innovation

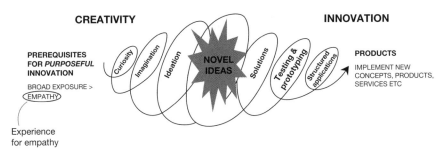

As this model shows, we all need to learn to integrate creativity and innovation. We need the spirit connection and openness to broad perspectives to ignite purpose-driven innovation; at the same time we need a pragmatic focus for implementing innovation. It is important to be open to diverse perspectives and to connect deeply with them, but we must then home in on specific practical solutions. The process starts with subjectivity through empathy, but it must end with objectivity.

Commercial innovation that connects

Who would have thought that emotions would contribute to better innovation and business success? Yet that is exactly what researchers have found: the best ideas and solutions come from better emotional connections. Empathy is now pretty much universally recognised as an integral part of the innovation process and a foundation for creative development. Bestselling business author Dan Pink believes empathy 'makes the world a better place' because it is all about 'standing in someone else's shoes, feeling with his or her heart, seeing with his or her eyes'.[1]

The *design thinking* approach to innovation, as popularised by Stanford d.school and the global design firm IDEO, has captured and developed the concept of empathy, to make it inseparable from the process. Design thinking is a powerful ideation and design process widely used by businesses today to come up with new products and services. Leading innovative companies such as Apple and Google use design thinking on a day-to-day basis.

The process focuses on looking at a challenge that may appear to have no clear solution, identifying the underlying problem at the heart of the issue, then trying to understand the different perspectives and needs related to the issue. The designer will initially identify the desires and needs of the users and, through an iterative process of prototyping, develop products, systems and services that best meet the user's needs. CEO and IDEO President Tim Brown describes design thinking as 'a human-centered approach to innovation that draws from the designer's toolkit to integrate the needs of people, the possibilities of technology, and the requirements for business success'.[2]

Brown also nominates an outward-looking perspective and empathy as prerequisites for innovation: 'A sense of inquiry, of curiosity, is essential for innovation, and the quickest way for removing curiosity in my opinion is to have organizations that are too inward-facing,' he suggests. 'A sense of empathy for the world and for the people whose problems they might be trying to solve — that's essential.'[3] Empathy provides the 'human-centred' focus in design thinking. It is the link between the person designing the new product or solution and the end user. By starting with empathy, the designer can understand and relate to the issues the user faces and therefore create designs that best meet their needs.

The importance of empathy and understanding the user's perspective when designing new products and services has been embraced by a wide range of companies. As an example of how this can work in practice, let's consider the challenge of shopping trolleys. Have you ever noticed how difficult these trolleys can be to negotiate around the supermarket aisles, how items become wedged or buried deep in the basket, and how frustratingly long it can take to get through the checkout process? IDEO was set the challenge of designing a new shopping cart (it's worth watching the ABC Nightline video that shows them going through the process[4]).

To deal with shoppers' frustration at having to wrestle a full trolley up and down the aisles, a number of years ago IDEO designers came up with ideas for carts that are more like skeletons providing a frame for baskets to be slotted in and stacked to allow for collecting and searching for a few items at a time. They added hooks around the edges of the skeletal structure on which shoppers can hang plastic bags. They then designed a cart concept with a scanner on the handle so shoppers can do the scanning as they place the items in the basket rather than having to go through the whole process at the checkout at the end. IDEO have continued applying these principles in a range of contexts over the years (for example, LA County voting, Ford Pill Pack, and so on)

This is a great example of empathy in business innovation, but let's go further. As design thinking is most often used as a means for designing commercial products, the emphasis can be on tapping into the *desires* of individuals mainly for commercial purposes — or even creating desires consumers didn't know they had and turning them into needs, as discussed in chapter 1. If we're not just looking at selling a product, the empathy described in this approach has its limitations. This can lead to the creation of a lot of useless and wasteful products. *Sustainable* and *transformational innovation,* on the other hand, connects with real-world *needs.* It helps to put the meaning and purpose back into innovation. IDEO has aimed to do this through their non-profit arm IDEO.org, which focusses on design challenges in poverty alleviation. This takes us back to the original core purpose of the concept of empathy, which was to understand another person's perspective in order to relate to their experiences, to feel what they feel, and ultimately to help improve their lives through connecting with them on a deeper level.

Taking this a step further, empathy can become a deeper, more transformational compassion: it becomes the sort of *authentic empathy* we have described when it takes the form of positive action that makes a difference in people's lives. This is the second stretch concept we'd like you to consider.

As an example of this principle at work, a number of useful inventions can be traced back to creative people who have attempted to understand and assist the disabled. Inventions such as the bendy straw, the telephone, the typewriter and icon-based keyboards have all come from inventors trying to help disabled people they knew. 'In empathizing with others, we create things that we might never have created for ourselves,' says a Co.Design article on the subject. 'We see past the specifics of what we know, to experiences that might actually be universal.'[5]

By using empathy as the starting point for the creative process, we can begin to ensure that innovation and progress are positive and purpose-driven. Before jumping into the mechanics of ideation and innovation, it is essential that we first make connections through *authentic empathy* by exploring diverse experiences.

> By using empathy as the starting point for the creative process, we can start to ensure that innovation and progress are positive and purpose-driven.

Shukanteki and *kyakkanteki*: elements of authentic empathy

The Japanese have a couple of useful terms for two contrasting perspectives on innovation.[6] The word *shukanteki* reveals why they believe it is important to embrace and empathise with all cultural perspectives rather than just taking one point of view. It refers to the concept of subjectivity and means literally 'the host's point of view'. The second word, *kyakkanteki,* takes another angle in referring to 'the guest's point of view', implying the ability to perceive oneself or a situation from the outside, as if as a stranger looking in.[7] Like the artist Shitao, the Japanese also believe that all phenomena can and should be seen from multiple points of view.[8] While westerners place high value on a detached, 'objective' perspective and an unemotional, scientific approach, the Japanese believe that each additional perspective contributes to creating a more comprehensive, connected and holistic picture.

Go Back to Where You Came From triggered deep empathetic connections. Rather than allowing us to indulge in vicarious and judgemental viewing and *schadenfreude* (the pleasure of watching others' embarrassment and misfortune) for the sake of entertainment, it *taught* us by forcing us to really see what others see and feel what others feel. A typically western perspective may be alienating us from the deeper meaning of what we do. A strong emphasis on science (reflected in the western artistic tradition) can lead to a detachment from emotion and purpose. By considering different cultural perspectives, however, we can potentially start to rediscover the purpose behind what we do.

Watching someone else in pain can give us some sense of going through the same experience ourselves. That's why seeing the deep emotional pain of asylum seekers in the *Go Back to Where You Came From* program resonated with so many viewers. This is not just the imagination at work; it is about triggering a deeper physiological connection through our innate ability to relate to what others go through. We can literally feel others' pain. Simply observing someone else receive a pinprick to their finger can elicit in us the same response in the same neuron. This is a survival mechanism: by learning from others through imitation, we can learn how best to survive. But researchers believe it is also a means of *connecting* us with others and helping us to relate to them through empathy. It helps us to access and understand the minds of others, which facilitates social behaviour.[9]

People who are more empathetic have been found to be more purpose-driven and more successful, mostly because they have a greater understanding of the reasons *why* they do what they do. They are able to embrace failure more readily (a core requirement for creative thinking, because it requires the ability to try, fail and try again), and they see setbacks as temporary obstacles and positive learning experiences rather than as indications of failure.

Philosopher Roman Krznaric proposes that *outrospection*, as an antidote for the introspective perspective of the twentieth century, can help develop curiosity and creative thinking and ultimately build better relationships and a better world.[10] By expanding your moral universe, and by understanding others' world views and beliefs along with the experiences that shaped them, Krznaric suggests, you can expand your thinking and open up possibilities for real transformative change. (It's worth watching Krznaric's animated video for a good overview of his ideas.)

We have argued that empathy is a foundation for creative thinking and the first essential step in the purpose-driven innovation process. It should also be the driving force behind *transformational* innovation. It is a simple yet potent tool for cultural understanding that takes us beyond our more limited perspectives and into the realm of the possible.

Sure, innovation may be triggered by a competition or hackathon, or it may arise from a casual observation or desire, but the purpose-driven innovation we are talking about here can only come from a connection with people's deeper needs. It is only through being able to see things from other angles, to experience things the way others experience them, that we can learn to get outside our own habitual ways of thinking and see things differently. This is a foundation for meaningful creative thinking and innovation. Authentic empathy ensures that whatever creative ideas are developed will actually connect with the end user by meeting a relevant deeper need or addressing a relevant challenge.

> Authentic empathy ensures that whatever creative ideas are developed will actually connect with the end user by meeting a relevant, deeper need or addressing a relevant challenge.

At the deepest level, if empathy requires that new innovations be sustainable and ethical, shouldn't true empathy extend to considering whether the battery in our phone was produced by child labour, or whether dangerous pesticides were used in the production of the cotton in the clothing we wear?

The problem is that empathy takes time. So here is an initial paradox for the race: that we need to take the time to really get to know the people and contexts we are innovating for and to develop the sort of 'spirit resonance' that will enable us to more deeply engage with others, yet often that time is not available. We also need to take the time to, at least metaphorically, 'travel far and wide' in order to gain the broadest perspective possible before zooming in on a particular experience.

By seeing and learning to accept different cultural perspectives, we can draw each other into our different experiences and overcome potential barriers.[11] Rather than using cultural comparisons as a basis for judgement, we should learn to use them as a basis for authentic empathy. This will help us really appreciate and understand different perspectives so we can put ourselves in the shoes of others and be of most service to them. We can use this heightened awareness to develop transformational sustainable innovations that can create a better world for all.

We are going to introduce here some reasons why it is important to take the time to understand other cultures in order to understand our own, and to take the time to get to know the people we are innovating for in order to get the process right more quickly and more accurately.

Are you a tourist or traveller?

We can all be guilty of viewing the world from our own perspective, especially when we duck in to visit another country briefly as a tourist. Thomas Cook Vacations has received some hilarious customer complaints from dissatisfied tourists over the years[12]. Here are some of our favourites:

> 'We went on holiday to Spain and had a problem with the taxi drivers as they were all Spanish.'

> 'There were too many Spanish people there. The receptionist spoke Spanish, the food was Spanish. No one told us that there would be so many foreigners.'

> 'I think it should be explained in the brochure that the local convenience store does not sell proper biscuits like custard creams or ginger nuts.'

> 'We had to line up outside to catch the boat and there was no air-conditioning.'

> 'On my holiday to Goa in India, I was disgusted to find that almost every restaurant served curry. I don't like spicy food.'

There was a time before we travelled far beyond our own borders, both physically and metaphorically, when cultural differences unsettled us and reduced our ability to learn from experience. Before we had the opportunity to be exposed to a broad range of diverse experiences, we were not so open to ways of thinking and doing things that were very different from our own.

Let's take traffic as an example. The first time we arrived in India we were confronted by the bedlam of incessantly honking horns, which we found extremely obnoxious. Honking your horn in the United States or Europe or Australia is usually considered rude and aggressive. In our home country we tend to sit in our own car bubble, mostly quite disconnected from those around us, very occasionally venting our anger by muttering obscenities or making an offensive hand signal. We think of this as normal.

In India, though, as we discovered, honking horns is a standard form of communication, and drivers use them to let others on the road know where they are. After spending time in Asia we learned to adapt and literally to 'go with the flow'. We now experience Indian traffic simply as a constantly running stream of noisy, honking fish moving in sync, and we are a lot more aware and accepting of the perpetual movement around us. Our travels in Asia have taught us just how important it is to build an awareness of what people around you are doing and to communicate effectively with them.

Being exposed to different cultures helps to increase our awareness (and our tolerance) of the rich variety of different life experiences there are out there and to broaden our thinking. Being exposed to only one culture is very limiting. You have only one reference point to work from, and that is your own personal perspective looking out. Broader exposure opens up many different ways of experiencing and doing things. It enables us to develop authentic empathy and to think more creatively. And the opportunities offered by travel—whether of the physical kind, through the media or, better still, through connecting with more diverse people within our own community—are something we can all enjoy and benefit from.

The journey theme that runs through this book was deliberately chosen. Research indicates that people who travel and who have lived in other cultures tend to be both more empathetic and more creative, which, as we have emphasised are critical foundations for positive innovation.

Travel stretches the open mind

Travel really does broaden the mind, opening it to new possibilities. If you allow it to.

So are you a tourist or a traveller in life? Are you someone who views and judges others from the outside, or someone who is open to learning from the differences you encounter? That can make a whole world of difference when it comes to developing empathy.

Producers of reality shows like *Go Back to Where You Came From* deliberately exaggerate differences by selecting very diverse groups of participants and putting them in a pressure cooker environment. This helps them dial up the tension and increase the drama—and, they hope, the entertainment value.

Rick McPhee knew that putting together people with very different backgrounds and opinions from their own, in tough conditions, would challenge them. In some instances the experiences they shared as they travelled together dramatically changed the outlook of those who had an open mind while consolidating the prejudices of those who didn't, which intensified the tensions even further. The participants' abilities to learn from other people and be transformed through the experience was either significantly enhanced or reduced, depending on their attitude.

Open-minded travellers have been found to perform better in measures of insight, association and ideas generation.[13] And simply imagining the travel can be as productive as physically travelling to other places. Spending time or living in other cultures can teach individuals to be more adaptable and flexible, which are also important traits in creative thinking.[14] Travel also helps us to recognise that a single thing can have multiple meanings, which

> **Open-minded travellers have been found to perform better in measures of insight, association and ideas generation. And simply mentally imagining the travel can be as productive as physically travelling to other places.**

allows us to deal with ambiguities and paradoxes better.

One study found that people who have been exposed to stimuli from two cultural perspectives (American and Chinese) write more creative stories than those who have been exposed to stimuli from only one culture. People who have lived abroad have been found to be 20 per cent more likely to solve a specific problem than those who have lived at home all their lives.[15]

Travel writer Rick Steves puts it like this: 'I was raised thinking the world is a pyramid, with us on top and everyone else trying to figure it out. And then I travelled and I realised that we have the American dream, and that is a great dream, but other people have their own dreams … Travel wallops my ethnocentricity.'[16]

Multicultural exposure at home can be just as significant,[17] as it also offers alternatives to entrenched cultural habits, exposure to new knowledge and diversity, and opportunities to synthesise new ideas.[18] So spending time with other cultural groups in your own area can be beneficial, and anyone can do this!

Even learning another language appears to be linked to increases in creative thinking. When we decided to live in Indonesia for an extended time, we felt it was important to learn the language in order to really understand a different perspective, and it did help us to connect with the local culture and open up to different possibilities in many ways. Early studies into the potential of bilingualism for creativity found that bilinguals performed better on divergent thinking tests than monolinguals. A recent study of Russian–English bilinguals and English monolingual speakers revealed enhanced performance in creative activities for the bilinguals. The researchers believed that the sort of 'double coding' required for bilingual speaking helped to facilitate greater mental flexibility, as the individual had to learn to code different concepts according to the language and move between two languages effectively.[19]

A study conducted by researchers in Iran compared a group of advanced bilingual language learners between the ages of 16 and 18 with a group of monolingual teens of the same age. They found that the bilingual language learners (who had been studying another language for at least six years) far outperformed the monolingual teens in all four areas tested. One of the factors the researcher believes was important was that bilingual speakers have to learn to switch attention between the two language systems.

This finding coincides with research into the ability to switch from one hemisphere of the brain to the other. It has been found that while predominantly logical, 'left brain' thinkers such as mathematicians are able to stay in this side of the brain for extended periods of time to focus on solving problems, highly creative thinkers such as dancers and jazz musicians are able to switch between the hemispheres more quickly. It has also been suggested that some languages are more conducive to creative thinking because they require faster brain switching.[20] To discover how quickly your brain switches from one side to the other (and how creative that might indicate you are!), visit www.the-innovation-race.com.

Israeli-American psychologist Daniel Kahneman describes how we have two systems that drive the way we think and make choices: a fast intuitive system (what he calls System One) and a more deliberate logical system (System Two). Kahneman illustrates how we can be aware of these systems at work[21], and how it's possible to access both systems at the appropriate times to achieve higher-level thinking.

An additional finding of the Iranian study was that teens' exposure through language to another culture and way of thinking effectively broadened their minds. The authors of the study point out that because other languages may not have the same constructs as our own, we need to learn to be creative to generate other equivalent possibilities, which links to divergent thinking, a critical part of creative thinking.[22] The way you learn a language may also impact your creativity. Collaborative and experiential language learning, for example, are more likely to foster creativity. It's interesting, in passing, to note some of the other benefits of learning a new language, such as in staving off Alzheimer's, multitasking, making better financial decisions and improving English language skills![23]

Considering the impact these findings could and should have on organisations today, it becomes clear that diversity within the organisation is essential for stretching thinking and expanding the brain's capabilities. Openness to diversity and, even more importantly, an ability to understand and empathise with different people with different perspectives can be critical for innovative development. Innovative global market leaders such as Google have learned the hard way how important this is after being criticised for significant gender and racial inequities,[24] but more on that later . . .

Fresh ideas from the fringe

The mythological Cyclopes of Greek and then Roman mythology had an all-seeing eye that could see forwards, backwards and sideways. Born of both the sky (Uranus) and the earth (Gaia), these gods were both visionary and well grounded.[25] The Roman god Janus had two faces, one that looked forward (to the future) and one that looked backward (to the past). Researchers have explored the importance of combining forward-looking cognitive capabilities, based on a map linking potential actions and outcomes, and the backward-looking capabilities that are based on experience.[26]

Go Back to Where You Came From did the work for us. They took us back through people's real experiences to enable us to better understand the present and prepare for the future. If we want to be smart about surviving the current innovation race and redefining innovation for the future, we perhaps also need to draw on the wisdom of the past, including our own and others' experiences.

For Mohammad Ali Baqiri, a 24-year-old minority Hazara Afghan refugee who came to Australia on a leaky boat similar to the one described at the beginning of the chapter, his traumatic experiences as a refugee have undoubtedly contributed to his ability to think innovatively today. Mohammad shared his harrowing story with us when he visited our comfortable home in Sydney, a very long way both physically and mentally from where he began. He and his family had escaped the Taliban when he was seven, then spent the next seven years trying to find refuge. They travelled first to neighbouring Pakistan then made the long journey to Indonesia. Neither country would support them. Finally they decided to attempt the dangerous boat journey to Australia. They got as far as Christmas Island, and only then reached land after another desperate refugee set the boat on fire and they all almost drowned. After months on Christmas Island and in the offshore processing detention centre at Nauru, living in appalling conditions and witnessing a wide range of traumas such as suicides and hunger strikes, at last Mohammad made it to Australia.

Despite the trauma he had suffered, and the fact that he had arrived in Australia at age 14 with no English and little formal education, Mohammad persevered to become school captain and went on to complete a double degree in law and commerce. Since then Mohammad has been working on innovative ways to help asylum seekers to get the help they need. He has even addressed the United Nations Human Rights Council in Geneva on the treatment of refugees. Without being able to draw on his past experience, it's doubtful he would have been able to make the strides he has in the present. (See an interview with Mohammad at www.the-innovation-race.com)

Many Latino children whose parents have made equally treacherous border crossings across the desert to 'El Norte' (the US) in search of a better life have also transcended their challenging background to achieve remarkable outcomes. A group of these 'undocumented' children in Arizona entered a prestigious innovation competition to build an underwater robot—and ended up winning it! These alienated school students had formed a robotics club under the guidance of their inspirational teacher Faridodin (Fredi) Lajvardi. When we spoke to Fredi about how, with no experience, only $800 in capital and some used car parts, the underdog team beat the country's reigning robotics champion team from MIT and fulfilled their dreams, he explained to us that they needed self-belief to succeed.[27]

They had drawn from the experiences of their past and built up new skills to create a better future. Fredi was able to tap into their emotion and, through *authentic empathy,* bring out the group's creative potential and channel it into a purpose-driven innovation. These specialised robots are being designed to dive longer and deeper than humans, and even to rescue people in peril. No doubt these children, keen innovators from diverse backgrounds who have triumphed through broad and challenging experiences, will prove to be incredible assets to companies seeking the best young talent.

Where will the next innovation come from? Some of our best minds might be out there now, on the boats or crossing harsh deserts, on a perilous journey to freedom. They might be living on the fringes of society, challenged by being labelled as outsiders or illegals. Yet their diverse experiences offer unique perspectives that can really make a difference. Forty per cent of Fortune 500 companies in the US were founded by immigrants and their children.[28] When people from different backgrounds become assimilated into our societies, and as tolerance and appreciation builds, greater mutual empathy and understanding leads to more creative solutions. The best ideas come from those on the fringes, and from those of us prepared to travel across cultures and to learn from others.

As we power ahead with our stage of the innovation race, grasping the baton that's been handed on to us by previous generations, we need to seek out new opportunities to become more *outrospective*—to explore, to travel, to expose ourselves to different ways of thinking, to empathise and build a real compassion with others in order to start to change the paradigm.

As the world is more connected than ever before, we can take the opportunity to open up to and connect with experiences and people from around the globe. This can help to ignite the creative process, but how do we convert this initial spark into innovative outcomes? What does the whole innovation process encompass, from imagination through to implementation, and how exactly does it work?

In the next chapter we will explore the innovation process as a whole and identify the fascinating tension that can either frustrate or fuel the innovation process.

PRODUCTION NOTES

Living vicariously through 'reality'

Reality TV is a contemporary social experiment that has revealed a great deal about who we are as humans. Some psychologists suggest watching reality TV programs may enable viewers to learn behavioural skills in a safe environment, as understanding other people's tribulations can sometimes help to save us from repeating the same mistakes. In a *New York Times* article titled 'Life Lessons Hidden in Reality TV', the writer argued that programs such as *The Bachelor* are contemporary versions of the Stanford Prison Experiment, and *Survivor* is about the 'inescapability of your being yourself, even when you have told yourself you can be someone different for 30 days'.[29] Other analysts talk about reality TV as an equaliser: making the unremarkable (ordinary people) remarkable, and making the remarkable (celebrities) unremarkable.

In the 'innovation race' we can find value both in looking back through history and in contemporary case studies, learning from the successes and failures of other companies and cultures. Such perspectives can remind us of the importance of empathy to really understand the challenges of the present and the future and to find positive ways forward.

EMPATHY CHECKLIST

- ☐ Do you feel emotionally detached or connected when you approach the innovation process?
- ☐ Do you expose yourself often to different cultural perspectives and spend time with people from different backgrounds?
- ☐ How often do you try to walk in others' shoes to see what they see, and feel with their hearts?
- ☐ Have you learned to develop an *outrospective* (rather than 'introspective') mindset?
- ☐ Can you identify what the customer or end user really needs?
- ☐ Are you able to learn from experiences to build innovative outcomes?
- ☐ Are opportunities to develop authentic empathy built into your organisation's innovation process?

4

PICASSO AND THE PARADOXICAL INNOVATION PROCESS

Understanding the challenges of the innovation journey,
from imagination and ideation to implementation

As we launch into discussing the complete innovation process, it will become clear that making the connection between the initial stage of imagination through to ideas and finally to full implementation is of critical importance. We may dream up novel concepts, but how do we then turn them into realities? And how do we harness the creative tension built up in the process for the most innovative results?

This chapter will help you to:

- *identify the different stages of the innovation process*
- *appreciate the importance of using imagination as a springboard towards innovation*
- *recognise the tension between the 'open action mode' of ideation and the 'closed action mode' of implementation*
- *manage this initial tension effectively to help to fuel the innovation process*
- *learn the importance of navigating between the relevant innovation 'paradox pairings' effectively*
- *develop the flexibility needed to follow through on the whole process.*

Key challenge: How to balance the paradoxes of purpose at each stage of the innovation journey.

'Son of a bitch! What the hell happened?'

These were the first words communicated to mission control at NASA and simultaneously broadcast around the world as Apollo 10 recovered from a deadly spin. Pilot Eugene Cernan's shocking unscripted and unedited exclamation became an early radio forerunner to reality TV shows. It captured the emotion of the event and drew the listeners in, enabling them to share something of what the astronauts were feeling at the time. This was a scary moment, when all the years of dreaming and scheming about space travel were being tested, and the potential for failure meant the stakes were extremely high.

It was 1969, just two months before the first lunar landing. The lesser known Apollo 10 mission was the fourth manned flight in the US Apollo space program, the 'dress rehearsal' for the first moon walk. It was basically a reconnaissance mission to test out the landing plan without actually landing. Apollo 10 had orbited the moon in the 'Snoopy' lunar module and descended to check the approach before returning to the 'Charlie Brown' command module. But not everything ran smoothly. As they were about to return to 'Charlie Brown' a series of small errors led to a malfunction in the guidance system and 'Snoopy' started to spin wildly, hurling the crew to less than 15 km above the moon's surface.

Following the lunar module pilot's dramatic outburst, mission control and all those tuned in back home waited with bated breath. At that moment it was as if the whole world was empathising with the crew and willing them to find a creative solution to the problem. Fortunately they eventually regained command of the situation, and one of the crew members, Tom Stafford, was heard to announce, 'Snoopy and Charlie Brown are now hugging each other!'—to the huge relief of all those who had vicariously shared the journey with the Apollo crew.

The mission had achieved its goals, but not without the heart-pumping recognition that the team had been moments from disaster. NASA was able to learn from the mission's mistakes, and the legendary first lunar landing followed only two months later. The rest is history.

What's even less well known about this mission and just as interesting is that the Apollo 10 crew had unknowingly entered the record book themselves. On their way back to earth the Apollo 10 was propelled through space and rocketed through the atmosphere, reaching a top speed of 39 897 km/h. This speed record has never been broken since, so the Apollo 10 crew remain the fastest travellers ever. They also have the distinction of having travelled farther from Earth than any other humans, reaching a distance of 408 950 km from Houston, another record that remains unbroken. Of course there are plenty of scientists out there working on this challenge, and it's just a matter of time before clever physicists and astronomers take it to the next level.

Space travel has ushered in a completely new era. In the 60 or so years leading up to that moment, and the 50 or so years since, travel has been completely revolutionised—on land from horse and cart to the Ferrari, steam train to bullet train; in the air from the Wright brothers to supersonic space travel. Where it had taken Magellan's expedition more than three years to complete the first circumnavigation of the world by ship in 1522, it is now possible to orbit the globe in a space shuttle in just 90 minutes. We can transfer data around the globe at around 1079 million km/h, almost the speed of light. That's more than 33 million times faster than the fastest postal horse could travel back in the 1800s! This is an indication of just how fast technology has progressed, and how far our creative and innovative powers have taken us.

During the past 100 years we have pushed the boundaries of our technical abilities to create and innovate as never before. But we have learned an important lesson along the way: it is important for imagination to drive innovation, but then the ideas generated by the imagination need to be assessed for their value and then refined and tested in order to be fully realised as innovations. It is often only the final outcome that is recognised as an innovation, as with the moon landing mission, but there are many small steps, involving a great deal of trial and error, on the way to the apparent breakthrough.

In the previous chapter we looked back to explore others' experiences, recognising that placing ourselves in their shoes for greater empathy was a starting point for the innovation process. In this chapter we look forward to imagining and implementing the future. Like the Roman god Janus, we need to be able to do both.

Imagination → Ideation → Implementation

Hollywood producers capitalise on the imaginative powers of creative writers. They rely on the imaginations of science fiction writers who have been able to envisage the future, for example, and they have produced a succession of movies that bring to life these imaginings, especially in the area of rapid global travel. Many movies and books about challenging around-the-world journeys have been created over the years. Perhaps the first grand-scale round-the-world adventure movies were *Around the World in 80 Days* (1956) and *The Great Race* (1965). Then came movies about still more ambitious exploration—of the ocean depths and outer space. The first epic movie to feature outer space travel, *2001: A Space Odyssey*, was released in 1968, only a year before the moon landing itself.

Many readers will already be aware of how fiction can prefigure reality, and how creative minds behind Hollywood science fiction stories have imagined inventions before they have happened. Consider how much of what has been imagined by novelists and screenwriters in the past has gone on to be realised in one form or another.[1] If you didn't already know, Jules Verne, in his books *Twenty Thousand Leagues Under the Sea* and *Clipper of the Clouds*, anticipated the invention of the submarine and the helicopter. The rocket and the moon landing were anticipated by H. G. Wells in his novels *War of the Worlds* (about a Martian invasion) and *The First Men in the Moon*. *Star Trek* inspired both the first mobile phone by Motorola and Apple's QuickTime.

The inventor of the helicopter, Igor Sikorsky, has often quoted Jules Verne as saying, 'Anything that one man can imagine, another man can make real.' It is this combination of *imagination* through to *ideation* and *implementation* that is the focus of the next stages of the integrated process — from curiosity to creative inspiration and finally practical innovation — a process that is not often well understood or fully utilised.

The complete purpose-driven innovation process

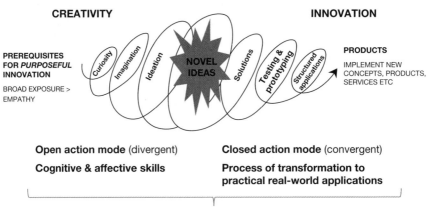

The complete integrated process – from imagination to implementation

Having established the importance of a foundation of empathy for *purpose-driven* and *transformational innovation*, in this chapter we are going to take some time to explore the complete innovation process. Before we do that, let's look a little further into interesting implications of developments from fiction that have become disturbing realities.

What if?

In the 1980s William Gibson wrote confronting science fiction stories that portrayed a hyper-connected global society in which computer hacking, cyberwar and reality shows are dominant features. Gibson, who coined the term *cyberspace*, was pretty much spot-on with his predictions. Long before him in 1914, H. G. Wells had imagined atomic bombs and warned of the problems of proliferation and of nation states potentially destroying themselves with nuclear weapons. He also imagined biological weapons and genetic engineering. Interestingly, he additionally envisaged a time machine that would allow its inventor to visit the future and learn from the destruction of the Earth that would be brought about by human folly. The time machine may not yet be a reality, but the idea of visiting the future to help us recognise and learn from our past and current mistakes is as pertinent as ever.

Science fiction has had a dramatic impact not only on technological development but also on social development, through helping to imagine possible futures.[2] Sci-fi writers in the early years of the twentieth century had presented a generally positive image of the future, but after two devastating world wars and the predicted invention of the atomic bomb depictions of dystopian futures became the norm. These visions of a frightening future under the rule of oppressive leaders have been a common feature of fiction and movies ever since, from novels like *1984* through to *The Hunger Games*. *The Hunger Games* in particular picks up on a number of themes of interest to us here, including the social impact of the reality TV concept and a central problem of the competitive race to the future we are all engaged in: the fact that although we are typically competitive by nature and we often prefer to compete vicariously, sitting on the sidelines and watching others enter into gladiatorial contests for our entertainment, rather than participating in positive social change ourselves. The German word *schadenfreude*, as introduced in the previous chapter, expresses the human impulse of taking pleasure in watching others suffer (even if only from embarrassment).

Frighteningly, such grim depictions of the future might not be that far from reality. Every year in January since 1945 an advisory board including some of the world's top Nobel laureate scientists convenes at the University of Chicago to determine how close the world is to global catastrophe. They adjust the minute hand on a Doomsday Clock according to how close they believe we are to 'midnight' (Doomsday), based on their assessment of the most serious perceived existential threats, most notably nuclear weapons and climate change. At three minutes to midnight (their current calculation), we are now closer to Doomsday than we have been since the height of the

Cold War in 1984, despite all our innovation efforts. So inventions alone won't get us out of this mess; that will take *responsible* innovation from connected, collaborative societies with leaders who want to use progress for the good of all rather than just to dominate, and a 'can do' mindset of enabled optimism.

Imagining potential futures is a critical part of the innovation process because it uncovers potential positive and negative consequences to help shape the development of ideas. This enables the innovator not simply to imagine the new ideas or products themselves, but to think through their potential impact. This means exploring a wide range of possibilities, while ensuring that the innovation process is relevant, realistic and responsible.

A number of companies have been capitalising on this concept of tapping into the imagination to trigger innovation. Google, Apple and Microsoft have all engaged science fiction writers to help stimulate ideas in *design fiction* sessions. This term was first popularised by science fiction writer Bruce Sterling in his book *Shaping Things* in 2005 and was applied in a business context in 2008 by Nokia researcher Julian Bleecker. Design fiction uses critical and narrative scenarios to imagine and raise questions about possible futures. This process has been used in the development of a domestic robot (by Intel) and of a mixed-reality immersive education desk (through Essex University). It has also been adopted to spark creative thinking around a number of challenges across the world, including entrepreneurship (Canterbury Christchurch Business School), the use of science and technology in business innovation (National Taiwan University), computer security issues (University of Washington), language learning (Shijiazhuang University, China) and community development projects (Leeds and Manchester universities). Other corporations have hired authors to create 'what if' stories to test new ideas. All these initiatives have helped to enhance imagination and the innovation process.

Another popular approach we have used in a business setting, the *pre-mortem*, helps project teams identify potential risks at the outset through a scenario planning approach, so the project can be adjusted and improved at the start rather than autopsied afterwards. But unlike a typical critiquing session, in which project team members are asked what might go wrong, the pre-mortem operates on the assumption that the 'patient' (project) has died (failed) and asks what went wrong. The team members' task is to generate plausible reasons for the project's 'failure'. Researchers have found that this type of *prospective hindsight* increases the ability to correctly predict future outcomes by 30 per cent.[3] This use of imagination and innovative thinking generates creative new ideas and approaches that may not previously have been considered.

We believe that the 'what if' process is especially important for purpose-driven innovation, and for ensuring that we consider the social and environmental implications of our innovations so they are of benefit for all. This can happen at all stages of the innovation process, from helping to generate the first sparks of an idea at the imagination stage, through to helping to test potential ideas at the implementation stage.

> The 'what if' process is especially important for purpose-driven innovation, and for ensuring that we consider the social and environmental implications of our innovations so they are of benefit for all.

The tension that frustrates or fuels innovation

How would you define the innovation process? As imagination *or* implementation? Ideation *or* application? It should be clear by now that there is no single narrow definition of innovation. As we have explored in earlier chapters, the concept is interpreted very differently in different contexts and by different cultures. Rather than having to choose one approach, isn't it possible that different interpretations can coexist simultaneously? Doesn't this provide us with the richest and most valuable model?

In previous chapters we have discussed different cultural approaches to creativity and innovation. Here we would like to focus on the specific dichotomy between the *creativity* side of our model, which includes curiosity, imagination and ideation, and the *innovation* side, which includes solution finding, testing and prototyping, and searching for structured applications. We have already discussed cultural connections to specific areas of the innovation process, for example, how Americans typically link innovation to ideation. American students typically outperform their Japanese counterparts in the sort of original and open thinking that characterises wild imagination.[4] Japan, by comparison, is considered one of the most innovative countries in the world, as already identified, yet the Japanese often interpret innovation as a process of gradual adaptation and implementation through prototyping, and this is where the Japanese students were found to excel.

These different perspectives could be related to different cultural traits. Openness to new ideas, for example, requires the ability and desire to seek new experiences, to be unconstrained by social expectations, to live with ambiguity and think divergently. *Adaptive innovation*, which works on building incrementally on existing ideas, is typical of a more conservative approach than the sort of creative thinking that seeks original, breakthrough ideas.[5] There are plenty of stories about how Asian businesses are great at finding more efficient and effective ways of doing things, for example, building on existing ideas rather than starting from scratch with new ideas.[6]

Yet it is by applying both of these modes simultaneously that innovation is best fuelled.[7] The following figure shows where the creative tension often lies, and illustrates how both parts of the innovation process are integral to the concept and can work together for maximum effect.

The tension that can fuel or frustrate innovation

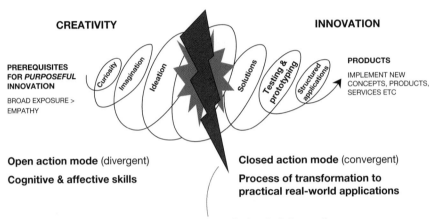

The tension between each mode that fuels innovation

Working together to cross cultural boundaries and utilise the best of both worlds will ensure that the innovative process continues to develop into useful strategies for the future. This is a fascinating paradox that in itself demonstrates an important innovative principle: innovation requires acknowledging and accepting ambiguities or contractions and working through the tension they create to come up with superior solutions.

In the initial creative thinking stage, thinking is opened up to search out all possibilities; this is where the brainstorming takes place, and where many ideas are needed in order to identify the best possible ones. The second half of the process, however—which leads towards practical innovation—needs to converge on the best solutions and the best applications for implementation.

You'll note that the spiral model in the figure includes both 'open' and 'closed' action modes.[8] Think of how the initial *open action mode* associated with creativity in the first half of this model takes openness, courage and a desire for novelty that tends to be more typical of the individualist philosophies. The *closed action mode*, typically associated with the application and implementation of ideas, tends to fit with cultures that seek to harmonise principles into an integrated system. The open mode is about knowledge generation (divergent thinking), while the closed mode is about knowledge integration (convergent thinking).

The open mode is needed for ideas generation (such as in brainstorming), while the closed mode is needed for implementation (such as in identifying specific solutions, testing and prototyping).

> The *open action mode* requires openness, courage and a desire for novelty, while the *closed action mode* seeks to harmonise principles into an integrated system.

Shadow and light: the power of paradox

We are told opposites attract. This principle is self-evident in physics, where similar electrical charges repel each other while opposite charges are magnetically attracted. In the dating game it's a little more complicated. Although people will often choose to marry those who are similar to them (for example in a similar social circle), when it comes to dating opposites often attract and complement each other. The challenge is that such relationships will inevitably lead to tension, and will succeed only if there is a clear *understanding* and *acceptance* of differences.

The different sides of the innovation process are both opposing and complementary, and where these differences are understood and respected they can provide a great foundation for transformational innovation.[9]

The Chinese yin/yang symbol encapsulates this core principle of the creative process. Within a circle a swirling black element with a small white core is balanced by a swirling white element with a small black core. The symbol is drawn from Chinese Taoist philosophy and described in ancient texts such as the *Tao Te Ching*. Yin and yang might be literally translated as 'shady side' vs 'sunny side'. The symbol represents how apparently opposing forces can coexist and achieve balance. An example given in Taoist philosophy is of the life cycle of a plant: it grows to its full height in summer (the sunny side), produces seeds and then dies in winter (the shady side), before the seeds germinate and the next generation of growth begins. Each part of the process contains the seeds of the other, and each cannot exist without the other. Think of how shadow cannot exist without light, and vice versa.

The ability to integrate opposing strategies is a critical aspect of the creative thinking and innovation process. Creative problem solving is not about choosing between black and white, but about seeing the potential for combination solutions. It involves identifying ambiguities and paradoxes and finding a way to push through these contradictions to better solutions.

A model that has helped to illustrate the importance of dealing with ambiguities, known as 'the umbrella challenge', was developed from work done by a Russian inventor who received his first patent—for the concept of an underwater breathing device—at the age of 14. Genrich Altshuller came up with a complex system for identifying and dealing with ambiguities to generate innovative solutions to problems.[10] After studying 40 000 patents he identified 40 key invention principles, incorporating them into his TRIZ model—an analysis and forecasting tool he developed from studying patterns of invention.

In 'the umbrella challenge' the participant is required to come up with an invention for an umbrella that satisfies the need for covering two people at once while not being so large that it catches the wind easily. Potential solutions included:

the SENZ umbrella, which cannot blow inside out, but also does not support two people.

an umbrella that works well but is inconvenient to carry.

The winning solution was an umbrella of large diameter with a hole at the top that forms a sort of valve.

What solution did you come up with?

The problem was solved by using the model to address the apparent paradoxes directly rather than shying away from them. It demonstrated how we can use creative tension to find better solutions.

Einstein and the ambidextrous organisation

We have already discussed how creative geniuses are able to see multiple perspectives. To take this idea a step further, they are also able to *synthesise* apparently opposing perspectives.

Picasso's art is the very embodiment of the integration of contrasts. He included both calm and chaos to create inimitable works of art. Einstein developed his theory of relativity by embracing the idea of an object being simultaneously in motion and at rest. Mozart worked with both concordance and discordance to compose inspired music.[11] What do these examples of creative genius have in common? They all married form and function to create artistic works of genius. They pushed out beyond current realities to imagine future possibilities. And they all demonstrated how the power of paradox can be put to work.

There are plenty of examples of how paradoxes can be effectively embraced for superior creative outcomes.[12] The yin/yang idea of balancing dynamic opposing forces was actually introduced into management theory as far back as the 1920s. Being able to hold apparently opposing ideas in creative tension is a key to creative success, and a critical part of thinking about how to build an innovative culture. Leaders and organisations that can recognise and work with these tensions are able to learn and grow the fastest, and to deal most effectively with complex problems. Being able to deal effectively with paradox in the organisational context can foster learning and creativity, build flexibility and resilience, and unleash human potential—all of which lead to higher energy and engagement and improved performance over the long term.[13] An ability to deal with paradox can, in fact, foster sustainability.

Remember the transformational innovation model we introduced back in chapter 1? We mentioned briefly the main paradox that has been explored in relation to innovation: the paradox of Exploitation vs Exploration (see overleaf). To refresh your memory, while some organisations will focus on 'exploiting' the resources they have and maintaining systems and processes to ensure stability, others will want to explore new options and push into new territory. There is a focus on small incremental innovations, on the one hand (Exploitation), or on breakthrough innovations on the other (Exploration).

> Being able to hold apparently opposing ideas in creative tension is a key to creative success, and a critical part of thinking about how to build an innovative culture.

Transformational innovation

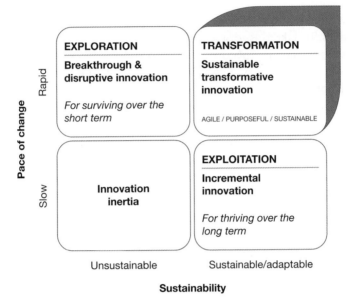

The ability to cope with the pace of change while simultaneously maintaining business viability in the innovation process has been referred to as *organisational ambidexterity*.[14] Organisations that are dynamic and organic will be better able to respond to changing world conditions than mechanical organisations will. This leads to what we have called *sustainable transformational innovation*: a foundation for growth based on the principles of being agile and sustainable, *and* having a clear sense of purpose built on a strong culture. An organisation's innovative success today will very much depend on how well it is able to adapt to these sorts of changes.

Smart organisations of the future will be able to embrace all of these perspectives and utilise them effectively. These organisations will be able to adapt as needed to different situations that require innovative responses. With a nod to 'situational leadership', we introduce the idea of *situational innovation*, ensuring that the approach to innovation fits the context and is appropriate to reach the desired outcomes. There will be times when ideation is needed, while at other times commitment to follow-through and implementation will be needed. There will be times when the organisation will need to focus on maintenance and ensuring stability, and other times or opportunities when it will need to be able to push forward with new ideas in order to remain competitive. Smart organisations should be able to embody these apparently opposing concepts simultaneously.

It's not enough to be mediocre in each of these areas. The research shows that organisations that have high levels of both exploitation *and* exploration do best.[15] What's more, the organisations that are the most successful have a culture that supports both approaches to innovation *and* maintains a focus on open learning. This research has been conducted in Taiwan, which has been recognised as technologically highly innovative culture but with a strongly entrenched traditional culture, which provides an interesting perspective.

Leading between the ponds and the pits

The most successful motor racing drivers achieve the best balance between use of the accelerator and of the brake. They also take the most efficient line on the track, without sliding off course. There is no perfect line for any situation — the line will need to be determined after considering the car, the corners, the strategy and the conditions. Often it involves swinging wide in the lead-up then pulling in close to the corner as you round it.

In a famous race in France in 1926 a number of Bentley cars that were looking unbeatable came into a mild bend known as White House Corner, where the driver of a French car lost control and the car ended up stalled and straddling the road. A series of nasty collisions ensued, from which only one Bentley survived — the one able to pick the best line and take it at the best speed, particularly taking into account the rapidly deteriorating state of the race. The others had come up to the corner too fast and failed to balance acceleration and braking optimally. The winning 'Old Number Seven' Bentley was the only car ever driven into the foyer of the Hotel Savoy lobby as a guest of honour at a celebratory banquet.

So what sorts of leaders will be needed to effectively manage these paradoxes and lead the ambidextrous organisation? The leaders of the future will of course need to be highly flexible, able to navigate their way carefully between extremes to find the best balance for any particular time and situation.

The latest management research shows that the most successful leaders are *integrative thinkers* — that is, they can hold two opposing ideas in their heads at once and come up with a new idea that contains elements of each but is superior to both.[16] This is the process of consideration and constantly adjusting synthesis (rather than superior strategy or faultless execution). These leaders consider multidimensional, non-linear relationships. They resolve the tension between opposing ideas and generate new alternatives. Jim Collins has said that 'leaders should be the genius of AND ... we must be able to embrace both extremes on a number of dimensions at the same time. Instead of choosing A or B figure out how to have A and B, purpose

> The latest research shows that the most successful leaders are *integrative thinkers* — that is, they can hold two opposing ideas in their heads at once and come up with a new idea that contains elements of each but is superior to both.

AND profit, continuity AND change, freedom AND responsibility'.[17]

It has been found that management teams tend to confront complex, dynamic realities with a language designed for simple problems,[18] but it's time to think and act more creatively as leaders. Creative thinking can happen only when people learn to think outside accepted parameters, when there is a cultural environment that allows creative ideas to flow (which we will discuss further when we visit Europe in chapter 6). To do that we need to encourage the synthesis of dualistic thinking.

In golfing you need to navigate the most effective path up the fairway and between the twin dangers of woods or deep ponds on one side and 'the roughs' on the other, with the occasional sandy bunker thrown in down the middle. Many racing sports—car racing, slalom and boardercross skiing, for example—require a similar form of navigation between the dangerous extremes that lie beyond the edges of the road or track. By choosing the best line between the two sides the racer is able to reach the finish line the fastest. Similarly, sticking to one default approach to innovation just doesn't make sense. It is neither efficient nor effective. But edge too close to one side or the other and you risk going off the road. It requires sophisticated calculations to navigate the best path based on the specific conditions. This is *situational innovation.*

In this book we aim to help you to navigate your way between the potential opposing 'extremes' on the route to innovation, to find the most constructive, efficient and effective course forward. As in *The Amazing Race,* from which we have been drawing parallels, we will be sending you off by air on a race around the world to find clues on how to navigate the best path ahead. When we interviewed veteran air traffic controller Grant Henderson, we discovered that when air traffic control plans a flight path the dangers are a little less obvious but potentially much more dangerous. Major danger points can be no-fly zones, war zones, mountains and storms. The pilot will use the data provided by air traffic control to decide the best course based on specific real-time conditions. Contrary to what you might imagine, although there may be no obvious obstacles in the air, it is not always possible to take a direct route. There are set air routes that aircraft need to keep to, but the planning team will also need to take into account factors such as air turbulence and storms. Pilots remain in constant contact with air traffic control to ensure they always have the most up-to-date information. Steering a course around a storm may add fuel and time costs but it is a standard (and prudent) practice. The more experienced the pilot, the more capable they are of handling the storms, but every pilot needs to know the sensible limit and choose the best course based on this. Once the course has been set there is a 3 kilometre radius within which the pilot can move before flying out of the 'safe' zone designated by the flight path. As the pilot gets closer to the runway that window decreases to a very tight 10 metres, but the pilot needs to maintain enough speed to keep stable.

Navigating the path between exploration and exploitation

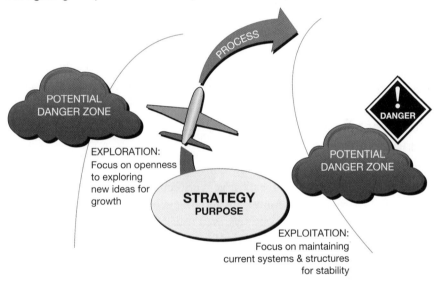

Business and self-help books love to sell the concept of 'easy steps' to success. When it comes to the 'innovation race', however, it is better to recognise that there is no clear path to navigate. Finding the right path to take requires that you assess the particular situation you find yourself in and use important principles to guide you. It will be important to recognise where your natural bias is in order to use it as a strength where relevant and to correct it where necessary. Over the journey chapters in Part II we will consider the four key paradox pairings that can impact a culture that supports innovation. We will identify where the boundaries are for these paradoxes, what extremes to avoid and how to use the full width of the road to your advantage, allowing you to push ahead at the highest speed possible on the shortest possible line in order to survive the 'innovation race'.

Any racing navigation team will be aware of where they are at any time and of where they need to go. It is vitally important to plan the route carefully and keep track of progress rather than randomly take the curves as they come and risk losing traction and going over the edge. In chapter 5, for example, where we explore the paradox of control vs freedom, you will find that if you move too far to the 'control' side of the road in an organisation you can veer off track into the dangerous territory of oppression, whereas if you veer too far on the 'freedom' side of the road you can find yourself in the dangerous territory of chaos.

> Many individuals and cultures are now learning to respect the values that different cultures bring and are seeking to embrace 'the best of both worlds'. There is a growing recognition of the need to find equilibrium in the midst of apparent ambiguity.

Many individuals and cultures are now learning to respect the values that different cultures bring and are seeking to embrace 'the best of both worlds'. There is a growing recognition of the need to find equilibrium in the midst of apparent ambiguity. Think about how we now want both individuality and community; flexibility and stability; doing, thinking and being; temporariness and permanence.

Creativity is in fact *the* contemporary value for our global village precisely because it allows for such adaptability and acceptance. Liberal Studies Professor Robert Paul Weiner from John F. Kennedy University sees creativity as a 'currency of exchange between conservatives and liberals, Americans and Asians, businesspeople and artists'.[19] As he says, even usually traditional religious leaders such as the Dalai Lama and the Pope speak of the importance of creativity because it cleverly crosses all boundaries.

Strategies for Purpose-Driven Innovation (PDI)

The process of continually synthesising the two apparently opposing paradoxes that are important in the innovation process creates a dynamic that powers innovation. Treating one as more important than the other will create an imbalance; effectively managing both, on the other hand, can build a highly adaptable culture that is ready to deal with new challenges in creative ways as they arise.

The challenge of balancing paradoxes has been compared to an acrobat on a high wire.[20] To remain on the wire — that is, to remain stable — the acrobat must rapidly move from one position of stability to another. On a high wire the concept of stability is actually constantly changing. The acrobat's arms must be able to move freely, because any inflexibility will contribute to instability. This image might help to explain the paradox of resilience, which involves the ability to constantly search for positions of stability and adapt to them, even if they are temporary, before moving on to the next position. Here instability and stability coexist and must both be embraced.

Research has revealed four key paradoxes that will typically need to be resolved at each stage of the innovation process, and these will be outlined in each chapter in Part II.[21] Our Purpose-Driven Innovation (PDI) model shows where these paradoxes need to be resolved in relation to the innovation process.

In the chapters that follow we will tease out the elements of the PDI model as follows:

1. **Strategy:** You will see from the model that there are four main strategies for purpose-driven and sustainable innovation: Liberate, Initiate, Motivate and Transform.

2. **Purpose:** For each strategy a positive purpose needs to be identified, which will involve resolving a critical paradox pairing. The four key paradoxes and potential resolutions are Control vs Freedom (synthesis: *guided freedom*), Focus vs Openness (synthesis: *targeted openness*), Individualism vs Group Engagement (synthesis: *collaborative engagement*), and Stability vs Flexibility (synthesis: *grounded flexibility*).

3. **Process:** As we have described in the first four chapters, there needs to be a process in place to support the delivery of an innovation. This model focuses on the four main modes: Enquire, Explore, Solve and Apply.

These different elements come together in this way:

STRATEGY	= PURPOSE (Paradox synthesis)	× PROCESS
LIBERATE:	Control vs Freedom > *Guided Freedom*	× Enquire
INITIATE:	Focus vs Openness > *Targeted Openness*	× Explore
MOTIVATE:	Individualism vs Group Engagement > *Collaborative Engagement*	× Solve
TRANSFORM:	Stability vs Flexibility > *Grounded Flexibility*	× Apply

This model emerged from the Creative Life Cycle model (see figure overleaf) we shared in our first book on this topic, *Who Killed Creativity?...And How Can We Get It Back?* The Creative Life Cycle model was developed after years of working with organisations and discovering that there are typical patterns that can be readily identified according to the direction leaders consciously or inadvertently take. Where there is an effort to create an open and supportive organisation, for example, the creative process is naturally initiated, which leads to higher levels of motivation and engagement, and ultimately deeper levels of culture change and organisational transformation. On the other hand, where individuals in the organisation are not empowered and equipped for the creative process, apathy and cynicism can soon set in and the culture can rapidly deteriorate. We have seen the impact when executive leaders change in an organisation, and the culture rapidly either grows or self-destructs, according to the direction they take.

Creative Life Cycle model

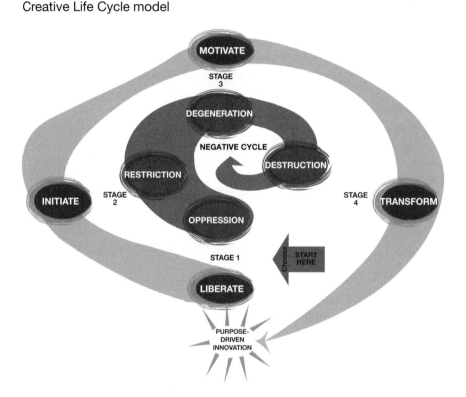

The Purpose-Driven Innovation (PDI) model that follows shows how all of these areas typically link together to form a practical approach to positive innovation (a virtuous cycle) that can counteract potentially negative trends (a vicious cycle).[22] These cycles describe complex chains of events that are reinforced through feedback loops, with the virtuous cycle producing favourable outcomes and the vicious cycle producing detrimental results. The model also shows how the potentially negative forces that contribute to the vicious cycle can be counteracted through appropriately synthesising the innate paradoxes. We use this circular pattern as a guide to reinforce the idea of the virtuous cycle as we make our global journey through the book (which follows the same clockwise direction).

In *Who Killed Creativity?* we demonstrated how individuals can build the cognitive (intellectual) and affective (emotional) skills needed to think more creatively. In this book we focus on how organisations and societies can build the structural capabilities to provide an environment and culture that best supports creative thinking and innovation.

The extended model that follows illustrates how these strategies fit with the innovation process overall, as we have discussed in Part I.

The Purpose-Driven Innovation (PDI) model (showing the links between strategies, purpose and process)

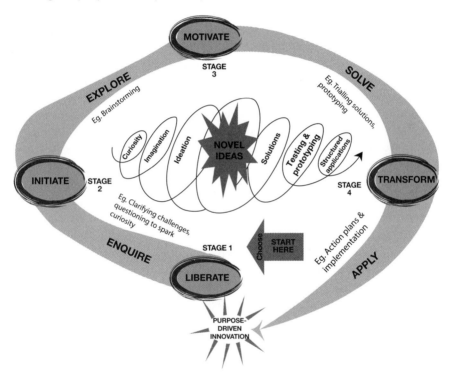

Navigating the path needs to be a conscious strategic decision, not an ad hoc spontaneous action based on egos or emotions, personalities or politics.

On the fast track to Mars

Some 50 to 90 per cent of new strategies fail to be implemented.[23] Research has revealed that the greatest failure of innovation programs in organisations is not a failure of the innovation itself, but a failure to follow through with it. Ultimately innovation needs to focus on the long-term *implementation* of the creative ideas that have emerged from the ideation process, yet this can be the toughest part of the journey to navigate.

Taking the innovation journey all the way through from imagination to implementation has never been more important than right now. That is how we can survive and escape the potential dystopian futures we have been warned of by the science fiction sages—and, perhaps more importantly, by most of the scientific world. So how do we ensure there is a focus on follow-through to implementation? It can be interesting to consider how our desire to go ever faster and further may reflect a fundamental belief in the 'innovation race' as a means to a better future. Yet by taking the time to focus on the *purpose* and *sustainability* of the forward momentum, rather than simply the *pace*, we should be able to do better in the long run.

Today the stakes are greater than ever before. As the long-term sustainability of our planet is more threatened, we are not just imagining how to get around the planet but starting to imagine how to get around our solar system. Some are imagining journeys into space to find alternative survival options. The Mars One project, for example, is exploring the possibilities of turning Mars into a viable alternative for human life by setting up a human colony on the planet, and they have been building prototypes here on Earth to test equipment and practise developing the skills needed.

When we spoke to Bas Lansdorp, the chief executive of Mars One, he told us that he believes the mission is on target. It has been claimed that 200 000 people have signed up to be the first people to take a one-way ticket to Mars in 10 years' time. Maybe Lansdorp is a dreamer, but maybe technological development will eventually catch up with his dream, as it has for some science fiction writers. The interesting twist is that the whole exercise has been planned as the subject of a reality TV show, which is a source of both funding and promotion. But consider how the objectives of reality TV run counter to the objectives of a successful science mission. Consider how the sort of crazy interpersonal dynamics that are well suited to TV entertainment would be most ill-suited to space survival.[24] It will certainly be the ultimate reality TV show if it ever gets off the ground!

The risks of failure of the Mars One mission are high. Two robots have survived the planet's extreme conditions, and two rovers have been based there for more than 10 years. However, of the 43 attempts to reach Mars, almost 50 per cent have failed.

Stephen Hawking believes we will have to get off this planet to survive. Although the Mars mission is still more in the realm of imagination than reality (many scientists still mock the idea of a human colony on Mars), perhaps it's an important start to imagining and implementing future realities. The critical element now, we believe, is to focus on building purpose-driven cultures to support the process of scientific and technological innovation. This is where so many other extreme missions have failed in the past.

Ironically, despite how clever we are and how much we have already achieved, future missions like these may never even get off the ground. Mission organisers have said that NASA's planned Mars mission has a $20 billion price tag, and the greatest risk is a failure not of equipment but of managing the human element. With four astronauts trapped in a spacecraft not much larger than your average RV for three years (the time it will take to get to Mars and back, with the research time included), the crew will need to be *very* compatible, and they'll need some pretty serious strategies in place to make it through successfully. (A previous Russian mission had to be aborted when one astronaut radioed back to Earth that the spaceship would need to be brought in immediately or there would be one live astronaut and one dead body returning home!)

We have explored the fundamental dilemma of contemporary innovation (chapter 1), considering, for example, the chasm between an Aboriginal and a white Australian perspective. We discussed the essential prerequisites for purpose-driven innovation, including broad exposure to multiple perspectives, as illustrated by the experience and vision of a distinctive Chinese Buddhist artist (in chapter 2), and the need for empathy, as explored through some responses to the plight of asylum seekers (in chapter 3). And in this chapter we have looked at the process of purpose-driven innovation itself, from imagination through to implementation. These stories have been included to help to prepare you for the race ahead.

We are now ready to unpack the *purpose,* or culture-change foundations of our PDI model, and begin our global journey towards creating a culture that *supports* purpose-driven and sustainable innovation. This is where we take you through the challenging paradoxes that can either frustrate or fuel innovation, and explore how we might successfully navigate a path through them. As we visit each destination, we will challenge you to think through the extremes and potential dangers of each polarised position, and then we will look at ways to synthesise the paradoxes effectively for better results.

How, exactly, can these paradoxes be effectively resolved? And how can that impact a culture for better innovation? Allow us to guide you through the possibilities!

PRODUCTION NOTES

The Innovation Games: 'Reality' as a platform for transformation

In the hit movie *The Hunger Games*, the announcement 'Let the Games begin' marks the moment when the rich and privileged elite of the dystopian society turn their attention to the popular annual televised contest in which representatives from the poorer working districts must fight to the death for the viewers' diversion. The producers at their consoles, particularly the 'game master', can at any time arbitrarily manipulate the environment to tip the odds against a contestant and increase the audience's excitement. The story has a satirical subtext that challenges our obsession with reality TV, politics in the new media age, class and competition in general. It reflects back to the audience our love for entertainment involving *schadenfreude* (the pleasure of watching others suffer), even at the cost of people's lives. It also satirises our obsession with celebrity. The author Suzanne Collins has said the idea for the Hunger Games books originally came from an evening when she was channel surfing on television. With one click she saw people competing in a reality TV show, and with the next click she was looking at footage of the invasion of Iraq, and she found the two began to blur in a frightening way.

The lines between reality TV and reality have become so blurred now that it is not unusual for a story on 'who won last night's show' to be treated as breaking news in major newspapers, and reality TV stars can leverage a successful crossover into politics.

To understand the 'innovation race', we may need to look into the future to see where our current trends and obsessions might take us and if there are alternative courses of action we should be taking.

INNOVATION SYNTHESIS CHECKLIST

☐ Are you able to look forward and imagine future potential?

☐ Do you use techniques such as 'design fiction', 'prototyping fiction', or 'pre-mortems' to help imagine future possibilities and work through to potential outcomes?

☐ Can you identify the potential tensions between the creativity and innovation parts of the process?

☐ Are you an integrative thinker? Are you able to successfully integrate the imagination and ideation part of the process and the implementation part of the process?

☐ Have you developed the essential quality of flexibility?

☐ Are you able to identify and take on both the 'open' and 'closed' action modes needed?

☐ Do you successfully see ideas through to implementation?

☐ Are you able to utilise *situational innovation*, adapting the mode to suit the particular situation?

☐ Have you or your organisation built ambidextrous systems and structures that can cope with ambiguities and synthesise them effectively?

PART II

DESTINATIONS

Through each chapter in Part II we visit different continents around the world to investigate one of the key innovation paradoxes that typically needs to be dealt with to create a sustainable culture that supports innovation.

Key challenges addressed:

- *How to ensure there is a clear foundation of purposeful principles for empowerment rather than simply relying on rules and regulations through 'guided freedom' (chapter 5).*
- *How to enable both individuals and teams to be both autonomous and interconnected through 'targeted openness' (chapter 6).*
- *How to capitalise on both individual passions and group synergy through 'collaborative engagement' (chapter 7).*
- *How to build both resilience and reliability through 'grounded flexibility' (chapter 8).*

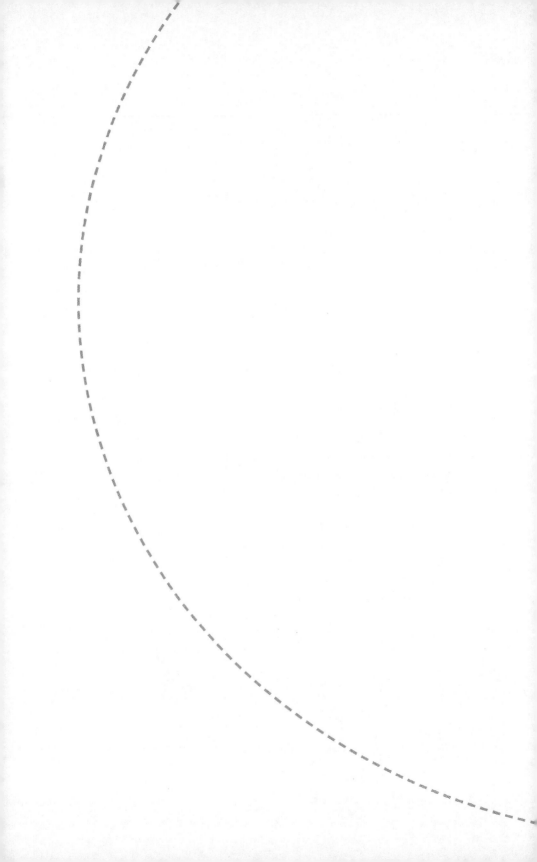

5

LIBERATE

How to liberate a culture for open innovation

Destination: Africa

Paradox: Control vs Freedom

Synthesis: Guided Freedom

In this chapter we will have the opportunity to explore the path between control and freedom, facing at one extreme the potential danger zone of oppression, and at the other extreme the potential danger of chaos. We will learn how to plan and navigate a route through guided freedom that will create a culture to best fuel purpose-driven innovation.

Key challenge: How to ensure there is a clear foundation of purposeful principles for empowerment rather than simply relying on rules and regulations through 'guided freedom'

The young Egyptian boy with the colourful flowers looked so sweet. He handed up one stem to us as we were sitting in a horse-drawn cart, ready to be taken to our next destination, and we appreciated his apparent gesture of generosity.

His sweet temperament was short-lived. No sooner had we taken the flower and thanked the boy for it than he demanded payment — a substantial one. We were late to a meeting and feeling manipulated, so we were keen to get away from this scene as fast as we could. We tried to hand the flower back, but he insisted we had taken it and therefore we needed to pay for it.

A long, uncomfortable negotiation ensued. In the end we gave him some money and moved on, but no one walked away happy with the outcome.

Where there is this sort of lack of freedom, development will be impacted — and ultimately, at some level, innovation too.

We had plenty of these sorts of encounters in Cairo. These experiences are uncomfortable because there is such a big economic and cultural gap between foreigners with money to travel and the impoverished street dwellers we were dealing with, so there will always be a sense of injustice. The sad thing is that many of these street kids are exploited by adults, and most face regular violence and abuse (according to Unicef 86 per cent of them say they regularly have to deal with violence). The needs of people without economic security are often so great that they will use any means to get what they can, and 'wealthy' tourists are fair prey. We know these people need the money, yet it is difficult to find a way to do this fairly.

The problem is that people like these are often victims of unfair and unjust systems simply fighting for survival. The incidents are most often symptoms of a much bigger problem, of systems and structures that fail to give them the opportunities they need. Where there is this sort of lack of freedom, development will be impacted—and ultimately, at some level, innovation too. The ramifications can be seen from street-level poverty and homelessness through to economic development and innovation at a country level.

Egypt has known such inequalities throughout its history, especially when oppressive systems have become entrenched in the culture. If you want to deal with these problems, you need to challenge the established systems and structures, not the individual victims. This takes courage, and an enquiring mind prepared to tackle the ambiguities head on.

Soon after the flower incident we were sitting on the deck of a traditional felucca boat drifting down the Nile, enjoying our break from the madding crowds and watching the ancient land slip by. We were amazed at how easily we were lulled into quiet reflection on the past as we floated along. You would step off the boat into the mayhem of active commercial centres, the cacophony of market sellers and donkey carters, before entering an ancient world of vast, awe-inspiring ruins that spoke of the grandeur of days gone by, then finally stepping back on board to watch the sun go down over mesmerising forests of river reeds.

It was by contemplating the history of these ancient civilisations, and contrasting them with the challenges of current-day experiences, that we started to identify the relationship between control, freedom and development—and the fascinating impact on innovation. Looking into the past, it is possible to detect some of the factors that could have led to the present. We started to consider how it is only by challenging established systems and structures to ensure they support freedom and growth that we can move forward and really make progress.

Challenging the systems

For this first mode of the innovation process we will be discussing how it is important to LIBERATE a culture. People need to feel free enough to challenge existing ways of thinking and doing things before they can begin on the innovation journey, and they need to feel free to consider alternative options. This mode starts with the preparation (broad exposure to multiple perspectives in order to develop authentic empathy, which helps to connect with real innovation needs). It then moves into defining the issues that need to be addressed for the innovation through asking questions at all levels to ensure the systems and structures in place will be sustainable and will support innovation over the long term (ENQUIRE).

This stage is critical to ensure you are building, not from an old, unsustainable, unsafe or irrelevant base—on ancient ruins—but rather on new, solid foundations. Challenging and clearing existing assumptions and expectations makes it easier to start with a fresh perspective.

We cover the practical process skills of this phase in our book on creative thinking *Who Killed Creativity?…And How Can We Get It Back?* (The specific tools provided for this mode are 'Strategy 1: Cultivate curiosity' and 'Strategy 2: Accept ambiguity'.) We suggest you look there for practical ideas and exercises for developing creative thinking strategies at each of the stages we are covering. This book, in contrast, focuses on the higher level, systemic culture change that needs to take place to support the innovation process.

Freedom to ask questions, freedom to challenge existing systems, freedom to imagine alternative futures and possibilities—these are foundations of a free society that supports innovation. And they are the philosophical principles that we are going to explore further in the first half of this chapter, before moving on to look at practical applications for the organisation in the second half of the chapter.

Purpose-Driven Innovation (PDI) in action: LIBERATE

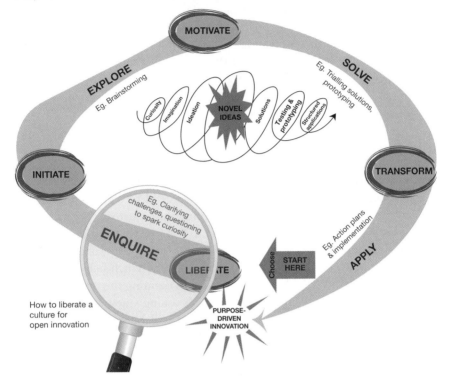

As we continue our exploration of the African continent, we will unpack the mindset that can block freedom, and discover the paradoxical principles that will assist with removing those blocks and finding better alternatives.

Oppressive control: behind the motives of mighty monarchs

Like all travellers to Egypt, we were intrigued by the massive, complex structures that had been built by early kings and queens, remnants of which are strewn along the banks of the river as relics of a glorious past. The imposing pyramids, the striking sphinxes, the vast palaces. We rode bikes up dusty tracks in the Valley of the Kings to see the intricate underground tombs that had originally been lined with gold and filled with precious jewels; we were fascinated by the architectural and aesthetic brilliance and grandeur of it all.

A country has to keep reinventing itself to stay at the forefront, and that involves innovation. It would have been easy for the Egyptian pharaohs to think they were great and invincible in their own remarkable developments, and we were certainly impressed by all they had achieved. But when we started to think about *how* it had happened we returned to the importance not just of the *outcomes* of development and innovation, but also of the *foundations* of development and innovation.

It was then that it hit us. We started to think about how so much of what is now venerated is the product of oppressive regimes. The grand relics of the glory days gone by, as majestic and awe inspiring as they are, often give testament to the ability of the powerful and the rich to exploit the poor for their own purposes. The grandeur of the rulers depended on the sweat of those they controlled, and any innovation may have been at the cost of exploitation.

If we were to believe Cecil B. DeMille's movie *The Ten Commandments*, we would assume that slaves from the south had built the pyramids. (If we were to believe some apostles of the paranormal, the master pyramid was built by giants, and humans copied their work to build the others on a smaller scale!) It seems increasingly likely, however, that Egyptian labourers built the pyramids. Egyptian society was organised along feudal lines with people owing service to a lord. The pyramid builders would most likely have been obligatory labourers, and their skeletal remains show evidence of arthritis and bone damage.[1]

The Great Pyramid, King Khufu's burial chamber, towered above the Giza landscape back in 2570 BC. It took around 20000 people to set in place the 2.3 million blocks of limestone with an average mass of 2.5 stones, and it remained the tallest structure anywhere in the world for 3800 years, until the building of Lincoln Cathedral spire in 1300 AD. But the striking self-confidence of the pyramid age was not to last.

Seeing these massive structures, most people would likely conclude that at one time Egypt was one of the most innovative civilisations in the world. With its complex architecture, religious beliefs and rituals, government structures, art and record keeping, in its time this advanced civilisation dominated much of the known world. Yet that grand civilisation is long gone.

When we first visited Egypt, millennia after its ancient heyday, we arrived in the short window between the Arab Spring uprising and the overthrow of the government that followed, and we immediately had the impression that

The architecture and plan of cities such as Cairo reflect a history of innovation for domination rather than innovation for progress.

Egypt had long since lost that apparent competitive edge. Looking at the dramatic changes that were sweeping through the country at the time we visited it was impossible not to wonder what had happened. How did a country that was once so innovative fall so far behind? Anthropologists who study modernised countries or cities in the African and Arab regions, such as Cairo, point out that the architecture and plan of the city reflects a history of innovation for domination rather than for progress.[2] This trend can be dated right back to the initial development of urban centres in the pre-dynastic period. Urbanisation brought specialised crafts, whose products were exchanged for agricultural produce. Eventually an elite social class developed and institutional dominance became established, as evidenced by the growth in individualised burial grounds.[3] Wealth led to great power, which then in turn often led to domination.

The problem is that although control through power and domination may produce spectacular results in the short term, it doesn't necessarily lead to cultural progress over the long term; in fact, it can significantly impede long-term innovation and progress by limiting collaborative dynamic growth at the grassroots level. Along with the great monuments of Egypt, there are many shrines in China and Meso-America that exemplify how cultures of control can produce creative and innovative outcomes.[4] The Soviet Union also produced amazing composers, writers, dancers and scientists, and were the first to launch a satellite into space. Yet these are examples of *controlled creativity*, as they do not involve and engage all people at all levels in the creative process, and they ultimately did not last.

How is it that these sorts of impressive developments based on power and ambition ultimately collapse so swiftly and completely?

The pride before the fall

A Zambian story tells a cautionary tale of ambition and innovation based on control. A man named Kamonu wanted to accumulate more objects and powers to rival his creator god, Nyambi. In his efforts to separate himself from the rest of the world Kamonu moved to an island, then to a mountain peak, before finally elevating himself into the sky: with his descendants he cut logs and built the tallest tower he could in order to reach Nyambi as an equal in the heavens. But the tower he built became top-heavy and eventually it came tumbling down, leaving his ambitions in ruins. The moral of the story is that an egotistical pride can often come before a dramatic fall.

The story of the Tower of Babel is another cautionary tale that warns of how development and innovation can come from selfish and controlling motives. The ancient Hebrews believed in a three-tiered universe comprising the underworld, the earth and the heavens. The powerful sought to reach the heavens in order to consolidate their position of power. According to the Book of Genesis (11: 1–9), following the Great Flood a giant tower was built in Shinar—an area in Mesopotamia spanning modern Iraq and Syria—precisely for that purpose. The Hebrews thought that they could build a tower so tall that they could control the world, becoming gods themselves. The story suggests that the ambition that drove them to control the world was the very thing that divided them and caused them to speak different languages, which in turn stopped them from achieving their goal.

In the middle of the Pacific you will find an example of a culture that faced a comparable challenge. Easter Island is best known for the giant *moai* statues that line the coast, but they have a sinister past. The islanders built at least 887 of these statues, the largest of which weighed 86 tonnes and stood 10 metres high, transporting them to auspicious locations around the island, where they could watch over the villages and protect the people from danger. Yet despite all the work put into them, these unique icons may also have been the cause of the island population's downfall. When the statues were built by the Polynesian Rapa Nui people, between the thirteenth and fifteenth centuries, there was strong competition between clan chiefs to build the biggest statue. The moai were symbols of power and were built larger and larger as the centuries passed. One incomplete statue uncovered would have stood 21 metres high—as high as a seven-storey building!

The problem was that through their desire to compete against each other in building these massive structures, the Rapa Nui people depleted the very resources they needed for survival. The moai were carved from huge slabs of compressed volcanic ash quarried locally. According to folklore divine power was used to command the statues to walk, but most likely wooden sleds or rollers and ropes were used to transport them to their final platforms. Vast numbers of trees were cut down to build moai, and by the time the last statue was built there were no trees left on the island. With the trees gone the bird population decreased, and the people were unable to build canoes for fishing. The deforestation also impacted the soil quality and crop yields. Food, fire and shelter became increasingly difficult to access. Soon the tribes that had until then lived together relatively harmoniously started to battle over the last resources. Environmentally and socially the island was devastated. You could imagine the literally earth-shattering impact as raiders attacked and toppled the statues of rival clans.

This story is a fascinating, terrible fable of the pursuit of power and control at the expense of long-term sustainability, a lesson that has significant ramifications for the global community.

It appears that many of the building projects of chiefs, kings and rulers in ancient times were based on pride and a desire for control rather than social purpose. They were pride-driven rather than purpose-driven. It has been said that the arrogance behind the fierce attitude towards dissent of the average Egyptian pharaoh would have done credit to North Korea's former leader Kim Jong-il.[5] The priestly elite controlled 30 per cent of the nation's land, which gave them a disproportionate share of the nation's output and income.[6] Ezekiel 9 records how prophets were sent to warn the pharaohs of their arrogance in setting themselves up as gods, and that for those who seek to rival the gods there would be dire consequences.

Professor Joann Fletcher believes that, 'The only way ancient Egypt could survive was through its own resilience and the strongest of leadership ... Being merely mortal was not enough. The Pharaohs needed to prove their divinity by exercising absolute control over their subjects.'[7] One pharaoh who ruled over 4000 years ago Seostris III, was portrayed with a scowling face to indicate he ruled with an iron rod and with larger ears to show he could hear plots.

What these stories have in common is an egotistic belief that it is possible to rival the gods through our own creative abilities. The clear lesson from the ancient texts is that innovation based on pride will not prevail.[8] Even in North Korea today the 'supreme leader' is believed to be a god with supernatural powers trying to demonstrate superiority. When we visited the demilitarized zone between North and South Korea, we discovered that the supreme commander in North Korea has been attempting to battle South Korea in a 'tallest neighbouring flagpole' competition, eventually building a pole 160 m high.

Innovation can come at a significant cost—if it is not based on a foundation of freedom. Domination may lead to short-term gains, but it will not lead to sustainable innovation. So while ancient Egypt, like other civilisations with absolute rulers, gained ascendancy in the 'innovation race' of its day, this did not lead to sustained progress. While the ancient Egyptians were busy ensuring their rulers passed comfortably into the afterlife with all possible benefits, they were too short-sighted to see that this dominance would not guarantee long-term success for generations to come.

History strongly supports the conclusion that without a culture of liberty there can be no sustainable growth and innovation. As mythologist Joseph Campbell puts it, 'Not authority but aspiration is the motivator, builder, and transformer of civilization.'[9] What does this mean for leaders today? Jared

Diamond believes, 'By focusing on the pinnacle of achievements while ignoring the foundations, leaders can become vulnerable in ways they never expected.'[10]

Are we scaling the pyramid?

When you climb the pyramids of Giza and look back at the vast view you are awed by the scale of these structures and the power they must have represented in their time. The Great Pyramid was the tallest monument ever built, and remains the largest stone monument in the world. It was 280 metres high when it was built, an elevation equalled only in the middle ages by the tallest European cathedrals, as mentioned earlier. It was certainly a significant symbol of power and success.

On the other side of the world, the Aztec pyramids in Mexico similarly embodied the power and dominance of the ruling elite. The Aztecs believed that the universe was created by the gods at the Teotihuecan site, 50 km northeast of Mexico City. The day we climbed the pyramids we were afforded a commanding view of the breadth of the valley leading up to the capital, and we could imagine how this complex would have dominated the once thriving city.

By contrast, the largest pyramid in the world, at Cholula, also near Mexico City, is underwhelming to visit, as most of it is now buried underground. All that remains visible from its grand past is a small mound on which a Catholic church now stands. Traces of the original construction have all but gone, with the Church having explicitly asserted its power and dominance over a defeated people.

Historically the tallest or grandest constructions in a populated area have typically represented centres of power.[11] Think of the tallest totem pole or community centre or the Papua New Guinean longhouse (in the Pacific); the castles, palaces and government buildings (in many developed countries); the great cathedrals and mosques; and, more recently, the cathedrals of commerce that are the skyscrapers in modern cities. All have been expressions of power and control in their time.

It is now the wealthiest institutions, the massive corporate offices, that dominate the skyline and claim the most powerful positions. Wealth is fundamentally associated with power, but think about whether this can exclude the vast majority of the world's population. The deification of commercial success can create a deep divide between the wealthy 'haves', who have all the resources and opportunities they need to be able to determine their own independent future, and the 'have nots', who have little power, little control and little choice in their lives.

While many of us in the developed world are looking to develop and innovate to bring more enjoyment and more fulfilment into our lives, many others have to simply focus on survival. Does this lead to the great divisions that determine who is able to participate in and benefit the most from innovation? Can it then become a vicious cycle?

Inequality impacts innovation, innovation impacts inequality

The grand 750 metre causeway stretching from the life-giving Nile to the city of the dead desert plateau in Saqqara, Egypt was built for the sole purpose of accommodating the great King Unas' funeral procession (2350 BC). Remarkably, it captures the tensions of the key paradox explored in this chapter, revealing distinctive drawings of the extremes of 'chaos' up one side of the causeway and 'order' along the other.

In this chapter we are exploring the principle of *guided freedom*, which can guide us between the extreme of oppression on the one hand (beyond order) and chaos on the other. As an essential starting phase for the process of innovation, we need to build an environment of freedom—balanced with clear guidance and support—that enables open enquiry and provides a platform for growth. Where there is no freedom there can be no initiation of the innovation process, yet most people in the world don't enjoy that foundation of freedom. They don't have the political freedom to make their own choices, and they don't have the material and financial resources or the opportunity to innovate, which immediately puts them way behind in the race.

While many of us in the developed world are looking to develop further and innovate to bring more enjoyment and more fulfilment into our lives, many others have to innovate on a simple level just to survive on a daily basis. The concept of Jugaad innovation we introduced in chapter 2 demonstrates this well. [12] Many of the people we met in Egypt did not have the foundation of freedom and security that would enable higher levels of development. As Wade Davis, *National Geographic*'s resident anthropologist whom we met in the first chapter, has so aptly stated, 'In reality, development for the vast majority of the peoples of the world has been a process in which the individual is torn from his past and propelled into an uncertain future, only to secure a place on the bottom rung of an economic ladder that goes nowhere.' [13]

According to humanist psychologist Albert Maslow's hierarchy of needs model (a model that fortuitously takes the shape of a pyramid), at the most basic level (equivalent to the bottom rung of Wade Davis's ladder), we all have physiological survival needs for food, water and shelter that must be met before we can focus on higher levels of development—if we are able to progress at all.[14] Once those needs are met, we concern ourselves with safety needs, which can be both physical and psychological needs. At the next levels our needs relate purely to our psychological wellbeing, including the need to be loved, to feel like we belong, to win the esteem or good opinion of others, and, ultimately, to realise our potential and thereby achieve 'self-actualisation'.

Maslow's hierarchy of needs

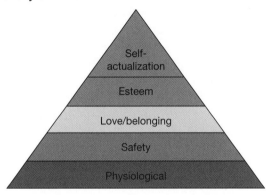

Many people misunderstand what self-actualisation means. Some find that once they have secured all the physical comforts and personal emotional wellbeing they need, they feel distinctly superior. Some think this 'superiority' gives them the right to dominate others. There are those, too, who will use power and dominance to try to achieve self-actualisation. This is not at all what Maslow had in mind.

It might be worth considering at this point where you stand, and how your position impacts your view of the world.

Where did that cheap t-shirt come from?

While we may comfortably believe we don't ourselves fit into the category of 'oppressor' and don't seek to dominate others, there are more subtle forms we may be guilty of.

> Think about how we boast about that super-cheap t-shirt or handbag we just bought, yet we often wilfully choose to ignore the fact that the purchases may have been made possible by the millions below us on the pyramid, often in unsafe, low-paying sweatshops.

Think about how we boast about that super-cheap t-shirt or handbag we just bought on sale at the department store, or the latest high-tech device we have acquired to add to our smart devices. We often unconsciously or wilfully choose to ignore the origins of these purchases, which have been made possible by the millions below us on the pyramid, often in unsafe, low-paying sweatshops.[15]

Globalisation was not meant to be about the 99 per cent at the bottom of the pyramid supporting the luxurious lifestyles of those on the top tier. Innovations produced under these circumstances are not positive, purpose-driven advances; they are the result of oppressive systems at work. Our aim here is not to morally judge if progress is right or wrong, or to comment on capitalism as a system to live by. We are more interested in sounding a warning about the potential dangers of following without question this or any system that allows for inequalities that can impact sustainable, purpose-driven innovation.

Just as Maslow's pyramid shows how until there is both security and a foundation of freedom it is difficult to progress, we believe it is difficult to reach higher levels of development and to innovate beyond mere survival without having these basic needs met.

What drives innovation?

INNOVATION TO MEET PSYCHOLOGICAL NEEDS AND DESIRES
The lofty realm of the wealthy

INNOVATION FOR PHYSICAL SURVIVAL NEEDS
The reality for most of the world's population

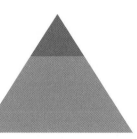

If you overlay this diagram with an economic pyramid showing the proportion of wealthy people to people living on or below the poverty line, you'll get a sense of just how few of us are living in comparative luxury, and how few of us enjoy enough basic security to be able to enjoy the benefits of higher level innovation and development.[16] The following 'Distribution of wealth globally' figure reveals that just 0.7 per cent of the world's population controls almost half (41 per cent) of the world's wealth, while more than 70 per cent of the world's population struggles to survive.

Distribution of wealth globally

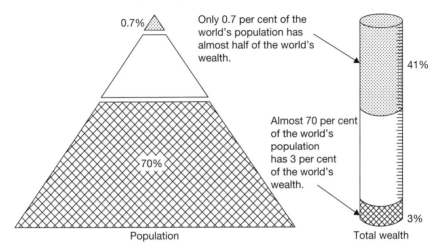

We can't be proud of our innovations if they lead to the kind of domination and exploitation we associate with despotic rulers of the past, and if our wealth and resources are used to prop up the lifestyles of the top 1 per cent. Sustainable innovation means we can all achieve a baseline level of comfort and security, and we can all enjoy the benefits of innovations that help to make lives more comfortable.

Do we still have modern-day pharaohs, pyramid builders or pyramid scalers based on an economic system that ensures those at the top live well and are luxuriously transitioned into the next life at the expense of their children? Will future generations inherit a world with catastrophic environmental problems, or are we innovating with everyone in mind? Surely we want our generation to be remembered as channelling our great knowledge, technology and innovation into solutions for the greater good of all?

The race to dominate

Egypt is just one small country in the northeast of this vast continent. The journey down the Nile takes you to the heart of the African continent, to lush jungles and vast plains of savannah teaming with wild animals, to lands where a different tragic story unfolded. This area is so remote that the full length of the river was first navigated only in 2004, a journey that took four and a half months to complete. The deeper you travel into Africa the more you discover how much of a struggle for survival life has been, and how much of that is owed to a race for superiority and domination.

Despite being the birthplace of mankind, or perhaps because of it, Africa's troubled history has inhibited the sort of growth that many other regions around the world have experienced. Invasions, slavery, colonisation, dictatorships, apartheid—all have oppressed the people and impeded their progress. Africa, it has been said, was 'Colonised, dismembered, raped of its resources (natural, human or otherwise) in order to support Western economies'.[17] The result is that Africa in general, and sub-Saharan Africa in particular, has by far the largest share of population living in absolute poverty (less than US$1.25 per day), so you can imagine the scale of the problems in this part of the world.

Africa has been subject to colonisation by a range of countries and cultures over the years, including countries from Europe and Western Asia. The colonisers brought innovation by introducing cash crops, which replaced vital food crops, with a dire impact on the quality of life for Africans. It was not *mutually beneficial innovation*. They also changed trading patterns and brought in indentured labour, for example from India—all of which undermined the traditional economy.

> The colonisers brought innovation by introducing cash crops, which replaced vital food crops, with a dire impact on the quality of life for Africans.

There is no doubt that European colonisation of Africa had disastrous impacts on its development over the long term. The slave trade took the healthiest and most productive young men and women, which often led to the demise of whole societies. There has also been the significant impact of colonialism in general. While some of the countries that have regained independence have been able to move forwards successfully, many have struggled with problems of corruption and war ever since.

Slavery was based on the desire for those with power to live off the involuntary labour of the many without power. Reimagining the pyramid as an iceberg helps us to get a feel for how the oppressed majority can end up supporting the elite minority, and what the hidden cost can be.

The potential cost of desire-driven innovation

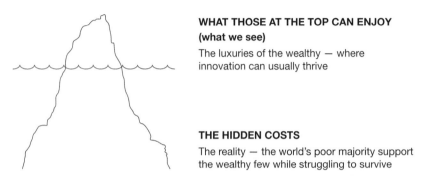

WHAT THOSE AT THE TOP CAN ENJOY
(what we see)
The luxuries of the wealthy — where innovation can usually thrive

THE HIDDEN COSTS
The reality — the world's poor majority support the wealthy few while struggling to survive

As was common practice in imperial projects worldwide, when the European powers first raced to carve out their own territories and areas of influence in Africa they studied their maps and divided up the territories arbitrarily based on sharing the lands, coastlines and water courses, rather than considering the existing relationships between peoples and ethnic groups.[18] The result was that previously harmonious tribal and ethnic groups were split and recombined with other groups quite capriciously, which naturally led to conflict. How many outsiders now judge Africa's enduring instability while failing to recognise the part our ancestors played in creating the conditions that led to these problems?

The colonisation of Africa was for domination and control, not to better society. It was based on parasitic rather than symbiotic relationships, oppression rather than liberation. Most introduced innovations were not intended to improve the local communities; they were designed to more efficiently extract the resources of the host country, so when the colonisers left the locals suffered.

Although most people would readily associate oppression with conquest and colonial domination, fewer are able to see the parallel deprivation and injustices suffered through systematic constraints in everyday life. Unquestioned norms, habits and symbols can lead to a structural oppression.[19] Oppression can become, as philosopher Marilyn Frye has identified, 'an enclosing structure of forces and barriers which tends to the immobilization and reduction of a group or category of people'.[20]

Education for empowerment

> *'Civilisation is the race between education and catastrophe. Let us learn the truth and spread it as far and wide as our circumstances allow. For the truth is the greatest weapon we have.'*
>
> H. G. Wells

Liberty or freedom from oppression has been identified as one of the six key areas people are universally morally concerned about,[21] as well as one of the key prerequisites for innovation.[22]

Brazilian philosopher and educator Paulo Freire studied the impact of oppression on the oppressed, and has described how it is possible to break the cycle of oppression and build a foundation of freedom.[23] In a nutshell, oppression can keep us trapped inside a 'box' from where we are unable to explore or develop new ideas freely, which is a critical foundation for innovation ('thinking outside the box'). Freire argued that oppressors, or dominators (as he has also referred to them), do not want the oppressed to be able to think for themselves in order to better their own status.

True education, says Freire, is the solution. Not the sort of teaching that merely involves depositing information for a passive recipient (what he has called 'banking' education), but rather the sort of education that opens up a world of possibilities and liberates for real growth. While banking education, he says, 'anesthetizes and inhibits creative power', real education can provide real freedom. To beat the colonialists at their own game, Africans have had to increase their own personal power through expanding their knowledge and capabilities. Ironically, the decolonisation of Africa has been achieved mainly by Africans educated in the European system.

History shows us that it is never possible to return to a previous state. Once there has been a massive intervention in a culture, that culture will never be the same again, and you can only move forward to create positive new futures. The indigenous communities of Australia and many other post-colonial countries around the world will never be able to go back to what they once had. They therefore need to find creative ways to deal with current realities and help develop a better future state.

> Once there has been a massive intervention in a culture, that culture will never be the same again, and you can only move forward to create positive new futures.

This is what creative development for innovation needs to be about. It is a form of targeted growth that empowers and equips for positive transformation for everyone, not just those at the top. Real education and empowerment need to be tools of this sort of social innovation.

There is no doubt that some guidance and organisation can be beneficial. Behavioural guidelines, for example, can help to reduce a lack of direction and keep society functioning smoothly. Some control can actually help to produce consistent and predictable behaviour, which can support the development of trust. Control can be coercive, relying on overt, externalised mechanisms of control, or it can be normative, or internalised and covert, relying mainly on a strong culture based on clear values. Where the control is normative, or based on a common understanding of meaning (purpose-driven), people choose to behave according to expectations because it is the right and natural thing to do rather than because they are feeling coerced to do it.[24] Too much control, though, can restrict freedom and lead to economic and social disadvantage. As freedom of thought and action have been found to be essential for creative thinking, a lack of freedom at these levels presents a significant problem for innovation.

This is the essence of the challenging paradox we face, and the lesson we can learn for how to transition to a culture that will best support innovation.

The Singapore sprint

Singapore is one of the few countries you can arrive in confident that everything will be spotlessly clean and will work. It stands out in the Asian region as a technologically advanced nation that has been able to leap ahead of its neighbours. Indeed it has managed to boost its GDP by an astonishing 3700 per cent, 10 times that of the US, since it was founded as a nation state in 1965.[25] It has also emerged as a highly innovative country prepared to challenge the status quo and do things differently. In fact, Singapore has been recognised as one of the most innovative cities in the world.

Founding President Lee Kuan Yew, who ruled the country for over 30 years, was a visionary leader who sought to bring innovative ideas to the country. In his inaugural speech he aspired to develop Singapore to become 'a first world oasis in a third world region'. He established what the locals have called an 'authoritarian democracy', which saw him navigate at the 'control' side of the spectrum, yet Singapore stood in stark contrast to a number of corrupt dictatorships among its neighbours in the Asian region. When the country entered the 'innovation race' in 1965, it started as a tiny, poorly equipped nation with few natural resources, even reliant on buying water from its neighbour, and yet soon emerged as a clear frontrunner.

Racing from the back of the field to the front, Singapore can now claim a number of trophies, including being rated as one of the best cities for investment potential for 16 consecutive years. It is also said to be the world's easiest place to do business, as well as Asia's 'most network-ready' and 'most transparent' country.[26] Bloomberg has placed it in the top 10 most innovate countries.[27] At the beginning of their race the focus was on quality control, then it shifted gears to focus on customer service. Now the focus is on innovation.

How did this happen? The mechanism Lee Kuan Yew put in place to drive the vision was a focus on developing talent (for example, through investing in higher education and attracting branches of top international universities), technology (in lieu of a lack of natural resources) and tolerance to attract the 'creative class' (according to Richard Florida's principles of what makes a 'creative class' as introduced earlier). For a country famously intolerant of publicly discarded chewing gum, the description of Singapore as 'tolerant' might come as a surprise. Yet the three major cultural groups (Indians, Malays and Chinese) had to learn to live alongside each other in the same housing districts to avoid cultural ghettos (and to allow for a sharing of perspectives).

From our conversations with Singaporeans, most don't feel that the current climate is negative and oppressive; rather they feel that some control has freed them to do business in a safe haven. This is why Singapore has managed to attract so much foreign investment.

The goal of most dictatorships is to ensure the smallest number of people enjoy the greatest amount of wealth and the greatest benefits of innovation (as in the wealth pyramid). Lee Kuan Yew, on the other hand, focused innovation on bringing *progress for all* rather than domination. It was control for the sake of progress, not control for the sake of domination, and this may have given the country an advantage as it moved into the future. Through maintaining control he was able to get things done quickly and easily and innovate faster, cutting through bureaucracy.

The question now needs to be asked: Are Singaporeans themselves innovative? Has this innovative focus from the government filtered through to all levels? Has a culture that encourages sustainable innovation over the long term been established? When we have asked Singaporeans specifically if they think Singapore is innovative, a typical response has been, 'Yes!, The government is very innovative!'. But what happens when a visionary creative genius leader moves out of the role; does it leave a vacuum? The next challenge will be to see if this sort of creativity moves beyond the visionary leader to each individual (for example, through having the freedom to ask questions, challenge the status quo and think outside the box).

The Singapore solution started as a short-term sprint, using methods that helped them get to the front of the pack, but it is in the process of transitioning to a more sustainable marathon. 'I believe Singaporeans can be creative,' says Professor Kirpal Singh of the Singapore Management University, 'but the creative eco-system needs to be firmly in place and entrenched as high value.'[28] (For the full interview with Professor Singh, visit www.the-innovation-race.com).

Think about the parallels for organisations today: How does the organisation transition from the visionary leader to an integrated innovation culture? How is it possible to transition to *guided freedom*?

More creative courage, fewer constraints

We started this chapter by looking at ancient civilisations that have veered so far off the path into dangerous territory using oppressive and often tyrannical practices that they were unable to find a way back. We then examined a culture that has found a way to navigate that challenging path between control and freedom to forge a way forward into the future. It's time now to cross over to the other side of the path—to consider the impact of freedom on an innovation culture.

Psychologists believe personal freedom through autonomy to be one of the key developmental stages that helps us grow from dependent children to responsible, independent and fulfilled adults. Most people identify freedom as one of our most important rights, and a lack of freedom as a major source of unhappiness.[29]

If you cross the Mediterranean from North Africa, you arrive at the birthplace of the concept of political freedom: Ancient Greece. Athens' first experiment with democracy took place in the fifth century BC. In the fourth century BC Democritus grappled with ideas around self-determinism and freedom, ideas later picked up by Aristotle. (We will explore the idea of freedom more when we travel to the Americas in chapter 8.) The concept of freedom has been associated with the Christian ideal of free will. Political theorist Hannah Arendt has interpreted it as 'beginning anew'.[30] Political freedom is one of the ideals of democratic societies, connoting a state of freedom from oppression, coercion and excessive constraints.

Freedom has also been found to be linked with creativity. We've discussed the importance of multiple perspectives for igniting creativity, and it's not hard to see how the engagement of diverse political parties and ideas produces higher rates of creative activity and output.[31] Such open societies contrast with 'insular societies' in which only one political philosophy or party is represented. Ethno-psychological studies have found that exposure

> Societies that are characterised by political freedom, particularly by the presence of diverse political parties and ideologies, have been found to produce higher rates of creative activity and output.

to multiple sources of power and information contributes to less compliance and conformity to pressure, and to a broader world view.

Democratic and pluralistic states use the rule of law to provide freedom of expression for all citizens, which encourages the development of ideas and talents. History has shown that countries run by democratic governments reduce opportunities for exploitation and provide more freedom to encourage greater development (and more peace).[32] Open creative thinking is a potential threat to autocracies determined to hang on to power and control. It means the elites could lose their exclusive access to the economic and financial resources of a country.

Data from the World Values Survey reveals that societies that rank highly on 'self-expression' (for example, interpersonal trust, tolerance and participatory decision making), rather than being stuck on 'survival values', tend to develop stable democracies that support development and growth.[33] This demonstrates again, recalling Maslow's hierarchy of needs, how important for higher-level exploration it is to have a secure foundation. Individualist cultures define and promote the self as autonomous and value independence and self-reliance, all of which assist the creative process.[34]

More democratic and individual freedom also helps to reduce corruption. An independent judiciary, freedom of the press and political opposition parties that work to expose corruption in the government are all inbuilt mechanisms that support responsible freedom. The Index of Economic Freedom (IEF) published by the *Wall Street Journal* and the Heritage Foundation in 1997 highlights the links between the availability of economic resources and economic freedom. Areas that are measured include freedom to hold property, to earn a living, to operate a business, to make investments, to trade internationally and to participate in the market economy.[35]

Can there be too much freedom?

Empowerment enables individuals to take responsibility for innovation. Open, dynamic, organic systems allow individuals to explore multiple ideas and options in a safe context. Mechanistic and controlled structures, on the other hand, typically hinder innovation.[36]

But here's the inevitable paradox: too much freedom can be counterproductive. As Paulo Freire expresses it, 'Freedom is not the absence of limits. What I have sought always is to live the tension, the contradiction, between authority and freedom so as to maintain respect for both.'[37] Or, as Nelson Mandela said, 'with freedom comes responsibilities'.[38]

Think about how too much freedom can lead to an economic crash. An undisciplined economy will inevitably collapse.[39] Unbridled economic freedom can lead to greed, pride and a sense of entitlement (qualities typically associated with tyrannical leaders, as we have argued), and these same qualities help explain the Wall Street Crash of 2008. Countries that had tighter banking regulations weathered the storm much better than those with fewer controls. Too much freedom of choice at the individual level can also lead to a state of anxiety.[40] Psychologist Barry Schwartz writes:

> Freedom and autonomy are critical to our wellbeing, and
> choice is critical to freedom and autonomy. Nonetheless, though
> modern Americans have more choice than any group of people
> ever has before, and thus, presumably, more freedom and autonomy,
> we don't seem to be benefiting from it psychologically.[41]

> ... if you shatter the fishbowl so that everything is possible, you
> don't have freedom. You have paralysis.[42]

Too much freedom can lead to chaos, which is obviously also not conducive to constructive innovative development. Unrestricted and uncontrolled empowerment can actually be counterproductive if the ideas that emerge are not adequately guided.[43] Silicon Valley has been described by a former tech startup employee as, 'a kind of kindergarten cult that plies its young charges with parties, toys, naps, playtime...' at the expense of having any real direction. 'One day, we are told the company will focus on big enterprise customers... Two weeks later, we're going back to selling to small businesses.'[44]

Guided freedom across all levels—as a balance between control and freedom—creates more opportunities. Successful organisations draw 'actions' boundaries through clearly defining the actions needed, the priorities, the level of responsibility and the level of empowerment needed to reach these ends. Behavioural guidance must be accompanied by redefinitions of responsibility as new processes are implemented. A strong organisational value system will help to ensure that this level of guidance is provided without veering into the dangerous territory of control.

In this context, the leader's role changes from Director to Guide. The leader becomes a custodian of the vision, ensuring that it provides sufficient guidance for empowered action. Leading with an assumption of incompetence leads to control, but an assumption of excellence based on a clear vision provides *guided freedom*. Eric Schmidt of Google has been quoted as saying, 'My job is to be the keeper of the vision, not the controller of the process.'[45]

The President of Pixar Animation Studios and Walt Disney Animation Studios, Ed Catmull, describes how this can happen in practice: 'During production we leave the operating decisions to the film leaders, we don't second guess or micromanage them. When production runs into a problem we do everything possible to provide support without undermining their authority.' At another level, he says, freedom is about ensuring that systems and structures are in place to assist, but that they don't become barriers to success. 'Everyone must have the freedom to communicate with anyone.'[46]

The deeper purpose: to dominate or to progress?

Egyptian rulers and European colonisers used power to dominate in the name of progress rather than for genuine, mutual and purposeful progress for all. Yet what about where the edges of acceptance are not as obvious?

Think of the two poles of control and freedom as the two sides of a motor racing track. Some people might say that countries like Singapore and companies and individuals like Apple and Steve Jobs have moved over to the 'control' side of the track, possibly dangerously close to the edge. This is still debatable. North Korean dictators, on the other hand, have hurtled right outside of the boundaries. You can tell when the boundaries have been crossed, as control becomes oppression. The challenge is to see where those edges are and to navigate efficiently without leaving the safe zone completely.

One way to check how close an organisation has moved to the 'edge' is to consider why that action has been taken. For example, in business, it can be helpful to consider if a company is taking a particular approach or action for progress, or for *political* or *market domination*. Those who get to the top of the pyramid can end up using their position to dominate rather than to help their people. The leader's role is to help get everyone to the top of the pyramid, not just the elite few, yet so often the leadership position is used as a opportunity for oppressive control rather than empowering guidance.

There is a continuum between control and freedom. The trick is to use *situational innovation* principles to know how close you are to the edge of the path at any time, and to avoid that danger zone where control turns into oppression or freedom turns into chaos. By empowering and trusting people in the organisation, it is possible to create a culture of 'assumed excellence', whereby everyone is motivated and equipped for positive, sustainable change.[47]

Bhutan has been making the brave transition from control to guided freedom when the King stepped down from the throne and gave the power to the people through the first democratic elections in 2008.

Through shifting to the concept of guidance towards progress, or guided freedom, it is possible to start making strategic PDI decisions. Future innovation and development will need to come from individuals at all levels, not just from those in positions of power.[48] This is the foundation on which a culture of innovation needs to be actively built for real long-term transformation.

DETOUR
China: Finding a foundation of freedom

Invention is an expression of innovation, and China has been the source of many important inventions. China invented the first iterations of the printing press, paper, paper money, the seed drill, the blast furnace, iron suspension bridges, textile production, the spinning wheel, gunpowder, chemical insecticide, the fishing reel, matches, the magnetic compass, playing cards, the toothbrush and the wheelbarrow! The game of golf originated here as far back as AD 1000. China was for many years way ahead of its time and way ahead of the pack.

In the next chapter we will explore how it was that China raced ahead in the early years. Today, however, the country is known more for its ability to imitate than to originate.[49] 'The Middle Kingdom', writes historian Niall Ferguson, 'once the mother of inventions, [became] the mediocre kingdom, wilfully hostile to other people's innovations.' He describes how one ingenious Chinese creation, the clock, was brought to Europe, improved on and later returned to China as a far superior concept. Today we still assume that the Swiss invented the clock.

How and why did this happen? Ferguson believes that the changing political environment was not conducive to a spirit of innovation. More central control, the removal of healthy competition, a mistrust of science, the rejection of capitalism and with it the entrepreneurial spirit — all of these contributed to a reduction in innovative thinking in China. Although China under Ming dynasty rule appeared both to thrive and to maintain equilibrium successfully, it relied on preserving a static social order. Innovation could threaten China's huge yet fragile social system. Only

(continued)

recently, now competing on the world stage, is China starting to recognise and re-emphasise the importance of innovation.

For a long time, it seemed, China eschewed the individual passions that can spur entrepreneurialism and innovation, while also failing to provide a collaborative social context that could benefit progress and innovation. By introducing a rigid, controlling system they lost the benefits of both.

When we spent time weaving through the crowded streets of Shanghai, the largest city in the world by some measures, we got a feel for the magnitude of both the potential of China and the challenges it faces. The murky Huangpu River, which snakes its way through this energetic city, splits the historic bund on the west bank from the futuristic high-rise buildings on the east side, old from new. The old banks and trading houses on the Bund comply obediently with the restrictive building code and boast classic intricate architecture from a range of eras, from the gothic to art deco. The elegant skyscrapers on the opposite bank are, in contrast, playful freeform experiments. In terms of skyscraper construction, Shanghai is one of the fastest growing cities in the world, with the tallest building in China and one of the tallest in the world. Shanghai itself embodies ambiguity.

The challenge for China will be how to build the foundation of political freedom that will enable individuals to follow their entrepreneurial passions while maintaining the sense of collective unity that can drive them towards solutions.

APPLICATIONS FOR THE ORGANISATION

Application 1: Ensure resources are used for mutual benefit rather than individual gain.

- Watch out for 'the hubris born of success'.
- Companies need to be rebuilt as communities.

Silicon Valley is seen (by those who equate innovation with technological development) as the epicentre of innovation in business today. The offices of the tech giants are vast and elaborate, rivalling, in concept at least, some of the awe-inspiring megastructures of the past. Are they pyramids built as monuments to power, or are they truly great places to work, designed to attract and keep the best talent for a greater purpose?

In the next chapter we will argue that for innovation to be best supported, workspaces need to be conducive to creative thinking and positive interaction. Large tech companies have paved the way with research into how to design workspaces that optimise creative thinking—that is, to build the ideal workplace. Leaders aiming to build big need to reflect on why they are building these structures: are they creating monuments to their own or their organisation's power, or are they genuinely wanting to create innovative places for their employees to work in (which, as we explore in later chapters, will attract the creative class), based on a purposeful vision that contributes to a wider community?

> The temptation will be to build empires, but shouldn't the mandate be to use these resources to contribute to solving the issues of the wider community?

The same question can be asked of every aspiring boss. Do they crave the large corner office, the prestige car or the fancy club more for personal display than for a greater purpose? (One company, Bethel Steel, found their employees were so obsessed with the prestige of a corner office that they built an office block in the shape of a cross to accommodate more of them—and went bankrupt as a result of the mindset that had manifested itself in the corner office obsession.[50])

A need for compensation for low self-esteem, or just a determination to climb the corporate ladder to get to the top (the pyramid image is relevant again here!), can generate a sense of entitlement. Taken too far this becomes narcissism, or even psychopathy with delusions of grandeur thrown in. (As many as one in 25 bosses has been found to be a psychopath; the rate among corporate managers is four times higher than in the general population.[51]) According to a definition from *Psychology Today,* 'Narcissists use people, objects, status, and/or accomplishments to represent the self, substituting for the perceived, inadequate "real" self. These grandstanding "merit badges" are often exaggerated. The underlying message of this type of display is: "I'm better than you!" or "Look at how special I am — I'm worthy of everyone's love, admiration, and acceptance!" '[52]

Every leader with grand aspirations should ask themselves, Why am I building big? Is my motivation for innovation *pride-driven* or *purpose-driven*? The US subprime mortgage crisis revealed in a particularly ugly way how power and dominance have become a problem in business ethics. The crisis emerged when mortgages were heavily promoted to push sales up as quickly as possible. During that time many executives of the big banks adopted what has become a pervasive style of leadership through power: they sat in their isolated office towers and announced arbitrary and irrational targets.[53] Instead of getting a realistic feel for what was going on at the ground level, these privileged few remained detached from the experience of the people they were selling their product to, out of touch with reality. The Lehman culture, for example, was not dissimilar to a Renaissance feudal court.[54]

When we gazed over the vast, crumbling pyramids of Egypt we were impelled to ask, 'What happened? How could such a powerful civilisation fall into ruins?' The same questions should be asked of our modern pharaohs of commerce. How do leading companies, seemingly invincible and with every competitive advantage, manage to blow it? The first indication of potential demise can show when the management becomes arrogant and develops a sense of entitlement (Jim Collins calls this the 'hubris born of success').[55] Another indication is an 'undisciplined pursuit of more' — more growth, more profit, more acclaim.

To innovate successfully a leader will need to check in their ego at the door. True innovation comes from the sort of humility that enables an understanding of and connection with the real issues at all levels. The values that need to drive a long-term sustainability-oriented leader must not be exclusive, but rather caring and inclusive. Leaders need to ensure both *security* and *liberty* for their teams to provide a safe launchpad for real innovation.

Application 2: Beware of 'controlled creativity'

- For a culture to be truly creative there needs to be evidence of creativity at all levels, and rigid and inflexible structures will not allow for this.
- A warrior culture can develop when aggressive employees are rewarded and the focus is on competition.
- It is possible to shift to a more empowered culture with open-source sharing of ideas and information.

Silicon Valley tends to be known as a collection of cowboys — individual creative geniuses who paved their way to the top through their highly successful ideas and strong, determined personalities, with well-known heroes such as Steve Jobs, Elon Musk and Mark Zuckerberg leading the way. Yet does having a creative genius at the helm of the company ensure that the company itself is creative at all levels?

Steve Jobs was indisputably an innovator, and at the helm he undoubtedly steered Apple to becoming one of the most innovative companies in the world. He was clearly able to identify and push forward good ideas and weed out the ideas that would waste money and time, but does that mean that the Apple culture as a whole is innovative, with consistent innovation at all levels?

Under Jobs' direction Apple continued to invent radical new products, which led to a huge international cult following, but after his death the momentum slowed down. Some say the market reached saturation, yet they had said the same thing just before the release of each of Jobs' major new inventions. It will be interesting to look back and reflect on whether innovation at Apple turns out to be a product of the controlling leadership style rather than of innovative, empowered individuals.

> Silicon Valley tends to be known as a collection of cowboys — individual creative geniuses who paved their way to the top through their highly successful ideas and strong, determined personalities.

We have discussed the concept of *controlled creativity* in countries. What about in organisations? Is it possible for an organisational leadership style to be controlling enough to stifle freedom even when the leaders are creative visionaries? In an interview, Steve Wozniak admitted that 'the most creative people in Apple who worked on the Macintosh, almost all of them said they would never, ever work for Steve Jobs again. He would directly confront people and almost call them idiots'.[56]

Although Apple has become known as a great technological innovator in terms of products, how sustainable and scalable is it, and what has been the cultural cost?

In our consulting work we met a former senior executive from another top tech company, who remembers a clearly controlling situation. An intern from an ivy league university suggested to the most senior leadership team the idea of 'apps', before Apple made apps famous. Not only was the intern's idea dismissed, but it was done so aggressively that the intern beat a hasty retreat and the idea was never raised at the senior level in the company again. Until it was too late. Perhaps not surprisingly, this company has now been all but eliminated from the unforgiving 'innovation race'.

We have seen that hovering around the boundary line on the control side has the advantage of enabling a leader to quickly cut through bureaucracy and to cull poor or 'unproductive' ideas, allowing for faster implementation. The visionary leaders of Singapore and Apple have done this. Ultimately the ability to rapidly identify the best ideas and eliminate those that would waste time and resources might have meant the difference between allowing the culture to become innovative and critically restricting innovation.

Many countries and organisations that have had this type of creative visionary leadership based on control have stumbled in their succession planning, and the loss of the inspirational leader has left a large gap. The list of companies that lost their way following the exit of a visionary founder is long.[57] These leaders typically do not adequately prepare for the future.[58] We've discussed that the difference between staying on the road and skidding off it can come down to ensuring there is a sense of purpose as opposed to allowing indulgent dominance, but it also needs to be asked how healthy is a 'command and control' leadership style for long-term sustainable innovation?

Apple was able to dominate the 'innovation race' for many years, despite this paradox, while the less visionary IT company was all but eliminated. At this side of the road it's a fine line between taking the most efficient route close to the barrier and skidding off the track.

Tech giant Microsoft had an entrepreneurial founder in Bill Gates, but Microsoft has had a different journey from Apple's.

Gates built a safer, sturdier bureaucratic platform before handing over to the strong though sometimes overbearing CEO Steve Ballmer. After a powerful start in the IT field (dominating the Windows market, possibly owing as much to being in the right place at the right time as to creative genius), they found themselves losing the lead. For some time Microsoft was known as having a 'warrior culture' that rewarded aggressive employees. This may have enabled it to get ahead of competitors with its dominant PC operating system, but it does not contribute to long-term growth and purposeful innovation.[59]

Since this 'eat what you kill' culture has lost relevance, Microsoft has been trying to adjust. In 2014 CEO Satya Nadella, only the third CEO for the company after Bill Gates and Steve Ballmer, talked of creating places where employees can innovate, of making sure there is open-source sharing of ideas and information within the company, and of embracing new things 'boldly'.[60] Microsoft employees, he says, will need to 'throw out' the old ways of thinking and embrace change. 'With the courage to transform individually, we will collectively transform this company and seize the great opportunity ahead.'[61]

Application 3: Engage employees with a sense of purpose.

- Shift from a focus on profit to a focus on purpose.
- Engage people in meaningful work.

Many companies state explicitly that their main aim is to please their shareholders by focusing on profit. The need for financial responsibility is a given, but beyond that what are we focusing on? It is becoming increasingly clear that we should be racing for more than just profit. Profit has been described as being like oxygen: we need it to live, but it's not what we live for.[62]

With a strong sense of purpose, employees can connect with the passion. This will help them to become motivated and empowered to participate in the change process. When we've joined client groups on their annual retreats, we've seen the way employees roll their eyes and recoil with despair or contempt when they are asked from the stage by passionate leaders on six-figure bonuses to give x per cent more to increase the company profit by y per cent. This can be discouraging when they feel they have already given their sweat and blood.

Yet employees are highly motivated to give of themselves when they can see the purpose (beyond just profit) behind what they are doing and they connect with it. Research shows that millennials don't just want a big pay packet (a share of the profit), as their bosses mistakenly typically believe. Rather, they are motivated by being part of a meaningful workplace and by personal development and training—by being part of a greater purpose.[63] This is the essence of normative control, or sharing strong cultural values, rather than coercive control.

More and more people today want to work for companies that are concerned about genuine mutual progress rather than domination for the sake of profit. They want to live a *purpose-driven life,* not just contribute to the company's bottom line—as Pastor Rick Warren and psychologist Martin Seligman have both emphasised. (Warren has sold more than 30 million copies of his book *The Purpose Driven Life*, which remained on the New York Times bestseller list for one of the longest periods in history.)[64] These days, it can be difficult for people to sell a product they don't believe in. If companies want the best employees to help deal with the 'innovation race', they need to decide on their most significant values and most important priorities.

It's no coincidence that the market leaders we have worked with who have consistently impressed us look beyond profit to building on purpose. Janssen (Johnson & Johnson) speaks with incredible passion on helping to bring health to developing companies, and on what measures they can take to ensure it's not all about profit. The Four Seasons Hotels and Resorts are relentless about providing a consistent customer experience to serve their clients the best way they can. Quiet achievers like Colgate Palmolive are successfully building a purposeful culture by deliberately avoiding dominating, personality-driven leadership styles, instead building up all individuals and a supporting culture as a whole. This company also has a genuine dedicated budget for corporate social responsibility and provides services not designed to seek the limelight.

One large international bank we have worked with rolled out a major Six Sigma–style program in different regions around the world. This program looked great on paper, yet ultimately it failed to reach its objectives. Why? Because they had not successfully connected a sense of purpose to the change management plan, there simply wasn't buy-in from the employees.

Returning to our opening story about *The Hunting Party* TV program: the Aboriginal people opted out because they saw no purpose to the ridiculous race, no significance beyond a ratings-grabbing TV show to dominate the market, which meant nothing to them. It was far removed from the Aboriginal experience, and they saw no point to it.

Surviving the 'innovation race' is not about dominating the field; it's about quiet achievement through a solid long-term strategy that carefully navigates the best path between the potential extremes of control and freedom. It requires a greater purpose and greater freedom for all.

Application 4: Identify if the system is too bureaucratic to support innovation.

- Systems can be sources of both constraint and opportunity.
- Too much bureaucracy can encourage conformity and stifle innovation.
- Building organic organisations will help to support the creative process; the resulting organisations have an experiential, risk-taking approach and decentralised power and decision-making processes.
- Build lean organisations with flat structures that support empowerment.

A neighbour of ours happens to work for one of the richest men in the world, Warren Buffett. He has talked about his work as CEO for Asia Pacific of Berkshire Hathaway's new insurance division, and about just how impressive he finds Warren Buffett. Our neighbour is particularly impressed by how unaffected Buffett is by his position and wealth.

Buffett has been ranked as the richest person in the world for many years, yet he chooses to live relatively simply. He continues to live in the same suburban home he had before he amassed his wealth, he still uses his local hairdresser and he doesn't drive fancy cars. He is someone who just happened to be good at investments, with no desire to dominate the world. He now channels much of his vast wealth into innovating to develop sustainable solutions to help solve the world's problems. Meanwhile his company has become one of the largest and most profitable in the world.

Even though the new insurance company that our friend is managing joined the race late, it is rapidly gaining ground. A combination of ensuring the organisation has a flat, egalitarian structure, and that it remains lean and connected rather than becoming bureaucratic and unyielding, has ensured that it can remain focused and competitive.

Our friend has observed how other companies he has worked for that were older, larger and more established were riddled with bureaucracy and suffered from inertia. The bureaucratic structure meant that over the years these companies slowed down until they struggled to stay at the front of the pack. As he described it, companies like this can end up spending so much time getting bogged down with systems and procedures that they are reduced to 'doing business with themselves', and opportunities for growth can be limited. In his new company our neighbour has the flexibility to move fast. The challenge will be to maintain that flexibility as the company gets more established and builds stability.

As another example of how it is possible to get past the bureaucracy to an organic, dynamic system, we once worked with a boutique hotel resort company that was the first of its kind. It was the first to come up with the concept of private villas, and the first to build bespoke properties in beautiful and unusual locations that reflected the local environment and culture rather than coming from a cookie-cutter corporate template.

This company had prided itself on working from core values and principles rather than policies and procedures. The organisation did not have a set Standards and Procedures Manual. Staff were instead required to understand and follow the company values as they applied in a specific circumstance. They employed managers who did not necessarily have a background in hospitality but did show a willingness to learn, and who exemplified the principles the company espoused. This created a powerful personal touch that differentiated the company from others.

As the company grew, however, it became impossible to maintain consistency and quality standards without putting more systems and procedures in place. When we interviewed leaders, they told us how there was debate within the executive team about the bureaucracy needed, and a gradual shift to a more systematised approach became inevitable. It was an unfortunate but realistic transition.

'Just as countries need a leadership structure and bureaucratic systems in place once they reach a certain size,' says Jared Diamond, 'so too do organizations.'[65]

As organisations grow, they tend to become more systematised and bureaucratic in order to survive.[66] This is typically a natural outcome of growth. It is very difficult to supervise and 'control' an organisation with a large number of employees, departments and functions. Joseph Wedgewood's famous pottery factory exemplified how the rise in bureaucratic structure became an organisational innovation during the Industrial Revolution in England. Despite the introduction of new forms of organisation such as matrix and network-based organisations, bureaucracy has become a necessary reality of large organisations.

Some organisations do it better than others. While some do it at the expense of innovation, others are able to include innovation as part of their growth strategy. Sometimes it happens through a strong leadership personality, sometimes it's a matter of being in the right place at the right time, and sometimes it results from following a strategic, conscious procedure. When leaders bring innovation through strong personality, though they may get the organisation off to a cracking head start, they are not necessarily creating a sustainable culture of innovation.

> **The sorts of rules and forms of control that can help provide stability for a large organisation are not conducive to creativity and innovation.**

The sorts of rules and forms of control that can help provide stability for a large organisation are not necessarily conducive to creativity and innovation. In fact, a staggering 40 per cent of tech companies that go public and set up systems and structures to support this find that their innovation slows down significantly.[67] As Harvard engineering professor David Edwards says in *The Lab,* 'specialisation of information and function discourages innovators and dampens dreams'.[68]

When it was launched, Virgin was a creative new starter in the airline industry that did things a little differently. In his biography, Richard Branson says that he started Virgin because he suspected British Airways was so tangled up in bureaucracy that it had become hopelessly ineffective. It's very hard now for national airlines to compete with the low-price independent carriers that have less bureaucratic red tape and fewer organisational barriers to get through. Malaysian Airlines struggled against Air Asia. Qantas Airlines in Australia started their low-cost subsidiary Jetstar as an attempt to bypass these bureaucratic issues and provide a less expensive alternative.

Application 5: Introduce dual operating systems.

- A dual operation system can solve the exploration/exploitation dilemma.
- Shadow networks can provide useful parallel structures for dealing with crisis.
- Avoid high 'power distance'.
- Ensure there are opportunities for innovative approaches ('doing things differently') as well as adaptive approaches ('doing things better').

Business entrepreneur and change management thought leader John Kotter has recognised the challenges of large organisations and suggested a dual operating system with hierarchy on one side and network on the other.[69] This enables the organisation to keep its systems and structures in place to ensure stability and consistency while having a parallel space that will support creative thinking and innovation through more flexibility. This is one way of addressing the exploitation/exploration dilemma and allows for:

- reliability and efficiency + agility and speed
- incremental or predictable change + constant innovation and leadership development
- management tools (e.g. budget, metrics) + accelerators (e.g. knocking down barriers).

This is a practical way of dealing with the ambiguities and paradoxes contemporary organisations will need to address in order to be most effective. Kotter proposes a management + leadership matrix[70] that will enable otherwise cumbersome organisations to respond to big opportunities when they arise. It involves having an urgency team alongside a senior leadership team.

This sort of approach can be particularly critical when responding to a crisis. In these situations there is simply not always the time to go through the formal procedures and processes. The creation of 'shadow networks', for example, can help to provide the sort of flexible parallel structures that are needed when responding to a crisis.[71] These are informal networks that are able to work with alternatives both inside and outside the dominant system. Shadow networks can also act as incubators for new ideas and strategies.

When conventional management politics failed to resolve the problem of repeated flooding of the Tisza River in Hungary from 1997 onwards, a shadow network of academics and activists emerged to look for solutions. Theoretically they were then able to feed the information back to the formal system, which could deal with the problem. Of course if a formal system also has a problem with implementation, as it did in this case, the application of the solution may be further stalled. As Frances Westley, Chair of Social Innovation at the University of Waterloo in Canada, and her colleagues have said, 'A more connected global society has the means to quickly respond to change and stimulate innovations on a planetary scale. Expert-driven, centralized, and top-down approaches to problem solving are not nimble enough to effectively address global challenges characterised by high levels of complexity and uncertainty.'[72]

We have already discussed how authoritarian forms of leadership can lead to controlled creativity but not true *systemic innovation*. Since ancient Egypt, dictatorships have revealed how a controlling, top-down approach can *enforce* certain innovations, but cannot necessarily *enable* a creative culture that supports ongoing productive innovation at all levels.

Problem-solving capabilities can be impacted in cultures where there is a high 'power distance' and a hierarchy that demands obedience. The series of South Korean air crashes at the end of the 1990s were not due to hardware failure or poor pilot training.[73] They could be directly related to the cultural norm in Korea that the co-pilot is always subservient to the lead pilot, whose judgement and decisions were never questioned or challenged, even when they were clearly wrong.

Bureaucratic systems and leadership styles can also limit the opportunities for creative thinking and innovation. A McKinsey report has found that a bureaucratic, hierarchical, fearful environment can actually stifle innovation.[74] Large organisations usually aim to accomplish known tasks in set and approved ways.[75] Social psychologist Max Weber believed that large bureaucratic structures require 'precision, reliability and efficiency'.[76] Catholic social activist Thomas Merton added that these sorts of bureaucratic structures put pressure on those working in the system to be 'methodical, prudent and disciplined' in order to maintain conformity.[77]

Application 6: Support both 'adaptors' and 'innovators'.

- Enable *associative* modes (systematic approaches to working through challenges based on set routines) as well as *bisociative* modes (being able to address separate, overlapping domains simultaneously to come up with novel solutions).
- Recognise that change involves risk and uncertainty.
- Look for opportunities where systems can be put in place to help support and increase creativity.

Bureaucrats and managers are often employed in crisis situations in order to maintain the status quo and fix the immediate problem rather than to come up with a different, superior solution that might challenge the status quo. In these cases, where the structural context of the problem is not being challenged, any solution is likely to be adaptive (that is, about 'doing things better'). When the structural context is addressed as part of the problem, though, the solution is likely to be more innovative ('doing things differently').

People at either extreme have been identified as 'adaptors' and 'innovators', with the adaptors being more likely to be employed to solve familiar problems in predictable ways, while innovators are more likely to find breakthrough solutions. You should be able to see by now how this fits with the exploitation vs exploration paradigm for innovation: adaptors will need to assist with maintaining control, while innovators will need the freedom to explore more openly.

> Adopting a more flexible and courageous approach to addressing the challenges, rather than simply following the status quo and maintaining control, can dramatically impact an organisation's ability to innovate rather than simply adapt.

There is another interesting approach to these differences. An *associative* mode of thinking is a systematic approach to working through a problem or challenge based on using a set of routine methods or procedures logically. Because associative thinkers follow established paths they are more likely to come up with more conventional solutions. *Bisociative* thinkers, on the other hand, are able to address separate overlapping domains simultaneously through a more intuitive and imaginative approach that defies the status quo to come up with more novel solutions.[78]

Adopting a more flexible and courageous approach to addressing the challenges, rather than simply following the status quo and maintaining control, can dramatically impact an organisation's ability to innovate rather than simply adapt. By its nature, innovative change involves increased risk and uncertainty, so there cannot be the same conformity to roles and social norms; rather, there needs to be a dramatic transformation.[79]

But here's a twist. Sometimes organisations systematise the creative thinking and innovation process in order to *increase* creativity and innovation.[80] Sometimes bureaucracy can *assist with* providing the sort of flexibility and adaptability that enables innovation. Sometimes providing rules and structures can create more opportunities to focus on unique areas for development. This is part of the paradox of control vs freedom. The important thing is to find the right balance.

Application 7: Empower individuals — listen to the garbage collectors.

- People who are free to respond to their own opportunities are often more innovative.
- When confronted with control, humans tend to either comply or defy.
- The 'if/then' reward system doesn't work for tasks that require creative conceptual outcomes, in which case autonomy is recommended.
- Where individuals feel they have the power to take risks without dire consequences, employee creativity is boosted.
- Rather than controlling from the top, middle management can assist with interpreting the strategic direction and supporting those who carry it out, which is known as *sandwiched innovation*.

One would not usually associate the career of garbage collection with innovation, yet studies in San Francisco found that the collectors who were free to select their own opportunities were indeed more innovative.[81] This says a huge amount about the need for freedom at every level, and the potential impact it can have on innovation. Yet many organisations still apply a controlling philosophy.

Business author Dan Pink suggests humans typically have two responses to control: they will either comply or defy.[82] Most organisations today, he says, still rely on an 'if/then' reward system, which means that *if* you do this *then* you will get your reward (simple causation thinking). Although this approach might work for simple tasks carried out in the short term, it is less effective for more complex areas that require creative conceptual outcomes. So organisations are reinforcing compliance rather than taking employees to the next step and ensuring they have the freedom and autonomy they need to come up with out-of-the-box solutions. Pink proposes a different model and a different form of motivation, one that focuses on autonomy and actively engaging employees.

Studies on psychological safety suggest that where individuals perceive they have the freedom to take risks in their work environment without dire consequences, employee creativity is boosted.[83] Where risk-taking is built into the group culture as a norm, with ambiguity tolerated and decisions often made with some uncertainty, creativity is promoted. Risk-taking and experimentation are critical to the development of innovative new ideas and products, and therefore freedom is an important facet of the organisational culture. An added benefit is that the opportunity to do creative work has been found to boost employee morale.[84]

An example of a company that has applied this principle is Netflix, which claims to treat its employees as 'fully formed adults'. The aim is to provide the maximum amount of freedom to help to support individuals in taking risks and innovating, without the usual bureaucratic barriers. The company created a comprehensive 124-slide presentation known as the 'Netflix culture deck', which outlined this culture of 'freedom and responsibility'. The highly successful US TV series *House of Cards* was the end product of this unique approach, with the creators being given the freedom to tell the story the way they wanted to.

> **The top management of continuously innovating organisations does not completely 'control' or 'direct' the innovation process, but rather provides the right environment and appropriate systems and structures to support exploration and experimentation.**

As Netflix's Chief Talent Officer Tawni Cranz has said, the company has been able to maintain an open culture from its early days through to its rise as a global company. 'The foundations of freedom and responsibility — not having a lot of rules, not having policies, not using sort of bureaucracy or hierarchy to govern — but instead really providing context to folks and giving them all the freedom to do their job and all the responsibility … continues to work.' By hiring the best and setting clear goals, Cranz explains, it's possible to empower your people and let them operate independently.[85]

The top management of continuously innovating organisations does not completely 'control' or 'direct' the innovation process, but rather provides the right environment and appropriate systems and structures to support both exploration and experimentation. Middle management can then assist with interpreting the strategic direction and assisting those who will carry it out, a concept that has been called *sandwiched innovation*.[86]

So what is the ideal balance for supporting the creative process? As far back as 1961 Burns and Stalker recognised that organisations need to be organic in order to support long-term innovation and development.[87] Dynamic organisations are characterised by an experimental, risk-taking approach and decentralised power and decision-making processes. The best environment to engage teams in creative processes has been found to be one that supports creativity, including shared goals, participative problem solving, close social connections and limited organisational control.[88]

CHAPTER SUMMARY

How to culture for open innovation

Navigating the path between Control and Freedom

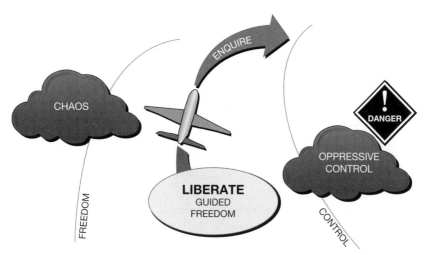

Key principles from the journey

Control usually comes at a cost.

- Where there is a lack of freedom, development, and at some level innovation, will be reduced. These problems usually need to be addressed at the systemic level.
- It is important to consider not just the *outcomes* of development and innovation, but also the *foundations* of development and innovation.
- Watch out when innovation and supposed 'progress' comes from oppression and domination (leading to exploitation), rather than from a deeper sense of purpose (e.g. Egypt, China, Meso-America).
- Urbanisation led to specialisation, which in turn led to the development of an elite social class and eventually domination.

Innovation for personal pride rather than mutual benefit cannot last.

- There are myths and historical case studies in which domination for power and control has led to collapse (e.g. the Zambian story, the Tower of Babel, Easter Island, the fall of the Egyptian empire).

- The pride described in these myths and case studies is usually based on an overreach of creative power—a belief in the ability to rival the gods in creativity.
- The tallest buildings in a society often signify the institutions with the greatest (economic or political) power; today it's the wealthy corporations that dominate.

Where there is no freedom there can be no initiation of the innovation process.

- Most of the world's population does not have the political freedom, economic resources, or physical and emotional security needed as a foundation for innovation.
- While some access the fruits of innovation for luxury products, others need to innovate on a basic level just to survive (e.g. Jugaad innovation).
- Domination can be expressed in different ways, for example through exploitation of those at the bottom of the pyramid.
- Wealthier people towards the top of the pyramid may be participating in a controlling system without realising it, for example through buying cheap products that have been manufactured unethically.
- Even people in so-called wealthy countries may not have the resources to innovate.

Innovation needs to be for the good of all, not just some.

- Slavery is an extreme example of how the many have been exploited for the benefit of the few, creating a parasitic rather than a symbiotic relationship.
- Many people are struggling to achieve the financial freedom that will allow them to access higher levels of development.
- European colonisers in Africa introduced innovations that benefited themselves but not the local Africans and that divided local communities, which led to conflict, corruption and cultural disruption.
- Going forward, for the sake of our own and future generations, innovation will need to be for the greater good.

A key to providing freedom is education and empowerment.

- Oppression can be an enclosing structure of barriers that can keep us trapped 'inside the box', unable to explore or develop new ideas freely.
- True education opens up possibilities; 'banking' education (depositing information to a passive recipient) anaesthetises and inhibits creative power.
- There is an inherent tension between authority and freedom, but both need to be respected.
- Liberty and freedom are among the six key areas of universal concern.
- Some control for guidance can be helpful—as long as it is normative (deriving from clear values and a strong sense of purpose) rather than coercive (externally enforced control).

Creativity needs to come from all levels rather than from a controlling leader.

- Powerful figureheads may be able to cut through the bureaucracy to innovate more efficiently, but where their creative efforts are directed against rather than for the mutual benefit of all people, they are not positive purposeful innovations.
- Transitioning to enabled creativity (rather than controlled creativity) will involve empowering people at all levels (e.g. Singapore in transition).

Freedom actively triggers creativity.

- Personal freedom through autonomy is a key developmental stage.
- Freedom has also been linked to creativity. Diverse political perspectives produce higher rates of creative activity and output.
- Only egalitarian institutions allow for full development of the creative potential of individuals and therefore of innovation.
- Democratic and pluralistic states can ensure the rule of law is used to provide freedom of expression for all citizens, which encourages the development of ideas.
- Organisations that rank well on higher-level 'self-expression' values (e.g. trust, tolerance and participatory decision making) can better support development and growth.

- The inbuilt systems of democracies limit opportunities for corruption, which can impact innovation.

Organisations need to find the balance between control and freedom.

- Identify the deeper purpose. Is it, for example, market domination or mutual progress for a greater purpose?
- Innovation and development need to come from individuals at all levels for long-term transformation.
- Build organic systems instead of mechanised systems where possible.
- Too much freedom can lead to anxiety and chaos.
- The principle of guided freedom ensures there is freedom without chaos or anxiety, control without oppression (e.g. Google, Pixar).

Applications summary

1. Ensure resources are used for mutual benefit rather than individual gain (case studies: Silicon Valley, US Subprime Crisis).
2. Beware of 'controlled creativity' (case studies: Apple, IT Company, Microsoft).
3. Engage employees with a sense of purpose (case studies: Johnson & Johnson, Four Seasons, Colgate Palmolive, International Bank).
4. Identify if the system is too bureaucratic to support innovation (case studies: Berkshire Hathaway, Boutique Resort Company, Wedgewood, Virgin).
5. Introduce dual operating systems (case study: Tisa River Disaster Hungary).
6. Support both 'adaptors' and 'innovators'.
7. Empower individuals—listen to the garbage collectors (case studies: Garbage Collectors in San Francisco, Netflix).

CHECKPOINT SUMMARY CHECKLIST
How to liberate a culture for open innovation

Paradox Synthesis: Guided Freedom

Is there a balance in your organisation between providing systems and structures and allowing *freedom*?

GUIDANCE

Sufficient discipline and structure to provide guidelines.

Are your employees stuck on the level of needing to have their security needs met, or are they able to reach the *blue sky imagining* stage? Are they receiving guidance without being subject to oppressive control?

Examples:

☐ **Security**	Employees have their basic physical and safety needs met, are provided with an environment where they are not afraid of making mistakes or suggesting ideas, and are kept informed of changes.
☐ **Limited bureaucracy**	Actions can be taken quickly and without fear of reprisal.
☐ **Guiding principles**	Procedures provide guidance based on purposeful principles rather than being restrictive.

FREEDOM

A platform for open exploration.

Are the pillars on which your organisation is built the principles of *oppression* or *liberation*?

Examples:

☐ **Democracy**	There are opportunities for participation in decision making at all levels.
☐ **Empowerment**	Employees are able to self-determine focus areas, tasks, career pathways, etc.

(continued)

☐ **Freedom of choice**	There is no obligation to follow specific paths (coercion), and options are not limited (constraints).
☐ **Limited power distance**	The organisation's structures and systems are not hierarchical.
☐ **Multiple sources of power**	Leadership responsibilities are shared.
☐ **Opportunities for growth**	The organisation supports enquiry and education.
☐ **Outward focus**	The focus is on improving people's lives and improving the world.

TRY THIS

How to provide guidance

- Check individuals have their basic needs met through the organisation (e.g. through a survey).
- Establish regular communication channels (e.g. newsletters, feedback sessions, active websites).
- Ensure there are clear principles to follow with clear directions when the stakes are high.
- Provide opportunities for quick actions to be taken with limited security when the stakes are low.

How to ensure freedom

- Design opportunities for participative decision making.
- Allow individuals to set goals in daily work and projects and to identify their own measures of success.
- Provide career guidance and open opportunities for career development.
- Establish flat leadership structures where possible and share these openly.
- Set up shared leadership responsibilities.
- Ongoing learning and development opportunities.
- Provide an outward focus through a strong corporate social responsibility program.

Preparing for the next mode

Now we have established the need for *guided freedom* as a foundation for the initial stages of innovation, it is time to start thinking about how to launch the ideation process. Freedom sets the stage for growth, but novel ideas will not be produced if the right connections are not put in place to extend thinking beyond the familiar and the known.

The next mode requires ensuring there is the autonomous focus needed to explore new ideas independently, as well as the diversity and openness to connections required to ensure concepts can be built on and developed. How do you build that sort of openness into the system and ensure it also continues to support an independent focus?

We next journey to Europe to get some clues to how this paradox can best be dealt with.

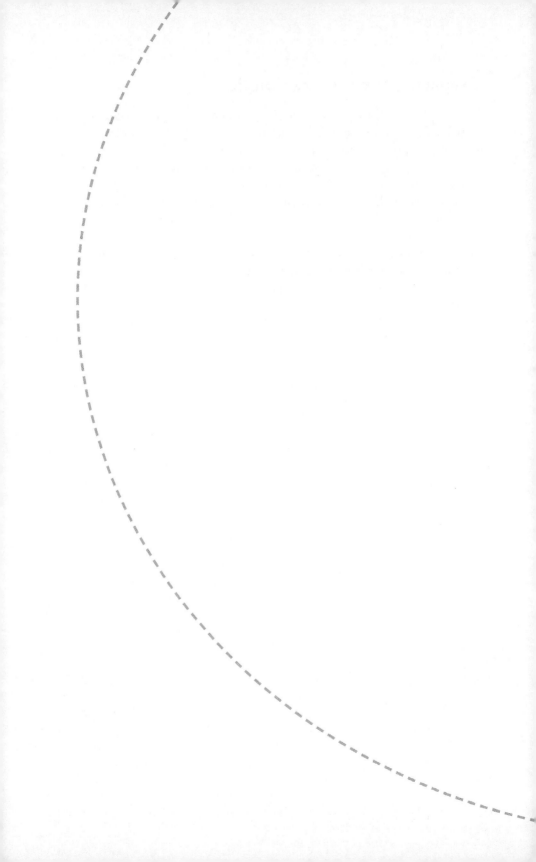

6

INITIATE

How to initiate the innovation process through open
connections for exploring diverse ideas

Destination: Europe

Paradox: Focus vs Openness

Synthesis: Targeted openness

*In this chapter we will explore the path between focus and openness through diversity
and connections, negotiating a line between, at one extreme, the potential danger zone of
insulation and, at the other extreme, the potential danger of a lack of direction. We will
learn how to plan and navigate a route through targeted openness that will create a culture
to best fuel innovation.*

*Key challenge: How to enable individuals and teams to be both autonomous and
interconnected through 'targeted openness'.*

It was mid winter, the shortest day of the year, and dusk had come early.
We were caught out by the rapid fall of night and had to find somewhere
to camp, fast. Finally, exhausted from the long drive through the craggy
Pyrenees mountains in Spain, we parked our campervan in the pitch dark.
We believed we were on the edge of a remote forest and imagined the
beautiful sights and sounds that would greet us when we woke. We were,
however, in for a rude shock.

We were woken not by the gentle patter of forest animals, but by the
stomping and screaming of excited schoolchildren. When we drew back the

curtains and peered out into the bright sunny day, we were greeted noisily by highly amused children with their disapproving parents. We must have looked like caged animals at the zoo. The parents hurried the children along, drawing them away from the dishevelled gypsy family, probably on their way to inform the school principal that there were undesirables camped on the school grounds. We hastily cranked up the engine, which struggled to catch in the ice-cold morning, and shifted our mobile home to a more suitable location nearby — the spot we had originally picked out but that had eluded us in the darkness the night before. Once settled again, we breathed a collective sigh of relief and took in the magnificent view, wondering how we could have got it so wrong.

Travelling overland through Europe can be like a tour through the random sets of a Hollywood film lot, never knowing what new surprises will appear next. A few hours' drive can open up dramatic changes of scenery, culture and language. European countries are so close that, for a bet, a pair of young Norwegians decided to try for a place in the *Guinness Book of World Records* by visiting the most European countries in a single day. They reached a total of 19 countries in a 24-hour period.[1] Coming from Australia, a massive, isolated island nation many thousands of kilometres away across vast oceans from it's nearest neighbours, we find it intriguing to visit Europe and discover the ease with which it is possible to skip from one country to the next.

This continent with relatively open borders between countries, and with close proximity and connections, holds some fascinating clues on how to navigate a path between focus and openness which can help to foster innovation.

Initiating innovation through openness

At this stage of the innovation process it is essential to start exploring a range of unique ideas through ideation. It will be important here to consider how to identify potential blocks to openness, and how to provide an unrestricted culture to support multiplicity.

The INITIATE phase needs the foundation of freedom (chapter 5), but then there also need to be opportunities to connect with and learn from others in order to stimulate diverse ideas (this chapter). A typical brainstorming process will do both. Ideally, brainstorming will start with individual ideas, coming from a position of empowerment, that are built on and developed through a shared process. By ensuring there is a diverse group of individuals involved in the brainstorming process it is possible to draw on a wide range of ideas and perspectives. (If you would like some practical tools to help you to execute this process, see our book *Who Killed Creativity?*, specifically 'Strategy 3: Unleash your imagination' and 'Strategy 4: Access all parts of the brain'.)

Purpose-Driven Innovation (PDI) in action: INITIATE

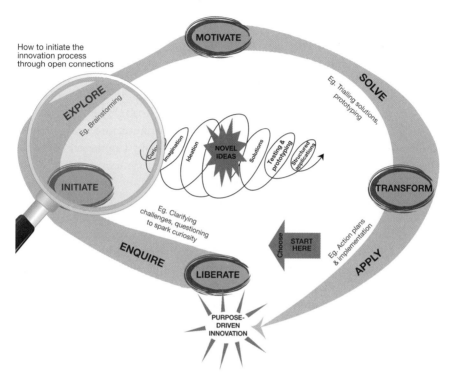

While the focus and autonomy of each individual needs to be respected and supported, there is a time when individuals need to come together to share ideas. Positive connections can grow possibilities exponentially—if they are managed effectively. So how is it possible to navigate the route between focus and openness? How is it possible to deal with potential blocks to openness, and to provide the best conditions for the sorts of open connections that really facilitate innovation? We will explore these principles further in the first part of this chapter, before going on to consider practical applications for the organisation in the second part.

A cultural safari in the minibus bubble

The proximity and ease of access between countries in Europe makes the campervan the perfect mode of transport for exploring the continent. How else can you travel freely carrying all you need with you so you can stop, eat and sleep anywhere you choose?

A campervan reminds you just how small the world can seem. But it can also feel like being on a cultural safari, watching the wild world go by from the insulated safety of your mobile home. And just sometimes, as in our Pyrenees experience, the roles can be reversed and you get the feeling that the locals are watching the foreigners pass by as though watching a bizarre travelling circus. The thin walls of the van can insulate you not only against the weather but also against the culture.

No doubt while we are busy enumerating the cultural differences we come across ('They drive on the *wrong* side of the road.' 'Their language is *impossible* to understand.' 'They eat *strange* foods.'), opinions are being formed about us ('Why have they not bothered to learn our language?' 'Why do they have to come and take over the country in their campervans?'). Perhaps the van acts as a barrier, preventing us from purposefully and positively connecting with the communities we visit.

Once we accidentally drove up the wrong lane of a main road while trying to find a place to park for the night. All our efforts to cross back over to the right side were blocked by a concrete barrier and neatly trimmed hedge, and we became conscious of having got ourselves and others into a highly dangerous situation. When we tried to stop on the side of the road to get help, we were berated by understandably angry locals in a language we could not comprehend.

The incident made us realise just how isolated we had become through our inability to sufficiently adapt. We had created a comfortable bubble for ourselves—a physical bubble that was reinforced by the language barrier. It dawned on us that this was a great contrast to the sort of travel we had believed in when we were younger. We had once been proud *travellers*, eager to immerse ourselves in the lives of the local people and to really appreciate and understand their unique insights and challenges. Now we had become the sort of *tourists* we had previously despised, looking at the world slip by as if on a TV screen, from the comfort of our own perspective.

> We had become *tourists,* looking at other worlds from the comfort of our own perspective, whereas once we had been proud *travellers*, happy to immerse ourselves in the lives of the local people.

Wealth and power can insulate us from the 'real world', just as wealthy travel can disconnect us from the communities we visit.[2] Years earlier we had travelled third class by train the length of India with our then two-year-old daughter. With 10 people squeezed onto a bench seat and no air conditioning, we were astounded by how everyone treated it as a happy community experience, sharing their lunches and chatting incessantly; how there was no recognition of or apparent need for 'personal space'. We were soon drawn into the close connections these people rapidly developed and and started to learn to see the world from their perspective.

Building on the differences between travellers and tourists we introduced in chapter 3, a key differentiator here is that travellers are open to learning and sharing—in fact, they see this as the whole point of travel—while tourists can remain closed and focused on their own needs and desires throughout their journey. Not only do travellers develop empathy as they open themselves up to new experiences, but this empathy enables them to think more divergently.

Innovation can only come about through an open mindset and a willingness to learn and share, and through fostering practical connections with diverse peoples and ideas. This is the foundation for ideation, an important initial phase in the innovation process.

Tourist traps

In her book *Willful Blindness*, business chief executive and entrepreneur Margaret Heffernan explores further how the ways we travel (literally and metaphorically) can impose distance between those who have power and wealth and those who do not, as in the pyramid model, and how wealth can often block creativity through a lack of exposure:[2]

> ...fly in the splendid isolation of...first class...limousines and catered lunches, personal assistants and flattering friends teach new habits of privilege and entitlement. While these may seem attractive luxuries, they come at a cost: isolation. The bubble of power seals off bad news, inconvenient details, hostile opinions and messy realities, leaving you free to inhale the rarefied air of pure abstraction...[Research shows] that the powerful appraise information differently.

Travel writer Paul Theroux would agree:[3]

> Luxury is the enemy of observation, a costly indulgence that induces such a good feeling that you notice nothing. Luxury spoils and infantilises you and prevents you from knowing the world.

Heffernan's research reveals that the more isolated we are from others, the more convinced we become that we are right, and this can kill our creative thinking. This sort of stubborn belief can lead to a fundamentalist approach that can become a significant roadblock for innovation. The psychological distance between ourselves and others means we can end up thinking in far more abstract terms, making real, concrete innovation much harder to implement.[4]

Familiarity does not necessarily breed contempt but it often does breed dangerous levels of comfort,[5] which, if we are not careful, can lead to insulation. As we have discovered, it requires *purposeful proximity* to survive.

This chapter examines how an extreme autonomous focus can become isolating and insulating. It can also inhibit creativity and slow down innovation, from the individual level through to the cultural level. In the heart of Europe, which has always been a hothouse for creative ideas and innovation, as we will explore further, being confined to our campervan kept us isolated. For creativity to flourish diverse elements need to be connected. Close connections through proximity are a great preparation for the ideation phase of innovation where we need an open platform to explore new ideas, but this just gets you to the starting line.

A risky experiment

Over the years Europe has given birth to and nurtured countless major innovations. Did you know, for example, that the motorised toothbrush we use today has its roots in Renaissance Europe? The mechanisms these toothbrushes use were initially conceptualised by Leonardo da Vinci, who was one of the earliest machine engineers. Leonardo's engineering skills originally came from developing his artistic talent, through training in art and sculpture, and by combining these with his growing skills in mathematics and science he became an incredible futurist and inventor. Da Vinci was fascinated by the idea of solving complex practical problems, and as a result he produced concepts for objects as diverse as textile machines, metalworking devices and clocks. He imagined, and brought to life in stunningly beautiful sketches, flying machines and flywheels, giant catapults and cogwheels, treadmills, submarines and armoured cars.

Throughout history, right back to the ancient Greeks, Europe has been a seedbed of creativity and innovation. While the Egyptians left evidence of astonishing engineering feats and the Babylonians proved to have an advanced knowledge of astronomy, only the Greeks developed the sort of *curiosity* that enabled them to innovate both critically and creatively. Einstein noted that the Greek invention of a formal logical system (in Euclidean geometry) was built on by the discovery of causal relationships through systematic experimentation in the Renaissance period.[6]

The Renaissance saw the launch of the scientific revolution and a torrent of new technologies. The inventions of the fifteenth century that would have the most impact on the world—for better or worse—were probably the printing press, the nautical compass and firearms, which heralded a new era in communication, cultural crossings and control, respectively.

Europe is still recognised as a world leader in innovation, and a number of countries within Europe consistently score well in innovation measures. Although Europe covers just 2 per cent of the Earth's surface and 6.8 per cent of its land area, and accounts for only 7.2 per cent of the world's population, the European Union leads the world in GDP. They are clear innovation race 'winners' in economic terms. In a risky contemporary social and political experiment, 28 fiercely independent countries have come together to align the way they operate and to leverage their combined potential. As Johanne Poirier has observed, 'While autonomy may be the best guarantee against oppression on the one hand, and territorial disintegration on the other, it can also have the effect of erecting a "Berlin wall" between people.'[7]

The European Union is a fascinating phenomenon that can be judged to have succeeded on some levels and has definitely been challenged on others.[8] With origins that hark back to the 1950s, the Union was formally established in 1993, only a couple of years after the dissolution of the Soviet Union in 1991. The Union has applied standardised laws to create a single market, enabling the cross-pollination and sharing of ideas, and one large marketplace to trade in.

Some of the most innovative countries in the world per capita are small countries in Europe, including Sweden, Switzerland, Finland and Denmark.[9] Of the 28 current member countries, 26 have a very high score on the Human Development Index.[10] Pawel Chaduski, co-founder of Point Nine Capital, believes this success is due to the fact that when startups in the fragmented and diverse continent build an online marketplace, they have to learn to work across multiple borders to be successful, which means they develop in a more robust and relational way than, for example, less diverse US companies.[11]

> Comprising 28 member states, the Union has applied standardised laws to create a single market, enabling the cross-pollination and sharing of ideas, and one large marketplace to trade in.

Why has Europe powered ahead in the 'innovation race' so fast and for so long? Some real progress, the sort of progress that impacts communities at the deepest levels, has come through the close connections and the innovations they have encouraged. Yet achieving these outcomes takes a great deal of dedication. It involves knowing how to bring together diverse autonomous elements sensitively yet effectively for purpose-driven transformational innovation.

Proximity and the printing machine

Do you know which country was the originator of a number of the elements that eventually came together as the printing machine, one of the most influential inventions of modern times? Most people assume Gutenberg invented the printing machine in Europe. If you look back carefully through the history books, though, you will discover that China was on its way to mechanised forms of printing long before Europe, but it was pipped at the post.[12] Although China had initially developed paper and (possibly along with Korea) the idea of movable type, the concept of mechanical printing didn't take off until its reinvention in Europe.[13] It was Gutenberg who was able to get all the glory and recognition when he printed his illustrated Bible in AD 1455.

The mysterious Phaistos Disk (found on the island of Crete), an early example of how seals were pressed into clay to leave a printed image, has been dated to around 1700 BC. The innovation of the printing press was inspired in part by the use of wooden screws in processing olive oil and wine. The Europeans then added to the mix advances in paper, movable type, metallurgy, inks and scripts—and a revolutionary invention was born. This illustrates the way Europe has pushed through major developments faster than other regions through maximising the opportunities that the proximity between European countries has provided. The broad exposure to different ideas made the difference.

Proximity has also been found to be a significant factor in the sharing, transfer and acquisition of knowledge that leads to creative thinking.[14] Societies that are located close to areas where cultural exchange can take place tend to have higher rates of creative output.[15] Those that have been embedded in major continents and exposed to their neighbours have in particular been found to benefit. Medieval Islam, for example, benefited from access to inventions from Asia on the one hand (China and India), and from Europe on the other (particularly Greece).[16]

Proximity can reduce uncertainty, and assist with coordination, learning and innovation.[17] The history of innovation has been referred to as the history of 'adjacent possibilities', a story of 'one door leading to another, of exploring the palace one room at a time', where ideas can 'bump into each other'.[18] For proximity to be truly beneficial, however, there also needs to be both a *constructive purpose* and an *openness and readiness to change*.

It has been found that populations benefit most from individual inventions where these ideas are shared openly to help maximise the opportunities for incremental innovations.[19] Just as evolution has depended on the random swapping of genes for experimentation, scientist Matt Ridley argues, 'Where you have people exchanging goods, exchanging services, and exchanging ideas, then you get extraordinary progress in human conditions.'[20] As astrophysicist Neil deGrasse Tyson says, 'We are collectively smart despite the limitations of each one individual.'[21] Edinburgh University has been found to be particularly innovative, for example, because disciplines are actively encouraged to mix and learn from each other.[22]

> **Proximity has also been found to be a significant factor in the sharing, transfer and acquisition of knowledge. Societies that are located close to areas where cultural exchange can take place tend to have higher rates of creative output.**

But proximity is not enough. When ideas are not shared openly, even where there is proximity, innovation will stall. The Mapuche farmers of southern Chile, for example, live in close proximity to each other but know very little about each other's farming methods. As a result their farming practices have remained at simple subsistence levels. This lack of innovative progress can be explained by the fact that they have developed social behaviours that limit the sharing of information and collaboration. The farmers actually deliberately keep information from each other to avoid envy and bad luck.

If Europe has historically been one of the most connected continents in the world, which inhabited continent has been the most isolated? The prize for this category should probably go to Australia, which remained largely isolated for many thousands of years before European colonisation began a little more than 200 years ago. Anthropologist Jared Diamond describes how the technology of Aboriginal Australians remained unchanged due to their physical isolation from the rest of the world.[23] This isolation meant limited opportunities and options. Although the Aborigines had a head start with natural resources, having some of the richest supplies of iron, aluminium, copper, tin, lead and zinc, and although they were one of the earliest societies to develop crafted stone tools, because of their isolation they didn't develop technologically in the same ways as other cultures.

Or maybe they just couldn't see a purpose!

Connected cities and lucky errors

So which are the most connected human populations? Cities, which represent the epitome of close proximity, have been found to be hothouses for creative ideas.[24] This is largely due to the opportunities they provide for collaboration between diverse individuals.

Urban societies have been found to be more innovative in technological terms.[25] Cities house 23 per cent of the world's population, while according to studies an overwhelming 93 per cent of the patent applications made around the world come from city-based inventors. Where there is a concentration of creative and talented people, there has been found to be more innovation (hence urban studies theorist Richard Florida's emphasis on how to attract what he calls a 'creative class').[26] There is no doubt that cities can exponentially increase innovation through the opportunity they provide to circulate creative energy and to cross-pollinate and share diverse ideas. What's particularly fascinating is that it has been found that cities that have more dense high-rise residential buildings (such as Hong Kong and Vancouver) thrive more on innovative ideas than cities that are more spread out (such as Mumbai).[27]

Cities have also been found to have a unique way of performing as they get larger.[28] Unlike animals, which get slower as they get larger, cities can move faster and become more efficient with size. The most highly innovative metro areas have large populations, which allows their workers and researchers to become highly specialised in their jobs, which in turn impacts innovation if these roles are well connected and coordinated.[29]

Inventiveness often comes from large populations because they are more interconnected and more likely to generate what have been called 'lucky errors' that can lead to innovation, and more likely to be able to diffuse these more widely.[30] Even more specifically, where there are influential people others are likely to imitate them, which helps to spread innovations through a culture. The relationship between the number of opportunities you have to learn from others in a social context and the probability of acquiring innovation is shown in the forthcoming graph. The graph illustrates quite clearly how the more connections there are the higher the probability is, and that this result increases exponentially. This is because technology begets more technology, and the whole process speeds up over time because the process catalyses itself.

The relationship between the number of learning ties and the probability of acquiring innovation

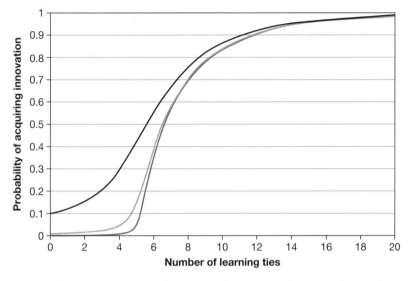

Source: Why societies vary in their rates of innovation by Joseph Henrich (www2.psych.ubc.ca/~henrich/Website/Papers/InventionInnovation05.pdf)

Interconnectedness has been found to be so important, that where groups invest in increasing the sharing of ideas through cultural interconnectedness the rates of innovation will be substantially higher than where there is an investment in raising the inventiveness of individual members only.[31] Also, the more cities grow the faster they innovate. In fact, the growth in innovation is exponential. A city 10 times larger than another isn't just 10 times more innovative — it's 17 times more innovative! This phenomenon was first recognised by urban activist Jane Jacobs more than 50 years ago and has become known as *superlineal scaling*.[32]

So here's an interesting thought. If density and proximity are important factors in the sharing of ideas and the development of innovation, shouldn't the capital city of a country like Bangladesh, which is one of the most densely populated countries in the world, be one of the most innovative? (While heavily populated Europe has a population density of 74 people per square km, Bangladesh has a total of 156.6 million people per square kilometre.[33]) There is of course the problem of resources here, or a lack of them, along with access to education, networks and market opportunities.

Although simple innovations that help to solve everyday problems can occur anywhere, no matter what the access to resources, innovation on a grand scale can flourish only where there is the access to adequate resources. This is a reminder that while proximity is one important foundation for innovation, it needs to be supported, and it needs to be *purposeful*—to have a useful function and purpose.

Cities can and should be hothouses where individual creative potential can be nurtured and fulfilled. They can be places where the world's greatest problems can be solved.[34] Yet there is now the concern that contemporary cities, such as a number in China, could become like Detroit: a large, thriving city in the 1960s, that filed for bankruptcy in 2013 following a steep decline. The sheer size of cities means that the potential for problems is increased, and a lot of deliberate systems and structures need to be in place to ensure the positive potential can be realised.

> Cities can and should be hothouses where individual creative potential can be nurtured and fulfilled, where the world's greatest problems can be solved.

Cities where the growth has been too rapid, for example, often trade public spaces for cheaper suburban comforts (behind the isolating 'white picket fence'), and are characterised by levels of growth and innovation that are unsustainable.[35]

Viral connections

Asia has developed a similar feeling of connection for business over the years, despite the oceans between many of the countries. This has no doubt been facilitated more recently by greater access to air travel. We were able to capitalise on the opportunities this created for business for a number of years, hopping between countries in the same way you might cross borders in Europe by car, but in early 2003 that suddenly stopped and our business in Asia all but dried up. We were no longer able to travel extensively around the region to visit our clients there, and conference calls replaced face-to-face meetings.

Do you remember what led to this sudden change? In 2003 a strange new viral epidemic swept across the world in record time: SARS. And there was more to the havoc it wreaked. SARS knew no political or cultural boundaries and created major tension between countries with different cultures, ideologies and political structures. Some countries openly declared their statistics to the world and welcomed assistance, while others shut out the rest of the world and failed to publicise the numbers of SARS deaths accurately in order to maintain their political pride and/or to maintain social stability.

Giving false statistics led to major mistrust with international organisations and the business community, which, as we will discuss further in the next chapter, impacts collaboration for innovation. The mishandling of the SARS crisis fed tentative calls for political reform and exacerbated a broad power struggle between several countries. News agencies in some countries tactlessly started naming victims, leading to considerable stress for the families involved. Many critics reflected on the panic, and gave the reminder that the odds of dying from the infection were actually minimal compared with the numbers of fatalities from ongoing everyday causes such as car accidents.

Rapidly increasing levels of international contact have meant a proliferation of new viruses are becoming the ultimate connectors. They can zip across the world faster than ever before. The increase in 'exploratory' travel behaviours (as opposed to 'returner' travel, where people keep returning to the same destinations) has been found to be linked with the spread of epidemics.[36] Pandemic flu viruses have emerged in the past in this way, but rarely before have they had such a global impact, and many experts believe it's only a matter of time before it happens again—with the big one yet to come.

Fortunately, the forces making microbes so mobile are also making them easier to track. A number of years ago, prompt communication was still a problem for many health departments. Today even the most remote surveillance stations are linked to the web-based Program for Monitoring Emerging Diseases. Once this process kicked in the SARS epidemic came to an abrupt halt. Perhaps governments finally saw just how high the stakes were and how dangerous the game they were playing politically was, so they moved away from self-imposed isolation, and scientists started to use available technologies to work together on finding solutions. It was a great example of how modern technology can provide opportunities for *purposeful virtual proximity*, which can go way beyond physical proximity and can lead to real and purpose-driven innovation.

Faster than the speed of light

The World Wide Web has connected us in a way that has not previously been possible, creating a global virtual proximity. The web represents proximity on a worldwide scale, dwarfing even the largest cities, and has the potential to foster rapid knowledge generation and problem solving of a magnitude never realised before.[37]

Open-source approaches are now being used to solve the world's technical problems. Imagine if they were also used effectively to solve the world's social and environmental problems! Social innovation platforms are starting to emerge and effectively bridge that gap. Platforms such as Kiva support microfinance, while Akvo and We Adapt provide knowledge sharing for improving sanitation and dealing with climate change.

Think about how the internet and mobile technologies are becoming accessible to people at all levels. Back when printing was first invented, the printed word was available only to the wealthy. Few could read, and few could afford the printed materials. The internet has become an incredible equaliser, democratising access to information and self-education in a way that has never been available before.[38] Europe has led the way with its 'Digital Europe' plan, with smart green digital technology making it potentially the most productive commercial space in the world and the most ecologically sustainable region on the planet.[39]

Different types of knowledge and competencies from people with different backgrounds need to be integrated to increase innovation, and this can be done effectively through strategic networks.[40] The world's largest health agencies have now created systems for sharing scientific research, as have researchers in a number of fields. Scientists are now sharing research findings and collaborating internationally, which is a critical step towards greater knowledge generation for problem solving.

For example, the ability of scientists to quickly locate the coronavirus that was responsible for SARS and coordinate throughout the world across cultural and political barriers was a miracle. In another case, a PhD student who was studying drug microbiology in Nigeria needed help with sequencing drug-resistant pathogens, so he used the social networking site for academics ResearchGate to look for solutions. He was able to connect over the internet and collaborate with an Italian geneticist who had the expertise and equipment he needed to analyse pathogen samples.[41]

In the business context, companies we have worked with, such as Salesforce, have used cloud marketing to connect with the customer way beyond the initial transactional buyer/seller relationship. They have streamlined systems that can link all parts of a customer relationship process and all people involved in the process. As a result of developing clever connections like these, Salesforce has been voted the most innovative company in the world by *Forbes Magazine* four years in a row.

If innovation happens as a result of adjacent possibilities, with groups physically connecting, increasing opportunities for ideas to rub off on others with purpose, this was accelerated to the nth degree when the internet arrived, removing the need for physical proximity. The transition that has emerged as a result of networking technology has been described as one from 'little boxes' (densely knit groups, linking people door-to-door) to 'glocalised networks' (sparsely knit but with clusters, linking households both locally and globally) to 'networked individualism' (sparsely knit, linking individuals with little regard to location).[42]

Three models of community and work social networks

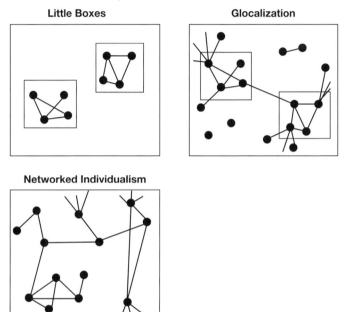

Source: 'Little Boxes, Glocalization, and Networked Individualism' by Barry Wellman[43]

While the 'little boxes' tended to be structurally and hierarchically organised, the 'glocalised' networks have flatter structures with more permeable boundaries that include more diverse groups of others and links with multiple networks. 'Networked individualism' has then arisen from the development of computer communication networks, which create the demand for collaborative communication and information sharing through the individual.

The internet as the ultimate enabler

With its lightning-quick capabilities, the internet accelerated the 'innovation race' to dizzying new speeds. Yet such systems are only as valuable as the openness and good will of their users will allow them to be. If anything constructive has come out of the SARS virus scare, it is a renewed commitment to these ideals. Scientists working independently in isolation in any one lab would have taken months or potentially years to solve the problem. They needed that specialisation and focus to find the initial clues to solving the problem, but once they connected and worked together it took them just weeks to come up with a solution.

The intriguing thing about this success is that no one person was in charge; no one at the top was dictating what was to be done. Each individual unit was autonomous and focused on their own work, yet each was connected by a higher vision, a greater goal that gave them a unified purpose. It enabled them to become unified in diversity. The collaborative nature of the SARS project gave each lab the freedom to focus on what it believed to be the most promising lines of investigation, and to play to its particular strengths, while also allowing the labs to benefit in real time from each other's data.

> Such systems are only as valuable as the openness and good will of their users will allow them to be.

Many people imagine it's the lone scientist who makes breakthroughs, but award-winning Nobel Laureate scientists are known to be the most collaborative scientists around, even when they find themselves in teams of people who are not as 'smart' as they are! Scientists are continually building on others' knowledge, and even the failures of the scientists who have gone before them can help to identify potential paths forward. SARS was one of the first international incidents of its kind to reveal the value of sharing knowledge for the benefit of all.[44]

Most inventors are actually building on previous work. A significant part of the innovative process is collaborative, rather than independent.[45] The light bulb, which is credited as being invented by Thomas Edison in 1879, was a development of other incandescent bulbs that had been patented 30 years before by other inventors. Alfred Russel Wallace contributed theoretical ideas to the theory of evolution, sending them directly to Darwin to view, even though we only ever hear of Darwin in discussion on the topic and only Darwin was credited with authorship of the landmark book *On the Origin of Species*. The Wright brothers' work was anticipated by Glenn Curtiss and others.

On the other side of the story, a number of scientific innovations were held back by petty feuds and a lack of collaboration.[46] The discovery of a retrovirus believed to be the cause of AIDS, for example, was reported to have been made first by the French, who sent their results to the Americans for their opinion, who in turn, a long time later, claimed it as their own discovery. The arguments between the research teams held up the research into actually treating AIDS for about four years. In an even more dramatic example, development of the marine chronometer, to measure longitude by celestial navigation, was delayed by about 60 years by an uncollaborative board.

Hyperconnection: the paradox of connection and isolation

The shift to *networked individualism* through technology, which allows us to rapidly connect with people all around the world, can be seen as a great advance for humanity, but there could also be potential problems. Some are concerned that although this form of networking enables us to present ourselves in multiple ways to multiple networked groups, it may also create the sort of compartmentalisation in people's lives that can lead to insulation. Are we losing connections with real people and therefore our ability to effectively relate to people? Comedian John Oliver thinks so: 'Do you remember the days when we actually physically had friends [before Facebook]? Where you would actually have a face-to-face conversation with someone in your proximity, instead of typing 140-character messages to people we don't know. It was awful, you couldn't tap people's faces to make them go away.'[47]

Modern technology has been an important a tool for surviving the 'innovation race'. But while it can help to lessen the problems of isolation, it cannot guarantee close connections. Ironically, if we are not addressing the need for real community we can end up as isolated and lonely as if we were in a vast empty desert, even though we have people all around us.

Today many of us have never felt so lonely. Our technology connects us, but it can also isolate us as we no longer have as much face-to-face contact as we had in the past. Twenty per cent of Americans experience long-term loneliness, and it has become such as problem that one social commentator has defined our times as the 'age of loneliness'. People are now twice as likely to die of loneliness as obesity, and equally likely to die early as they are from smoking heavily—and the philosophy of individualism may be to blame.[48] Older citizens living in cities have also been found to have less contact with neighbours than in rural communities.[49] We are social creatures who need to connect, yet we are ignoring the psychological warning system that feelings of loneliness should provide.[50] A study on Facebook use has found that loneliness has led many to use the site. (Clearly people who aren't lonely also use Facebook, but they tend not to be so reliant on it and to have a number of personal relationships too.)

Too close for comfort: is there such a thing as too much openness?

Although musicians will often perform in public in a group or an orchestra, they will usually practise alone. The innovation process similarly involves the focus of individual ideas and energies coming together in a productive way. Most of us need that focus time to really engage our critical and creative thinking, but that needs to be balanced with an openness to adding new information and ideas in collaboration with others.

Open office environments may be conducive to the sharing of information and ideas, but they can also lead to too many distractions and to inefficiency and ineffectiveness (as we will explore further in the Applications section later in this chapter). Workers in a Chinese factory who had a curtain put up around their team to allow them to focus on their task were found to be 10 to 15 per cent more productive than those who continued to work in a completely open environment. They also tended to experiment more.[51] This might indicate that while there is a certain level of openness that can enable us to think creatively, too much openness can end up stifling our creativity.

We have discussed the potential benefits of proximity, but there are also potential problems. Ironically, although proximity can provide great opportunities for open innovation, the downside of proximity can be a lack of openness and flexibility.[52] As we have seen, just because people or societies are in close proximity to one another it doesn't mean they will be willing and open to share ideas. The danger is that sometimes in large group contexts we can retreat into our own cultural ghettos and become insulated. So it is important that there is an opportunity not only to share with those immediately around you, but also to be open to those at a distance as a source of innovation.

One researcher has identified six types of proximity and has shown how each of these can be impacted in the exteme.[53] Cognitive proximity, first of all, can cause a lack of novelty, which leads to 'lock in'. So here's the paradox: just as too little openness can lead to insulation, *too much openness through proximity* can also lead to insulation! Too much organisational proximity, secondly, can lead to bureaucracy, while too much social proximity can lead to a lack of direction or a lack of economic rationale. Too much institutional proximity can lead to inertia, and finally, too much geographical proximity can — again ironically — lead to a lack of openness.

Big city connectedness can also lead to conformity.[54] Simply accommodating a large group of people in one area does not ensure innovation. It can still lead to isolation and groupthink, which can reduce creativity and innovation. If we build on the learnings from the last chapter, proximity without the right balance of control *and* freedom can lead to oppression. An imbalance can create a situation known as 'the contagion of conformity', which potentially supplants critical thinking.

Another potentially detrimental side-effect of large cities is that they can foster prosperity, which, perhaps surprisingly, hinders development.[55] Think about it: where there is success and complacency, there is less motivation to continue to innovate and progress. Cities such as Detroit in the US and Manchester in the UK, which also declined after a period of rapid advances in technology, can be seen to have suffered from this problem. These cities had both wholeheartedly embraced new technologies, but they had failed to consider the human impact of these technologies. It is perhaps a classic example of the tortoise and hare principle at work. Cities can create opportunities for innovation, as they bring together diverse people with diverse experiences and ideas, but these opportunities need to be actively recognised and capitalised on.

On another level, too much connection in societies where there is a strong familial orientation has been found to be linked to corruption. A strong sense of obligation coupled with close connections can impact the potential for real openness.[56] Restricted access to opportunities along with a stress on economic success will typically lead to higher levels of corruption. Open access to opportunities coupled with a low achievement motivation, on the other hand, will typically lead to lower levels of corruption (for example, in Scandinavian countries), as measured by the World Values Survey 1990–1993.[57]

> There has to be a deliberate breaking down of potential barriers and an openness to sharing to facilitate this process — this is what *purposeful proximity* is.

Countries in Europe enjoy the geographical advantage of proximity, but this alone doesn't guarantee more connectivity and more positive sharing of information and ideas. There has to be a deliberate breaking down of potential barriers and an openness to sharing to facilitate this process—this is what *purposeful proximity* is. Or, to take it even further through the paradox synthesis of this chapter, this can lead to *targeted openness*. Once the opportunity of proximity is maximised through an authentic openness it can be more effectively utilised.

There needs to be some focus to ensure actions are targeted, while maintaining the general principle of openness.

Targeted openness

When information is effectively shared across borders in *targeted openness* the results can be astounding. Coming back to printing, the revolutionary invention of the 3D printer has crossed international borders. The invention started in Japan in 1981 when Hideo Kodama used techniques of Additive Manufacturing (AM) in developing methods to create a 3D plastic model using photo-hardening polymer. Then in 1983 engineer Charles 'Chuck' Hull was experimenting in a small lab in Colorado in his spare time when he came up with the concept that has become the foundation of 3D printing technology today. One night he realised he could instantly convert a liquid plastic gloop ('photopolymers') into a solid using ultraviolet light, and he came up with the process of stereolithography. He was so excited he called his wife to get out of bed and come down to the lab. 'This had better be good!' was her initial response.

Little did they know just how big this concept would become. 3D printing has now advanced in a number of different ways, one of the most exciting being 3D bio printing. China developed the most advanced 3D bio machine in the world, successfully printing body parts from organic material. As Chuck Hull has said, 'The whole premise of this technology has been to foster creativity, and change in product design and manufacturing.'[58]

To recap, although China invented the concept of printing, it was only the physical adjacent possibilities that enabled the first printing machines to come together in Europe. The 3D printer was invented on the same premise of adjacent possibilities, but this time, thanks to the internet, the concept travelled very rapidly around the world, as if all those involved were in the same room.

These principles are as applicable to individuals and organisations as they are to countries and civilisations. Two of Google's top 'Innovation Principles' stem from the idea of open collaboration through close connection:[59]

Open will win: [Google] shares everything we can with you and with everyone else … the more information you can share, the more collective knowledge we all have …

Ideas come from anywhere: [Google's] greatest ideas and innovations have come from outside our industry and from people we've met through different types of conversations.

We found when we changed from travelling in a campervan to participating in a home-exchange program, where we could stay in the home of a local family in Europe while they came to stay in ours, that we started to connect with European culture as never before. This was a unique opportunity to, almost literally, 'step into the shoes of others'. Living where the locals lived and doing what they did, our learning went much deeper. We met the neighbours, got to know the local shop vendors, spent time exploring a local area to become familiar with its features and the people living in it. While maintaining our own cultural identity, we also aimed to learn about and respect the local culture by trying to learn the language and customs. We developed a newfound empathy, and it triggered the first stage of the innovation process: a curiosity and motivation for ideation that opened up a world of possibilities. (On a humourous note, the highly popular home rental company Airbnb may have taken this concept a little too far in a tweet campaign that ended up sounding creepy rather than comforting: 'Sleep in their beds, so you may know their dreams ... Sit at their tables, so you can know their tastes ... Go look through their windows, so you can understand their views.' One reader responded, 'Airbnb's tweets from today sound like instructions an axe murderer would write for himself'!)

Think about how this relates to organisational culture. Individual autonomy and focus need to be respected and individual differences need to be celebrated to ensure unique qualities are a source of strength. At the same time, closer connections need to be made based on strategic networks and with respect for mutually agreed guidelines. This is a powerful foundation for initiating creative thinking and innovation.

DETOUR
Switzerland's secret

Switzerland can be seen as a microcosm of Europe and a unique meeting place of its three larger neighbours — France, Germany and Italy. When you travel through Switzerland you will notice the signs are in three languages: German, French and Italian. Switzerland has three distinct cultural and language groups, but there is a fierce pride in the Swiss identity that transcends individual cultural and language differences. In this it is a microcosm of the European continent. Respect for diversity has been of critical importance, and Switzerland has embodied this principle for many years.

Switzerland excels in all three areas identified by Richard Florida as essential for attracting a 'creative class': talent, technology and tolerance. Not only has it invested over the years in information and communication

(continued)

technologies and structures that support innovation, but it has also invested in human capital and ensured a cross-pollination of knowledge. Switzerland invests more in the health, education and talent of its people than any other country worldwide. These principles have been found in all of the top 10 economies as ranked by the Global Innovation Index. Switzerland ranked as an innovation leader, coming top of the index for four consecutive years.[60]

Perhaps not surprisingly, these principles have probably contributed to Switzerland being one of the happiest and healthiest countries in the world.[61] The fact that it has few natural resources has meant that the government has had to focus on the development of its best resource, its people. Switzerland is ranked as one of the happiest countries in the world by the UN's *World Happiness Report*. It has the eighth lowest rate of depression, it is the leader in disability support, and it has one of the highest rates of literacy in the world. These are just a few of the areas in which it has excelled. Purposeful proximity, close connections and tolerance for diversity (along with talent and technology) have all come together successfully in this country.

As Saadia Zahidi, Senior Director of the World Economic Forum, has said, 'Countries that invest in human capital end up getting returns in terms of economic growth, and then countries that have that economic growth are able to reinvest further in human capital. So you have this virtuous cycle that's established.'

It's no wonder that Switzerland is, in relative terms, racing ahead when it comes to innovation.

DETOUR
Lessons from the Soviet state

In comparison to countries like Switzerland, and the European Union in general, why did the Soviet Union fall apart? And why did it struggle in the race for innovation? Is there a connection? Overspending on the military during World War II was undoubtedly a major factor, along with corruption and poor policies and planning. Also significant was that there was overall an isolation and a history of rigid, autocratic systems and excessive bureaucracies limiting freedom and creating resentment. Rather than recognising and respecting different individual cultures, the Soviet Union tried to create a monolithic state based on a uniform political and economic system.[62] This isolation had a major effect on its ability to keep up with innovation.

DETOUR
Papua New Guinea's impassable chasms

Jared Diamond has outlined the challenges for Papua New Guinea. Like Aboriginal Australia, for thousands of years this country remained cut off from the main development routes. With more than 600 outer islands and an extremely rugged and mountainous main island, opportunities for exposure to outside ideas and resources were limited. Vast mountain ranges and swamps on the mainland kept the population fragmented and isolated in small pockets and inhibited unity and development. Indeed the people have been so fragmented by the inhospitable terrain that they are believed to have developed as many as 1000 different languages (one-sixth of the total number of languages in the world), which in turn further restricted exchanges of ideas and resources. Some of these languages have had as few as 500 speakers at a time. Many people who live in the highlands travel no further than 16 km from their homes, which means they have had extremely limited exposure to different people and new ideas.

In contrast to tropical countries where communities can remain in the one place long term (Vanuatu, for example, has a similarly large number of languages), colder countries, where there has been a need to migrate with the seasons, most often have less linguistic diversity. China, for example, with a population (at 1.3 billion) nearly two hundred times greater, has just eight main languages. The Chinese were able to race ahead with innovation because of their connection through common language, which allowed for more sharing of ideas. As we will see, though, to survive in the 'innovation race' requires the alignment of a number of different factors, and while China has scored highly on innovation through much of its history, it fell behind by the nineteenth century due to other factors.

Gold prospectors in 1930 made contact with many distinctive peoples in the PNG highlands, whom they discovered living in ways that had remained pretty much unchanged since the Stone Age. One area of isolated mountains in the north had no record of any outside visitors before 1979.

Isolation (whether physical isolation or through language) seems to lead to insulation, which can be a major obstruction to innovative development.

APPLICATIONS FOR THE ORGANISATION

Application 1: *Manage autonomous focus for better creative ideas.*

- Individual focus and team diversity need to be balanced and managed for the best results.
- Individual autonomy needs to be recognised and respected.
- Autonomy should be encouraged to allow for broad, uninfluenced thinking for ideas generation.

Just as a country's physical isolation can restrict its innovation and development, organisations that become isolated and can't keep up with innovative technological advances can be impacted by disruptive innovations. Business borders are being crossed as never before, which is creating a more highly competitive market than ever before.

For years the top three luxury car makers, with equal market share, vied for a competitive advantage that would allow them to dominate the market. Research has shown that the younger generation would rather own a luxury phone than a luxury car, so a company on a path that was once a sure bet could find themselves tripped up and left behind in the blink of an eye. Who would have expected the CEO of Daimler/Mercedes Benz, the auto company whose origins date back to the early prototypes of the automobile, to express surprise and admiration for Google's progress towards the next generation of self-driving vehicles? And who would have imagined Rolex watching in frustration as Apple and Samsung started competing in the watch market? When they launched, the revolutionary accommodation company Airbnb and mobility company Uber didn't themselves own a single hotel or vehicle, but through coming up with a new idea and exploiting new digital technologies they quickly became the biggest players in their market, changing the competitive landscape completely. In recognition of the dangers of trying to live off previous successes, Daimler's Chairman Zetsche has said, 'We should be defined by our future, not by our past.'[63]

The global super-connectedness we experience today means there is now the opportunity for new contestants to enter the race at any level and for them to compete on a fairly even playing field. But for those organisations that want to survive over the long term, there are some important rules for the game. Ensuring there is a reasonable balance between autonomy and diversity to support both the generation of original ideas and their implementation is an essential initial step.

Application 2: Design diverse teams to reach superior creative solutions.

- Heterogeneous teams produce better solutions.
- Homogeneous teams can lead to *homophily*, which increases social pressure towards conformity, increases levels of comfort and complacency, and can lead to insulation.
- Where both autonomy and diversity are well managed, on the other hand, teams can become incredible sources of strength.
- Tolerance for diversity is not just about simply accepting different types of people, but about being open to and proactively including diversity.

What happens when you gather together diverse groups of independent, autonomous individuals to come up with new ideas or solve problems? How effective are they? Diversity has been found to be linked with innovation (specifically cultural diversity)[64] and better economic performance.[65] Diverse groups can be the most creative of all types of collaborative groups — but only if they are managed well.

A focus on social diversity emerged in the 1980s out of a concern about ensuring inclusion of different genders and ethnicities. It has since been high on the agenda of a lot of organisations concerned that they might not be including people from a broad range of backgrounds. Yet it is not an easy policy to implement.

Social networks, which can be defined as relatively enduring patterns of connections between people and groups, can either foster creativity or stifle it. While teams of like-minded people from similar backgrounds solve problems faster, the solutions they come up with are often mediocre compared with the potential of diverse teams. The tendency for people to associate with individuals similar to themselves is known as *homophily*, and homophilic groups have been found to exert particularly strong social pressure towards conformity. Where social groups are homogeneous, there is more likely to be social reproduction.

Heterogeneous teams (of people from different backgrounds and experiences) take longer to solve problems and have more trouble with the process, but the eventual outcome is superior.[66] Although research has shown that group diversity can lead to greater perceived conflict and a lack of trust[67], it has the advantage of throwing a lot of different experiences and perspectives into the mix, and there is less opportunity for groupthink to creep in and take over. Diverse connections also create opportunities for higher levels of creativity and innovation through helping to cross boundaries.[68]

Comfort, as we have discussed, can lead to insulation. For example, do we insulate ourselves by reading the blogs that we already agree with and the social media news made popular by Facebook? Do we read the books recommended by Amazon, which has identified our key interests by analysing our previous choices, and listen to streaming stations that keep us within the realms of what we already know and like? Companies that manage online sales are making a scientific art out of the interpretation of big data, helping their clients pinpoint exactly what the data says their customers need next.

While this sort of 'predictive intelligence' might help take some of the fuss out of shopping, narrowing our options (and therefore our exposure to diverse information and ideas) will not deliver new perspectives or help us to become more creative and innovative. Researchers in Italy have found that this narrowing of sources of information reinforces our own existing values and beliefs, turning us into 'echo chambers'.[69] As comedian Steven Colbert has summarised it (with reference to Sarah Palin opening her own TV channel), we create 'a safe space where like-minded folks can hear things they already agree with, from someone whose opinion they already know'.[70]

Although English has become the common business language globally and many of us speak it as our first language, we know that monolingualism can be isolating. Even within one language isolation can be created, for example through using slang, nicknames and jargon. Nicknames can create cliques, which can insulate homogeneous groups from others. Jargon is often used as a secret language to speed up the communication process for people who know it, but it excludes those who don't. Investigations into the Enron scandal in the US revealed the large number of code names used for illegal activities, along with the significant number of times outsiders were referred to in a derogatory way.

A number of Silicon Valley tech companies released data on their organisational diversity (or the lack of it), particularly in terms of gender and race, and the results were concerning.[71] These companies and more like them refused to provide data for a diversity report, even taking out a court order to block the push. One of the companies revealed that

70 per cent of employees were male and 62 per cent of the company's U.S. employees were white. The non–white breakdown was 30 per cent Asian, 4 per cent mixed race, 3 per cent Latino, 2 per cent black and 1 per cent 'other', and other companies have had similar results.[72] The stats on women in tech companies in particular have actually been getting worse.[73] Hundreds of millions of dollars have since been pledged to an effort to improve this balance.

How can homogeneity be so damaging? Strong ties between individuals can build protective walls that become barriers to new ideas. Where these ties are based on similarities they are likely to become a form of exclusion rather than inclusion. Research has found that groups with shared norms tend to have access to the same sorts of information, which in turn limits their exposure to different information.[74]

> **Strong ties between individuals can build protective walls that become barriers to new ideas. Where these ties are based on similarities they are likely to become a form of exclusion rather than inclusion.**

Where both autonomy and diversity are well managed, on the other hand, they can become incredible sources of strength. Richard Florida reminds us that tolerance for diversity is not just about simply accepting different types of people, but about being open to and proactively including diversity.

If the global 'innovation race' was being judged by a panel, the panel might well take into account the harsh, isolating environments imposed on Australian Aboriginals and Papua New Guineans over which they had no control. However, the judges might be less empathetic to the teams that had all the right conditions in place (common language, close proximity) yet didn't capitalise on the innovative opportunities that diverse ideas can bring.

Application 3: Manage diversity for better overall innovation.

- Highly diverse teams can be planned to avoid potential subgroups or cliques of like-minded people.
- Diversity has been linked to greater innovation, enhanced financial performance, and implantation of and adaptation to organisational change.
- Diversity is enhanced by high levels of autonomy, and well-planned diversity ensures that perspectives are not assumed to be the same.

- Open systems support diversity in teams, which require openness and humility.
- Communication in diverse teams is important and is linked to interpersonal engagement.

Team members may differ in a number of ways, and researchers have found that the impact of diversity depends on how well these characteristics are aligned.[75] Teams that use their interpersonal differences as an advantage have generally been found to be better at resolving complex cognitive tasks involving multiple possible solutions, such as decision-making tasks requiring creative thinking. The greater the autonomy in completing a task, the better the benefits of team diversity.

A danger can arise within diverse groups when subgroups or cliques emerge, which can split the team and reduce cohesion. The authors of this research have suggested that when designing teams:

- managers should be aware of the structure of diversity they create to ensure the team is not at risk of splitting into subgroups
- managers can alter the team's task so they can become more autonomous, considering work specifications such as decision rules, working methods and planning tools.

If managed well, diversity ensures different perspectives are considered and there is the opportunity for different sorts of information to be included, which leads to better problem solving and decision making. Studies of diversity have revealed that when we are with people who are similar to us we are more likely to make assumptions that perspectives and information are shared.[76] When we are with people who are different from us, on the other hand, we are more open to sharing ideas and information, as there is the assumption that different people in the group will have different perspectives.

Ethnic and gender diversity especially have been found to be linked to greater innovation and enhanced financial performance. In simple murder mystery problem-solving tasks, as explored in one research study, groups with greater ethnic diversity will share information more openly and solve problems more effectively. Another study found that ethnically diverse juries will exchange a wider range of information about a case than homogeneous groups. A study of innovation-focused banks has

Ethnic and gender diversity have especially been found to be linked to greater innovation and enhanced financial performance.

revealed that there is better financial performance where there is greater ethnic diversity.

Greater financial gains have also been found to correlate with more women in leadership positions in companies where innovation is prioritised. Diversity is similarly recognised as essential for doing research and innovation effectively.[77] Studies have additionally shown that political diversity can prompt greater thought and discussion, which can lead to more diverse ideas.

The successful management of team diversity has been found to relate to better working conditions and faster implementation of and adaptation to organisational change.[78] The ability to deal with differences in a diverse team is vitally important, as is a willingness to share opinions and voice objections. Strong cohesion within a team is conducive to rapid action, but the team's culture must also allow for the expression of a range of diverse points of view.

Interdisciplinary approaches are required in order to transform the concept of knowledge from a closed system to an open system that can support diversity. In the 2011 RESCUE (Responding to Environmental and Social Challenges for our Unstable Earth) project, it was found that humility and openness were required in order to achieve positive results. The emphasis in this project was on 'seeing things differently' rather than on 'doing more of the same but better', so it required broader insights.[79]

> The successful management of team diversity has been found to be related to better working conditions and faster adaptation to organisational change.

A diverse team's success has been found to be most closely connected with the patterns of communication team members use. MIT's Human Dynamics Laboratory closely examined patterns of communication in a client call centre company, and found that the best indicator of team success was how engaged in communication team members were outside of formal meetings.[80] The opportunities to connect randomly through physical proximity, and to share in discussions through a common language, produced more creative collaborative options.

Based on this finding, the MIT consultants recommended that the company adjust their coffee break times so there were more opportunities for informal communication. As a result there was a 20 per cent drop in average handle time in lower-performing teams, and an overall decrease of 8 per cent. The manager went ahead and changed the break schedule at all 10 of the bank's call centres, which triggered an increase of more than 10 per cent in employee satisfaction. These changes will impact a total of 25 000 employees and are predicted to increase productivity by $15 million a year. This company made a conscious decision to extend the opportunities available to them and accelerated their progress.

As Rico and his colleagues found in their research and so beautifully summarised, 'In [autonomous] teams [with no subgroups], the need for communication and collaboration created a climate appropriate for exploiting differences between team members, merging the differences in expertise, and facilitating the development of high-quality solutions.'[81]

It is important that differences are not merely tolerated but valued, which can require intensive character education, not just training.[82]

Application 4: Connect cubicles.

- We can face the problems of isolation and insulation through the way our work environments are set up.
- We can create office environments that support both openness and opportunities for independent focus.
- Everyone has a different psychological makeup and different cognitive preferences—some are more 'focused', while some tend to be 'mind wanderers'—so working environments will need to suit both styles.

Source: Dwayne Booth/Mr.Fish

Despite our ever more overcrowded cities we may be in danger of creating a climate or even a culture of insulation. As we have already identified, being in the city might offer a competitive advantage for innovation, in that it gives the potential for connectedness through proximity, but it does not guarantee it. It might seem a long way from the Australian outback to the urban corporate/organisation office, but we can also face the problem of isolation and insulation through the way our work environments are set up.

Remember: isolation can lead to insulation, which can become a roadblock to building a culture of innovation. In our offices, while we design proximity into the workspaces, we are not necessarily making it purposeful. Connection and an openness to connecting, on the other hand, can allow for innovation. Indigenous Australians and Papua New Guineans could only work with the restricted environmental conditions they found themselves in. They had a purpose (to live in harmony with their environment) and complex kinship and trading networks that facilitated survival, but a lack of proximity to other countries meant that technological development did not progress in the same way as on other continents, which is not necessarily a good thing or a bad thing, just a fact.

If we decide we do want to develop and grow in the workplace we have much more choice. We can create office environments that support both openness and opportunities for independent focus.

The mockumentary TV show *The Office*, created by English comedian Ricky Gervais, was a huge hit in the UK before being remade for the US market. The series portrayed regular office workers in a regular office environment. They were notably working in cubicles. As journalist Kevin Craft wrote, *The Office* 'made its audience feel better about their professional lives by showcasing a workplace with even drabber décor and more grating co-workers. [The show] meditated on the tribulations that arise when a group of people who occupy the same space out of necessity rather than choice try to form meaningful social connections.'[83]

Somehow the contemporary working environment needs to foster connections that may not be natural but need to be viable. Simply placing people side by side will not do this. The office environment has historically been through a few significant transitions: from the workers lined up in an open space, their desks in neat rows, busily tapping away at their typewriters, to closed private offices, to cubicles, and back to open space again. Open offices emerged in Germany in the 1950s to support the easy flow of communication and ideas. The cubicle was introduced in 1967 under the name 'Action Office II' to help workers to concentrate without distractions. More recently there has been a return to the concept of open offices to increase the opportunities to collaborate and share ideas—both of which are essential for creative thinking and innovation. Open-plan offices with more creative layouts are now coming back into fashion.

Cubicle workers have actually been found to be the least satisfied of all types of office employees. Workers in these environments have the worst of both worlds: limited space and problems with noise interference, and not enough privacy to really focus on getting work tasks done. Office workers are interrupted on average every 11 minutes. This can be a problem for modern workers given that it takes 25 minutes to get into a creative and engaged work flow in which you are able to perform to your full potential.[84] Studies in Finland, the USA and Australia have all confirmed that 60 per cent of office workers in cubicles are dissatisfied on a number of different measures. Simply breaking down the cubicle walls and opening up the office space more is not the solution, though, because open-space office workers have been found to be only slightly more satisfied.[85]

Everyone has a different psychological makeup and different cognitive preferences—some are more 'focused', while some tend to be 'mind wanderers'—so working environments will need to suit both styles.[86] There will obviously need to be a smart blend of privacy for focus and open areas to encourage connection between people. It will mean setting up specific systems and putting structures in place that actively foster collaboration, rather than simply expecting creative collaboration to take place naturally. One contemporary office, for example, has designed the space with open casual seating in the middle and more private office spaces around the outside. Some new desk designs are like business-class seats on airplanes—with very private lounge spaces in small individual 'pods', and shared communal lounge spaces in between.[87]

Application 5: Create convivial communities.

- In future the dominant concept will be of a 'convivial workplace', a workplace that promotes social interaction but also offers opportunities for privacy and for productivity.
- The office performs an important social function, so it needs to provide a special kind of experience centred on social contact.
- Organisations can be designed as communities where people can connect and ideas will collide.

In the future, the dominant concept will be of a 'convivial workplace', a workplace that promotes social interaction but also offers opportunities for privacy and for productivity.[88] Workplaces will look less like *The Office* and more like someone's living room, or a trendy bar or café. Progressive technology companies like Google and Facebook have pioneered the concept of distinctive workspace designs as a way of expressing and establishing a clear organisational identity and creating a positive culture, which helps to attract the right kind of employee.[89] These proactive companies recognise that by creating purposeful proximity in clever collaborative spaces they can create hothouses for innovation.

Consider how most people's work can these days be completed on a laptop at home (or anywhere else for that matter). Why, then, do we need offices? Clearly the office performs an important social function, so it needs to provide a special kind of experience centred on social contact. Companies like Google have made a science out of creating innovative work environments. Take the canteen, for example. While canteens were initially introduced into organisations to help improve productivity, they are now much more about helping to create a feeling of community in the organisation, as eating brings people together.[90] The Google workplace became so community oriented and 'home-like' that some employees chose to live 'on campus' to save money, one setting up in a campervan for two or three years.[91] Google created an environment where they all spoke the same language, a place where people could constantly connect with each other.

> Proactive companies recognise that by creating purposeful proximity in clever collaborative spaces they can create hothouses for innovation.

Many Silicon Valley companies have provided their employees with a huge range of perks. While some have seen that as an indication of a caring company, other more cynical critics believe it has been a clever way to keep employees at work longer. These companies created a self-sufficient, independent environment with such services as shuttle transport, cafeterias, pools and gyms, post office services, hairdressers, doctors, chiropractors, dentists, laundry services and banks providing for all basic needs.

Work canteens are like a modern European marketplace, where individuals can come together to cross-pollinate and share ideas. Taking the concept even further, Google has researched the eating habits of employees and has provided healthier food in their staff canteens to ensure better employee welfare.[93] An in-house study nicknamed 'Project M&M' looked into whether consumption of the most popular sweet might impact happiness and productivity. After moving the M&Ms to opaque containers and making healthier snacks such as dried figs and pistachios more accessible, the company managed to dramatically reduce consumption of the less healthy snack. They were also successful in dramatically increasing consumption of water by using a similar tactic — making the sweet carbonated drinks less accessible.

Was all this effort put in just to be nice to employees? Maybe, but there were also other things at stake. Firstly, these incentives and perks were being offered to attract the best of the best to the organisation. Secondly, these companies realised that proximity with a purpose is the most powerful and effective way to bring about innovation. The ability to share ideas in a safe, relaxed environment where everyone is close to each other and talks the same language provides the vital 'fast forward' card that has kept these companies racing ahead with innovation.

We have designed an experiential diagnostic exercise intended to identify some of the blocks to creative thinking in an organisation culture through a Clue/Whodunit-style board game called 'Who Killed Creativity?'. When we ran this exercise with an Asian client company it emerged that the employees consistently indicated that creative thinking was being killed by the suspect 'Pessimism' wielding the 'Negativity' weapon at 'The Coffee Shop'. Intrigued, we spoke to the CEO to see if we could find out what was behind this. Rather than being concerned, the CEO indicated he was proud. He boasted to us that he was hoping to improve productivity by making the food in the company cafeteria so bad that it encouraged everyone to get back to work faster! What he had failed to see was the impact this would have on individual motivation and the organisational culture, which would ultimately reduce productivity, innovation and profitability — something that was immediately obvious to us.

Zooming further out, whole communities could and possibly should be built to support better connections of ideas. Many cities were originally designed around the dominant transport structures of the time rather than directly connecting people. So in Los Angeles and Las Vegas, where the dominant transport system has been the private car, there is little opportunity for connection with others — people remain in their bubbles!

The CEO of Zappos, Tony Hsieh, has tried to counter this problem by building on an interesting vision: he is trying to turn Las Vegas into a community. This $350 million project, a personal investment for Hsieh, includes repurposed shipping containers for use in bars, retailers and small businesses in his Downtown Container Park. Hsieh has also invested in the arts and education, tech startups and small businesses. He has been described as being an early adoptor of the shift from closed innovation to open innovation.

Hsieh is a multimillionaire, but instead of building pyramids or monuments to his own power and wealth, he is building urban community development centres that benefit all. And he is deliberately designing these communities so they become places where people can connect and ideas will collide.

Application 6: Capitalise on broader networks.

- Work environments of the future will need to ensure both independence from pressures and opportunities for collaborative connections.
- They should also connect with the local community, and the greater society needs to avoid isolation and ensure responsibility.
- There will need to be the opportunity for open learning and growth.

In the final season of the American version of *The Office* one of the characters interacts with a member of the fictional film crew that has been filming the 'documentary'. The office employees learn that they are the subjects of a documentary titled 'The Office, An American Workplace' and are horrified by the personal details that have been revealed. They had been highly connected internally, but they had not made the external connections necessary to know and understand their real context.

Contemporary workers in modern offices need to feel connected externally as well as internally. There needs to be an authentic approach to promoting openness and connections that helps to meet the needs of all people for genuine connections at all levels. Organisations today can also end up becoming isolated and insulated, and if they are not connecting to other organisations as well as to other communities and cultures they could be in dangerous territory. Just as we became insulated in the comfortable bubble of our campervan and needed to learn to find new ways to keep the connections open, both within our family and with the cultures we were visiting, organisations today need to ensure they are connecting on both levels.

Even a company like Google can be in danger of becoming isolated and insulated. Google became such a great place to work that it created its own internal comfort zone. People would be ferried to work in a Google bus, eat at the Google canteen and exercise at the Google gym; indeed they could live their entire life there, physically isolating themselves from the rest of the world. Imagine this scenario: 10 people sitting in the Google bus on their way to work from San Francisco to Silicon Valley, passing the depressed suburbs of the city where people struggle to afford transport, passing the local communities and local businesses in Mountain View where the headquarters is based, driving straight into the self-sufficient compound where all of their daily needs are conveniently provided for. Of the 10 people on that bus, eight will be male and two female, six will be white, three Asian, and one may be black or Hispanic. All 10 of them will be speaking in jargon, using terminology and acronyms that any outsider would be hard pressed to follow—just like us in our campervan in Europe. Like us, they are close to yet so far removed from others that it's possible to fail to connect with them, and therefore to fail to gain the full benefits of the experience.

Apart from its lack of internal diversity, Google came under fire for its lack of community support externally. Perhaps this is an example of the sort of 'lock-in' principle we introduced earlier that comes from too much proximity. In some ways Google cut itself off from the external world. In 2014 the company was accused of bypassing the local community completely, and there were protests in San Francisco and Mountain View. Unfortunately the large number of employees with high disposable incomes moving into the San Francisco area pushed up the local housing prices, which created additional resentment in the local communities.

Despite the best intentions to live up to their innovation principles, and their attempts to support innovation internally using purposeful proximity, Google has had the challenge of ensuring they are also connected externally. Fortunately, the company has taken these issues to heart and they have looked into how to best deal with these challenges. The paradox of growth is that as companies become more successful and grow, they can end up becoming isolated in the process. It's easy to skid across the path without realising it's happening.

As an important side note here, it has been found that community engagement and corporate social responsibility can actually lead to better innovation.[94] Opportunities for purpose-driven innovation can be enhanced by ensuring company social awareness and values are strong.

As individuals we can fall into the same traps. Despite the promises of a more open and connected world, if we are not making *constructive connections* with people from all walks of life and in all parts of the world, we are in danger of becoming insulated, and therefore of losing purposeful connections. By continuing to tap our usual sources of information we may be closing ourselves off to different possibilities, and before we know it we're constructing our own roadblocks. By connecting only with the people we typically connect with, we may be closing ourselves off to wider possibilities. We can remain in our own bubble by giving in to the temptation of doing what the media tells us to do, the internet taking our cookies and giving us more of what we want, keeping us isolated in our autonomy rather than exposing us to diversity.

We have the opportunity to help launch a renaissance, to create new marketplaces that foster both independent thinking and collaborative innovation through harnessing diversity. Let's move forward into this new possibility.

Application 7: Balance autonomy and connected diversity.

- Focused autonomy and self-efficacy have been found to be strongly related to idea generation, so it is important to continue to support these.
- Both 'open' and 'closed' action strategies in the innovation process need to be introduced, so everyone's skills and capabilities are appreciated and engaged.

Focused autonomy and self-efficacy have been found to be strongly related to idea generation, so it is important to continue to support these.[95] The more people think independently and focus on developing new ideas — free from external pressures and expectations, and secure in the understanding that they have the independence and opportunity to explore different options — the broader the creative thinking and innovation outputs will be. When this is combined with opportunities to connect and collaborate with a diverse group, the results will be magical.

The 'open action' strategy that is used here assists with generating and exploring different ideas. It involves divergent thinking — opening up to all possibilities. When cultural specialists Trompenaars and Hampden-Turner were called in to assist the Advanced Micro Devices (AMD) factory in Dresden in East Germany, one of the most innovative semiconductor factories in the world, they discovered a company in conflict.[96] They needed to work out how to integrate the skills of the American, East German and West German employees, who were not able to work together effectively. The Americans, they discovered, were optimistic and empowered in their approach, whereas the West Germans wanted to do everything absolutely correctly and thoroughly, to the point that they were in danger of falling prey to 'analysis paralysis'. The East Germans, on the other hand, had learned to be innovative under Communism. They smuggled in machine parts, for example, but when they broke down they could not call up anyone to fix them, so they had to come up with resourceful solutions for themselves. This was an example of ingenious solutions resulting from practical problem solving, innovation arising from necessity (remember Jugaad innovation introduced in chapter 2).

Trompenaars and Hampden-Turner set out to combine the Americans' natural bias towards open thinking and freewheeling brainstorming and ideation, and the Germans' instincts to prepare thoroughly before revealing ideas openly. They used both 'open' and 'closed' action strategies in the innovation process, so everyone's skills and capabilities were appreciated and engaged. Simple changes to the brainstorming process, such as giving people the opportunity to write their ideas down privately before posting them up on boards, made a difference in accommodating their differing needs and approaches. The factory was soon breaking production records *and* reducing errors, which the company executives have credited to this new multicultural approach to innovation.

Imagine the incredible results you will be able to achieve when you effectively manage autonomy (for more independent ideas) and connected diversity (for a greater range of ideas) in the organisation. This will enable a more highly innovative culture that supports open thinking and innovation. As long as these are the basis for continuous learning and growth,[97] the organisation and the individuals within it will benefit enormously.

CHAPTER SUMMARY

How to initiate the innovation process through open connections for exploring diverse ideas

Navigating the path between focus and openness

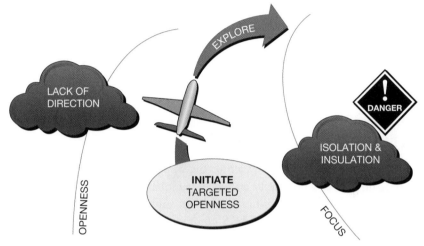

Key principles from the journey

Isolation can lead to insulation.

- By focusing on our personal needs and goals we can become isolated from others, which in turn can lead to insulation (e.g. tourists vs travellers).
- Autonomy and individual focus is critical for independence (e.g. each EU member country's sovereignty and independence can be eroded).
- Independent focus can lead to isolation, polarisation and a lack of solidarity.

A balance of autonomous focus and diversity with respect leads to more openness and more innovative ideas.

- Where diversity is respected and utilised as a source of strength there are significant benefits (e.g. the challenges and achievements of the European Union and Switzerland).
- Richard Florida has found that tolerance is a major requirement for attracting a 'creative class'.

We need to plan for purposeful proximity.

- A lack of proximity can impact development and innovation (e.g. Australia's and Papua New Guinea's historical isolation).
- Proximity can foster connections and lead to higher rates of creative output (e.g. the invention of the printing machine).
- Cities are an interesting experiment on the impact of proximity and the links to innovation and can potentially solve many of the world's problems.
- Proximity needs to be purposeful and connections need to be capitalised on to avoid complacency, a lack of openness and flexibility, conformity and corruption.

Opportunities for targeted, open connections need to be deliberately designed.

- Digital technology has given us the opportunity for superlineal scaling of our proximity and greater global connections. It can also enable collaborative problem solving on critical issues (e.g. responding to the SARS epidemic and inventing 3D printers).
- Technology can also isolate rather than connect (e.g. we are facing the 'age of loneliness').
- Too much openness can be overwhelming and can lead to a lack of direction.
- New strategic collaborative networks need to be built and integrated (e.g. health agency networks, research networks, Salesforce in business).
- These networks need to be built in a way that supports individual autonomy while encouraging collaboration.

Application summary

1. Manage autonomous focus for better creative ideas (case studies Mercedes Benz/Daimler, Google, Airbnb, Uber).
2. Design diverse teams to reach superior creative solutions (case studies: Silicon Valley Tech Companies).
3. Manage diversity for better overall innovation (case studies: RESCUE Project, Call Centre Company).
4. Connect cubicles (case studies: *The Office*).
5. Create convivial communities (case studies: Google, Zappos).
6. Capitalise on broader networks (case studies: Google).
7. Balance autonomy and connected diversity (case studies: Advanced Micro Devices (AMD)).

CHECKPOINT SUMMARY CHECKLIST

How to initiate the innovation process and improve connections for greater diversity of ideas

Paradox synthesis: Targeted Openness

Is there a balance in your organisation between supporting *autonomous focus* and ensuring *openness* and *diversity*?

FOCUS

A solid foundation for generating ideas

Is there evidence of individual focus that will support the ability to think and act independently without external pressure?

☐ **Individuality**   Individuals are encouraged to recognise their own talents and lead from these.

☐ **Independence**   Individuals feel free to express their own ideas and act on them where appropriate.

☐ **Personal space**   People have the personal space (time) and physical space both to focus on individual tasks when needed, and to collaborate when needed.

OPENNESS

An open and inclusive environment for greater variety of ideas

Is there evidence of diversity in the organisation that will help to expand thinking?

☐ **Heterogeneity and diversity**   There is a variety of different opinions, ideas etc. rather than evidence of conformity (e.g. groupthink), complacency or insulation (e.g. use of jargon, nicknames).

☐ **Tolerance**   There is an acceptance and respect of diversity.

☐ **Opportunities to dialogue**   Communication is a meaningful, two-way exchange rather than a one-way message.

(continued)

OPENNESS *(cont'd)*

Are connections actively established and encouraged through purposeful proximity?

☐ **Openness** — There is an openness to new ideas and different ways of thinking in the organisation.

☐ **Connection** — There are clear opportunities to connect in meaningful ways.

☐ **Love of learning** — The culture supports education and growth.

☐ **Learning from multiple sources** — Learning from multiple sources is encouraged.

☐ **Internal + external connections** — Connections are established and maintained both internally within the organisation and externally with outside stakeholders.

TRY THIS

How to ensure autonomous focus

• Set up autonomous team tasks (e.g. decision rules, working methods, planning tools).

• Set up independent workspaces where people can focus.

• Remind individuals of the importance of autonomy when generating ideas.

How to build openness

• Recruit diverse employees (different backgrounds, cultures, sexes).

• Expose people to different cultures, classes etc.

• Ensure teams have a diverse mix.

• Build a culture of tolerance and trust (e.g. through sharing positive stories about this in meetings, newsletters).

How to manage openness to diversity

- Check teams won't form subgroups or cliques due to similarities.
- Facilitate groups effectively.
- Establish values of openness and trust (e.g. through identifying values for vision).
- Ensure there are opportunities for interpersonal engagement and constructive communication (e.g. through setting up social spaces).

How to build connections

- Be aware of the potential for loneliness.
- Set up the office environment in a way that allows opportunities for connection as well as personal focus time.
- Encourage the establishment of deliberate social networks.
- Use technology as a connecting tool, rather than allowing it to become an isolating factor (e.g. set up social networks).

Preparing for the next mode

As we have discussed, navigating the path between focus and openness is critical for stretching thinking to new ideas without losing aim. Typically, in most contemporary cultures, the individual will want to maintain autonomy and keep information and ideas to themselves if individual actions are recognised and rewarded. And yet the organisation will promote the idea that collaboration is important.

Putting people in close proximity can be a good start, but it's not enough. For the solution-finding SOLVE mode, the next phase in the innovation process, a collective and collaborative approach is essential. If only it was as simple as declaring, 'We should all collaborate for better innovation.' But what happens when what's best for the individual is not best for the group? Does the logic of individual interest lead to collective disaster? Collaboration can be more complicated than at first glance.

As we continue our race around the globe and visit the Asian continent, we explore further this dichotomy and the potential power of a strategic resolution.

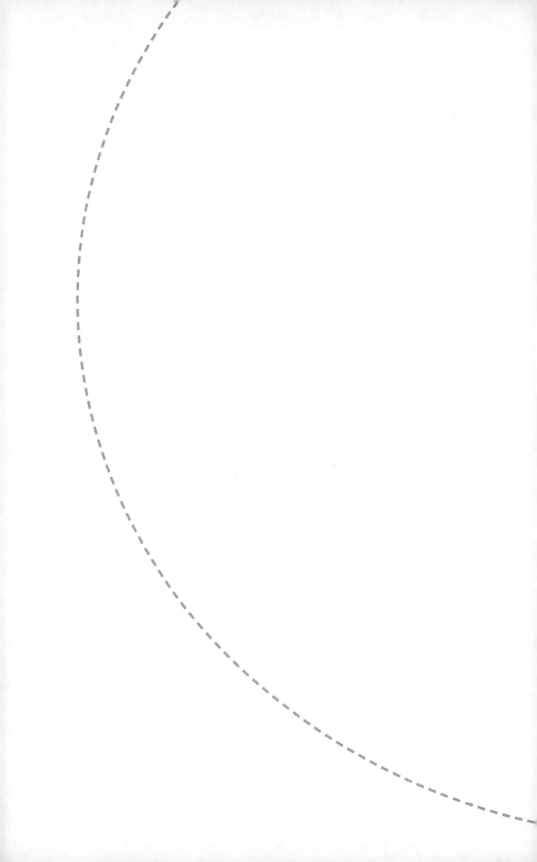

7

MOTIVATE

How to motivate individuals and teams to come up with unified solutions

Destination: Asia

Paradox: Individualism vs Group Engagement

Synthesis: Collaborative engagement

In this chapter we will have the opportunity explore the path between individualism and group engagement, facing at one extreme the potential danger zone of apathy and disengagement, and at the other, the potential danger of obsession. We will learn how to plan and navigate a route through collaborative engagement that will create a culture to best fuel innovation.

Key challenge: How to capitalise on both individual passions and group synergy through 'collaborative engagement'.

Hurtling down a steep, muddy jungle track on the back of a suspect truck overflowing with pigs and chickens was positively terrifying. Yet by the time we found ourselves in this particular circumstance there was no turning back. We were on our way to a 'secret surfing spot' near an isolated village in the central Philippines. It had quickly become obvious why this location had remained 'secret' and rarely visited, but we needed a break, so we gritted our teeth and hung on for dear life.

This was supposed to be our chance to recuperate after some intensive lecturing work, but the journey wasn't quite what we had bargained for.

Yet the trip would end up being an incredible learning experience on the contrast between communal engagement and individualism that tends to characterise our world today.

When we finally reached our destination we gratefully, if not so gracefully, extracted ourselves from the truck and stumbled into our simple thatched bungalow, thoroughly relieved. What we found was entrancing, but also quite daunting. We were on an idyllic white sandy beach with a few thatched sleeping bungalows scattered along it and one communal lounge and dining hut in the centre for guests. A small cluster of village huts sat a little further back from the beach, but that was all there was. Period. We wondered how we were going to amuse ourselves for three weeks with so little to explore or to entertain ourselves with. This was before the internet, so there were no portable electronic devices to keep us amused, and there was also no electricity in the village. We had brought some books and notebooks, along with the compulsory surfboards, but apart from eating, sleeping, swimming and surfing, reading and writing would be all we would be able to do.

Our first week swung wildly between heaven and hell, from periods of delighted appreciation to the agonies of tech withdrawal. We were forever checking our watches, silently (and sometimes openly) urging the minutes to pass till it was time to walk the 10 metres down the beach to the eating hut for our next meal, just to give us something to do. By the second week, though, we were gradually learning to wind down, and we started to experience some amazing new creative insights. We also started to get ourselves out of our own individual activities and engage more with the local community. By the third week we were positively chilled, going with the flow and enjoying the simple rhythms of village life. It took three full weeks to get through the tech detox and successfully complete the modern-life withdrawal process, but by that time we had come up with some original ideas and just about solved the problems of global poverty.

The sad irony was that during the time we were there, while we learned to live without our usual modern conveniences, we witnessed the village's transition in the opposite direction. During the first week we had watched the children happily playing around the village together (as they would have done for generations), content with the simple playthings their natural environment provided. The adults had gone about their daily work, interacting with one another in a casual, comfortably familiar way. At night everyone gathered around the gas lanterns and the fire to share the day's events. In the second week electricity was hooked up for the first time, and the natural rhythms of the villagers started to change. People stayed in their own huts more, and there was less communal time. At the beginning of the third week a TV was ceremoniously carried into the village and set up in the communal hut. From then on the blinds were closed during the day and the children remained indoors, transfixed by the magical entertainment machine. By this time we had no desire for a TV and were contentedly living without electricity.

When TV came to town

It was disturbing to get an outsider's insight into just how much modern technology can impact a community. While we were learning to disconnect from the individualism of technological 'innovation', we saw first-hand how quickly communal engagement can be displaced by individual pursuits to the detriment of the community.

Interestingly, this experience ended up being a social experiment that was similar to what India had gone through when the media market suddenly opened up in the early nineties, but on a much smaller scale. Up until 1991 there had been only one national television channel in India, the public service provider Doordarshan. Much of the programming was controlled by the government and was often propagandistic. In 1991 new government economic reforms led to a sudden and dramatic shift to a global media market through satellite TV. This led to a transition to more than 200 digital channels by 2005, and almost double that again by 2013. With about 45 per cent of the Indian population illiterate in 1991, television was the dominant source of news and information.

> While we were learning to disconnect from the individualism of personal technological 'innovations', we saw first-hand how communal engagement be impacted.

This huge growth in the offering ultimately led to more freedom of information, which as we have discussed is critically important for innovation, but it also had negative social impacts. The statistics indicated a rise in crime rates and an increase in violent and anti-social behaviour across India at the time. Given that even kissing had never previously been seen on Indian TV or in movies, the sudden exposure to sexualised TV shows like *Baywatch*, *Dallas* and *Dynasty* had a huge impact on social norms. Conversations with Indians living abroad have revealed a broadly held view that Indians have in general become more individualistic since that time.[1]

In this chapter we will explore the tension between individualism (which is predominantly seen to be a western value) and collectivism (which is a predominantly seen to be a philosophy of eastern cultures). There are of course both constructive and negative elements in both of these traits. For example, individualism can be driven by personal passion, but it can also lead to apathy and disengagement from the group. Group commitment and engagement can come from a regulated and disciplined approach, so it sometimes lacks the passion or incentive of the individual single-minded drive. Group contexts have, for example, been found to lower accountability and individual motivation to perform at a high level[2], yet, on the other side, collaborative groups can produce higher levels of creativity.[3] We will focus here on the apathy and disengagement that can come from extreme individualism, and the engagement that can come from a heartfelt collectivism.

Motivation for finding collaborative solutions

This third mode of the innovation process involves bringing together the diverse ideas of individuals into unified team solutions. It requires a transition from individual attention and focus to utilising the benefits of a collective approach.

Once there is a foundation of empowerment that enables individuals to challenge current systems (as discussed in chapter 5), and openness to make new connections for diversity in the ideation phase (chapter 6), it is then important to bring together these ideas into united solutions (this chapter).

This can be a long and intense process, as it can involve combining, pulling apart and recombining different concepts until unique and practical solutions emerge. It can involve testing and prototyping to come up with structured solutions. It is an iterative process that builds on possibilities to find the best options and outcomes. It requires combining the passion of individuals with the synthesis of a group approach (moving from knowledge generation to knowledge synthesis). The culture therefore needs to be able to MOTIVATE both individuals and teams for success in this area. (Remember, for some practical tools to help you to execute this process, please see our book *Who Killed Creativity?*—and in particular, 'Strategy 5: Reconstruct common concepts'.)

Bridging that apparent divide between ideation, which is a divergent thinking process, and solution finding, which is a convergent thinking process, can be especially challenging, since this is typically where you will find the greatest tension in the paradoxical process. Yet only by doing so effectively will you really solve the issues and generate unique results.

Purpose-Driven Innovation (PDI) in action: MOTIVATE

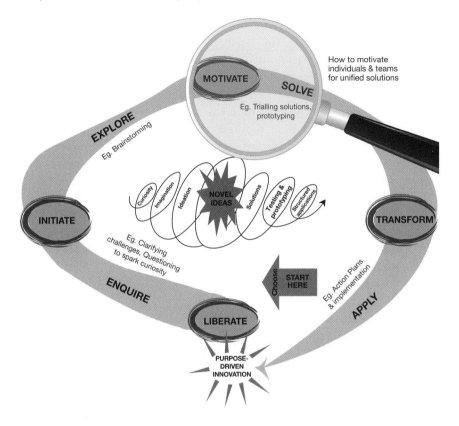

Engagement is related to how well individuals are able to integrate into a group, and—building on the previous chapter—how open and willing they are to help others in the group, rather than simply focusing on their own needs.[4] At this stage of the innovation process, after unique ideas from individuals have been explored and collected, a collaborative effort will be required to come up with practical solutions that best meet the innovation need. So how do you deal with those two apparent contradictions effectively?

Ancient wisdom and modern metropolises

The contrast between individualism and collectivism we discovered through our remote island experience is one of the easiest comparisons to draw between East and West.[5] It has become clear that Asia is a continent of stark contrasts that has been working on balancing these apparently opposing philosophies for quite some time.

As well as learning how to build more collectivist and collaborative cultures, many of us in western societies look to the East for wisdom on how to simplify our lives, for example through meditation and other Buddhist principles. At the same time, many from the East want to catch up technologically and are shifting to more individualistic behaviours and living patterns. While we are trying to simplify our lives after years of consumerism and unnecessary accumulation, and to reconnect with communities (the contemporary expression of that desire is often through social media), in Asia there is a growing desire to have what many westerners take for granted. As a result much of Asia is now 'developing' in a technological sense, but we are wondering how much may be lost in the process. Many countries across the region are seeing a dramatic clash between traditional communal values and modern innovation.

Western travellers have long been enchanted by the vibrant energy these countries exude through their strong collective spirit. While in western culture individuals are often isolated inside their nuclear family homes behind picket fences (living in the sort of isolated 'bubbles' we described in chapter 6), many Asians still live with their extended families in open communities and spend most of their time in communal spaces. The resulting collective energy is evident in towns and cities across the region, their streets alive with people going about their daily tasks: the street vendors, tricycle peddlers, couriers, shoe shiners . . . and often the beggars. The urban spaces in these countries are among the most densely populated in the world, with China and India in the lead (apart from small self-governing states like Monaco), and one consequence is that many are living on the edge of poverty. Yet somehow even the poor don't appear to be psychologically and physically isolated in the way they are in the western world.

Studies into how individualism and collectivism relate to social strata have found that the top echelons of society are consistently the most individualistic. It appears that the wealthier we get the more we want to isolate ourselves and the more we *can* isolate ourselves (remember the pyramid image!), not just through travel, as already discussed, but in our lives in general. Many of the inventions at this level are about giving us more privacy. It's interesting to note that sometimes the poorest of the poor become individualistic in order to fight for survival, but typically most of the less affluent rely on community for support. Couple that with the fact that most eastern countries and cultures have collectivist roots, and you start to get a picture of just how pervasive collectivism is worldwide. In fact, it has been estimated that at least 70 per cent of the world has a collectivist orientation.[6]

Historically, nomadic hunter-gatherers who had searched for their food individually or in small groups became more collectivist when they recognised the advantages of working together to hunt for larger animals. Once people adopted an agrarian lifestyle, they became almost exclusively collectivist, as agricultural practices and limited resources meant they needed to cooperate to survive.

Outwit, Outplay, Outlast

A popular story in business tells of two hikers who wake up in the middle of the night when they realise that a tiger is pacing near their tent.[7] When one of the hikers grabs his running shoes, the other warns that he couldn't possibly outrun a tiger. The first hiker replies that all he has to do is outrun his friend.

Like the metaphor of the 'shark tank' from the reality show we opened with, this story reduces the competitive business environment to a brutal, survival-of-the-fittest survival contest. By immediately going for his shoes rather than thinking how he might collaborate with his partner, he demonstrates opportunistic and individualistic behaviour. In this action he has made the assumption that his partner will also behave opportunistically. Yet do all people automatically behave that way?

We have discovered that while competitive games work well in western countries, they don't always work in Asia. They can be perceived completely differently here because of the generally collective cultural orientation. For this reason TV programs that work well in the West don't always translate as well in the East.

Many western reality TV programs, such as *Survivor,* are advertised as team events, as if the goal is for individuals to work together to achieve unified team outcomes, but the truth is these are individual competitions. There's only one winner at the end, and although the individuals often work together in the short term, ultimately remaining a team player won't win them the competition. Many companies use the 'Survivor' theme in team-building programs, but how often have they really thought through the implications of this? The theme title 'Outwit, Outplay, Outlast' clearly gives away the fact that this program is about fighting to the end to win—for yourself.

The big twist in many of these shows (including *The Apprentice*) comes in the last episode when the whole team is brought back and the finalist has to harness the power of the team to achieve the task. Those who burned their bridges along the way will face the consequences at this point.

At a point in *The Amazing Race* known as an 'Intersection', each team is required to pair up with another team and collaborate on all tasks and decisions until further notice. The 'Salvage Pass', introduced in season two of the Australian version of the program, was awarded to the winners of the first leg. The team who receives the pass is able to choose to give themselves a one-hour head start in the next leg of the race or to save the last team to arrive at the Pit Stop from elimination.

Any number of reality TV shows lay on the tension between individual and group goals. It's usually built into the formula. The sort of passion and drive that impacts activity starts from individual motivation. Unity, on the other hand, relates to collective engagement at a broader community level. These different motivations create ambiguities that can work against each other if the individual is pushing towards individualised goals and outcomes, or can work in harmony if the individual ensures that the momentum is towards a common goal.

The paradox that emerges in this chapter is the fundamental question asked by political scientist Robert Axelrod when researching his landmark work on 'Cooperation Theory'[8]: What happens when the right decision for the individual is the wrong one for the group? This leads to a basic problem that occurs when the pursuit of self-interest by each individual leads to a poor outcome for all.

The polar opposite of this resolute selflessness is the extreme individualistic selfishness of 'Homo Economicus'[9], a personality type identified by the American Psychiatric Association as sociopathic, typified by a willingness to lie and exploit to achieve personal aims. Individualism can appear as mere selfishness. Just how productive is that individual passion and drive to achieve, and how does it impact the potential for group engagement? What happens when tenacious drive becomes ruthless competition? Is it possible, then, to balance competition with collaboration? Can they coexist?

Social relations and economic exchange always take place in a certain context, which can lead to (as some theorists have found) self-aggrandisement or trust, individualism or collectivism, competition or cooperation among participants. Yet economic progress and innovation require both kinds of behaviours, synthesised effectively, not just one or the other.[10] Economists typically argue for competition rather than considering the positive economic roles of cooperation, trust and reciprocity.[11] Sadly, the competitive focus permeates business jargon, freely promoting ideas like 'Outwit, Outplay, Outlast' as metaphors for business success. Perhaps it's time for this focus to change.

The competitive advantage in the 'innovation race' might come from leveraging the human ability to take initiative in cooperation; it also may rely on 'exploiting the organization's … purpose and diversity to enhance both learning and its use in creating innovations and purposive adaptation'.[12] Organisations typically fail when they are unable to provide the social context necessary for building trust, commitment and, ultimately, cooperation.

The neuroscience behind the tragedy of the commons

The tension between single-minded individualism and community engagement has a long history. One of the best-known historical examples of how this can play out is known as 'the tragedy of the commons'[13], a description first coined in 1833 by William Forster Lloyd, an Oxford economist.

By law, villagers in pre–Industrial Revolution England had the right to graze a certain number of sheep and cattle on common land. If everyone collaborated and the numbers of animals were kept low, the grass had time to grow back and the practice was sustainable and mutually beneficial. If any farmer decided to improve his own financial situation by grazing additional animals, however, although he might benefit in the short term, the whole community suffered over the long term.

The tragedy of the commons has become a popular analogy when describing the challenge of balancing self-interest and communal good. The core principle revolves around two competing human interests. Firstly, that innovation should be something from which everyone will benefit. This requires a commitment to the group and to group welfare. Secondly, its counterweight: the individual desire to use innovation for personal advantage. Individuals who betray a common social agreement in order to better their own situation are known as *defectors*, and while they can gain a short-term advantage in the race, defection usually comes with long-term consequences. It's all about the need for trust, and the negative consequences of broken trust.

From an evolutionary perspective, the dynamic interplay between competition and cooperation makes sense. Cooperation among individuals has been needed for security, such as to meet basic needs for food gathering and mate selection and for protection against predators. Competition provides individuals with selective advantages in these areas. The evolutionary perspective on social cognition would therefore recognise the roles of, on the one hand, altruism and cooperation, and, on the other, mechanisms for competition such as coercion, deception and manipulation. This is the nature of the paradox in this particular challenge.

A study in this area has revealed that we are neurologically wired for both competition and cooperation, and that when we engage in these activities we are accessing the same parts of the brain.[14] The areas we access (the right superior parietal cortex and superior frontal gyrus, as well as the anterior insula) are those that are responsible for helping to monitor our own behaviour in relation to another individual, along with our sense of agency. Both cooperation and competition have been found to help humans to make choices about the best courses of action in new situations and to monitor that action (executive functions),[15] as well as predicting the behaviour of others in social situations (mentalising).[16]

But there are some significant differences between the two states of mind. Competition requires more energy for processing (medial prefrontal activity), while cooperating appears to be more socially rewarding (indicated by the activation of the medial orbitofrontal area).[17]

This means that there are natural systems in place to reward cooperation—so long as we can deal with that competitive urge we have identified here (as first introduced in chapter 1), which impacts our ability to collaborate effectively and 'drains the brain'.

The rice paddy principle

We have ourselves seen the principle of the tragedy of the commons play out during the 30 years we've been travelling to Bali in Indonesia. In Kuta, which is now a highly developed tourist mecca, a few thatched huts originally lined dirt pathways between rice paddies leading to pristine, palm-fringed beaches. There were no freeways then, no traffic lights, no shopping malls and only a handful of larger multistorey hotels. Most of the hotels were confined to a small separate area that lacked arable land and was therefore pretty useless to the Balinese themselves. Tourists were kept isolated in the gated community of Nusa Dua to reduce the impact on the local communities and environment. But it wasn't long before Kuta became filthy and overcrowded. The physical beauty that had originally made Kuta appealing for tourists was gone.

Much of the Balinese landscape had actually already been reshaped by farmers by 1000 BC, but traditionally the land was converted into rice paddies.[18] The process was environmentally sound, with the farmers growing their own seeds and needing no pesticides or fertilisers, and they had developed natural forms of irrigation.

The whole system of irrigation has traditionally relied on close collaboration between the owners of neighbouring fields. The water from the mountain lakes and streams is efficiently channelled down from the mountain and through the myriad paddies on the hillsides and plains, so it is essential that this collaborative system be maintained. By making offerings to the temples of upstream neighbours (placed at each branch point in the canal network), individual farmers can ensure that the system continues to work. They need to be able to rely on and trust each other, and they need to work together towards a common goal.

Nobody directs or oversees the system, and no priest demands supplication—all give freely on the understanding that the system benefits all. The irrigation system is an expression of the important Balinese religious philosophy of Tri Hita Karana, the belief that there are three important sources of happiness: people's relationship to God, to each other and to nature. Everything had run incredibly smoothly and harmoniously in this way for thousands of years. Until, that is, the tourism industry took off. Suddenly, with the arrival of mass tourism, land prices rose as land was snapped up for hotel and villa developments. Up until recently the average Balinese could only earn $4000 a year from farming rice, but the farmer could sell that same land for $250 000 per 100 metres square.[19] As a result, up to around 1000 hectares a year have been converted from rice fields to buildings, and the trend continues to increase. As soon as one farmer defected from the traditional system of collaboration by selling their land, the flow of the irrigation system was impacted, which ultimately led to jealousy and distrust in relationships. One defector, and the system was in a shambles, which soon led to a landslide of others selling. (Ironically, for a foreigner a villa in the middle of a rice paddy began as a stunning investment, but the same villa in the midst of a suburban sprawl lost much of its value.) As the Balinese could no longer live off their land once the money ran out, and they couldn't produce enough rice to support their own communities, there was an economic crisis.

Encouraging cooperation without the ties of kinship can be challenging. Although we are naturally wired to work together with people we are related to, we need more convincing when it comes to collaborating with broader groups. It is in these circumstances that free-riding becomes more

> Nobody directs or oversees the system, and no priest demands supplication — all give freely on the understanding that the system benefits all.

of a problem. We have had to develop moral systems and guidelines to help deal with this problem and ensure cooperative behaviour for the good of the community.[20]

$1000 buzzers and booths

Let's demonstrate the real problem with defectors by exploring a specific scenario originally discussed by science journalist Matt Ridley.[21]

Imagine you are sitting in a booth with a buzzer in front of you. Your booth is one of many booths — in fact, 50 other people are sitting in similar booths with buzzers in the same large auditorium. You have been told that each of you will receive $1000 — if everyone gets to the end of one hour without pressing the buzzer. On the other hand, any person who presses the buzzer anonymously before the end of the hour will receive $100. What would you do? What would you imagine would be most likely to happen?

Obviously, the best mutual outcome is for everyone to wait until the end of the hour for the big pay-off. Yet, if there is no trust most people will expect that someone will 'defect' and take the $100, so they figure it might as well be them. This story and others in this chapter demonstrate a principle famously captured in 'the prisoner's dilemma', which illustrates how rational individuals might opt not to cooperate, even if it is, on the face of it, in their best interests to do so. The game offers mutual gains from cooperation, but also allows for the possibility that one player motivated by selfishness can exploit all the others. This logic leads inexorably to collective disaster. So what happens to innovation when the right decision for the individual becomes the wrong one for the group?

We have run exercises posing a similar dilemma with groups of people all around the world. Simulations we have designed such as 'Win as Much as You Can' and 'What Happened to WAT?' use a game theory[22] model to set up a system whereby everyone will win more if all work as a collective team through a number of rounds, while a few will have the opportunity to gain more if they defect and play for the individual win. Typically when we play these games, people may have high ideals for a few rounds, but as soon as one person defects, distrust sets in and they end up competing to deceive each other and win the most for themselves.

We work a lot in competitive corporate environments that operate according to individualistic western principles, so this result is not surprising. What can be scarier is that defectors can then feel they have a position of power (the control we described in chapter 5 set in Africa) and can end up oppressing those who chose to collaborate. A minority can end up oppressing the majority once they have gained a position of superiority through defection. This principle is well known and has been tested in social experiments. Interestingly, studies have found that when the 'Win As Much as You Can' game is renamed as 'The Wall Street Game' there is a 70 per cent defection rate, but when the name is changed to 'The Unity Game' the defection rate drops to around 30 per cent. This reveals just how important language and focus are for creating a culture of collaboration and for determining values and outcomes.[23]

The real surprise for us came when we ran the exercise with our university classes not long after we started lecturing at the Central Philippines University on an education development program. Immediately the groups behaved very differently. They interpreted the *you* in the title 'Win as Much as You Can' collectively rather than individually, and they approached the game with a collectivist mindset. It was the first time we had seen everyone collaborate so readily and reach a mutually beneficial outcome so well. The collectivist mindset meant everyone made progress, not just the competitive few, and the whole game was played in a highly collegial atmosphere. They also won more money than any other group we had ever played it with, including CEOs. They didn't need competition to provide the motivation. Motivation came naturally from the desire to see everyone achieve. This approach literally blew us away.

It is easy to see in this game how individual competition and the tendency to defect for potential greater individual gain can impact collective outcomes, particularly in individualistic business contexts. Yet it is possible to find a positive balance through drawing on the collectivist principles that can bring mutual gain.

The power of the collective

After living in the Philippines for a while we had started to appreciate just how deep the collectivist mindset ran. We learned the importance of the word *bayanian*, which literally means 'cooperative endeavour'. It refers to the collectivist approach the Filipinos take when working on projects.

Few countries have experienced such a peaceful transition from dictatorship to democracy as the Philippines did in its 1986 'people's revolution' that ousted the corrupt despot Ferdinand Marcos and brought Cory Aquino to power. The lingering visual memory we have is of tens of thousands of people in yellow t-shirts, a symbol of peace, thronging together in solidarity to pray for a peaceful resolution to the crisis.

We were further struck by just how deep this principle went, when we trekked into the highlands to visit tribal villages who shared their limited resources so willingly, offering us meals when we knew they were struggling to feed their own families. The generous spirit was a moving demonstration of their natural inclination to share what they had for the common good. As we ate one meal, we asked our host how she could afford to be so generous when we knew she had so little. Her response was, 'I would rather eat bananas with my community than feast with kings.'

It occurred to us that some societies inherently understand and live these collective principles, right down to the language they use. The Filipino language Tagalog has two words for 'we': one is a less inclusive interpretation (*kami*, which refers to the speaker and a few other close people but not the listener) and a broader, more collective term (*tayo*, which refers to the speaker and the listener and possibly others). Malaysian and Indonesian also have two words for 'we' that have similar meanings: *kami* and *kita*.

Gotong royong, which literally means 'cooperation in a community' or mutual aid, is a very powerful guiding principle in Indonesia.[24] The principle suggests that everyone in a community must contribute to the community's success. We learned that when there is a wedding or funeral in Bali everyone pitches in to help. When someone's house has been damaged, that person can rely on the village community to contribute to the repairs. When the Balinese celebrate, everyone prepares for the celebration together and enjoys the celebration together. It's not a personality-driven, concert-style event but a focus on the community.

On quite a few occasions we have introduced international corporate groups to Balinese communities to help them learn about these incredible collaborative principles. We have sat CEOs on the bamboo floors of basic huts to listen to the challenges of the poorest of the poor, to learn their secrets to collaborative survival, to see the small space where a large extended family might lie out side-by-side to sleep. We have encouraged corporate groups to participate in local celebrations and feel the energy of a collective commitment. It is rare that a group walks away from this experience without having been deeply moved.

Many other cultures have their own interpretation and indeed their own word for the principle of mutual assistance—for example, *gadugi* (Native American), *talkoot* (Finnish), *harambee* (Kenyan), *imece* (Turkish) and *meitheal* (Irish). Governments in a range of countries have tried to promote the idea of community spirit for 'nation-building' purposes using collective-oriented terms. But rather than using this concept as a means for external *control*, it should instead provide a foundation for *freedom* and *openness*—and the opportunity for authentic collaborative engagement.

This is the point where it is possible to work on finding innovative solutions based on mutual trust. Yet even the concept of trust will need to be clarified to ensure it is completely inclusive.

Trust in the tribe

During the time we lived in Bali we met a rich Indonesian who was part of the corrupt Suharto dictatorship gang. He gave a speech on trust and integrity to a conference group we were working with, emphasising how the Suharto system would bring the country together. The presentation was designed to be an inspiring motivational talk, but we were stunned by the implications. Perhaps it would have been motivational had his own ties with corruption not been so well known, but we found it incredibly disturbing. When we discussed this with another observer, he pointed out that the trust referred to was within the tribe, the powerful Suharto tribe, not outside of it. That created a completely different dynamic. With a lack of security and autonomy, as there was in Indonesia at the time, we could see that real trust in the government in general would be difficult to achieve.

> Trust is a critical social glue for binding individuals together in communities. What many people may not know is that trust has been found to be linked to good governance and high economic performance.

Authentic trust goes way beyond simple reciprocity and is a critical social glue for binding individuals together in communities. The level of trust between leaders and employees has also been found to impact the organisation's ability to take certain technological innovations on board. The stakeholders' sense of what is 'right', 'just' and 'fair' is closely linked to trust, and in turn impacts commitment and innovation.[25] In general, the sort of trust that is based on consistently positive experience built up over time has been found to be linked to good governance and high economic performance.[26]

We mentioned in chapter 5 that the right sort of control can actually assist with the development of trust. Control that is not coercive, but rather is based on a common understanding of agreed values and cultural principles (normative), can help to produce the sort of consistent behaviour that facilitates trust. So where there is a strong sense of purpose and there is buy-in to that purpose (such as through a clear and authentic vision and mission), it is easier to develop trust. What's more, developing strong organisational values and culture can be actively used to help to facilitate what's known as *identification-based trust*, which is an ongoing internalised form of trust built on the individual's personal identification with and connection to the organisation. It is a *purpose-driven* trust, which facilitates purpose-driven innovation.[27]

Within trusting relationships built on strong cultural values, individuals typically freely share knowledge and collaborate to generate new, combined ideas in the process of innovation. Finland (a country considered to be doing well in the current 'innovation race') has been found to have a high level of collaboration between firms. It has been suggested that the US has more recently floundered in innovation when compared to other countries because there has been a failure to keep a strong focus on the sorts of values that engender collaboration and trust.[28]

We all have to trust a large number of people in our daily lives, usually without even realising it. A report from the National Institute for Safety Management in the US found that the average American will trust about 2000 different people a day, most of whom will be strangers.[29] This can include anyone from airline and vehicle safety regulators to food inspectors to elevator maintenance technicians to factory workers and teachers. What is interesting is that we would not usually meet many of the people we have to trust. When you think of it like this, the level of trust we have learned to build up is astounding.

Trust has been found to be linked to economic prosperity.[30] Trade and commerce really flourished in Europe only when standard weights and measures were agreed on, which impacted levels of trust. Once there was a common language and common approaches, trust developed more quickly. Researchers have now found that countries with higher levels of trust (such as Germany, Sweden and the US) have stronger economies than those with a lack of trust (Colombia, Sudan and the Congo at the other extreme).[31]

Countries without trust typically end up trapped in poverty.[32] Extreme poverty, where the focus shifts to individual self-survival, is naturally not conducive to building trust, and so the cycle continues. Where there is no trust there is higher corruption, and conversely when there is more corruption there is less trust.[33] Trust has been found to be essential for the development of 'relational capital'. Once this form of social glue starts to give way and trust diminishes, more resources are devoted to security, detailed contracts and legal proceedings. People also become more anxious and health is impacted.[34]

As was the case with the Suharto crony we met, it has been found that poorer countries do have certain levels of trust, but typically these apply more within their own tribes. Not only has human nature been found to be inherently selfish, but there is also a group bias that supports community development, particularly within our own tribe.[35] While we have a number of mental mechanisms to promote our own interests in competition with our peers, we also have mental mechanisms that help us to promote our own group's interests in competition with other groups. We have interlocking sets of values, norms and practices that help to control self-interest and make cooperative societies possible. Laws like 'Thou shalt not kill' turn out to apply only to our tribe.[36] In the same way, as discussed in the previous chapter, cliques within companies will often build their own set of values and norms to protect their own interests.

> It's time to stop seeing life in terms of tribal boundaries and interests. Our fragile planet is now so interconnected that we need to realise we are all one tribe. By attempting to beat other tribes we may end up destroying ourselves.

Many people and cultures will continue to want to race ahead with innovation, beating others for the sake of the survival of their tribe, which can start with friends and family groups and extend to their socio-economic or cultural group, religion or country. A US Senator and presidential candidate summed up the sense of hopelessness the prisoner's dilemma engenders by arguing there was no point doing anything about climate change when other countries would not make the effort. He also claimed that because the US is a country rather than a planet, America should not feel any responsibility.

It's time to stop seeing life in terms of tribal boundaries and interests. Our fragile planet is now so interconnected that we need to realise we are all one tribe. In our efforts to beat other tribes we may end up destroying not only ourselves and our own tribe, but our planet. Astronomer Carl Sagan writes, 'Human history can be viewed as a slowly dawning awareness that we are members of a larger group. If we are to survive, our loyalties must be broadened further, to include the whole human community, the entire planet Earth.'

Can there be too much of a collectivist approach?

As with all of the paradoxes we have been exploring, it is possible to have too much of a good thing. When it comes to collectivism, there can be a problem if there is too great a focus on collectivism without a respect for individual diversity and autonomy.

Japan, for example, has been found to have developed higher levels of trust and collaboration because restrictions on immigration have limited the impact of rival 'outsiders',[37] and yet some commentators believe their insulated 'monoculture' and lack of trust of outsiders is now impeding their opportunities for economic growth.[38]

For the Philippines, the collectivist orientation has been found to be linked with compliance.[39] So the strong emphasis on maintaining 'smooth interpersonal relationships' may have made the Filipinos more vulnerable to being controlled by dominant defectors. They can also demonstrate a fatalistic attitude that 'tomorrow will look after itself' (*bahala na*, a concept we will explore more in chapter 9). Leaders we have interviewed have recognised that the economic development of the Philippines has actually been held back by the limitations of a combination of collective and fatalistic mindsets.

You need to note here also that a collectivist approach does not guarantee more engagement in the creative process. A study that compared the impact of Japanese and Chinese collectivism on creativity found that while the group enhances the individual creativity and creative outcomes in the case of the Japanese, it can suppress individual creativity for the Chinese.[40]

Ultimately, too great a collectivist focus — particularly if it is externally imposed rather than internally selected — can lead to coercion and control, which is ultimately counterproductive for the innovation process.

> Countries with individualistic cultures have higher rates of innovation and economic growth, while collectivist cultures are more conducive to collective action in the innovation process. So what's the bottom line? We need both!

So what is the bottom line? We need both the individualist's single-mindedness, which can drive innovation forward in a focused way, and the collectivist approach, which can help bring ideas to fruition in the more broadly engaging social context they need to thrive. To ensure the group brings out the best in individuals there needs to be *collaborative engagement*.

Research has shown that industrial urban cultures tend to be individualistic, while traditional agricultural/rural cultures tend to be collectivist.[41] When this is matched with the findings that countries with individualistic cultures have higher rates of innovation and economic growth, while collectivist cultures are more conducive to collective action in the innovation process[42], it's possible to start seeing the individualist vs collectivist quandary.

But is it possible to balance these effectively for better innovation?

Solving the prisoner's dilemma

When researcher Robert Axelrod tried to find a solution to the prisoner's dilemma, he set up a competition for people to submit models to demonstrate if there is a way to really 'win' it. The book he wrote on the topic, *Evolution of Cooperation*, considers the premise, 'Under what conditions will cooperation emerge in a world of egoists without central authority?'

Traditional Balinese rice growers, with their system of mutual respect that didn't allow egoists to dominate, were perhaps exceptional, as the system survived without a central authority. This unusual case gives an important clue to what might work. Countries and companies today may have central authorities to deal with defectors and free-riders, but in the bigger picture of global innovation there is still no central authority. Yet we still need to collaborate. In his foreword to the revised edition of Axelrod's book, ethnologist and evolutionary biologist Richard Dawkins poses three key questions that we believe will need to be answered if we are to ensure sustainable innovation for the future:[43]

- How can a potentially cooperative strategy get an initial foothold in an environment that is predominantly uncooperative?
- What type of strategy can thrive in a diverse environment composed of other individuals using a wide range of more or less sophisticated strategies?
- Under what conditions can such a strategy, once fully established among a group of people, resist invasion by a less cooperative strategy?

These are critical questions that need to be addressed in the 'innovation race'.

There have been plenty of computer models run on the prisoner's dilemma scenario, with the 'tit for tat' strategy being the most effective solution (collaborating in the first round, then following what the other does in the remaining rounds). However, none of these are very innovative solutions, because they all involve 'in the box' thinking. The fascinating book and movie about reality TV, *The Hunger Games,* actually provides an 'outside of the box' alternative.

As we introduced in chapter 4, the dystopian story of *The Hunger Games* is, among other things, a metaphor illustrating the importance of collectivism. When the group compete in the bloodthirsty games as isolated individuals for selfish motives (and for the Capitol's entertainment), the possibility of meaningful achievement is reduced. By playing by the rules, they can hope for material gains (their own life, money and fame), but they lose out on vital collective interests (emancipation of the group). As we shall discover when we unpack the prisoner's dilemma, there are no real winnable solutions.

The answer to this puzzle ends up being to change the rules. The two main characters work together, agreeing that each will take their own life at the same moment rather than kill the other to win. They sacrificially commit themselves to protecting others, in defiance of the rules imposed by the games organisers (and, by extension, of modern psychological and economic expectations). Refusing to be mere pawns, they challenge and change the whole premise of the game.

Let's revisit the 'Win as Much as You Can' game we described earlier, which is based on the principle of the prisoner's dilemma. As a reminder, the game offers mutual financial gains from cooperation, but also allows for the possibility that one player motivated by selfishness can defect, which can lead to everyone defecting. People 'fail' when they treat each other as opposing tribes. The best chance of winning is when there is dialogue, empathy and collaboration. Research has found that when people didn't know each other before the exercise they typically left the room with 21 per cent of the maximum earnings, because they didn't have the chance to develop the trust needed to collaborate successfully. When participants were allowed a single discussion opportunity they achieved 50 per cent of the maximum earnings, and with repeated discussion opportunities they reached 73 per cent. The best result—93 per cent of the maximum earnings—was gained when the groups were able to communicate *and* they were able to develop their own rules. These groups were effectively able to combine the trust needed for collaborative engagement *plus* ensure all individuals benefited.

To come back to the 'buzzers and the bells' example (where people could either wait for a collective payout or defect and ring a bell early to ensure an individual payment), imagine taking part in a discussion on changing the game to stop people defecting. Imagine how different the results might be! How about if the cubicle walls were removed, for example (creating a more open environment)? Or if the bell was disconnected? These creative alternatives reveal how it is possible to come up with more collaborative solutions when we put our minds to it.

Solving the prisoner's dilemma involves creative thinking, which takes us away from a simplistic, dualistic, either/or, 'inside the box' mindset. It probably never occurred to the producers of *The Hunting Party*, who were committed to the concept of a win-or-lose race, but when the Aboriginal people changed the game they might have transitioned the show into a completely different type of show. The Aboriginal Australians couldn't see any purpose in the race, possibly because the idea of such a competition simply was not in their vocabulary, and the start and finish lines were too arbitrary to have any real meaning, so they simply stopped competing. What might have happened if the army and Aboriginal teams had collaborated, combining their considerable skill sets for a greater purpose? This could have been a game-changing approach to innovation, and it's one we will continue to explore through the book. Had they done so, this could have been a prequel not to an *Amazing Race* show, but rather to a collaborative version of Bear Grylls' *Man vs Wild*.

HOW TO WIN THE GAME THEORY CHALLENGE OF THE PRISONER'S DILEMMA[44]

- Recognise/challenge defectors and seek out collaborators to establish a mutually beneficial approach.
- Sideline defectors and free-riders by building a strong culture of collaboration.
- Build up emotional bank accounts to ride on reciprocity and reputation.
- Divide the labour and share the resources and rewards.
- Focus on a goal bigger than the sum of its parts to provide a greater vision.
- Discover healthy competition that enhances performance rather than destructive rivalry.
- Use positive language and quality metaphors that connect rather than divide.

Authentic collaboration — beyond 'tit for tat'

Cooperation must now go beyond a basic strategy of 'tit for tat' or selfish reciprocity. It needs to go deeper to become authentic collaboration. Like the Filipino university students we worked with, perhaps we need to redefine the word *you* when we talk about 'winning'. Perhaps we need to adopt the much more inclusive conception of *we*.

When, six months later, we went back to visit the remote Filipino community we described at the beginning of this chapter, we were dismayed to discover that the move indoors had been maintained over the longer term. What's more, when the children did occasionally come outdoors to play, their games were more violent and competitive, inspired by the kung fu movies they had been watching. It takes a long time for communities to lose their values altogether, but here we saw clear evidence of a rapid transition to the sort of individualism that can undermine collaboration.

Similar scenarios would have played out time and time again in communities all around the world, but it is an evolution that few of us have the opportunity to witness first-hand over such a short time period. The steady erosion of traditional communal values as western culture and technologies invade all corners of the earth is unmistakable. The challenge is how to find a balance between the two systems: how to capture the entrepreneurial energy and drive of individual passion while maintaining the more traditional unifying power of trusting, collaborative communities — how to engender the sort of trust on a large scale that can bind us together at all levels for more sustainable, purpose-driven innovation.

DETOUR
Destructive competition in Cambodia

At Angkor Wat in Cambodia, the past is mysteriously entwined in the present. Gnarled, mossy tree roots wrap themselves around the stone pillars of ancient temples, growing out of the relics of days gone by. When we visited the area we clambered over these enormous roots to delve deep into the mysteries of the past. There was a distinct eerie feeling as we wound through the botanical mazes, trying to imagine what once was.

The Khmer empire was a mighty power in its day. The city of Angkor around the thirteenth century was a thriving metropolis with no apparent threats.[45] Rather than freeways, the city had a complex canal network that stretched from the city centre out to suburban satellites. One reason for the city's eventual collapse was that the canal system silted up because the rulers were too focused on building monuments to properly maintain the public services (think back to chapter 5 and the message of the pride before the fall). Many cities today have similarly failed to anticipate extreme weather conditions caused by climate change, which partly explains the devastation caused by Hurricane Katrina in New Orleans.

The great civilisation of Cambodia was thought to have been rapidly destroyed after the city was plundered. It is now believed, however, that the demise of the city may have had much earlier roots in the elite's greed and corruption. The city appears to have become victim to the sort of destructive self-interest that still plagues modern cities today. History continues to repeat itself.

The greatest lesson seems to have been that the rulers of Angkor pursued their own personal goals at the expense of the communal good, which led to a lack of trust and ultimately the downfall of a once mighty kingdom.

DETOUR
Will robots replace humans in Japan?

While many countries in Asia are embracing technology relatively slowly, Japan has raced ahead. The robotics industry, in particular, has become a huge industry. Robotics factories employ more than 250 000 workers in Japan, a number that is expected to quadruple in the next 15 years.[46] The types of robots that are being developed include human-like androids, robots that assist with mobility and domestic tasks, robots designed for social interaction, robots for security and rescue roles, and robots designed to go into space.

After visiting the home of ASIMO (one of the first 'personal robots') in Tokyo and seeing the robot in action, we were curious to hear from the founder and director of another Japanese company that had produced a similar type of android at a global event we were also speaking at. This man proudly explained to an audience of highly successful entrepreneurs how his company's robot could take over a number of different functions. As he spoke, it was difficult not to think about the potential impact on people, about how advances in technology threatened to make some forms of employment obsolete. As if reading our thoughts, the speaker explained that the use of robots in factory lines would free up people to spend more time on higher-level tasks, and that nothing else would change. Given the country's declining birth rate, very low immigration rates and consequently shrinking workforce, we could see it made sense for the Japanese to be focusing on robotics as a solution for the future. The speaker also focused on how, with an aging population, robots would be able to keep the elderly company and perform some of the physical tasks they had difficulty doing themselves. With a clear focus on sustainable innovation, the man was very convincing.

Despite his careful framing of the issue, however, the first question that came up in question time was from a young American CEO who asked, 'How long will it be till I can sack all my workers and replace them with robots?' The Japanese director looked horrified. It appeared that the thought hadn't even occurred to him. Coming from a collectivist culture, his assumption was that technology would supplement rather than substitute for human capabilities. It was clear that these two people were seeing the technological innovation very differently.

The exchange presented us with an interesting contrast between the individualistic, utilitarian western approach to innovation as an economic benefit, and the more collaborative eastern view of technology as potentially enhancing our social welfare. Technology is not necessarily going to solve the world's problems. We need to ensure that the end goal is not the technology itself, but rather a better, more collaborative outcome.

APPLICATIONS FOR THE ORGANISATION

Application 1: Inspire individual passion.

- The implementation phase of the creative process requires motivation and perseverance, working towards combined outcomes – and yet a high percentage of employees lack motivation.
- Performance (P) is a product of motivation (M) and ability (A): $P = f(M \times A)$
- Two major factors have been found to assist with innovation implementation: individual motivation, and the ability to gain buy-in through relationships, or networking ability.
- Geniuses don't just rely on high IQ; they are also often highly creative and highly motivated.
- The 'tournament' competitive approach, where winning means making others lose, does appear to motivate workers, *but* there can be a cost in less collaboration.

There comes a time when the rubber needs to hit the road. In order to keep testing and trialling different possibilities, and to find and apply solutions, it is important to be able to push potential ideas through to practical implementation. This is the part of the process—the *solve and apply* stage—that is most likely to fail or to be neglected. It is where convergent thinking rather than divergent thinking becomes the focus, where the 'closed' action strategy of knowledge integration takes over from the 'open' strategy of knowledge generation.

The implementation phase of the creative thinking and problem-solving process requires a great deal of perseverance and motivation, along with a willingness to work towards a unified outcome. The transition from idea to implementation involves two significant factors: individual motivation and the ability to develop strong relationships.[47] The motivation to engage in idea implementation is referred to as *implementation instrumentality*, and the ability to gain buy-in through developing social relationships is referred to as *networking ability*.

A passion for the issues and for finding solutions is a critical first factor for success. Individual motivation has been shown to be a critical factor in idea implementation. Motivational psychologist Victor Vroom developed a popular formula for this in which performance (P) is a product of motivation (M) and ability (A)[48]:

$$P = f(M \times A)$$
$$\text{Performance (P)} = f(\text{Motivation} \times \text{Ability})$$

Research has found that those who generate variety and are able to come up with a number of different ideas, typically corporate founders and entrepreneurs, are often individualistic. This stage in the innovation process requires individual initiative and creativity. The next stage of the process, however, requires leveraging resources to come up with solutions, and this depends on efficient relationships that require a collectivist mindset.[49]

Contrary to popular perception, the achievements of 'geniuses' correlate most closely not with IQ, but with the ability to think creatively and the willingness to *persevere*. They are highly motivated. A study of 1500 children with extremely high IQs aimed to identify whether they would eventually become geniuses.[50] Two Nobel Laureates did not have high enough IQs to make it into this study; they had instead relied on that combination of creativity and perseverance to reach their goals. An Australian Nobel Prize winner, Barry Marshall, has demonstrated the importance of this sort of creative passion. Marshall believed that stomach ulcers were linked to bacteria rather than stress, but he was not permitted to conduct studies on humans. He was so confident in his theory that he decided to drink a batch of specially prepared bacteria himself to test the outcomes. Through this act of sheer determination he proved that the bacteria did in fact cause an ulcer, and that certain antibiotics could be used to cure it.

Although motivation has been found to be critically important for success in life and work, research has revealed that more than 50 per cent of employees lack the motivation to continue learning and improving in their jobs.[51] An Australian study of 23 firms found that where companies offer substantial pay rises to try to increase motivation and engagement, they do succeed in getting people to engage in the job more, but these workers also become more selfish (for example, not sharing tools) to protect their newfound success. The 'tournament' competitive approach, where winning means others lose, does appear to motivate workers, *but* there can be a cost in reduced collaboration. Tournament-style motivation means assessing whether each individual worker's efforts to improve performance will have a more significant overall benefit than its potentially negative impact on collaboration.[52]

Application 2: Enable collaborative engagement.

- Star performers aren't just individual achievers with high motivation—they also collaborate better.
- Perhaps there should be other elements to Vroom's formula—greater engagement from collaboration: $P + E = f(M \times A) + C$
- Encouraging motivation through individual financial reward can be counterproductive; instead reward collaborative teams.
- Recognising collaborative teams can lead to higher engagement and therefore more productivity.

The 'star performers' in an organisation—those who will throw themselves into their work as high achievers without external motivation—can outperform their peers by working to the level of three average people, and can give back to their company 88 times their salary.[53] Contrary to expectations, though, while star performers are highly motivated individually, they are not individualistic. They are, in fact, highly collaborative.

Highly motivated individuals will become collectively engaged when the collaborative actions of teams are supported and rewarded. According to a Right Management survey of almost 30 000 employees from a broad range of industries internationally, engagement is critical for organisational effectiveness.[54] Engaged employees have been found to be 50 per cent more productive and 33 per cent more profitable than non-engaged employees. Engagement impacts a number of different areas of organisational performance, including customer satisfaction, profitability, loyalty, quality and innovation. Yet the study also found that only one in three employees is actively engaged in their work, with that number dropping to one in ten in Japan.

> While 'star performers' are highly motivated individually, they are not individualistic. They are, in fact, highly collaborative.

Here we're going to use a little licence to add some ideas to Vroom's formula. We'd like to suggest that the ideal outcome might not be just performance (P) but performance *plus* engagement (E). We'd also like to suggest that superior outcomes require not only individual motivation and ability, but also a collective, collaborative mindset (C). So an adjusted version of the formula with these principles included might look something like this:

$$P + E = f(M \times A) + \mathbf{C}$$

Performance (P) + Engagement (E) = f(Motivation + Ability) + Collaboration (C)

Let's consider how we can introduce that collaborative mindset in the western business context to help balance the individualistic drive that is typically already present.

Application 3: Harness basic human drives.

- Creating teams with distinctive identities and purposes can help to meet the need to belong and foster collaborative engagement.
- Rewarding team achievement rather than individual achievement can foster a spirit of collaboration rather than competition (e.g. stockbroker teams).
- Involving individuals in the process of identifying and implementing the organisation vision and mission will build unity.

Identifying the keys to engagement will involve tapping into the basic drives and motivations of individuals.

Here's something to consider in this light: What do food and sex have in common? They are more closely related than you might initially think! Did you work it out? Food and sex are two of the most primal human drives, and they are also, perhaps surprisingly, the motivating factors behind a lot of behaviours, including collaboration. Both are necessary for survival: one contributes to physical survival over the short term, and one contributes to survival as a species over the long term. They are human experiences that are common across all cultures, as they have been throughout human history.

Since at least the Stone Age the stronger men could bring in more or better meat and attract women sexual partners more easily. Like the drive for sex, the drive for food also led to more collaboration. People needed to collaborate to hunt for large sources of meat, so hunger may in fact have helped to promote collaboration. This is true for a number of different, apparently individualistic drives.

Consider other drives that may be more relevant to the workplace: the drive for belonging, for achievement or for self-fulfilment (working our way up through Maslow's hierarchy of needs). These, too, can be effectively utilised and harnessed for the collective good. So creating teams with distinctive identities and purposes can help to meet the need to belong and foster collaborative engagement. Rewarding team achievement rather than individual achievement can encourage a spirit of collaboration rather than competition. Involving individuals in the process of identifying and implementing the organisation's vision and mission will build unity.

Consider also the all-consuming drive for money as a supposed means to reach self-fulfilment and happiness. We have been able to see the impact of this potentially more destructive drive in stockbroking groups we have worked with. In stockbroking, if one individual goes for the quick trade, he or she may gain the fast bucks in the short term, but there is the risk of damaging the reputation of the team and/or the company over the long term. This can set off a chain reaction, with each individual stockbroker out for themselves, creating a dog-eat-dog culture.

When we were once called in to assist with a particularly challenging cross-cultural stockbroker team based in Japan, we soon discovered the 'team' was made up of individualist mercenaries, most of whom had been brought to Japan as expats from a number of different countries. They were obviously planning to make their millions before the lifestyle burned them out. These expats were ruthless, highly competitive and completely focused on making money at all costs in contrast to the more relationship-orientated Japanese members of the team. The jobs were so high powered and so well paid that a first-class trip to Aspen for a skiing weekend was considered a standard way to unwind for a few days!

We started our work with this group by giving them a nice academic model showing the need for collaboration. We had some good discussions around this in a morning workshop session, but in the afternoon the leader had organised for the group to play paintball. Immediately they switched into an aggressive, competitive mode that torpedoed any discussion of collaboration. They all cheated so much that it ended in a brawl. Afterwards some of the traders shared with us how common it was for an individual to go in for the quick, short-term profit at the expense of relationships that their colleagues had built up with the banks over the long term, and at the expense of the relationships they themselves had built up with their colleagues. The paintball aptly reflected the reality of their situation: they walked into the office each day ready to do battle, not only with the market but also with each other.

We were able to frame some exercises to enable the 'team' to discover these issues for themselves, and they soon came up with a simple but highly impactful modification to their work environment: they decided to move their desks—which had been facing outwards and away from each other—to form one central table with a shared focus. This simple adjustment encouraged them to collaborate more effectively, and along with significantly increasing their collaboration and engagement they eventually tripled their revenue as a team. They made a conscious choice to shift from a strongly individualistic mindset towards a more collective approach, and the results were outstanding.

Application 4: Balance competition and collaboration.

- Cooperation, commitment and trust have been found to be the top qualities exemplified by the 100 Best Companies, yet business teams are commonly more competitive than collaborative.
- The human ability to collaborate in large numbers and be flexible sets us apart from the animal kingdom.
- The most collaborative teams in organisations are those that debate ideas openly rather than competing.
- Balance the individual drive for competition with the need for collaboration.
- Trust should be understood and modelled in the organisation at all levels.
- Combine different individual preferences in the creative process.

The organisation Great Place to Work has identified the top qualities exemplified by the 100 Best Companies. Of these qualities, cooperation, commitment and trust (they define trust as credibility, respect and fairness) come out as a major factors for success. Yet business teams (like the stockbrokers) are commonly more competitive than collaborative. They may try to maintain the appearance of being a cohesive team while conducting turf wars behind the scenes.[55] This obviously impacts team performance, productivity, engagement—and ultimately innovation.

At one time Sony dominated the market for small music player devices, then they lost their lead to Apple. So what happened? For a number of years Sony had thrived with a highly competitive culture. Engineers were encouraged to outdo each other rather than work together on projects. Yet while this had worked well for some standalone products they had produced in the past, it was destructive when it came to newer projects requiring collaboration among different divisions. As an example, Connect, Sony's version of iTunes, relied on five Sony divisions in both the US and Japan that typically worked in competing silos.[56] Since the organisation was set up to compete rather than collaborate, the project was soon floundering.[57]

Perhaps we can find inspiration in the animal kingdom. Bats, for example, can actually learn how to build a culture of collaboration.[58] Because they tend to roost in the same places for long periods of time (as long as 18 years), they get to know each other individually. And they learn that by feeding themselves without contributing food to the community they may do well individually, but they will impact the welfare of the group over the long term. The only scenario in which all bats do well is when they feed each other. Baboons, as another example, will reject new members who try to come into the group if those new members don't appear to be collaborative — or they will insist that new members change to become more collaborative. This could be seen as reciprocity (tit for tat), but at a deeper level, when examining long-term sustainability that recognises the mutual gains from cooperation, 'trust' might be a better word.

> Baboons will reject new members who try to come into the group if those new members don't appear to be collaborative — or they will insist that new members change to become more collaborative.

You may remember that in chapter 2 we raised the question as to why humans have innovated more than other animal species, and we discovered it was related to our ability to be flexible, along with our ability to *collaborate in large numbers*.[59] So while a swarm of bees can collaborate successfully, they do not have the flexibility that humans have. If we were able to harness this capability more successfully we would have a very powerful basis for sustainable innovation.

One central New Guinean tribe devised a new version of football that ensured a collaborative approach when the relations between tribes could be so aggressive and alliances so unstable.[60] In this version the game is played until both teams have won the same number of goals. There is no direct losing team and everyone who scores a goal is considered to be a winner.

It has been found that the most creative teams in an organisation are those who have the confidence to share and debate ideas openly rather than competing for recognition and holding back ideas for themselves.[61]

So what do collaboration and trust look like in the organisation? Trust can be described as *credibility* (including a sense of respect and fairness) + *reliability* + *intimacy*. Where individuals are authentic and have integrity, they develop credibility. Where they have shown themselves to be consistently reliable over time, they develop reliability. And where they open up and allow themselves to become vulnerable to others, they can develop intimacy. Where these qualities are understood and modelled in the organisation at all levels it is possible to build a culture of trust, which in turn will support collaboration for innovation.

Application 5: Utilise collaborative expertise.

- Practise working through different potential solutions.
- Combine individual motivation and group relationships to push through to implementation.
- Innovations typically result from a systematic collective approach.
- Interdependent players need a common belief in a future vision.
- Three key approaches appear to help individuals and groups manage some of the paradoxes of belonging (autonomy vs unity): maintaining a focus on the task; valuing differences; and reducing power distance.

When Kennedy launched the national effort to land an American on the moon a huge amount of coordination was required to pull together the 400 000 people involved in the project, which of course included the important Apollo 10 dress-rehearsal mission we examined in chapter 4. Moreover, Kennedy's ambition was to achieve this goal by the end of the decade, so the pressure was on. NASA space teams that had previously been focusing on an Earth orbit adjusted to come into alignment with Kennedy's vision and complete a lunar orbit instead. Other teams focused on manned spacecraft did the same. We all know the result of that goal!

Creative thinking and the potential for growth can become stifled by the greater desire to protect and maintain a specific position. Visionary teams and organisations, on the other hand, focus on bettering their own position rather than on trying to beat the competition. Success can be a natural by-product of that, but it is not the end goal. As we have discussed, innovations typically result from a systematic collective approach.[62]

When implementing innovative ideas, it is difficult for an individual entrepreneur to get significant results without a collaborative focus. Unified and coordinated action is required for high-level system change. To achieve this, the interdependent players need a common belief in the future vision.[63] For example, members of successful string quartets have been found to be aware of and manage well the paradoxical tension between their desire for personal autonomy, on the one hand, and the need for clear leadership to unify the group, on the other.[64]

So how do you help to move independent elements towards a unified collaborative outcome? Researchers have identified three key approaches that appear to help individuals and groups manage some of the paradoxes of belonging (individualism vs engagement): maintaining a focus on the task, valuing differences and reducing power distance.[65]

As an example of how this sort of unity can be achieved, some companies that are usually arch-competitors have decided to band together to develop semiconductor technology.[66] Companies such as TI, Intel, Motorola and AMD have come together in this way after considering the market opportunities. Pharmaceutical companies have also contributed their proprietary R&D work, which is usually a highly competitive space, recognising that this may help in getting a drug to market faster.

Thomas Malone, an MIT Sloan School professor, has attempted to bring together the best minds to help solve global problems in a systematic way through the Center for Collective Intelligence. In the Climate Collaboratorium, which is a web-mediated discussion and decision-making forum that is a part of the centre, the 'best minds' are working together to try to solve global climate change issues.[67] 'To solve the climate problem,' Malone says, 'we need a huge range of expertise. We've got to know things about the physics of the upper atmosphere and the chemistry of the oceans and the economics of carbon taxes and the psychology of consumers who are making decisions about when to drive versus take public transportation. Collective intelligence mechanisms are ideal for bringing together those diverse kinds of knowledge.'

Application 6: Recognise complementary contributions to the creative process.

- The innovative team recognises the different creative skills and abilities each individual brings to each stage of the creative process.
- Businesses need to develop ecosystems to support collaboration around new innovations.

The innovative team recognises the different creative skills and abilities each individual brings and seeks to harness these effectively to reach a unified goal. The FourSight tool, developed by the head of the International Center for Studies and Creativity, Dr Gerard Puccio,[68] and based on the Creative Problem Solving (CPS) model introduced by Osborne and Parnes,[69] has identified different preferences individuals tend to have in the creative thinking and problem-solving process.

First, according to this model, there is the Clarifier, who is good with detail and is able to focus on specifying the challenge. The Clarifier will ask a lot of questions and ensure that the process is kept on track (this relates to the ENQUIRE process from our PDI model). Next, the Ideator will be the one who can come up with the most diverse ideas. They will have no trouble with the brainstorming process (EXPLORE). The Developer will work on these ideas, following different potential pathways to see which ideas might work best (SOLVE). The Implementer will then take the process through to completion, ensuring there are practical applications from the process (APPLY).

> The innovative team recognises the different creative skills and abilities each individual brings and seeks to harness these effectively to reach a unified goal.

Pixar, which we introduced in chapter 5 as a company that is able to empower with guidance, is also a great example of how an organisation can harness the collective creativity of the team. Professor Linda Hill, who researched Pixar and other similar companies over a decade, found that, 'Innovation is not about solo genius ... it takes about 250 people four to five years ... You have to unleash the talents and passions of many people and you have to harness them ... [it's] a type of collaborative problem solving, usually among people who have different expertise and different points of view.'[70]

At the next level, organisations need to collaborate more effectively with other organisations. Rather than seeing the business as a single individual entity and keeping the focus internal, a company should see itself as part of an ecosystem that crosses a variety of companies and industries. 'In a business ecosystem,' says business strategist James Moore, 'companies co-evolve capabilities around a new innovation: They work cooperatively and competitively to support new products, satisfy customer needs, and eventually incorporate the next round of innovations.'[71]

By creating an open organisation culture, individuals can be encouraged to develop collaborative behaviours that foster both the incremental and the radical innovation practices needed for transformational innovation.[72] They will also have greater incentive if they can draw on shared interests, goals and values, and see the ultimate benefit for all — which enables purpose-driven innovation.[73] If the process is well coordinated, it is possible to see how individual passions can pull together for a unified creative purpose.

Many of us are living in a 'tragedy of the commons' without realising it, competing every day for limited resources without thinking about how we could be sharing resources for mutual benefit, through developing trust. Our systems are too often set up to encourage defection, or at best a shallow reciprocity of tit for tat (reciprocated altruism or punishment).

Yet here's an irony: if we create too much of a collaborative system we become vulnerable both to defectors dominating it and to free-riders taking advantage of it. To achieve true collaboration there needs to be a deeper engagement in the individual and in the culture of the organisation. Because we operate so individually, we fail to recognise the richness of the community that supports us.

Our societies would fall apart without the level of collaboration and trust we all rely on. We often fail to consider how our society has been designed to support us in our daily lives and work. For example, our children can think that milk simply comes in cartons from the supermarket, with no appreciation of how farmers milk cows in the countryside. Similarly, in business, despite our dependence on intricately interwoven networks to support us, we still assume that our survival needs the focus to be on the individual.

We watched the shift from collectivism to individualism within a single week on that remote beach in the Philippines. We saw a similar transition over about a decade in Bali when the farmers started to sell their arable land for foreign tourist ventures. We saw how a shift of focus and power can tip the balance away from community, how for the Balinese the temptation of selling the rice paddies to make more money became too great. We have also seen how, in the case of a small group of stockbrokers, the balance can be shifted back.

CHAPTER SUMMARY

How to motivate individuals and teams to come up with unified solutions

Navigating the path between individualism and engagement

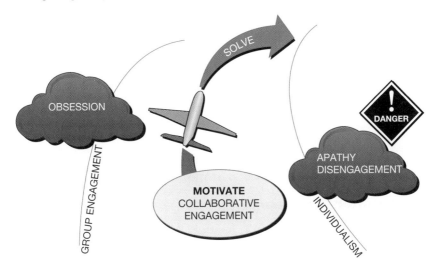

Key principles from the journey

Recognise the impact of modern individualism.

- Traditional communal engagement is being supplanted by the individualism of modern influences (e.g. through technology).
- The tension between individualism and collectivism is a typical contrast between East and West.
- We need to ensure that the end goal of innovation is not individual modernisation, but rather a means to combine individual passions for a more collaborative and sustainable end (e.g. *The Hunger Games*, development of robots in Japan).
- Balancing competition (individual drive to achieve) and collaboration (working together for the communal good) will be essential to future collective development (e.g. lessons from Angkor, Bali and *The Hunger Games*).

To balance individualistic objectives and the need for collectivist engagement, build trust in the broader tribe.

- Trust is the catalyst for the shift from pure individuality to community (e.g. the way trust developed in Europe after common measures were agreed on).
- Trust has been found to be linked with good governance and high economic performance.
- Trust breaks down when people take advantage of communal efforts and 'free-ride'.
- Trust and commitment need to go beyond our immediate tribe to the broader human community (e.g. Suharto story).
- We need to develop moral guidelines to engender cooperation and collaboration in the wider community (e.g. the tragedy of the commons).
- We should work from a foundation of freedom (e.g. the need for China to explore principles of democracy to support innovation).

Applications summary:

1. Inspire individual passion (case study: Nobel Laureates).
2. Enable collaborative engagement.
3. Harness basic human drives (case study: Stockbroking Company).
4. Balance competition and collaboration (case study: Sony).
5. Utilise collaborative expertise (case studies: NASA, Center for Collective Intelligence).
6. Recognise complimentary contributions to the creative process (case study: Pixar).

CHECKPOINT SUMMARY CHECKLIST
How to foster engagement through trialing practical solutions to challenges

Paradox synthesis: Collaborative Engagement

Is there a balance in your organisation between supporting individual activity and ensuring group engagement and unity?

INDIVIDUALISM

The motivation for actively pursuing potential solutions

Is there evidence of individual passion and purpose?

☐	**Purpose**	There is the sense that people have a purpose in the work they do and that they are working towards constructive goals.
☐	**Motivation**	People continually pursue interests and passions.
☐	**Drive**	Employees consistently initiate projects and see them through to completion.
☐	**Opportunity to disconnect & reconnect**	There is the opportunity to disconnect from old, habitual ways of doing things in order to find fresh new solutions.

ENGAGEMENT

Disciplined engagement in the process as a team

Do individuals feel that they have a common vision and are working towards a common goal to find the best solutions?

☐	**Vision**	There is a commitment to the vision and values of the organisation.
☐	**Retention**	Individuals believe in the organisation and are committed to it over the long term.
☐	**Trust**	Individuals believe in and trust each other.
☐	**Support**	People feel supported in the work they do.
☐	**Satisfaction**	Individuals indicate significant work satisfaction.
☐	**Engagement**	There is voluntary involvement in higher-level projects and activities.

(continued)

☐	**Connection**	People actively connect with each other.
☐	**Cooperation**	There is an atmosphere of non-threatening cooperation when developing new ideas.
☐	**Building**	Individuals build on others' ideas in order to achieve the best outcomes.
☐	**Collaboration**	People actively collaborate with each other to achieve common goals.

TRY THIS

How to ensure individual needs and passions are addressed

- Undertake personality / behaviour profiling to identify individual strengths.
- Profile positions to match individuals with their most ideal jobs.
- Hold regular reviews to check individual goal setting and progress.

How to ensure group engagement

- Involve the group in setting the vision and mission.
- Identify and deal with defectors and free-riders.
- Analyse employee retention information to understand why people are or are not staying with the organisation.
- Run employee satisfaction surveys.
- Put in place strong support structures for individuals.
- Practice facilitative leadership.
- Facilitate regular social events.

How to build collaboration

- Set ground rules for discussions and innovation sessions.
- Encourage people to build on others' ideas in innovation sessions.
- Set up teams to work on projects.
- Reward teams rather than individuals.

Preparing for the next mode

We've seen so far that we need *guided freedom* as a foundation for fresh innovation (chapter 5), and that we need *targeted openness* through diversity and connectedness to develop novel ideas (chapter 6), and in this chapter we have identified the value of *collaborative engagement* for working through to solutions. But there is one more stage to ensuring leaders can create a culture of innovation that drives deep into the human psyche, fundamentally challenging our beliefs and mindsets, and that impacts the way we interpret and understand the world around us and our position in it.

This transformational mindset will be the decisive factor in determining whether solutions translate into valuable purpose-driven innovations, and whether these innovations will enable us to stay in the race.

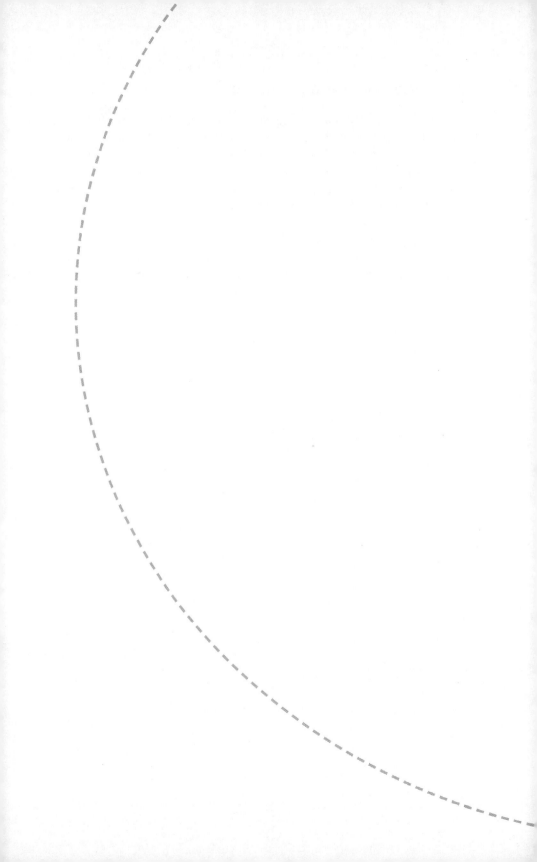

8

TRANSFORM

How to transform a culture for implementing innovation

Destination: The Americas

Paradox: Stability vs Flexibility

Synthesis: Grounded Flexibility

In this chapter we will have the opportunity explore the path between stability and flexibility, facing at one extreme the potential danger zone of rigidity from pessimism and/or fatalism, and at the other extreme the potential danger of a lack of reality and an inability to implement. We will learn how to plan and navigate a route through grounded flexibility that will create a culture to best fuel innovation.

Key challenge: How to build both resilience and reliability through 'grounded flexibility'.

We are on an expedition to take Hollywood star Val Kilmer surfing, flying down the freeway with the windows down and a warm spring wind tossing our hair every which way. A native of Los Angeles, Val is best known for a string of popular films including *Batman Forever*, *Top Gun*, *The Saint*, *The Doors* and *Heat*. Val had decided he would like to write a movie about surfing, and he wanted to brush up on his skills and immerse himself in the surfing culture a little more. He had been connected to us for that purpose.

We ended up spending some time with Val and his girlfriend, playing tennis, having dinner and generally hanging out with a surfing crowd, as well as taking him on a few surfing expeditions to help him get into the right mode. Like a true artist, Val would become a recluse for a few days, mulling over ideas, then suddenly announce he was ready to *do something*. He would swing around in his car to pick us up and off we'd go, Val hanging his head out the window, shooting the breeze and watching the scenery pass by as we combed the coast for the best surf, in his element with the wind blasting his face.

In the water Val struggled to regain his surfing ability, pushing himself through wave after wave to try to improve his skills. On one particular expedition a forbidding-looking black cloud hung over the horizon, but Val was keen to go ahead anyway. It wasn't long before heavy rain and lightning struck with a vengeance. We didn't want to be known as the people who had led Val Kilmer to his death so we urged him to leave the water, but he was determined to keep going until he got his technique right. When he finally left the water it was in the nick of time, just before a dramatic lightning bolt hit the water frighteningly close.

It became clear to us just how driven Val was. He would immerse himself in the experience to reach his end goal of making the movie. His singular focus and unbounded energy that kept him going through the challenges gave us an insight into his success. It reminded us how although many people might assume that success comes easy for some people, inevitably it is optimistic determination, sweat and incredible resilience to keep trying and trying again that leads to success.

This is arguably the essence of the American spirit: the confidence to decide on a goal and the energy to push through to its completion. The American Dream, a national ethos, is built on many of the principles we have been exploring: freedom, openness, passion—and a broad and flexible optimism. Spending time with an optimistic American who has had a successful career encouraged us to think about how it is possible to convert great ideas into action: how to ensure the sort of idealistic optimism that seeds great ideas does not remain a pipe dream but instead is converted into positive, practical outcomes. This is the basis of the sort of culture change needed to support the final critical stage of the innovation process: *innovation implementation*.

The implementation challenge

When it comes to the crunch, you can have all the great ideas in the world, but if they are not translated into action they will never come to fruition as innovations. This is where many organisations fail in the innovation process. Curiosity, imagination and ideation are only a small first part of the innovation process: after the divergent thinking 'open action mode', all these ideas need to come together into practical solutions and achievable actions.

This is the convergent thinking 'closed action mode' that channels energy with a laser-like focus into the final outcomes.

For the conversion of structured applications to practical implementation, once all the problems have been ironed out following the testing and prototyping phase, it is important to ensure the culture change process is cemented at all levels to support the innovation. This TRANSFORM stage ensures all the purpose-driven innovation strategies are being put into practice for long-term sustainable change. This is not just window-dressing; it needs to be the real deal to ensure authenticity is maintained and cynicism doesn't set in. It involves a deep values shift for genuine change.

Take a look at *Who Killed Creativity?*, paying particular attention to 'Strategy 6: Explore different paths' and 'Strategy 7: Embrace optimism' for practical ideas and exercises to assist with navigating this implementation phase successfully.

Purpose-Driven Innovation (PDI) in action: TRANSFORM

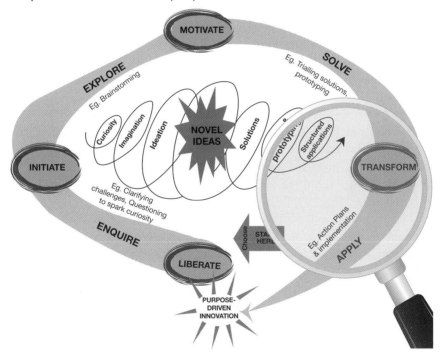

As we travel through North America before journeying south to the South American continent for contrast, it becomes clear how principles of optimism and flexibility balanced with a grounded stability can lead to a powerful resilience, which helps to navigate a path through the challenges of the implementation phase. These principles can be difficult to balance effectively, however.

Let's start by exploring the opportunities and obstacles this mindset can lead to in this potentially game-changing transformation stage.

Unpacking the American Dream

The US is a prolific patent producer and has strong copyright laws to protect innovations, which has encouraged innovative growth. In this chapter we are going to explore the mindset that may have contributed to US success in innovation—the optimism that has kept the country buoyant through the challenges.

Nate Silver summarises the distinctly American link between self-belief, self-determinism and innovation well when he says, 'If there is one thing that defines Americans—one thing that makes us exceptional—it is our belief in Cassius's idea that we are in control of our own fates ... Most of our strengths and weaknesses as a nation—our ingenuity and our industriousness, our arrogance and our impatience—stem from our unshakable belief in the idea that we choose our own course.'[1]

For many Americans freedom is built on opportunity and passion, and the resolution to follow through to see where opportunities lead. According to the American Dream you can be whoever you want to be—and Hollywood can help you get there! This is the pioneering approach that defined the first European settlers and the equal determination with which the indigenous Americans tried to deal with the pioneers. (It's interesting to note that Kilmer is himself part Cherokee, so perhaps an interesting blend of both perspectives.)

The central belief behind the American Dream—that everyone has the opportunity to achieve whatever they want to achieve—has been challenged by economic crises, yet Americans have remained upbeat about the possibilities. A survey found that, overall, Americans are satisfied with their lives and optimistic about their future.[2] In contrast, in many societies your path is mapped out for you before you are born, and it can be difficult to imagine, let alone hope for, a different future. In many cases you will be born into a class and have a pre-established role in life (a predestined fate), so a shoemaker's son is destined to become a shoemaker, a girl destined for the role of wife and mother, a beggar's child destined to become a beggar. Yet in the US you are told you can be whoever you want to be and become whatever you want to become. One senator has described the country as consisting of 'haves' and 'soon to haves' (in contrast to the usual term comparing the 'haves' and the 'have nots'). This is a uniquely optimistic contemporary perspective that may be influencing the persistent pursuit of innovation.

Yet the US is also facing some major challenges and could be falling behind, according to recent OECD results, while other countries are fast catching up — at least in the technological race.[3] We have already mentioned Japan as a strong contender; Taiwan, Korea, China and India are also rapid-growth markets that are racing ahead. John Doerr, a well-known venture capitalist with a Silicon Valley firm describes the sort of transition that has been taking place: 'When our company shifted our attention to clean energy, we found the innovation cupboard was close to bare. My partners and I found [that] the best fuel cells, the best energy storage and the best wind technology were all born outside of the United States.'[4]

Among the challenges the US is currently facing is the fact that innovation may not be translating to economic growth and employment.[5] This could be explained by the fact that the US has been identified as focusing more on ideas than processes, which are just as important in the innovation process. As we have already identified, Americans seem to be good at ideation, which requires a great deal of optimism, but to also focus on the follow-through required to push ideas through to implementation it will be essential to develop a deep, grounded resilience too.[6] Additionally, research universities, which have been an essential foundation of the innovation ecosystem, are now facing severe financial restraints, and the country is less welcoming to skilled immigrants than it once was (which means the country could be losing out on the value of diversity and connections).[7]

The essence of the entrepreneurial spirit

Thinking back over what we have covered so far, it's possible to see how these principles could be contributing factors to America's apparent decline. With less emphasis on pushing through ideation to implementation, with less investment in collaborative development, less diversity and fewer connections (by being less welcoming to immigrants), innovation will simply not have the conditions needed for growth.

One problem could be that the US, compared with other industrial nations, has less of an overarching innovation strategy to coordinate and support individual initiatives.[8] Has the US reached the point where it is now relying on an optimistic and flexible entrepreneurial spirit rather than a strategic plan? Paradoxically, as American Nobel Laureate economist Elinor Ostrom has commented, the opportunities for entrepreneurship that complexity can provide may have carried the US innovation system this far. Ostrom has extensively documented the adaptive advantages of the type of open, institutionally diverse systems the US has had over linear-designed systems, which helps to explain the successful development to this point.[9]

It is interesting to consider the contrasting approaches of the US and Singapore. While we discussed how the Singaporean people we spoke to were hesitant to describe themselves as innovative but attributed the country's innovative position to the government, the American people might describe themselves as innovative and believe themselves to be innovative, but this isn't necessarily coming from a strategic government plan. So perhaps America's past success in innovation may have been due to the optimistic and resilient mindset that individuals in the country seem to have developed. Or contrast the US with Japan. While, as we have discussed, Japan has been successful in technological innovation due to a strong iterative approach and a high commitment to follow-through, the US appears to have relied on the ability to ideate well. The strongest qualifications for surviving the innovation race could be a combination of individualistic optimism and ideation, supporting government strategy and a high commitment to follow-through.

How do we convert the kind of idealistic optimism that generates novel ideas into a grounded strategic focus that will lead to long-term success? We need to dig deeper to identify the foundation of optimism: is it built on vague dreams and hopes, or is it grounded in a more realistic position that will enable flexible action? Where does it undermine long-term sustainability (for example, if built on ideals but not grounded), and where does it contribute to sustainable purpose-driven innovation and development over the long term?

> How do we convert the kind of idealistic optimism that births novel ideas into a grounded strategic focus that will lead to long term success?

Perhaps we need to define *optimism* better to see what aspect of optimism will lead to 'can do' implementable innovation and what might be more of an explanatory mindset to cope with life's problems.

It is worth taking a quick trip back through history to pick up on a few interesting illustrations of how the country has had an optimistic mindset and innovative focus.

From cultivators to innovators

When Columbus arrived in America stories of the ingenious inventions of the Indigenous peoples started to spread in Europe. These people had developed early versions of such popular contemporary products as: hypodermic needles (they used sharpened hollowed bird bones attached to small bladders to inject medicines, irrigate wounds and clean ears); baby bottles and formula (with a dried bear intestine as the bottle, a bird quill as a nipple, and pounded nuts, meat and water as the formula); pest control methods (such as ground buffalo gourd to repel garden pests and burned lemon verbena to protect crops); and bunk beds (which apparently are not an original Swedish invention courtesy of Ikea!).

Most of the early European settlers arrived from England after 1600 in search of famed riches, and they were welcomed by the Native American people, who shared their traditional wisdom and taught them how to survive. But the Europeans brought with them their foreign industrial ways and dangerous diseases, and it wasn't long before the lives of the Indigenous people were disrupted. The ordeals of the Indigenous Americans after white settlement were not dissimilar to those of many indigenous peoples around the globe, including the Indigenous Australians. No doubt these people would have had a different perspective on 'progress' and the sort of 'developments' that technological innovations can bring.

Skip a few centuries forward, and by the time millions of immigrant workers and farmers arrived from Europe during the twentieth century, boosting the workforce and the economy, the US was well on its way to becoming the world's leading industrial power.

It was this climate of openness to diversity and new connections that enabled new ideas to flourish. The rapid growth in population, however, led to a number of social problems that challenged the quest for liberty and equality. Americans had to think creatively and to focus on innovation and technological development to try to solve these problems. This led to a collaborative focus on finding solutions, which was another major stepping stone in innovation success.

For example, the spectacular growth of New York's population throughout the 1800s threw up a range of public health challenges, not least of which was the disease and stench related to overwhelming volumes of horse dung. By the 1890s the streets were crammed with up to 100 000 horse-drawn carriages producing more than a million kilograms of horse manure *every day*.[10] The crisis exposed the need for major technological innovations—and led to the acceleration of the mass production of a new, affordable 'automobile', Henry Ford's Model T. Meanwhile, the city of Chicago came up with another creative solution. Engineers used 'jack screws' to hoist up the whole city, building by building, block by block.[11] Only in a climate of strong optimism would someone have had the confidence to propose such a bizarre project!

This action not only enabled the city literally to rise above the street muck, but because Chicago was a flat city it gave them the opportunity to build sewerage pipes on an angle so sewage could drain successfully. The concept also led to a revolution in building beneath the city, with underground trains, pedestrian walkways, water and sewerage pipes, and electrical cables forming complex subterranean systems.

By the time French politician Alexis de Tocqueville arrived in America in 1831, the unusually positive attitude of the nation was already apparent. Tocqueville saw democracy as a simple equation: a balance between liberty and equality, with a focus on both individual and community. He believed this was the foundation for a successful society and contrasted it to the fading aristocratic traditions in France. Tocqueville noted with interest the quality of optimism he found among the Americans he encountered in his travels—which may have been both due to and/or a shaping force in the drive for democracy.[12]

The world's most optimistic country?

'Americans have all a lively faith in the perfectibility of man ... They all consider society as a body in a state of improvement.'

Alexis de Tocqueville, a French observer of American life in 1831

Visitors to the United States throughout its subsequent history have continued to comment on this quality of comparative optimism, and recent research has confirmed it.[13] Americans seem to have a greater hope for their future than their counterparts in other developed countries.

Despite the recessions and terrorism fears, and the setbacks that have come with these, Americans manage to keep upbeat about their expectations for the future. Ten years of data from the World Values Survey reveals that close to 40 per cent of Americans consistently rate themselves as happier and more optimistic than the populations of a wide range of other economically advanced nations. When asked whether they are having a 'particularly good day', Americans will typically respond more affirmatively than their European and Japanese counterparts. In an interesting related finding, a high percentage of Americans feel their success in life is determined by forces inside their control—a significantly higher percentage than the global median.[14] Although an inverse relationship has been found between optimism and GDP per capita, with greater wealth correlating to lower optimism, the US goes against this trend.

Percentage of people who describe their day as a 'particularly good day'

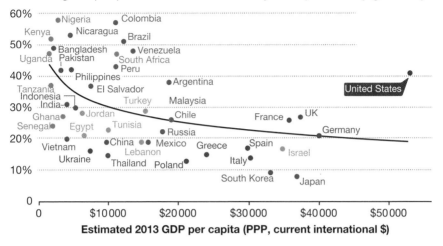

Source: Spring 2014 Global Attitudes Survey. Data from GDP per capita (PPP) from IMF World Economic Outlook Database, April 2014. Graph prepared by the Pew Research Centre.

A number of additional factors support this finding. Optimism about the potential for innovation and economic growth has often been seen in the climb of the Dow Index on Wall Street, for example. Despite continued concern about America's political and economic state, most Americans believe the country will improve.

According to the Perfectionism and Optimism–Pessimism Lab at the University of Michigan (yes, there is a lab devoted to researching just this!), American values of freedom, liberty and rugged individualism will translate into perceptions of personal control that impact optimism.[15] (Of course, any inferences from these stated values need to be tempered with the reality that the US has the world's largest prison population, and a habit of intervening in international affairs!)

Religion may also play a part in this optimism, as Americans are typically more religious than their counterparts in other wealthy countries. Research has revealed a connection between religion and optimism, yet as we shall discover further on in the chapter there is an innate ambiguity in this — as optimism (even if only of 'those who see their prospects favourably') does not necessarily lead to innovation and creative thinking, and religion (or more precisely the mindset behind some forms of religiosity, which is the underlying principle we want to focus on) can relate inversely to innovation.

A specific optimistic approach can have a huge impact on the ability to determine the implementation of innovative solutions. There could well be a relationship between Americans' optimism and their ability to attain some of the highest rates of innovation in the world (although no doubt also having the economic resources to back the implementation of innovative ideas makes a difference). It will be important to go on to define optimism further in this chapter to see the mindset that leads to innovation.

> A specific optimistic approach can have a huge impact on the ability to determine the implementation of innovative solutions.

But first we are going to take a long journey south to the South American continent to consider some comparisons and contrasts that may be helpful to the discussion.

Bodyguards and bombs

A journey across the equator takes us through extraordinary contrasts of landscape. At its narrowest point, the isthmus of Central America that joins the two vast continents is bisected by the Panama Canal, one of the most complex, challenging and expensive engineering feats ever accomplished. It is the only canal to connect two oceans. Ironically, splitting the continents apart has enabled them to stay better connected—two utterly different continents, in terms of both geography and population, now with easier access between them. Bringing together the lofty desires and aspirations of the north with the rugged, grounded survival mentality of the south, this is an area we have found particularly fascinating.

It was down in El Salvador that another celebrity surfing scenario unfolded. We were there during the bloody 12-year civil war, and this time we were surfing alongside a family member of the President of El Salvador and a bevy of bodyguards. This was in stark contrast to our home country, where we had seen our prime minister surfing on his own without a bodyguard in sight.

We had woken the night before to the sound of a bomb going off in the electoral office not more than a few hundred metres from where we were sleeping. This sort of disturbing event is normal here, and the people have had to learn to live with it, but it gave us a sense of what it must be like to live in such constant fear that it becomes a part of your psyche. In this part of the world, where your life can readily be threatened without warning, you don't take your freedom for granted. It wasn't long before we decided it was not a place where we felt comfortable. It felt way too dangerous to us. Yet, perhaps unsurprisingly, it was here in these extreme conditions that we met some of the most resilient people we have ever come across.

What struck us about this region, which is another part of the world that has struggled with internal conflict and corruption, poverty and pain, is how flexible and resilient the people have become. Exploring the history of this region may help to shed a little more light on the way resilience can develop.

The great Incan Empire, for example, spread across four climate zones and therefore required a flexible approach to farming to meet the potential challenges of seasonal and climatic change. Importantly, while at the micro level each family could produce its own food, families were also part of wider kinship groups known as *ayllu* that owned farmland collectively. By owning land in both the highlands and the lowlands, the *ayllu* could ensure they had a range of crops they could rely on in different conditions.

The Incas also developed sophisticated food storage facilities that enabled them to prepare for the hard times. By building intricate terracing, canals and irrigation networks, the Incas maximised land use and ensured optimal returns on their efforts. The ancient citadel at Machu Picchu offers a fascinating insight into the capabilities of the Incas. With 170 buildings, 300 terraces and 16 fountains, this city perched high in the Andes mountains represents an astonishing engineering feat. The fact that much of it still stands today is a testament to the ingenious skills of the Incas.

This is the continent where companies like SEMCO in Brazil have learned to adapt to a changing economic environment. SEMCO has been recognised worldwide for setting up a flexible leadership matrix and diversified innovation process (as described further in the Applications section). A number of South America's urban centres are now included among 'the world's most resilient cities'. It has seen the emergence of a number of high-impact agricultural and environmental innovations to assist with long-term sustainability, such as sensory and GPS software to monitor seeding and irrigation; creating ethanol out of waste; extracting oil from plastic waste; the world's first solar-powered stadium; and using aeronautical and space technology to develop custom-made blades for wind turbines to produce energy.[16]

This intersection between idealistic optimism on the one hand, and pragmatic resilience on the other, provides an interesting framework for the final stage of the innovation process. We will explore what happens to innovation when these principles are pushed to the extreme later in the chapter.

Hurricane survivors and adaptors

Hurricane Katrina, which struck the Gulf coast of the US in 2005 with deadly ferocity, brought a great deal of trauma and suffering in its wake, and has become a strong collective memory for the American people. The survivors of the hurricane responded to the disaster in different ways. The immediate response of most was to support each other to get through the crisis. There's the story of the owners of a severely damaged local bar who set up a tarp and gave away bottles of cold water, another of how a couple outside of the impacted area offered a second home rent-free to hurricane survivors, and yet another of the pharmacist who helped to provide medications to those needing relief.

Research has found that, as a general rule, in times of disaster or crisis people tend to become more highly adaptive, and most engage in altruistic and protective behaviours rather than negative behaviours.[17] So it appears to be in our nature as humans to find ways to cope with the distress and support each other when things go wrong.[18] Specific coping mechanisms kick into action to support the sort of flexibility and resilience needed to get through. First, the situation will typically be appraised to ascertain the dangers; second, practical responses will be weighed up; finally, the response or coping method, which is usually either problem-focused or emotion-focused, will be executed.[19] Where people are optimistic about potential solutions or alleviation options, they will tend to take a problem-solving approach. It follows, then, that an optimistic outlook will assist with the ability to deal constructively with this sort of stress.

Yet there is another clue here to coping. When added to an optimistic outlook, often (though not always) a sense of empowerment, a belief that you have the capability to take action and make a difference through your actions, can lead to a real inner strength. People who are pessimistic or even fatalistic, believing that a crisis just has to be suffered and endured, will more typically adopt an emotion-focused coping strategy. Some examples of how emotional coping strategies can manifest themselves are through avoidance or denial, self-control or self-blame, expressing or sharing feelings — which are all strategies for trying to reduce the impact of the emotional distress.[20]

> Where people are optimistic about potential solutions or alleviation options, they will tend to take a *problem-solving* approach. People who are pessimistic or even fatalistic, believing that a crisis just has to be endured, will more typically adopt an *emotion-focused* coping strategy.

Ultimately, both of these coping approaches (problem-focused and emotion-focused) can contribute to greater resilience during a crisis, particularly in combination, but it is important eventually to move on from the emotion-focused approach to a problem-focused approach in order to reach resolution. While the problem-solving mindset leads to innovation, the emotion-focused reaction is less likely to do so.

This brings us to another stretch concept, a concept that is designed to take you beyond the normal bounds of thinking. While optimism can be perceived as not much more than a form of positive thinking—in fact, the *Oxford Dictionary* defines it as 'hopefulness and confidence about the future or success of something',[21] and the *Merriam-Webster* dictionary as 'a feeling or belief that good things will happen in the future'[22]—we'd like to introduce the stretch concept of *enabled optimism*. Beyond a simple state of positive thinking, it is this empowering optimism that enables the sort of development that can drive innovation. This term refers not just to *having* positive beliefs, but also to *behaving or acting* according to these beliefs in order to bring the aspirations to fruition. This is a stretch concept because acting on optimistic beliefs requires a great deal of flexibility and adaptability in behaviours and should lead to resilience. So perhaps we should be drawing on the different approaches of North and South Americans to provide a powerful force for change.

The power of enabled optimism

	Disempowered	Empowered	
Optimism	**Fatalism** A positive outlook but limited opportunities to innovate	**Enabled optimism** Positive outlook but also empowered — most ready for proactive innovation	*This position leads to flexibility and resilience*
Pessimism	**Learned helplessness** No opportunities to innovate	**Active pessimism** In touch with reality, but limited opportunities to innovate (less ideation)	

Optimism has been found to be linked to flexibility, as optimists can learn to vary their behaviour to face specific challenges.[23] Being flexible when applying a number of different resources and skills to solving a problem and working towards a goal is a crucial human strength and a critical component for innovation, and optimists appear to excel in this area.[24] Optimism has also been found to be closely linked with perseverance in setting and achieving goals.[25] Optimists have been described as 'those who see their prospects favourably and thus will continue efforts to reach their goal'. They are also quick at assessing negative information and apparently unsolvable problems, disengaging from them, and identifying possible better alternatives.[26] Bringing this all together, it becomes clear that the ability to flexibly draw on and apply as many different resources and skills as necessary to solve a problem or work towards a goal is a feature of optimism.[27]

On the other side of the coin, what happens when optimism is absent? A lack of enabled optimism has been found to be related to mental illness, especially depression. A negative correlation has been found between optimism and depression: that is, the more optimistic a person is the less depressed they will be. More than that, where there are feelings of a lack of self-mastery (what we are referring to here as empowerment), the impact is greater.[28] Anxiety in particular can narrow our vision significantly. Because energy is expended on focusing on a potential danger, it becomes difficult to see information that may be on the periphery but may nevertheless be very beneficial for solving a problem.[29] According to the World Health Organization, approximately 350 million people around the world suffer from depression, which is recognised as a leading cause of disease and disability worldwide, so this will be a critical insight to consider for the future mental health of our societies.[30]

> Creative thinking — in particular the qualities of flexibility and originality — assist with emotional recovery after a crisis.

Enabled optimism through practical empathy (for example, through positive feelings towards others and performing acts of kindness) has been shown to help manage depression. The *outrospection* of empathy and compassion for others (as discussed in chapter 3) may therefore help develop more optimism and resilience. Some of those who embrace the optimistic American spirit would say you can conquer any challenge, even illness, through optimism and positive thinking. According to research this is not strictly true, but there is a relationship between positive thinking and a stronger immune system, so the benefits of this kind of optimism on all levels can be significant.

Relying on resilience

Interviews with survivors of Hurricane Katrina found that creative thinking—in particular the qualities of flexibility and originality—assisted with emotional recovery after the crisis.[31] What's more interesting is that these two specific qualities were found to be a significant reliable predictor for the African-American population but not the Caucasian population. Although these qualities were perceived to be important for all survivors, and Caucasians most often mentioned them, African-Americans most often *demonstrated* the qualities. The study certainly revealed the importance of creative thinking (most specifically flexibility and originality) in resilience.

Organisations can also demonstrate resilience. At this organisational level resilience refers to a system's capacity to cope with stress without leading to collapse.[32] Resilient systems have been found to be linked to diversity, response to feedback, and continuous experimentation and improvement.

With a foundation of diversity, as has already been discussed, a wider range of ideas can emerge that can help to deal with the challenges. The optimism and flexibility to be able to continue to play with possibilities until suitable solutions are found is also significant. Resilient social systems are built on a foundation of diverse and independent subsystems, so even if one of these subsystems collapses other solutions are still available. A resilient society must have cultural diversity (which we showed in chapter 6 is important for innovation) and must have the opportunity for creativity to flourish. Among the key concepts linked to resilience are the ability to take risks without fear of making mistakes or failing, and the ability to face uncertainty and chaos.

So how do our contemporary societies rate today? There seem to be two opposing trends. On the one hand, corporations are getting bigger and more standardised, which is linked to greater fragility. On the other hand, a lot of small players are now entering the social system through greater socio-technical opportunities, with greater agility and flexibility to deal with change. Organisations are going to have to deal adequately with the tension between simultaneous stability and change. While they will need to maintain stability to provide a solid foundation for growth, they will also need to be able to continue to adapt to cope with changing needs and demands.[33] To enable innovation, institutions need to allow for virtuous cycles of innovation, expansion and mutual prosperity.[34]

> Resilience will be a disruptive concept that can lead to radical transformation.

As the University of Arts in London's 'Cultures of Resilience' project has identified, another paradox has emerged out of recent realities that we need to consider now: it will be important to move away from the typical dominant ways of thinking and doing things in order to make our societies (and organisations) more resilient.[35] As we explored in the previous chapter, when we visited Asia, there will need to be a shift of focus away from individuality and towards values of sharing, collaboration and reciprocity. This means resilience will be a disruptive concept that can lead to radical transformation. However, the reasons behind why we are resilient and optimistic (the mindset) have a deep impact on how we view innovation.

The cosmic bet

We grew up with the story of a man who was the victim of an interesting bet, a man who demonstrated remarkable optimism and resilience under incredibly challenging circumstances. The bet was between two powerful figures and long-term sparring partners: we will refer to one (the head of the largest company around) as the *boss*, and the other (a partner who had been kicked out of the company and then set himself up in direct opposition) as his *adversary*. The victim who was the subject of this bet we will refer to simply as the *worker*.

The worker was successful and rich and had everything anyone could ever want, and he was in line to be the next partner. The boss was proud of him and boasted about him. One day the adversary tired of hearing how great the company was and how devoted its employees were, so he challenged the boss to test the loyalty of this particular worker. The boss had just finished talking about how dedicated his favourite employee was, to which the adversary responded that the worker was only loyal because he was so successful. He challenged the boss to take away all the opportunities the worker had and to leave him with nothing. The adversary was convinced that once the worker experienced some hardships he would reveal his true colours and turn against the company, and would curse the boss to his face.

The boss accepted the bet and set about proving the point. First he sent the employee to a distant posting with incredibly tough conditions. One day the worker received the news that a robbery had gone terribly wrong and his family had been shot and killed. Then he got word that his house was destroyed in a fire. Soon after that he learned that all his stock options had crashed in a financial crisis. As he was still transitioning to the new role and country, his insurance company refused to pay out and declared him bankrupt.

The worker had no shortage of colleagues prepared to offer their opinions and theories on why everything went so horribly wrong. Some hinted he must be being punished because of something he did wrong back at HQ. Others thought he was just whingeing because he was a spoilt brat who wanted his wealth back. Still others suggested it was his boss's fault so he should sue his boss. His friends lacked empathy, and because they were unable to solve the mystery of his suffering, they jumped to conclusions about the reasons behind it. The debate raged on as the worker's life went from bad to worse. The stress triggered a terrible, excruciatingly painful illness, yet he still remained loyal and never questioned the will of his boss.

Finally the worker was allowed to return home (alone, having lost everything). The boss was pleased with the outcome, and especially with the fact that throughout his ordeal the worker had retained his personal integrity. So he rewarded the worker with a new house much larger than the one he had owned previously, and gave him a massive pay rise and promotion. The loyal worker ended up remarrying and having more children, taking up a life even more privileged than that he'd had before. He remained optimistic and resilient throughout the ordeal, but two questions need to be asked: Why did he stay so positive? And did this lead to any innovation?

What we've set out here is a modern-day version of the story of Job from the Old Testament, with the core of the story pretty much unchanged.[36] It is the story of two celestial powers (God and the Devil) involved in what Jung called a 'cosmic bet'.[37] Not unlike producers and directors in a string of TV shows and movies—think *The Hunger Games*, *The Truman Show*, *Wayward Pines*, *Pleasantville*, *The Stepford Wives* or *Ascension*—the higher powers were in full control. In this case, they put the individual through a series of tough challenges to test his faith and stamina to the absolute limit. Although the participant suffered greatly, he did in the end 'win', if it can be called winning. He picked up some big prizes: a new wife, family, job, health, wealth and a long and prosperous life.

> Typically we can behave either as pawns (with a fatalistic outlook) or as players (from a position of self-mastery and enabled optimism).

The story from the Book of Job could have been a forerunner to a reality TV show. Job is an unusual section of the Bible placed halfway through the Old Testament and also referenced in another holy text, the Qur'an (Surah 21 (The Prophets), Ayah 83). In context it's meant to be read as an allegory, but it has raised questions and heated debate about how much control we actually have over our lives. Regardless of what might be happening in the heavens, this story can prompt us to think about the mindset we adopt, how it relates to resilience and how it impacts innovation. Looking back at the figure 'The power of enabled optimism', you can see how Job displayed disempowered optimism, which made him resilient enough to sit out the crisis, but not innovative enough to deal with it.

Typically we can behave either as pawns (with a fatalistic outlook) or as players (from a position of self-mastery and enabled optimism). We can believe we have either little to no control or a lot to full control, and the mindset we choose greatly impacts our willingness and ability to innovate.

In the hands of higher powers

We were reflecting on this story about Job after returning from working in the orphanage run by a courageous local church in war-torn El Salvador. We have visited a number of orphanages around the world where disempowered children appear to be passive victims of their circumstances. What struck us with the orphanage in El Salvador was the proactive sense of responsibility that every child in the orphanage had. They were active in completing their many daily tasks, and positive in the process. This sort of outlook required not only optimism and resilience, but also a sense of empowerment.

The juxtaposition of experiences caused us to reflect on how our response to challenges can depend on either an external locus of control (the belief that external forces, such as fate or luck, determine our fate) or an internal locus of control (the belief that we determine our own destiny). In the bible story, Job left his fate in the hands of the higher power, believing there was nothing he could do to change his circumstances. His initial optimism and resilience was impacted by the fact that he did not feel empowered or enabled to make a difference. It made us question our capacity to determine our own destiny—whether we think we are pawns in the game or have the chance to be active players in the process. It also made us think about the power of the stories we tell—the dominant narratives we live and work by—and how these can impact our beliefs and behaviours.

Throughout history there have been raging debates about the nature of the higher powers (most often referred to in English as 'God' or 'the gods', although these powers go by many other names) and their influence on humanity. We have discovered that most cultures have expressions for the conviction that an external source determines the direction humans and humanity will take, as a way to explain the authority of a higher power. The Latin supplication *Deo volente*, expressing this mindset, was equivalent to the English 'God willing', 'Inshalla' (in Arabic), 'Que sera sera',

'Ojalá' and 'Si Dios quiere' (in Spanish) and 'S'il plaît à Dieu' (in French). Sixteenth-century Christian theology, under the influence of the French Protestant John Calvin, and even more fervently his right-hand man, Theodore Beza, subscribed to the philosophy of predestination. Martin Luther argued that because God is omnipotent and has sovereignty over all creation, humans cannot ultimately have free will.

We felt the impact of this mindset in the back of a car in Bahrain, gripping the door handle as the car swung erratically through the ancient city streets. In a situation like this you can really feel the locus of control shifting away. People's behaviours typically reflect their beliefs. Many drivers we have met in our travels in this region feel they do not need to wear seatbelts, use their indicators or follow the traffic rules; some would not even think it necessary to look left or right when crossing intersections. Motorcyclists often don't wear helmets or, if they do, fail to do up the straps or do them up only when approached by police. Although the top five major risk factors for road deaths have been found to be excessive speed, drink-driving, and the failure to use helmets, seatbelts and child restraints,[38] restrictions in these areas (other than drink-driving) are not necessarily enforced.

Does this fatalistic approach come from the conviction that a higher power controls the future? Do many citizens in this region fail to connect this fatalistic philosophy with the inordinately large number of road deaths? Is there a connection with the fact that at one time Saudi Arabia was reported to have had the world's highest number of deaths from road accidents, and Iran, Iraq and Oman have been found to be up in the top 6 per cent of road deaths?[39] We'd like to discuss how this mindset might lead to consolidating optimism but not innovation. Fatalism, determinism and predestination can be seen to be related in this context, so it's worth considering how they can all impact innovation, directly or indirectly.

The Job story could be interpreted as showing how optimism, resilience, and loyalty to and trust in a higher power can lead to fulfilment. While the ancient Greeks and Indo-Aryans of the Vedic period saw the gods as unpredictable and fickle, other philosophers might question how an all-powerful, all-knowing, omnipresent power could also be a loving being. Rather than examining this contested question here, we'll focus on how certain mindsets impact innovation.

It's important to note that the fatalistic approach exemplified in the story of Job is not the exclusive domain of the religious. You will often hear secular people declare, 'That's the way the world works' or express fatalistic optimism ('Things will work out for the best' or Nietzsche's 'What doesn't kill us will make us stronger'). All could illustrate an optimistic mindset and resilience to challenges, but the cost could be a lack of empowerment. As we introduced in chapter 2, 'post-traumatic growth' through surviving adverse circumstances can lead to greater empathy and more creativity.[40] Yet, as has been suggested, 'Most adversity most likely results in post-traumatic stress disorder.'[41] If it leads to depression, anxiety and helplessness, then it is difficult for innovation to flourish.

The fact that we have limited or no free choice to determine our own futures could be a depressing thought, yet some research suggests that religious people with these sorts of beliefs are in fact more optimistic than the average non-believer.[42] This could spring from the belief that a higher power 'will do the best for me' so it is 'out of my hands'; it could, in other words, be a 'passive' response rather than a 'proactive' sense of empowerment. Another antithesis to resilient and enabled optimism may be fatalism. The Merriam-Webster dictionary describes optimism as 'a doctrine that this world is the best possible world' and 'an inclination to put the most favourable construction upon actions and events or to anticipate the best possible outcome'.

Whereas an *enabled* optimistic mindset or culture would often indicate we are endowed with the ability to change things and to some extent shape our own future (for instance, through innovation), fatalism indicates that there is nothing anyone can do to change things and the future is predetermined. Stephen Hawking questions the consistency of a fatalistic mindset: 'Even people who claim everything is predetermined and that we can do nothing to change it, look before they cross the road.'[43]

> Giving people an empowered mindset to overcome and push on no matter what the challenges will lead to completely different outcomes than giving them the expectation that there is nothing anyone can do to change the course of events.

This mindset, as we shall see, has a profound impact on whether it is possible to build a culture of innovation, and on face value it's easy to see why. As an example, where they believe their actions can contribute to their fate, people tend to behave more cooperatively and less opportunistically.[44] There are also deeper implications.

If the 'innovation race' to date was thought of in terms of *The Amazing Race*, enabled optimism could be the equivalent of a 'Fast Forward' card, and fatalism could be a 'Detour' or 'Roadblock' card. The 'Optimism' card (linked to belief in a higher power) becomes a means of coping with being stuck at the roadblock, rather than of directly dealing with it. These cards would have a profound part to play in determining the position of each contestant in the race. Giving people an empowered mindset to overcome and push on no matter what the challenges will lead to completely different outcomes than giving them the expectation that there is nothing anyone can do to change the course of events.

The inverse relationship between fatalism and innovation

Despite the link between religion and optimism, there is a deeper paradox to wrestle with that might surprise you: within the US, the most religious states are also the ones that are least innovative.

This inverse relationship is evident on a larger scale too: the most religious countries also appear to be the least innovative, at least in scientific or technological terms.[45] Princeton economists unveiled this finding in a recent paper: higher levels of religiosity relate to lower levels of scientific innovation.[46]

It appears that where religion predominates, the sort of inquiry that can lead to more innovative thinking may be taking a hit. Religion and science appear to be mutually exclusive. Indeed, research on the brain has shown that there are two opposing domains in constant tension: an analytical network of neurons that enables critical thinking, and a social network that enables us to empathise and to think spiritually.[47] A healthy, flexible and innovative brain is actually able to fire up one side at a time (while simultaneously suppressing the other), but some people are only able to engage one side and not the other.

We want to unpack this finding and look at the deeper question of 'why' to find out what is the real roadblock behind this and how it might impact all of us. And we believe this goes way beyond certain religious beliefs. Although it would not be right to assume causation, there must be a deeper mindset at play.

The researchers who found the inverse relationship between religion and innovation have also found that the power of the state impacts innovation. Is there something in these taboo topics, religion and politics, that might help us understand the reasons behind this? This brings us back around to our discussion in chapter 5 on liberation and the importance of guided freedom as a culture to support innovation. The most supportive political approach was not found to be the oppressive theocracy, in which both state and religion suppress science, resisting new ideas and restricting their diffusion in order to maintain ideological control. (Of course this is not to take away the important role religion can have when weighing in on the ethics of science and technological innovation.) We feel that examining the different mindsets behind optimism may help us to understand the paradoxes of and relationships between fatalism, politics and innovation, and the research into these relationships.

We don't want to paint religion with too broad a brush. The word *religion* actually covers a very wide range of beliefs and behaviours, from peace-loving Quakers or Sufis to hardline Zionists or jihadists, from sequestered meditating monks to the boisterous expressions of faith at Pentecostal mega-churches.[48] We are touching on this topic not to debate religion or politics, but to look at the mindset that can be behind a fatalistic mentality. As Jonathan Haidt, social psychologist and Professor of Ethical Leadership at New York University, has noted, 'Morality binds and blinds. It binds us into ideological teams that fight each other as though the fate of the world depended on our side winning each battle. It blinds us to the fact that each team is composed of good people who have something important to say.'[49]

Throughout the ages religious people have expressed their faith in magnificently creative ways. Yet the sort of creative artistic expression aimed at giving glory to God is not necessarily linked to the sort of developments that lead to innovations. Artistic creativity and innovation are not one and the same thing.

The fatalistic mindset that disempowers people, freeing them from personal responsibility for their actions, can be found anywhere — even in science, which is often considered to be the antithesis of religion. The scientist could also argue that our lives and actions are predetermined: whereas chaos theory has it that the world is no more than a series of random, unpredictable and unconnected events, scientists will argue (after Newton) that 'every action has an equal and opposite reaction', which is perhaps a kind of predestination at molecular level. Richard Dawkins describes this fatalistic survival mechanism as the 'selfish gene'; he thinks of humans as 'robot vehicles blindly programmed' to survive — that is, we are almost pre-programmed to behave in certain ways.[50]

Learned helplessness or enabled action?

A mindset can either liberate you or hold you captive.[51] The fatalistic mindset can impede progress and development (and therefore innovation) because it can lead to 'learned helplessness'.

This concept of learned helplessness was originally developed by the psychologist Martin Seligman after conducting research on dogs back in the 1960s.[52] In a series of experiments, Seligman placed dogs in boxes with two compartments separated by a barrier that the dog could jump over. Typically when dogs had learned that there is no way to escape the shock before they were placed in the box, they failed to try to escape the shock. They simply lay down and endured it. Those dogs that had learned that they did have some control over a shock before being placed in the box, however, (by being able to press a button with its nose) would readily jump over the barrier to escape the shock when placed in the box.

Helplessness is crippling, but we can potentially deal with it if it is a temporary state or is created by particular circumstances. An oppressive boss in the workplace, for example, is quite different from a culture of oppression, whether in the workplace or anywhere else. When fatalism becomes a mindset that expresses a deeper, more entrenched belief system, it can have a powerful long-term impact that can impede growth. It can make it difficult to see the obstacles it brings or blind you to the reality of the race. Ignorance can be bliss, but it may mean being sidelined from surviving the 'innovation race'.

Fundamentalist beliefs have directly impacted innovation throughout history.[53] The Islamic Golden Age saw important developments in mathematics (in algebra and trigonometry, for example), in chemistry and medicine (such as the use of the experimental method), and technology (such as the development of navigational instruments and the clock), but by the thirteenth century a conservative wave of fundamentalism introduced a resistance to new knowledge and virtually halted this period of rapid innovation.

A similar pattern can be seen in Europe's history. Tolerant scientific and philosophical approaches from the Greek tradition were subdued in the name of faith by the Roman Church from the fourth century. In the seventeenth century Galileo, one of the greatest scientists and thinkers of the Renaissance revolution, was made to stand trial by the Holy Inquisition of the Church for proposing and defending a scientific explanation for the way the world works that challenged the rigid mindset of Church tradition. Rather than leading to healthy dialogue, these 'heresies' saw him persecuted.

The baleful influence of the Holy Inquisition had a dramatic impact on the adaptation of new technologies and, consequently, on economic development. The suppression of free thought and scientific development that characterised religious fundamentalism in different regions with different beliefs has its parallels in the business world — for example, the fixed mindset that imposes a strict literal interpretation (such as the boss's interpretation) that blocks dialogue and the chance to test ideas against reality. As a rigid interpretation that tends towards intolerance, it can impact progress and development. This could be as straightforward as a dogmatic commitment to a single explanation for the origin of the cosmos, a simple solution for the problems of society, an absolute faith in science or atheism,[54] or an inflexible view on innovation! If we accept that a fundamentalist fatalistic mindset can become an impediment to innovation, the question needs to be asked: How and why do people develop such a potentially inhibiting mindset? And are any of us immune to this? We will explore this deeper level further in the following chapter.

Is it possible to be too optimistic and flexible?

We have already discussed how an optimism that is not enabled can be an obstacle to action. It can also lead to a disconnect with reality, an inability to see things as they really are.

People are actually often overly optimistic and a little too flexible with the truth when it comes to assessing themselves. When they describe themselves in relation to some type of desirable dimension, for example, most people will typically rate themselves as better than average. Here are some humorous examples of research that has revealed this:

- When nearly a million senior high school students were asked to rate themselves on their leadership abilities, 70 per cent said they had 'above average' leadership skills, and only 2 per cent felt they were 'below average'.[55]

- 94 per cent of college professors think they do above-average work.[56]
- Doctors making a diagnosis for pneumonia with 88 per cent confidence have been found to be right only 20 per cent of the time.[57]
- 80 per cent of men say they are better looking than the average man.[58]

People will also notoriously exaggerate their attractions when advertising themselves on a dating website. Men, in particular, will typically add a few thousand dollars to their salary and add a few inches to their height. Woman in contrast typically take a few kilograms off their weight and under-report their age! Being out of touch with reality can lead to some bad first dates, when the person on the other side discovers they are meeting someone quite different from the description. When you take this principle to the organisational level, being out of touch with reality or overestimating positive qualities can lead to dissatisfaction and disillusionment for employees and customers. Being out of touch with or ignoring reality can keep organisations from dealing with the real issues and solving the real problems. This is a problem for innovation, as it means that innovations will not be meeting the right needs.

The solution is to develop a *grounded flexibility*—a positive adaptability that, working from a stable foundation, enables action (John Kotter's 'dual operating system' model is again a good model to draw on here). In a loosely coupled system where there is structure but also some capability to flex, the independent autonomous partners can shift their goals and strategies more easily in alignment with the vision and goals of the group and organisation.[59]

Perhaps ironically, we need some stability in routines to provide the foundation for flexibility and adaptability.[60] Routines help to make things more efficient by reducing complexity and the chances of failure, but they can lead to inertia, locking organisations into rigid patterns. Think of how in music learning the scales and learning to sight-read music can provide a foundation for learning to improvise. Only when we have the foundations and routines established can we then use them as a springboard for trialling new ways of doing things.

By learning to operate from a position of *grounded flexibility* it will be possible to take the innovation process right through to implementation —and transform the organisation in the process.

DETOUR
Harmony from chaos in Paraguay

We described in our first book on this topic, *Who Killed Creativity?*, how the rubbish-dump dwellers on the outskirts of Mexico City had built a livelihood from the trash at the dumps, making a living from recycling and repurposing the rubbish of others. Their resilience, ingenuity and ability to see potential in what the rest of the world treats as useless waste is astounding. Kites are made from old plastic and broken wood, toys from can lids nailed to sticks, homes from discarded tin sheets and discarded timber, gardens from old rusty tins and tyres. (See www.the-innovation-race.com for a video).

In Paraguay, this concept has been taken a step further: young musicians from a slum there have toured South America playing instruments constructed out of waste products collected from around their homes.[61] Landfill worker and musician Favio Chavez came up with the idea of the Recycled Orchestra when he saw how the children who lived in the slum area of Cauteura could not afford to buy musical instruments but could create their own. The shanty town, perched on top of a landfill site next to the Paraguay River, receives 1500 tonnes of waste each day, and its residents are exposed to critical levels of pollutants. Here is an example of resilience through perseverance, of innovation from elimination, and of a community that moved beyond being pawns to becoming players.

APPLICATIONS FOR THE ORGANISATION

Application 1: Challenge and confront paradoxes for deeper transformation.

- When transformation is needed, there can be a struggle between the old and the new – the transformation process will be simultaneously a process of destruction *and* of construction.
- Most often, in the process of 'sensemaking', people frame the new realities from the perspective of what they have known in the past.
- Unfortunately the qualities that initially enable an organisation to grow can become the very factors that impede its growth.
- The key factor here is the ability to learn—to transform through the change. This will involve challenge, open communication and confrontation, and paradoxical leadership.
- Education is a critical factor in helping people to transform and grow through change, and this includes challenging current frames of reference and opening up communication.

When transformation is needed, old assumptions or beliefs can carry over into the new setting, which can lead to paradoxical tensions. There can be a struggle between the old and new, between what's known and not known, between the security of the past and the insecurity of the future. The process of transformation (also often referred to as transcendence) will be simultaneously a process of destruction *and* of construction—breaking apart the old through critiquing in order to build the new.[62]

You would think that as soon as people perceive inconsistences from changes in the environment they would do something about it, but often they don't. Most often, according to the concept of 'sensemaking', they will frame the new realities from the perspective of what they have known in the past.[63]

Unfortunately the qualities that initially enable an organisation to grow can become the very factors that impede its growth. The boutique resort company we have worked with (introduced in chapter 5) learned this the hard way when they had to decide whether to work from a basis of principles or procedures. There's the paradox again. So, for example, as organisations become more complex, their focus can become narrower and their approaches simpler. Learning can become stunted and the organisation can become paralysed. Fear of change can lead to a regression to the more comfortable, known systems and behaviours, which can limit the opportunities for creative breakthroughs and innovation.

The key factor here is the ability to learn — to transform through the change. So, again, a critical element is education. Educational approaches that enable individuals and organisations to move beyond the potentially paralysing impact of change and to start to learn and grow again can include:

- *challenge* — challenging a current frame of reference to help people see the limitations of the current situation (for example, through presenting information in an unexpected new way)
- *open communication and confrontation* — helping to surface divergent insights and frames of reference (for example, through experimentation)
- *paradoxical leadership* — leading through understanding and analysing the tensions rather than suppressing them.

Application 2: Be flexible — operate 'outside the box'.

- 'We see not the world "as it is" — but we see the world in a way that proved useful in the past'... 'We process the information that fits the expected world, and find reasons to exclude the information that might contradict it'.
- Most people need to create a box or a set of parameters to work within, and tend to look for solutions inside this space.
- If we can learn to see the unexpected, we can often start to spot creative solutions that were possibly there all the time but we failed to notice.

The director of the modern-day optical illusion centre Lottolab, R. Beau Lotto, believes, 'The whole concept of an illusion is predicated on a misconception. We see not the world "as it is" — but we see the world in a way that proved useful in the past. Our brain constructs what it knows by searching for useful patterns in sensory information.'[64]

Survivalist researcher Laurence Gonzales helps to explain why people have trouble being creative (and why we are so easily fooled by magic) when he says, 'We construct an expected world because we can't handle the complexity of the present one, and then process the information that fits the expected world, and find reasons to exclude the information that might contradict it. Unexpected or unlikely interactions are ignored when we make our construction.'[65]

Within this quote lies the main reason why many of us struggle to use creative thinking and to think flexibly. If we can learn to see the unexpected, we can often start to see creative solutions that were possibly there all the time but we failed to see them. When our brain does this it can restrict creative thinking. Of course we need this normal pattern-seeking brain behaviour to survive normal everyday life. Without patterns and 'norms' our brains cannot make sense of the huge amount of stimulus we receive each day. But there are times when we need to let go of these pattern-making predispositions. Many tortured souls are unable to recognise when or how to switch between these two states, and others who have been driven to creative insanity by not being able to relax into familiar patterns. The key here is that we need to know when and how to access our creative brain actively, and when to leave it to run passively in the background.

Most people need to create a box or a set of parameters to work within, and tend to look for solutions inside this space. There is nothing wrong with this, but the research shows that a creative genius goes way outside these boundaries, and in some cases even has no box, or has a 'less intact' box, which is why many creative geniuses lean towards eccentricity or madness.

When it comes to seeing ideas through to practical implementation, it can take a combination of American 'can-do' individualistic brashness, the flexibility and resilience of impoverished communities that have had to adapt to survive, and an eastern communal focus to get the right balance, but managing that cultural dynamic is not easy![66]

Application 3: Ensure the culture enables.

- Adaptable systems and structures need to be set up in organisations to support *grounded flexibility*.
- Challenge restricting leadership styles, limiting access to information and ideas, and systems that fail to engage and stifle individual passions and needs.
- Look out for comments such as 'This is the way we've always done it in this organisation', 'You can't change the way things are' and 'There's no point trying to do anything differently — we've attempted that before', as these sorts of comments reflect a limiting pessimistic approach.
- Look for signs of learned helplessness.

We once worked with a major telco company in Greece. Greece was found to be the most pessimistic country in the world in the Gallup poll mentioned earlier in the chapter, and we saw evidence of this mindset when we ran a simulation for middle-level managers. 'The Chocolate Factory', as we have called the simulation, involves experiencing a dysfunctional 'factory' process that is deliberately designed to fail as a result of such factors as siloed structures, time pressures and disconnection from the customer.

By taking participants through creative thinking and innovation skills training, we can demonstrate how the process could be redesigned and improved. Yet the participants clearly in this particular group felt disempowered, telling us they were afraid to change anything and felt any changes weren't going to make a difference anyway. 'We can't sneeze without HQ intervening,' they declared. 'So why bother trying to make changes?' Digging deeper, we could see that at the organisational level they felt restricted by a controlling, hierarchical structure, and at the cultural level they felt disheartened by the economic climate.

When we have tried to teach the value of creative thinking in a number of organisations we have worked with, a common response has been, 'What's the point?' So many people feel there is nothing they can do to make a difference. This happens when the 'higher power' (in this case management or the 'boss') so controls the situation that there is a general defeatist attitude and a feeling of learned helplessness. Or when the leader is so charismatic or authoritarian that they create a culture in which workers work and only the leader innovates. We refer to this as a mindset because, regardless of the situation you are in, this is a belief rather than established truth.

You'll see how at this point we are starting to bring together all the principles we have examined in this second section of the book:

- Consider how organisations can try to keep employees 'inside the box', and, how leadership can restrict employees as a way of limiting freedom and keeping control (chapter 5).
- Consider how workplaces can isolate and insulate employees from outside information and ideas through employing like-minded people, or through physical separation (for example, in cubicles) and/or insulating language, such as jargon (chapter 6).
- Reflect on how individual passions and needs can be subjected to organisational requirements (chapter 7).

Now, in this chapter, we are asking you to consider how deterministic, pessimistic and fatalistic approaches can limit opportunities for positive action. Comments such as 'This is the way we've always done it in this organisation', 'You can't change the way things are' and 'There's no point trying to do anything differently—we've attempted that before' reflect this limiting, pessimistic approach.

So what are the personal and business implications of this sense of disempowerment? The challenge is that for an organisation to grow it needs to innovate, and to innovate there needs to be a culture of constant challenging, questioning and critiquing. To do that we need diverse people, a high level of tolerance for diversity, and a willingness to dialogue about ideas without feeling threatened or stood over.

Application 4: Help employees make the transition from pawns to players.

- It's possible to help people make the shift from fatalistic pessimism (pawns) to enabled optimism (players).
- This transition to a more empowered position will help to activate a more innovative culture.
- Build a dynamic organisation that can adapt with challenges and keep the employees committed through shared values.

In any group there will usually be both hardcore fatalists/fundamentalists *and* people who believe they are capable of making a difference. But most people sit in the middle of the bell curve, and it's these people who can develop either a fatalistic pessimistic mindset (pawns) *or* an enabled optimistic mindset (players). For an innovative culture to succeed, the majority of people sitting on the bell curve need to move from believing they are pawns to a conviction that they are players.

The attitudes and doctrines of the 'higher powers' will, to a great extent, influence the mindsets of the large majority in their organisation. This is why it's so important to look at the culture of an organisation and the beliefs that drive them to see how innovation is impacted. Over time, in a conventional workplace, the supporters will stay and those that felt uncomfortable with this belief system will move on. In the workplace, where a fatalistic culture becomes the norm, most likely it will attract people who feel comfortable in this stage (people who love authority). The people at a higher stage (those who are more likely to be innovators) will leave for greener pastures.

The Brazilian corporation SEMCO, which we introduced earlier, is often referred to as a company that has applied the sorts of optimistic and flexible transformational principles that have enabled them to continue to grow through challenging times. The CEO and majority owner of the company, Ricardo Semler, has introduced innovative business management policies that have attracted worldwide attention, and has featured in such influential media as *Time* and the *Wall Street Journal* as a result.

When Semler first went to work for his father's firm (then called Semler & Company), he clashed with his father over the autocratic leadership style he used. Young Ricardo threatened to leave the company, but instead his father resigned as CEO and gave his son majority ownership in 1980, when he was just 21 years old. By setting up a leadership matrix and diversifying the product offerings through an extensive innovation process, Semler was eventually able to rescue the company. When there was a severe downturn in the Brazilian economy, employees at all levels demonstrated how committed they had become to the company when they agreed to significant wage cuts. They were included in financial decisions and given the opportunity to make suggestions on how to improve the business.

The company demonstrated how it is possible to enable and empower people at all levels, and ultimately support the innovation process effectively and sustainably.

Perhaps the balance in this challenge can be best summed up by the simple Serenity prayer for 'the grace to accept things that cannot be changed, the courage to change the things that can be changed, and the wisdom to know the difference'.

Application 5: Create ambidextrous organisations.

- Institutional structures can be sources of both constraint and opportunity, and contradictions and conflicts within institutions can actually enable creativity.
- A company must effectively balance ongoing management and maintenance needs (exploitation) and innovative activities (exploration).
- There needs to be a differentiation between a circular transformation and an axial revolution.

Building a solid platform for transformation requires setting up parallel structures that provide both the stability and the flexibility needed. In terms of leadership, it will require moving across the continuum, away from complete control and towards a form of guidance that offers support when needed but also steps back and provides autonomy rather than stifling creativity and innovation. Researchers have found that institutional structures can be sources of both constraint and opportunity, and that internal contradictions and conflicts within institutions can actually enable creativity.[67] A number of theorists have concluded that a company must effectively balance ongoing management and maintenance needs (exploitation) and innovative activities (exploration).[68]

As introduced in chapter 4, organisations must become 'ambidextrous'—that is, able to simultaneously pursue both incremental change that keeps the organisation stable, and discontinuous or radical innovations that will propel the organisation forward into an unknown future.[69] They will be able to support those in the organisation who are more inclined to the open action strategy of knowledge generation (breakthrough innovators), as well as those who are inclined towards the closed action strategy of knowledge synthesis (adaptive innovators).[70] A B2B technology firm found their operating income was boosted by 300 per cent when they implemented these principles. In another example, a federal government organisation that was targeted to be closed down became a model facility.

Whenever there is change in the organisation (which is pretty much a constant state of being these days), dichotomous tensions can arise. These tensions are likely to be destabilising. Change management therefore requires highly flexible thinking and a resilient mindset at the individual level, along with highly adaptable systems and structures at the organisational level. The most productive approach to dealing with the tensions is transformation (also referred to as transcendence as mentioned previously).

Change will require an 'axial revolution', a revolution in which there will be a different way of thinking about the issues (as opposed to a 'circular revolution', in which similar things are done repeatedly).[71] An axial revolution requires the use of non-conventional tools and approaches that allow individuals to question current assumptions and beliefs. This is the only approach that will enable us to truly change organisations and deal with the global challenges we face.

CHAPTER SUMMARY

How to transform a culture for implementing innovation

Navigating the path between flexibility and stability.

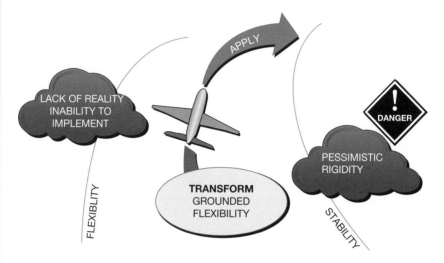

Key principles from the journey

Enabled optimism and flexibility can lead to greater resilience and better problem solving.

- Freedom can be expressed in open possibilities and free choice, through a balance of liberty and equality (e.g. the American Dream).
- These qualities impact perceptions of personal control, which in turn can impact optimism.
- Optimism combined with flexibility can provide resistance to challenges.
- The two concepts are linked, as optimists can assess information more quickly, identify possible alternatives, find resources, set goals more easily and learn to vary their behaviour to face challenges.
- In times of crisis people tend to become more highly adaptive, which assists with resilience.

- The more optimistic people are, the more likely they are to take a practical problem-solving approach in a crisis rather than being immobilised by an emotional response.
- Enabled optimism, where there is an internal locus of control and the individual feels empowered to take independent action, provides the best foundation for coping and success. A lack of empowerment and a pessimistic outlook, on the other hand, has been found to be linked to depression.

It will be important to build resilient organisations for future survival.

- At the organisational level, resilience refers to a system's capacity to cope with stress and resist collapse. Resilient systems have been found to be linked to diversity, response to feedback, and continuous experimentation and improvement.
- Corporations are getting bigger and more standardised, which means less resilience, while smaller players with more agility and resilience are entering the market.
- Organisations will need to maintain the stability to provide a solid foundation for growth; they will also need to be able to continue to adapt to cope with changing needs and demands.
- To increase resilience in organisations there needs to be a shift of focus away from individuality and towards values of sharing, collaboration and reciprocity.
- To enable innovation, institutions need to allow for virtuous cycles of innovation, expansion and mutual prosperity.

An external locus of control can lead to pessimism and fatalism, which undermines development and innovation.

- Religious people may be more optimistic than the average person, but where this is due to a fatalistic attitude it is not an enabled optimism.
- Enabled optimism is required for innovation.
- Where they believe their actions can contribute to their fate people tend to behave more cooperatively and less opportunistically.
- Fundamentalism (the strictly literal belief in source materials that can be found in any religion or philosophy, secular as well as religious) can breed a fatalistic mindset.

- Where fatalism leads to learned helplessness, it can hold back progress.
- Innovation flourished in Islamic and Christian countries when there was openness to the rational sciences, yet when a narrower, more fatalistic theological doctrine held sway innovation slowed down.
- Religion has been shown to have an inverse relationship with empathy and with innovation.
- Most people pass through a fundamentalist stage at some time in their lives. Moving beyond fundamentalist doctrines requires greater flexibility and openness to all possibilities, not just what has previously been explored.
- Where a brand or company culture is too strong, there can be a fundamentalist, quasi-religious approach and growth and innovation may become limited.
- A truly innovative company should aim to lift people to higher stages of development where they are constantly questioning, challenging and critiquing.

Applications summary:

1. Challenge and confront paradoxes for deeper transformation (case study: Boutique Resort Company).
2. Be flexible — operate 'outside the box' (case study: Loottolab).
3. Ensure the culture enables (case Study: Telco Company Greece).
4. Help employees make the transition from pawns to players (case study: SEMCO).
5. Create ambidextrous organisations (case studies: B2B Technology Company, Federal Government Organisation).

CHECKPOINT SUMMARY CHECKLIST
How to transform a culture for sustainable innovation

Paradox synthesis: Grounded Flexibility

Is there evidence of resilient action in your organisation—a balance between stability and flexibility for better implementation of new ideas?

STABILITY

A solid platform for supporting change initiatives and innovations stemming from self-mastery

Is there evidence of enabled optimistic mindsets and company culture built on a stable confidence?

☐	**Internal locus of control**	People are optimistic and feel they have control over their actions and can impact outcomes.
☐	**Self-mastery**	People have the opportunity to develop personal skills and see the impact of their actions.
☐	**Shared ideals**	There is evidence of cooperative rather than opportunistic behaviour.
☐	**Empowerment**	There is a hopeful belief that individuals can design and create change—rather than a fatalistic trust in the 'higher powers'. Individuals are open and responsive to change.
☐	**Positive language**	The language used reflects this optimism and adapts to the changes rather than becoming jargon.
☐	**Practical problem solving**	New ideas are actively being implemented and problems are actively being solved.

FLEXIBILITY

Adaptability for resilient action to deal with and pre-empt rapid change

Is there evidence of resilient action at both the individual and organisational level stemming from an enabled optimism?

☐	**Resilient individuals**	Individuals display qualities of resilience, including an ability to deal with challenges and crisis, assess situations, find alternatives, set goals and vary behaviours accordingly.

(continued)

☐ **Resilient systems and structures**	There is a shift away from an individual focus towards values of sharing, collaboration and reciprocity.
☐ **Constructive open culture**	There is a culture of questioning, challenging and constructively critiquing.
☐ **Effective change management**	There are individuals with flexible and resilient mindsets, and highly adaptive systems and structures that can manage and pre-empt change effectively.
☐ **Opportunity to safely fail**	Failure as a result of genuine good effort is seen as a learning opportunity rather than a disaster.

TRY THIS

How to ensure stability

- Ensure the vision and mission can be translated into practical actions.
- Set clear role descriptions.
- Establish regular routines.
- Provide opportunities for self-mastery so individuals can see progress.
- Focus on implementation follow through and report success.

How to build flexibility and adaptability

- Teach employees to practise using the vision and mission to guide behaviour choices.
- Set up opportunities to question, challenge and constructively critique the system – (for example, through surveys, question boxes, set sections in the review process).
- Identify and develop principles of enabled optimism.
- Set up support systems to support individuals and teams through times of change.
- Establish structures that will allow for appropriate failure in the innovation process.
- Develop change management strategies.

PART III

THE FUTURE OF
THE RACE

Destination: Antarctica

Part III takes us to one of the least visited and perhaps least understood regions on Earth to consider the deeper implications of the innovation journey.

Key challenges addressed:

- *How to develop motivation and mindsets for purpose-driven innovation (chapter 9)*
- *How to innovate responsibly to deal with a rapidly changing world (chapter 10).*

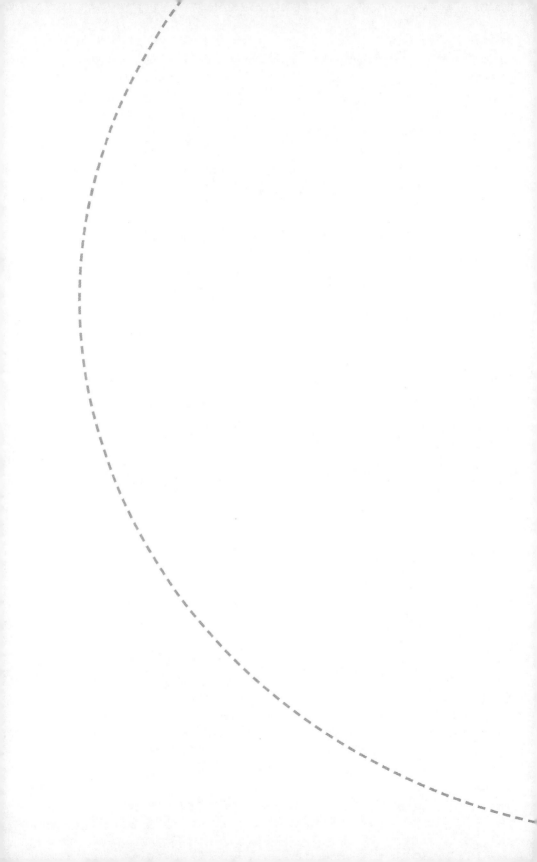

9

PAWNS AND PLAYERS

Who really wins in the end?

'A wise man learns from the experience of others, a smart man from himself, and a fool never learns.'

Russian saying

This chapter will explore the deeper culture-change challenges that can lead to mindsets that either foster or impede innovation. The chapter will help you:

- *consider your innovation orientation*
- *identify inactive and proactive responses to issues and the attitudes behind them*
- *understand a developmental stage model that can help to ascertain potential for innovation according to mindset*
- *appreciate why being in a stage of conformity can limit innovation potential*
- *recognise the importance of enabling people to move to a questioning, challenging and synthesising stage*
- *appreciate that to create a culture that supports innovation, there needs to be a shift in values from compliance (acting positively to gain rewards and avoid punishment) to internalisation (acting positively because it is congruent with your values)*
- *ensure there is an alignment between the organisation's values and individuals' values for better acceptance of innovation principles*
- *rise above the position of 'pawn' or even 'player' to a higher level of empowerment in order to change the game.*

Key challenge: How to develop motivation and mindsets for purpose-driven innovation.

Here's an interesting cognitive challenge: If you stand at the South Pole, which country will you be looking towards if you face north?

It's a fascinating puzzler when you stop to think about it, isn't it? If you stand at the South Pole and spin 360 degrees, you will *always* be facing north! All longitudinal north–south lines meet at the South Pole. Likewise, if you head south from any country in the world you will always be led to that single point in the middle of Antarctica. Our final continental destination should therefore provide us with the perfect metaphorical vantage point to pull together all the ideas we have explored and see the challenges from the past and leading into the future from a unique 360-degree perspective.

Antarctica gives us a particularly interesting perspective on the problem of climate change. The increasing threat to the continent—it is now identified as one of the fastest-warming regions on Earth[1]—could point to dire consequences for the rest of the planet. The 'ozone hole' over Antarctica, first detected in 1985, now covers almost the same area as the continent itself. It has an interesting paradoxical effect on the continent. Ozone depletion actually leads to cooling temperatures, which intensify the westerly winds, known as the polar vortex. This traps the cold air over the continent and the edges of the peninsula reach higher temperatures, which in turn leads to increased melting. Fascinating sequential pictures from satellites, the more objective, distanced view from outer space, reveal that large sections of the continent are breaking off with global warming and the continent as a whole is dramatically changing.[2]

As Antarctica plays a vital role in the equilibrium of the world's oceans, any change in this continent impacts the oceans in general, which impacts the planet as a whole. Atmospheric gas- and mineral-enriched water from Antarctica sinks 4 km to the bottom of the ocean and is then circulated throughout the world's oceans, allowing the oceans to 'breathe'. But in 1997 it was discovered that as the Antarctic Ocean gets warmer it is less able to dissolve and disseminate carbon dioxide.

Climate change issues are a major current concern, yet people tend to respond very differently to the apparent threat. We typically react to confronting issues from the position of our belief system. We often tend to place more importance on the information that supports our existing beliefs, and less on the information that challenges what we believe.[3]

Long after science had disproved it, many people maintained their entrenched belief in the flat earth theory, for example. Today we face a similar situation with climate change. From the anecdotal evidence in our interviews with polar expeditioners we've met through to the overwhelming scientific consensus, the evidence is irrefutable—yet not everyone currently accepts it.

It takes innovation to solve a problem, but our innovation orientation is impacted by our belief system. In this chapter we will explore how we develop an innovation orientation, and the impact this can have on the way we see and deal with challenges.

Innovation roadblocks and fast-forward enablers

To navigate the controversial path towards transformational innovation, it may be helpful to have a model to explain the motivations and belief systems that can lie behind attitudes and approaches to innovation. Following along the lines of Jean Piaget's stages of cognitive development and Lawrence Kohlberg's stages of moral development, stages that we all typically progress through in life as we age, James Fowler believes we also all go through developmental 'stages of faith'.[4]

We first came across this model when studying for a postgraduate degree in theology back in the 1980s. We immediately saw the value of the model for understanding our values and belief systems in general, and we believe it is a useful model to draw on here to help us make sense of the innovation race. Fowler sees faith as the individual's 'attempt to give meaning to life', which gives the concept a broader interpretation beyond religious belief. It is fundamentally about identifying our reasons for doing what we do. The model has interesting implications for all people, no matter what their beliefs, but critically for business and innovation. Think about this possibility as we run through the model.

The initial stage (stage 0: 'Primal or Undifferentiated' faith) is heavily linked to the need for safety and survival (as in Maslow's hierarchy of needs model). Fowler believes we begin by progressing through phases that are impacted by the beliefs of our parents and community and are characterised by literal interpretations and conformity (stages 1 to 3). We then become more individualised as we struggle to interpret our beliefs for ourselves, before reaching a stage where we can acknowledge the paradoxes of life and accept the complexities (stages 4 and 5). The final stage is an 'enlightened' phase in which universal principles of care and justice supersede all others and people are seen as part of a connected universal community (stage 6). The forthcoming table (overleaf) summarises how these interpretations of the world can impact the potential for innovation.

Fowler's 'Stages of Faith' table linked to innovation potential[5]

Lower levels: Innovation 'roadblocks'			Innovation potential
Stage 1	Intuitive–Projective	an imitative stage based on imagination unrestrained by logic	Innovation potential is limited through acceptance of conventional ways of doing things
Stage 2	Mythic–Literal	a literal interpretation of the world based on myths and stories	
Stage 3	Synthetic–Conventional	unquestioningly taking on the perspectives and boundaries of a peer community	
Higher levels: Innovation 'fast-forward enablers'			
Stage 4	Individuative-Reflective	taking personal responsibility for beliefs, capacity for critical reflection on identity (self) and outlook (ideology)	Innovation potential is enhanced through: • a focus on questioning to challenge existing assumptions
Stage 5	Conjunctive	moving away from self-certainty, alert to paradox and the truth in apparent contradictions	• a desire to seek new solutions • a desire to confront paradoxes
Stage 6	Universalising	a tolerance and inclusiveness of all beings and a unifying force	• an openness to diversity

You will note that people may typically resist innovation where they have not developed the ability to think reflexively, as in the lower levels.

Are you smarter than a third grader?

As a start, think about how the opportunity to develop innovative mindsets can be restricted when thinking is limited to the conformity stage. The *bandwagon effect*, the *herd mentality* and *groupthink* are all terms used in psychology to describe the brain's bias for going with the group. We are naturally wired to want to go along with the majority view, even if that view is shown to be objectively incorrect. The brain has a natural confirmation bias that means people tend to seek information that reinforces a pre-existing belief, which leads to the formation of the 'echo chambers' we described earlier.[6] This is especially notable in relation to social media. A group of Italian researchers found that people tend to 'friend' and follow those who have similar beliefs and values to themselves while filtering out those they don't agree with.[7] For this reason many people stagnate in the synthetic–conventional stage, which limits their potential for innovation.

The brain has also been shown to produce an 'error' signal when an individual chooses to differ in opinion from others in a group. We are wired to conform, and are chemically rewarded with dopamine in the area of the brain that processes social rewards when we choose to go along with the ideas and behaviours of others — particularly our 'in-group' or the group we associate most closely with.[8] Even when individuals initially have a divergent opinion, the desire to conform is so strong that they will typically go along with the opinion of everyone else in their group.[9] An accompanying behaviour is that members of the in-group will often not trust outsiders. We discussed in chapter 6 how Margaret Heffernan refers to this as a 'willful blindness',[10] but according to Fowler's model another reason could be that this person is trapped by their isolated synthetic–conventional surroundings.

Fowler points out that keeping a population at synthetic–conventional stage can be easier for a society in that it reduces dissention and fosters a willingness to go with the flow. Keeping people in a state of ignorance can help to shore up power and control. A researcher has studied the act of wilfully spreading confusion and deceit to maintain a state of ignorance, naming it *agnotology*.[11] Think back to the impact of oppression on innovation (chapter 5), and the paradox of leaders of countries or companies we have previously discussed who move dangerously close to the extremes of control. These leaders were not known for encouraging critical reflection (usually associated with the higher stages of development). Since they themselves were both visionary and creative *and* they had an end goal to improve everyone's lives (altruistic), innovation happened despite their controlling approach.

Some people with this synthetic–conventional mindset appear to prefer a controlling leader who can give them the direction they feel they need. A recent sampling of 1800 registered voters in the US has revealed that while a number of different factors (including education, income, gender, age, ideology and religiosity) had no significant link to what candidate a voter prefers, two factors did stand out as having statistically significant links: authoritarianism and a fear of terrorism.[12] People who have been labelled 'authoritarians' typically follow and obey strong leaders and strongly dislike outsiders. With these sorts of fundamentalist beliefs so strongly ingrained in many cultures, perhaps it's not surprising that strong, dominant leaders end up being a popular choice for some, even if they are light on wisdom, experience and content. Authority is often justified by an entrenched moral hierarchy.[13]

Authoritative leaders can use what is known as 'emotional contagion' through 'mob psychology' to create groupthink. This style of leadership (especially in politics) plays on people's fears, appealing more to people who think that life is getting worse. A common use of this tactic might be, 'There is going to be a recession unless you vote for me.'[14] A distinguishing feature of conformity is that it feels voluntary, and we willingly give to the most charismatic leaders, or perhaps the best 'con-artists'.[15] Research increasingly suggests that human reason is more of a tool for justifying what we've already decided to do rather than a tool for logically deciding what to do.

Leaders can take advantage of this conformity bias without realising how it can impact the ability to innovate. An analysis of the speeches of presidential candidates in the US assessed the language level of some candidates as being just above third-grade level, using both fewer words and words of fewer syllables than the higher-level speeches.[16] The speeches at this level were seen as being more emotional, simpler in structure and content, and angrier. Rather than discussing the complexities of domestic policy or international affairs, these speeches tended to degenerate into emotional tirades. In recent years there appears to have been a decline in the complexity of political speeches, and whether this is a symptom or a cause, it does show that stage 3 synthetic–conventional thinking is flourishing in many communities today. Perhaps not surprisingly, as the format of reality TV shows shape reality, their oversimplified and dramaticised formulae shape the political sphere.

It is important to remember here that of course there is a spectrum between strict fundamentalism on one side, where we are simply 'pawns', and enabled optimism on the other, where we become 'players', but some of us will tend to swing towards one side, while others tend to swing towards the other. Identifying default positions can help us to identify possible blocks to innovation, along with potential solutions.

Changing the status quo

The Czech Republic is a fascinating country in which very different generations demonstrate the two common approaches to innovation. When we worked with the enthusiastic young director of the Innovation Centre Česká inovace, a venture set up to encourage companies to innovate, he told us how he remembers his parents always being too scared to ask questions. Having lived for so long in compliant fear under an oppressive government, never raising their heads above water, they were shocked by the new generation that felt free to challenge and question the status quo. The current generation, on the other hand, is working with Česká inovace to build an 'innovative playground' that will 'inspire people and companies to be creative, promote new ideas and support each other'.[17] The group talks enthusiastically about 'evangelising' innovations, and creating an 'ecosystem' to support ideas and innovators. The country has obviously come a long way since the director was young.

Government control and press censorship may to some degree keep a society stable and functioning, but they will slow down shared communal innovation. That sort of control for the sake of dominance, says Freire (the Brazilian educator and philosopher we introduced in chapter 5), 'anesthetizes and inhibits creative power'.[18] In this chapter we will go further in seeking to understand why and how this happens.

It has been suggested that the best way we can compare countries in the 'innovation race' today is by looking at the walls that have divided countries down the middle and their impact, such as eastern and western Europe (Berlin) and North and South Korea.[19] You can literally see how one side went on to innovate as they saw themselves as players, while the other side went on to stagnate as their population were treated as and believed themselves to be pawns. People in North Korea had been brought up to view their leader as god-like, for example. Too afraid to question this, some lived in fear of even thinking otherwise, believing that Kim Jong-il could read minds.[20]

The apparently indestructible Egyptian empire was finally brought to the brink of annihilation following years of domination at the end of the third millennium BC. The catalyst for change came when a major drought dried up the Nile, the source of life for the Egyptians. When the Egyptians started to believe the gods had abandoned them and the uncertainty led them to question the current beliefs, they took their futures into their own hands rather than simply continuing to believe in fate. The tradition emerged of recording undesirable events or curses on clay pots, and then breaking the clay pots to symbolise a newfound control over the outcome of these events. Common people also started to make unusual linen masks that gave them a feeling of power and control over their own destiny. Gradually, there was a shift from fatalism to empowered optimism. Similarly, countries from the Eastern Bloc, having unshackled themselves from governments that used their power to dominate, are now freer to focus on innovation.

The synthetic–conventional stage brings with it a sense of identity within the group. Remember in chapter 5 we discussed the tendency for people to commit to and trust their own tribe while finding it difficult to extend that trust beyond the tribe? This sense of tribalism can be typical of these lower stages. Since the dawn of time humans have sought a sense of safety through defining themselves as belonging to a tight-knit in-group and ostracising or even demonising outsiders. For many years, for example, traditional tribal groups typically defined themselves as 'the people', with outsiders considered non-human.[21] We have discussed how social psychologist Jonathan Haidt identifies that a belief system can both 'bind and blind' us. The way beliefs hold us together can either, as he has said, bind us into 'ideological teams that fight each other as though the fate of the world depended on our side winning each battle', or, blind us ' ... to the fact that each team is composed of good people who have something important to say'.[22]

Because innovation comes from creative thinking, and creative thinking starts with questioning and an openness to new and different ways of seeing things, it is possible to see how remaining in Fowler's lower stages can limit innovation. Thinking 'outside the box' usually means venturing beyond the standard ways of thinking, beyond what others think. This sort of creative thinking is clearly going to challenge the status quo.

The inherent value of ethical innovation

In areas that involve ethical and moral decisions many companies remain at Kohlberg's[23] and Fowler's conventional lower stages. People at the lower stages will do the right thing only where they risk getting caught if they don't. By staying at this level, however, they will not be able develop the authentic ethical base that enables them to see the inherent value that ethical choices offer. A truly innovative company should be aiming for a culture of people at the higher stages, where they are constantly questioning, challenging and critiquing as they work towards the *best possible* mutually beneficial decisions based on a strong ethical foundations. Big brands caught using sweatshops to produce their garments apparently reformed as a result, but then reverted to their old practices once they thought no one was looking. Part of the genius of these brands is to elevate their products above ethical or environmental considerations in the minds of consumers. 'Commodities take on a life of their own, overshadowing that of the hapless factory worker who makes them.'[24] These strategies work best with consumers who don't ask questions.

Other industries have also been caught paying lip service to the rules to appease the system rather than because they are following a deeper principle. Some of the big banks decided to speak out on ethics only after they had been caught being unethical. VW and Mitsubishi Japan tried to get away with building cars that passed the emissions tests but did not actually comply with emissions requirements. Some companies appear to submit to regulations on diversity to avoid sanction and punishment rather than because it is the right (and most beneficial) action to take. In each case, the company fails to understand the value that the higher stages of morality and ethics can bring.

Compare these companies to strong ethical companies such as Patagonia, 3M, Colgate Palmolive, Visa, Timberland, Country Road and Fairphone, and to fair trade chocolate in general, whose sales are growing at a significantly faster rate than normal chocolate. (You can find out more about the most ethical companies at BWA[25] and Honorees[26] or by using the Good On You app.) So there is profit in taking the moral high ground, but this is not the reason these companies do this. Their higher level of integrity has become an important part of their brand. It is inherently valuable for creating a culture of innovation and attracting the creative class.

Can strong company cultures block innovation?

We have a friend who works for one of the most successful retail chain stores in Australia, a chain so successful that it has wiped out most of its competitors. The commercial success of this company is often attributed to the strong company culture they have created. They are known for providing a fun workplace with opportunities for growth, for focusing on building effective leaders and teams through training and motivational programs, and for ensuring that the staff retain close connections socially as well as professionally. In return, employees give their heart and soul—working long hours, remaining loyal through challenges (for example, not making worker's compensation claims when they could and should) and tolerating inconvenient postings without complaint. The culture is actually so strong that the employees have learned to conform rather than to question. So while the company would like to think they are creative and innovative, opportunities for innovative growth are actually limited.

Having a strong company culture is important, as all management theories will attest, but a culture that is *too* strong may actually encourage the sort of synthetic–conventional thinking that limits growth and innovation. One of the points of transition from belief to doctrine, Sam Keen suggests, is when expressions of faith are represented as sacred scripture.[27] Think too about how organisational ideas and beliefs, once captured in writing, such as in vision and mission statements, can actually limit growth—unless they are constantly revisited and revised according to the changing needs of the organisation and the individuals within it.

The TV documentary *Secrets of the Super Brands*[28] made a clever connection between these sorts of high-commitment companies and religion, showing how there is the same sort of neurological response in individuals in both cases. The sort of fervour and loyalty that religious faith can engender can also be invoked by powerful companies and their brands. We know a former employee of a large IT company who brought up the fact that he had heard their products were being produced in sweatshops. This challenge was raised in a meeting with an important executive from the US, a meeting designed to reinforce the strong company culture. Most of the employees and executives present were so invested in the strong company culture that they felt it was almost blasphemous to question it and were horrified at the apparent lack of loyalty. This employee was told that maybe he didn't belong there, and it wasn't long before he left. At that point he took his questioning (and potentially innovative) mind elsewhere!

Out of the shark tank

People often stick with what they have always believed to be right without questioning it. But what happens when an individual starts to question the beliefs they have long taken for granted? In Fowler's model, signs that individuals might be starting to move beyond the lower stages may include contradictions, paradox and debates between valued authority sources, along with marked changes in the policies or practices of leaders. Those still at the synthetic–conventional stage might refer to the transition to a higher stage as 'backsliding' or 'disloyalty' as it looks to them like a loss of faith.

Galileo was condemned by the Inquisition for challenging the accepted beliefs of his day about how the world worked. Questioning the status quo can often be met with suspicion, distrust or even contempt. By encouraging open debate and openness to change, organisations can find ways to transition to more open models and systems. This in turn can lead to real transformation over the long term, but the organisation needs to be ready for this sort of change.

Although the transition to the higher level stages might be interpreted as a loss of faith or a sign of disrespect to those still in the synthetic–conventional stage, it will feel like a natural development to those who have made the move. At this stage the individual is starting to take seriously their responsibility for the consequences of their own actions. This enabled and empowered stage involves authenticity and taking a huge leap of faith. 'To enter into stage 4', says Fowler, 'means to spring out of the fish tank and to begin to reflect upon the water.'

The metaphor of creative thinking being 'outside the box' is overused, but maybe Fowler's model gives a deeper meaning to this, with people in the higher stages being the first to be able to truly break out of the box. Or, in the case of the *Shark Tank* program, break out of the competitive 'tank'. To use another well-known business metaphor, higher stage thinking will lead to the type of innovation that will create real 'blue ocean' strategies — that is, it will open up creative possibilities outside of where the general competition is looking.

People locked in the synthetic–conventional stage are more likely to think of problem solving from what a cognitive scientist has called a 'direct causation perspective', or dealing with a problem through direct action. The following types of statements are typical of causation thinkers:[29]

> 'It was very cold today — so global warming doesn't exist.'
> 'Refugees are flooding into our country — so deport them/build a wall/stop the boats.'
> 'If criminals use guns to kill — then arm everyone else.'
> 'There was a tsunami — we must have done something wrong.'

'After decades of the world being made simple for our entertainment (for example, through reality TV),' says Dr Raymond Orr of the School of Social and Political Sciences at the University of Melbourne, 'we have begun to think it actually is that simple.'[30] Those who are able to see such issues as more complex recognise *systemic causation*. Rather than looking at single explanations it is essential to recognise and embrace the ambiguities. Innovative thinkers need to be able to hold multiple ambiguities in their mind at any one time, embrace paradoxes and use authentic empathy to see things from others' perspectives. This leads to a dialogue, which can result in genuine collaboration between opposing groups, and solutions will start to be found from an empowered 'can do' attitude.

The sociological equivalent of splitting the atom: transitioning to higher stages

Historically cultures have naturally evolved towards higher stages. This can be seen in the shift from a dependence on agricultural production, which is vulnerable to fluctuations in climate and the will of the higher powers, to a dependence on man-made technologies from the end of the eighteenth century.[31] Industrialisation led to a period of intellectual 'enlightenment' and significant political and social change. The greater dependence on technology led to greater specialisation, and capital was invested and reinvested. There was now an expectation of continual development and progress, and change took on a constant, autonomous momentum.

As more and more people at all levels became a part of this change and empowered by it through a process of questioning and continual improvement, laws were questioned and revised too. Where once seen as immutable and divinely ordained, laws now needed to be adapted to respond to changing modern demands. The Renaissance period in Europe saw a liberation from the lower stages of fundamentalist faith to more creative, individual thought. Anthropologist Wade Davis refers to the period as the sociological equivalent of splitting the atom.[32]

All the definitions of creativity and innovation we have discussed in this book point towards the higher stages of Fowler's model. Someone in the higher stages develops a humbling 'second naivety'; the sort of openness and curiosity we have identified activates creativity. This stage is all about *embracing paradox*. The individual is able to accept the multiple perspectives and dimensions held together in paradoxical tension, acknowledging the need to transcend beyond thinking in black and white, and to relate to the reality behind the symbols of inherited systems rather than to the symbols themselves.

By the final stage the individual is able to truly transcend differences and include all perspectives. Richard Florida, as we have discussed in earlier chapters, identified tolerance as an essential quality for building a creative class. Individuals at this level experience a shift from the self as the centre of experience—away from dominance based on personal ambition and towards mutual freedoms (chapter 5), away from a closed mindset and towards diversity and open connections (chapter 6), away from the individual focus and single-mindedness, and towards authentic collaborative engagement (chapter 7). These people are connected (chapter 6) and are making the shift away from inflexibility and towards greater enabled optimism and adaptability (chapter 8). They 'create zones of liberation from social, political, economic and ideological shackles'. Their community is universal.[33]

We are not here to debate the best system for life (whether political, religious or economic) or what will work for everyone, but rather to show how best to manage the 'innovation race'. It should be clear by now that moving up through Fowler's stages of faith will put an organisation (as with a country or culture) in a winning position for the long term.

The challenge will be to assess what may need to be questioned and confronted in the organisation in order for transformational, sustainable innovation and progress to take place.

True organisational culture change

To create a culture that supports innovation, there needs to be a shift in values from *compliance* (acting positively to gain rewards and avoid punishment) to *internalisation* (acting positively because it is congruent with your values). Compliance means accepting values from an outside source and attesting to them because you believe you should rather than because you really believe in them; by internalising values you make them your own. It has been found that where employees feel there is alignment between the organisation's values and their own personal values, where there is an internalisation of the values, there is likely to be more commitment to innovation and enthusiasm around the implementation of innovations.[34]

Organisational culture is not easily definable and not easily identified. It is intangible, subject to change (albeit often imperceptible), and it is usually unique to an organisation. Micro-level factors can resist change; macro-level factors can become barriers to change. Both affect the pace and type of change.[35] At the core of organisational culture are values, and values are represented through practices.[36] Changing the *values and practices* will impact the climate and culture and eventually lead to transformation.

In a truly innovative organisational culture innovation is absorbed into rather than tacked onto the culture and management practices.[37] Innovation is not a line item objective; it's a natural way of thinking and working. The culture will impact how well creative solutions are supported and implemented. The leadership style that most supports innovation has been found to be the 'change-oriented' style, while the 'structure-oriented style' usually has a negative or neutral impact on innovation.[38] Research suggests that the climate is greatly influenced by the manager and management style, and that risk-taking, dynamism, freedom and debate have been found to be the critical climate dimensions that influence radical innovation rather than incremental improvement.

> Risk-taking, dynamism, freedom and debate have been found to be the critical climate dimensions that influence radical innovation rather than incremental improvement.

Deciphering the code

Culture is often reflected in language, and in order for there to be a deep culture change there must also be an analysis of the language used in the organisation. Imagine what organisations today would be like if we took away the corporate jargon? What if we were no longer able to use the terminology and common idiom that have defined the ways we communicate for so long? All organisations have their own distinctive vernacular, but many people have been exposed to the language for so long they don't realise how pervasive it is.

We mentioned in chapter 6 how language can isolate. Language is a key barrier to innovation, but it can have even more dangerous implications for innovation: it can disempower and disable, entrapping us at the synthetic-conventional stage. Sam Keen believes: 'Every institution and profession —religious or secular—creates its lingo. It is the nature of professions and organizations to invent special languages that are understood by insiders but are otherwise opaque; to be a professional is to speak in code. For the uninitiated reading [the texts] ... is like deciphering code. It is not uncommon for professionals of all kinds ... to use obfuscation, complexity, and mystification to claim knowledge—and thereby power—unavailable to the layperson.'[39] Keen believes that to cut through jargon that may no longer be relevant all organisations should go on a corporate linguistic fast:'It would be interesting to see what would happen within corporations if, for one hundred days, it was forbidden to talk about profits, losses, stockholders, competition, or market share. Some workers might wonder out loud if what they were doing with fifty or sixty hours a week truly reflected how they wished to spend their fleeting years. Others might wonder whether the product being promoted was ecologically viable, or if their contribution to a global economy was likely to benefit those on the planet who needed it most.'[40]

Through this process, says Keen, it will be possible to reconnect with the original meaning and power of the organisation.

So who really wins in the end? We spoke about how refugee Mohammad Ali Baqiri refused to remain a pawn and rose up to become an empowered player. His mindset of *enabled optimism* gave him the power to move forward, to innovate, to change things for the better and not simply accept the way things were. Mohammad changed the game through becoming a lawyer. He is now involved in groups seeking to change government policy, especially towards children in detention. Mohammad has progressed rapidly from pawn, to player, to game changer.

Up to chapter 8 we looked at how to create a culture that supports the 'innovation race'. This chapter seeks to understand the deeper *why*. Why can we or can't we innovate? At this point we can suggest:

- Pawns won't have the opportunity to innovate. They can only passively observe or allow themselves to be manipulated by the producers (even if they are optimistic about their situation).

- Players (participants) can take control and therefore have the opportunity to innovate.
- Wise players can even change the innovation game, rising up to become producers.

This is what these final chapters are about—how to change the game, rather than simply going along with it as pawns or even trying to manage it as players.

We've adopted the analogy of a race, and some readers will have assumed that means it's all about winners, losers, elimination and how to stay ahead of the pack. Yet it becomes clear that higher level players, using enabled optimism as a powerful intervention, can change the game in such a way that we can *all* do better and win. This is not about *the* 'innovation race' or *my* 'innovation race' or even *our (tribal) group's* 'innovation race', but rather *the global* 'innovation race' for survival. This signifies a shift from 'what's in it for me?' to 'what's in it for us?' It's about how to win the universal race for the benefit of all.

Throughout this book we have been talking about how to get ahead through creating the best environment to support innovation, but trying to 'win' and 'be the best' at the expense of others can be dangerous. Right at the beginning we mentioned a second theme paradoxically running through the book: looking at purpose, the big picture of progress, even whether there should be a race at all. We have discussed collaborative engagement, exploring the benefits of mutual gains over individual wins. We described how we may need to change our interpretation of the words *you* and *we* to become more inclusive (as illustrated by the different forms in the Filipino, Malay and Indonesian languages). We might learn from such indicators how we can stay in the race in a way that is mutually beneficial rather than at the expense others.

By drawing on the resilient spirit these people embody, we might learn not only how our organisations can get ahead in innovation through times of dramatic change, but how we can start to change the game to ensure that innovation is sustainable and benefits all.

It's interesting to note that Antarctica is the only place on Earth where nations have put aside their differences to focus on a common goal: the future of the planet. Antarctica is possibly the most sustainable and ecologically well-protected continent—and the most politically neutral. A number of countries agreed in a 1959 treaty to prohibit activities that could harm the fragile ecosystem of the continent, including mining, military activity, nuclear explosions and the dumping of nuclear waste. There are no permanent inhabitants on the continent, but it houses up to 5000 people at the different research stations located there.

In Antarctica it's possible to see what a winning innovation strategy might look like. People living and working in Antarctica have a strong sense of purpose, and they must learn to see from multiple perspectives and develop a deep empathy. They work from a foundation of *guided freedom* (working together with a framework of shared principles), and *targeted openness* (accepting diversity and building connections), with *collaborative engagement* (authentic mutually beneficial cooperation between countries) and *grounded flexibility* (enabled optimism with a stable foundation). Researchers are there because they believe they can make a difference, and use purpose-driven innovation to solve complex problems.

We have talked about the concepts of winning, losing and eliminations in the context of the 'innovation race'. It should now be becoming clear that if we don't *all* win, we could all lose and be eliminated.

Does Antarctica offer a model for how we can collaborate creatively to solve our most urgent problems? In the final chapter, we will offer some suggestions for a future innovation agenda to ensure these principles can be actively implemented for long-term sustainable change.

GAME CHANGER CHECKLIST

☐ Can you identify reactive and proactive responses to issues and the attitudes behind them?

☐ Can you identify if conformity is a potential innovation block?

☐ Have you identified the importance of enabling people to move to a questioning, challenging and synthesising stage?

☐ Is there a need for a shift in values from compliance (acting positively to gain reward or avoid punishment) to internalisation (acting positively because it is congruent with your values)?

☐ Do the organisation's and individuals' values align?

☐ Are you and your team able to rise above being a 'pawn' or even a 'player' to a higher level of empowerment in order to really change the game?

10

FUTURE TRENDS

The new innovation agenda

*'We were making the future ... and hardly any of us troubled
to think what future we were making. And here it is!'*

H. G. Wells

*As we launch into the future, we need to reimagine and reinvent the ways we do things
to ensure more sustainable solutions at all levels. We recommend:*

- *systemic change that generates viable alternatives to our current economic structures,
  along with creative and innovative cultures*
- *new definitions of innovation that recognise a move away from technological
  measures towards integrated and sustainable systems*
- *a shift towards purpose-driven innovation, exploiting business opportunities
  associated with solving the world's biggest problems, while maintaining a clear
  priority on ethics and integrity.*

*This chapter offers food for thought on where we could go next by providing a new
innovation agenda for changing the game.*

Key challenge: How to innovate responsibly to deal with a rapidly changing world.

Our wildly courageous friend Matt McFadyen, extreme adventurer, does
not look like an elite athlete. He has a stocky frame and solid build, but this
physique has actually been well suited to the sorts of polar expeditions he
has undertaken. Matt was the youngest Australian to sail to Antarctica. He
also told us of a particular expedition he took to the North Pole, which
(unlike Antarctica) offers no firm land mass, but only shifting, drifting ice.

Matt conveyed to us the incredible energy and determination needed to hike for hour after hour, day after day, over pressure ridges of rough broken ice and crevasses, dragging all your supplies in a sled behind you. You burn so many kilojoules that you have to eat slabs of pure butter to keep your weight up and keep warm. Yet because of the shifting ice, you can wake in the morning to discover you are kilometres behind where you stopped the night before. So a few hours of trekking are added to your schedule each day ... and still find you are further from the Pole than when you started.

The perils of shifting sea ice have challenged sailors and explorers across the ages. RMS *Titanic* sank when it hit an iceberg in the North Atlantic on its maiden voyage in 1912, with the loss of more than 1500 passengers and crew. Ernest Shackleton's ship *Endurance* was trapped in a drifting ice floe for months before finally breaking up under the pressure and sinking in the Antarctic Weddell Sea. As recently as 2007 a tourist cruise ship, MS *Explorer*, sank when it hit an iceberg in the Southern Ocean.

Another arctic explorer we spent time with over the years, the late Peter Malcolm, had the dubious honour of captaining the fourth ship to sink in Antarctica after it was crushed by moving ice. A quietly spoken man who readily admitted his errors and downplayed his significant achievements, Peter travelled to Antarctica 15 times over a period of 21 years, and after the early sinking disaster he learned the lesson of how to adjust to the changing environmental challenges.

An interesting solution to the problems of sailing through ice was an innovation originally devised in the 1890s by the Norwegian explorer Fridtjof Nansen when he invented an 'ice-proof' ship. Previous attempts to reach the North Pole had failed when the ships were crushed by the ice. Even hulls that were especially strengthened to push through would eventually get stuck and submit to natural forces. At that time no one really knew whether the Pole was located on ice over the Arctic Ocean or over a land mass, and no one had succeeded in designing a ship that would not be crushed by the shifting ice, so people had begun to accept that all attempts to reach the Pole were doomed to failure. Nansen was determined to prove them wrong.

Nansen knew the polar ice was constantly changing and drifting, but he also hypothesised that an arctic current constantly pushed the ice westward and that he could harness this natural east–west current to reach the Pole. And just as important, Nansen had designed a ship for the purpose, with especially strong cross-bracing and a rounded hull that, under pressure, would lift the ship above the ice rather than allowing it to be seized and crushed.

Nansen had found a way to rise above one of the challenges that polar expeditioners such as Matt typically experience — to effectively change the game. To do this required real innovation. He didn't just build a stronger boat, he built a completely different type of boat.

It's time for the real game changers

As a civilisation we are now in a bind, at a point where innovation has become critical for our survival. We have created a world in which we must continue to innovate to stay alive, yet we seem unable to keep up with the pace needed. There can be times when, like Matt McFadyen in the Arctic, we feel like we have made progress, only to discover we are behind where we started from. So we are at a dangerous crossroads, facing a raft of problems, many of which we have ourselves created. Global warming, pollution, species extinction, a number of modern diseases — these are problems that threaten our very existence but that humanity itself is responsible for. If we don't find a way to rise above the challenges and change the game our future could be devastating.

The writing is on the wall. As proposed in the previous chapter, real transformation is required — in society in general, and in governments and organisations in particular. Transformation demands a change in forms, rather than a superficial external makeover. This is not about renovating, touching up and repainting to present as new; it's about remaking from scratch, jettisoning old ways of doing things and reconstructing new futures.

Transformation needs to happen at all levels and in multiple ways. As Nansen had learned of ship design, improvement on current methods is not always enough. We need to change individual and organisational beliefs and mindsets in order to break through to the next level of thinking required.

We have discussed how one of the greatest challenges for organisations today is the need to balance stability and flexibility, to continue to perform reliably and consistently while at the same time being flexible enough to adapt to fast-paced change. Transformation at all levels — individual, team and societal — is vital in these challenging times. Only through dedicated and deliberate sustainability leadership will we be able to move towards a more sustainable society. As sustainability researchers are saying, 'Our challenge is to shape, define and effect deliberate transformation in ways that will enhance human well-being and sustainability.'[1]

A number of radical transformations will be needed for real change to take place, in order for humans to shift from being passive observers to collaborative producers.

The innovation agenda

We have touched on a range of long-term issues and challenges in this book. In summary, we believe the following dramatic changes will be needed for socially responsible and sustainable responses to current and future business, societal and global challenges:

A. Systemic change

We believe two levels of systemic change are needed: viable alternatives to our current economic structures, and the design of creative and innovative cultures.

1. Viable alternatives to our current economic structure

It could be time to challenge the economic system that we have assumed for so long will bring peace and prosperity. Capitalism can support collaboration and raise living standards through innovation. Yet the 2008 financial collapse revealed the dangers of unrestricted capitalism and the unfettered greed it can promote. As those who advocate 'conscious capitalism' tell us, 'It is unquestionably the greatest system for innovation and social cooperation that has ever existed. So much has been accomplished, and yet much remains to be done ... We are collectively less prosperous and less fulfilled than we could be.'[2]

Measures of innovation success have typically started with economics. If an invention or new idea is commercially successful, it is lauded as an innovation breakthrough. Yet is this the best measure of the value of innovation? The mindset of focusing on economics and growth at all costs could have dire consequences. The challenging landmark book *Limits to Growth* (and more recent updates) has revealed how the current economic model has led to humans consuming more than the Earth is capable of supporting.[3]

Consider the practice of comparing countries according to their GDP (gross domestic product). This seven-decades-old practice, which started after WWII, may now not be broad enough to measure all areas of progress. Robert F. Kennedy believed a country's gross GDP measured 'everything except that which makes life worthwhile'. Many people are now concerned that GDP measures market transactions but takes no account of human wellbeing and welfare or environmental costs.

New systems that benefit humans and the environment will need to be developed. Founder and co-CEO of Whole Foods Market John Mackey has been actively putting these principles into practice through his unusual organisation. Through the philosophy of conscious capitalism, business leaders such as Mackey are advocates for a higher purpose, for stakeholder integration, for building a consciousness culture and for developing conscious leadership. Another idea is *innovationism*, which shifts the emphasis from the availability of capital to tested innovation.[4] In this model ordinary people are able to contribute to progress through trialling products and services, and through this trial and error there is a continuous process of purpose-driven innovation that connects with real people's needs.

Visionary political economists say that true leaders will be able to step back, analyse the current system, and search for more collaborative and innovative alternatives that will work over the long term.[5]

2. A focus on creative and innovative cultures

Let's look at the big-picture changes that need to be made to our economic system from another angle. We could start to think about what sort of economic system will be optimistic and flexible enough to support holistic and sustainable innovation. Richard Florida and his Global Innovation Index team believe, for example, it will need to be a new system of 'creative capitalism': 'Capitalism is in the midst of an epochal transformation from its previous industrial model to a new one based on creativity and knowledge. In place of the natural resources and large-scale industries that powered the growth of industrial capitalism, the growth of creative capitalism turns on knowledge, innovation, and talent.'[6]

It is clear that the parameters need to change from metrics based on technology and industry to ones based on valuing creative ideas. We have already referred to Richard Florida's ideas on how to attract the 'creative class' through talent, technology and tolerance. Technology is just one ingredient of creative success. The others require people development: developing talent for more creative thinking and innovation skills and capabilities, and developing creative tolerance for greater diversity. Florida and his team built a 'Global Creativity Index' to measure these three areas, and in the 2015 edition Australia came out on top of the 139 countries measured[7]—not because it has the most patents, which we believe is a very limited measure, but because it scores highly in the areas of talent and tolerance.

This report outlines how creative economies are more productive and competitive (according to the World Economic Forum's Global Competitive Index), are associated with higher levels of human development (according to the UN Human Development Index) and are more egalitarian (according to the World Bank's Gini Coefficient). Tolerance has the highest correlation with economic output, so by increasing diversity and supporting diverse populations in our cities and in our organisations we will ultimately be improving productivity. The correlation between the Global Creativity Index score and economic competitiveness is actually stronger than GDP per capita as a measure, and measures of entrepreneurship from the GCI are stronger still!

The Scandinavian nations successfully combine high levels of creative competitiveness with relatively low levels of inequality, which appears to meet both demanding economic needs and critical human development needs. Says Florida's team, '... a high-road path to prosperity where the fruits of economic progress are more broadly shared is not only possible . . .it can actually be better for economic performance.'[8]

As we move forward we will need not only more advanced *technological innovations,* but also more advanced *creative thinking and problem-solving skills.* As computers and robots take over more of the simpler work functions and workplaces become more automated, there will be fewer low-skill jobs available, and humans will be required to take on more advanced problem-solving roles. The new jobs that will emerge will require emotional and social intelligence, and critical and creative thinking, rather than task-specific skills that can easily be automated.[9] Individuals and organisations need to be able to think critically and creatively in order to effectively solve 'wicked' problems (for example, issues that are difficult to define and socially complex).

B. New definitions of innovation

There are two levels at which we might usefully redefine innovation: moving away from purely technological measures and moving towards more holistic measures, along with introducing integrated and sustainable systems.

1. A move away from purely technological measures

As we have discussed, measures of creativity and innovation (such as patents, R&D budgets and inventions) are typically positively correlated to growth in innovation, but of course this refers to *technological innovation.* So naturally, according to measures such as these, America and Europe usually dominate. Perhaps it's time to start thinking of additional measures that recognise the innovation talents of other countries and cultures. Think of all those creative concepts and innovative ideas that might otherwise never see commercial success (again Jugaad innovation, introduced in chapter 2, springs to mind).

There are many other ways to measure progress and success that may be more appropriate—or at least as relevant. Anthropologist Wade Davis writes, 'Were societies to be ranked on the basis of technological prowess, the Western scientific experiment, radiant and brilliant, would no doubt come on top. But if the criteria of excellence shifted, for example, to the capacity to thrive in a truly sustainable manner ... the Western paradigm would fail.'[10] Although western societies generally boast a longer life span, better medical care and lower death rates by homicide, they typically do not provide as much social support as other countries.[11] The Bhutanese, for example, measure progress according to a Gross National Happiness (GNH) Index as well as a GDP (which is also increasing). When you visit the country, the only remaining Buddhist kingdom in the world, you can feel the focus is on community and general well-being. Our definition of innovation also needs to expand to embrace these psychological and social measures.

Because there has been such an emphasis on innovation in technology, the technological gap between advanced and lagging countries has tended to widen rather than narrow over time. This is due to what economist Jeffrey Sachs, Director of the Earth Institute at Columbia University, has referred to as 'positive feedback mechanisms', in which innovations lead more rapidly to further innovations. 'Technological innovation operates like a chain reaction in which current innovations provide the fuel for future breakthroughs.'[12] So it will be extremely challenging for those already lagging behind technologically to get ahead in this field.

Technology can also impact general wellbeing measures. If, for example, you simply look at the measures of life expectancy and wealth over time, you will see that significant technological innovations correlate with greater health and wealth. Two hundred years of incredible progress has not been evenly distributed within and between countries. Hans Rosling, a Swedish medical doctor and statistician, does a great job of demonstrating how dramatic this difference is in his famously exuberant lecture style, which includes dynamic graphs showing changes over time.[13] If we take a new approach to innovation and start to define it as a means of improving the lives of people around the world for the mutual benefit of all, we can see how valuable creative thinking and innovation can become.

Rather than leading to inequality, innovation can be a great equaliser. Advances in transformative technologies mean useful technologies are increasingly accessible to those who need them most, and this now needs to be a focus. In developing countries in Africa, for example, while business as well as personal use of mobile phones is on the rise, in many villages without access to electricity it has meant a long trek to a neighbouring town just to charge the phone. The introduction of solar panels to provide local energy sources is helping to change that.[14] Other innovation initiatives that are helping to equalise opportunities for developing countries include small power plants that can convert rice husks into electricity, biogas chambers that can convert cow manure into fuel and electricity, and small hydroelectric dams that can use local streams to generate power. Imagine how once these communities have access to power they can start to utilise 3D computers for broader access to manufacturing, greater communication and connectivity to enable, for example, community-supported agriculture, in which urban consumers can pledge an amount in advance to cover farming costs—all of which will foster consumer involvement and build social capital. Innovation in the future should be more about solving social and environmental problems for the good of all rather than solely for the sake of commercial advantage, or technological development for its own sake.

Rosling believes that with 'aid, trade, human technology and peace', every country can in the future progress into the 'healthy and wealthy' corner of the growth graph. As economies open up, so will opportunities. The spread of capital markets has ensured that there is more access to capital and labour across borders, and multilateral trade agreements are helping to support this.[15]

Queen Rania al Abdullah, queen of the Hashemite Kingdom of Jordan, sums up the challenges well: 'What good are these technologies if they cannot be shared and enjoyed by all—especially the people or nations who need them most? Or if a lack of security and stability prevent people from accessing them? In other words, what good is technological progress without moral progress? Answer: It's nothing more than the illusion of progress.'[16]

Take a look at our website (www.the-innovation-race.com) for a list of some great alternative measures of development and innovation that have emerged in response to this growing trend.

2. Integrated and sustainable systems

The future is a hyperlinked and *integrated* world, where our lives will be less segmented and innovation less isolated from real-world needs. There will need to be closer and more purposeful connections, as we have discussed, which will become essential for identifying challenges and developing more creative and innovative ideas. As analysts have commented, 'In today's hyperlinked world, solving problems anywhere solves problems everywhere.'[17]

Technology will more consciously enhance our lives through supporting real-world learning and connections rather than providing an alternative to real-life experience and so isolating us from it.

The future will depend on how well we can integrate technology into our daily lives, suggests CNN host Fareed Zakaria. 'And that depends on skills fostered by the liberal arts, such as creativity, aesthetic sensibility and social, political and psychological insight.'[18] Zakaria believes that creativity and innovation emerge at the intersection between different disciplines, where there is the opportunity for cross-pollination, so it is essential that education remains broad. As examples he points to how Steve Jobs' experience with learning calligraphy influenced his focus on the aesthetic of Apple products, and how Mark Zuckerberg's early studies in psychology impacted the development of Facebook.

The point of integration will be to provide greater sustainability. Sustainability is about doing things differently economically, environmentally, socially and individually so they are more workable over the long term. Sustainability needs to prioritise a broad range of values rather than simply focusing on economic value.[19] In this context, environmental costs and rising personal and social costs will need to be considered. We can no longer focus only on the stakeholders that benefit financially from the organisation's success; we also need to focus on the stakeholders who will benefit emotionally and socially. Organisations of the future will lean towards a 'coordinate and cultivate' leadership approach that focuses on values, freedom and flexibility.[20]

We need to work through Maslow's hierarchy of needs, whereby all of humanity's basic physical needs are first dealt with before other higher order needs such as freedom are addressed, so that sustainability, inclusivity and equality are ensured.[21]

C. A move towards purpose-driven innovation

There are two additional ways, finally, that we might be able to make a greater shift towards purpose-driven innovation.

1. Business opportunities from solving the world's biggest problems

Rather than doing business solely for the sake of profit, we need to explore how we can use business to help solve the world's greatest problems. 'Businesses are the greatest platforms for change and can have an enormous impact on improving the state of the world,' suggests the founder and chairman of the World Economic Forum. 'As business leaders we are in positions of influence, and responsible for more than just shareholders. We are accountable for the well-being of an extended community of employees, customers and partners, as well as our fellow beings on this planet we inhabit.'[22]

An inspiring 'wish list' of more than 50 breakthrough technologies that could defeat poverty has been put together by the Institute for Global

Transformative Technologies at the Lawrence Berkeley National Lab. This list focuses on potential developments in the areas of: basic physical needs such as health, food and agriculture, water and electricity access; human rights needs such as education and gender equity; and environmental needs such as climate change and the environment. The authors of the report believe that real breakthrough innovations, not incremental changes, are needed to meet the challenges.

The list includes vaccines for major diseases (for example, HIV/AIDS, malaria and tuberculosis), smart educational textbooks accessible to all, new low-cost and scalable methods for desalination, low-cost solar irrigation pumps, affordable homes resilient to extreme weather, and low-cost transportation for families using renewable energy.[23] If organisations could focus even some of their creative energy and resources on designing and producing these products, imagine how much better the world could be for all.

The world's biggest problems could also be the world's biggest business opportunities and the best way to create billions of dollars' worth of value might be to positively impact the lives of billions of people.[24] Now, more than ever, is the time for this to happen. The growth in mobile technology is democratising knowledge access and helping to include the people who need it most in the innovation process, assuming they first have their most basic needs met.[25] Technology can now be leveraged by organisations working at the bottom of the pyramid to assist the world's poorest, such as through using real-time data to track the use of mosquito nets or monitor agricultural practices.[26]

Bill and Melinda Gates have already demonstrated how it is possible to make development needs a priority. The Gates' personal wealth now equals twice the GDP of Kenya,[27] and they top the Forbes list of the 50 highest givers in the US.[28] When he first focused on bringing connectivity to impoverished communities in Africa, Bill was struck by the fact that much more basic needs had to be met. For those at the bottom of Maslow's pyramid no amount of IT connectivity was going to solve the basic food and security needs they faced. Gates describes how he had arranged for a computer demonstration for a group of impoverished children, and a generator had to be brought in — a generator that would be taken away from the community again after the demonstration. Then he visited the local hospitals and saw people dying unnecessarily of treatable diseases, and he realised that he had a responsibility to assist with the most basic of needs before even thinking about the continent's connectivity problems. The foundation now focuses on fighting disease and reforming education, two areas of fundamental importance for the continent's development over the long term.[29] Microsoft has partnered with USAID on a Global Development Lab that aims to eradicate extreme poverty by 2030.

Gates believes that we need to apply principles of 'creative capitalism' to improve the world, and that organisations like Microsoft have a moral and business imperative to lead the way. Organisations will need to change their focus and their culture, inside and out, to support this ideal.

2. Ethics and integrity as a priority

Critical for business success will be ensuring there is a foundation of ethics and integrity so everyone wins the race over the long run.[30] Think about what this actually means. What would you do, for example, if you discovered that the furniture you were buying had been made in sweatshop conditions in an impoverished country where child labour was used? Would it matter if the customer didn't know about it, and if it was the most cost-effective way to buy furniture? This is the sort of dilemma that can really test an organisation's values and determine the motivation behind innovation for the future.

We recently worked with the general manager of a hotel who was proud to tell us about his company's wonderful mission statement. To us there was nothing outstanding about it, as it included the key words we saw in mission statements all the time: integrity, honesty, passion and so on. But in this case the GM wanted to ensure that this was not merely an outward-facing PR exercise, that the values would become integral to the way the whole organisation operated. After some investigations, he learned that the furniture he had been sourcing for the hotel was relatively inexpensive because it came from a sweatshop that used child labour. He knew that even though the guests wouldn't necessarily know where the furniture was sourced, if he was really going to live up to the values of the mission statement he was going to need to change suppliers and check more carefully in future. He demonstrated how important it is to act from a values base to maintain integrity.

Another hotel GM we have worked with managed a property in a developing country. The GM discovered that the sewage shipped out in trucks never made it all the way to the official depot. To save time and hassle, the truck driver was dumping his load at a beach down the road. Out of sight, out of mind. When he found out, the GM arranged for a senior staff member to travel with the truck each time to ensure it ended up where it was supposed to. The guests wouldn't know the difference, but the GM knew it was the right thing to do for long-term sustainability.

For many companies these values can be difficult to align with the need to provide economic value to stakeholders. This creates a paradox that inevitably leads to tension. These days companies need to make sense of their values and use them as a foundation for more than just superficial marketing purposes. Enron had long proudly boasted about honesty in their values before being exposed in one of the greatest corporate scandals in history. By contrast, companies like Patagonia have carved out a niche in the market by sticking to authentic core beliefs and by doing so have won real respect and loyalty from all stakeholders.

Psychologist Howard Gruber first introduced the idea of *moral creativity*, arguing that creativity should be harnessed for moral purposes.[31] We have a responsibility to use creative thinking and innovation to solve the world's most overwhelming problems with integrity.

How to change a culture to change the game

We have whipped around the world in 100 000 words, looking at (using TV game shows as an analogy) the winners, the losers and how to 'get ahead'. In business-speak that translates into reviewing the challenges and the best practices to deal with these. This has involved looking for common threads in countries, companies and cultures, to see if we can find some common themes and answers on how to win the innovation race, and what this might mean.

We started exploring the concept of the race in the Australian desert with a mismatch between two very different teams. The outcome raised questions about the very concept of a 'race' and why it had become so accepted as a metaphor for innovation. We discussed how innovation is about much more than just technical progress. We entered the life of a seventeenth-century Chinese Buddhist artist to explore the importance of emotional connection and multiple perspectives, before boarding a leaking boat with celebrities and asylum seekers to discover the importance of empathy — all critical starting points for purpose-driven innovation.

We travelled to four continents (taking a few detours along the way) to learn first-hand some very different perspectives on how we might find a balance within the four key paradoxical pairings that lead to creating a sustainable culture of innovation: Control vs Freedom, Focus vs Openness, Individualism vs Group Engagement, and Stability vs Flexibility.

Finally, we took our journey of exploration of the race to the Poles, to Antarctica and the Arctic, to find how our technological progress and innovations have affected these farthest corners of the Earth, and the critical impact this could have on the future of our planet. We also noted that Antarctica is the only continent where all nations have set aside their differences to work on a common goal, and it is perhaps from this model of collaboration that we can draw our greatest hope for the future.

Most importantly, as we have been emphasising, we have learned that this race can and should be a collective race, *our* mutual collaborative challenge. For those who still enjoy the concept of the adrenaline-charged thrill of the chase, maybe we can start to consider that rather than racing *against* others, we can race *together*—against contemporary challenges such as climate change and ecological destruction, against nuclear proliferation and injustice, to find more efficient and effective methods of survival, and to alleviate poverty and suffering. We now need innovation to move ahead, yet we need to redefine innovation to ensure it is holistic and benefits everyone.

Just as Nansen built a better rather than a stronger ship to rise above the ice, we need a better metaphor for innovation rather than simply trying to run a faster race.

Consider the problems inherent in the concept of always trying to get ahead of others. Coming first often has its challenges. In plenty of episodes of the reality TV show *The Amazing Race*, as the contest approaches its climax the audience is sure the current leaders will triumph, only to find they miss out at the end and face elimination. This, of course, makes for good drama, but it also demonstrates how tenuous and temporary success can be. The dominant players who push ahead may not be ready for the possible outcomes of racing at all costs. Sometimes those who have been eliminated in past rounds are brought back in just before the grand finale and have a say in the conditions of the final leg. This is when those at the front of the race will reflect on how they treated others along the way.

So what are the alternatives? Some interesting stories of races around the world give a completely different perspective on how we can see competition.

Every Easter the small provincial Italian town of Panicale hosts 'a sporting event that combines elements of bocce and yo-yo', a race that involves rolling a 4 kg round of Pecorino cheese all the way around the town walls. The contestant who takes the least number of strokes to get the cheese over the line is judged the winner and, quite literally, takes the cheese. What matters isn't crossing the finish line first, but rather getting the cheese over the line most efficiently. This tradition provides an interesting twist to the concept of competition: it is the process that matters more than coming first.

The New Guineans have a traditional log-rolling race in which teams roll logs down a hill as fast as they can towards a finish line. Yet the aim is not for one team to reach the finish line before the others, but for all teams to reach the finish line *at the same time*. So if one team starts to fall behind, individuals will break away from other teams to help them catch up with the others. There is great excitement and celebration when all the teams fly over the finish line at the same time. They take joy in the shared experience of 'winning together'.

Yabusame is a traditional Japanese equestrian sport in which arrows are shot at a target from a moving horse. There is no rivalry between the riders, and they don't compete for money. Rather they do it 'for the gods' and believe that if they hit all three targets health and prosperity will flow not just to the individual rider, but to the whole region.

An anthropologist once proposed a competitive game to some children from an African tribe. After placing a basket of fruit near a tree, he told them that whoever could get to the tree the fastest would be able to enjoy eating the sweet fruits. As soon as they started to run, the children grabbed each other's hands and ran together, and then when they reached the fruits they sat together to enjoy them. When asked why they had run together, the children used the word *Ubuntu*, which means 'I am because we are'. 'How can one of us be happy if all the others are sad?' they said.

The first British woman to reach the North Pole, Helen Jomoa, has told us how it is critical to collaborate in extreme conditions for the mutual survival of the expedition team. (See an interview with Helen Jomoa at www.the-innovation-race.com). What great examples of how competition can help all to reach a mutually beneficial goal, and what great inspiration for our world today!

Doing things differently

To get a better feel for the dramatic impact of this shift, let's return to a story related to the one we started with. The last Indigenous Australians to come into contact with Europeans emerged from the desert the year before *The Hunting Party* went to air. The family group that came to be known as the Pintupi Nine entered the modern world in 1984, 20 years after they had become separated from their tribe.[32] Their appearance caused a big stir in the media at the time, with headlines announcing the arrival of a 'lost tribe', but the Pintupi family were frustrated by this description. They claimed they were never lost; they were simply living the way their people had lived for countless generations.

So back to that question. Who have we discovered are the real winners? Who are the real survivors? Surely those who learn to walk that fine line between innovation for the mutual advancement of society and innovation for the sake of it. The why of progress and the purpose of innovation are critically important here.

It was probably never even considered at the time, but imagine if the *Hunting Party* scenario had been developed differently, not as a contest between two opposing groups but as a collaborative race. If they had realised how ill-suited their original script was and learned to adapt and change (dare we say *innovate*) even as the story was unfolding, perhaps the producers could have carved out a new, more fruitful path. They could have designed a narrative around collaboration, providing opportunities to combine the unique innovation skills of the tech-savvy SAS soldiers and the deep knowledge, experience and wisdom of the Aboriginals. With a sense of enabled optimism, the two teams could have collaborated and raced together to solve a bigger problem more purposefully.

A documentary was later made about the leader of the Aboriginal group in *The Hunting Party*, David Gulpilil. The title of the documentary, *One Red Blood*, came from a quote by David: 'We are all one blood. No matter where we are from, we are all one blood, the same.'[33] In this single quote the wisdom of the ages captures the principles of the future of innovation we are recommending.

The CEO of Salesforce, Marc Benioff, wants to see businesses take the lead through a similar collaborative approach. Salesforce is a company we have had the opportunity to work with, and we have been impressed by their commitment to social change. Benioff believes that given their current position, for better or worse, 'Businesses are the greatest platforms for change and can have an enormous impact on improving the state of the world. As business leaders we are ... accountable for the well-being of an extended community of employees, customers and partners, as well as our fellow beings on this planet we inhabit.'[34]

Pawns, players—or empowered producers

It's time to rise above the playing field and look at better alternatives. And we can only do that by shifting perspective from being pawns or even players to becoming producers. From this position we can coordinate a better future.

Bruce Cohen, Academy Award–winning producer of movies such as *Silver Linings Playbook*, *Milk* and *American Beauty*, describes how a good movie-producing process engages and involves all players at all levels:[35]

> Part of the challenge of the job of producing is as the movie gets going, you're creating. But also discovering, probing, learning about, well, what is the organizational structure of this film? Who are the players? What do they do? Who's got the power? Who thinks they

have the power? Who wants the power? Who doesn't have the power? And how can I recreate that to be what it should be? ...

Also what is the forum for decision making because that goes from the extreme of a movie where the Director makes every decision and no one has any say in anything on one side, to a movie where 12 people stand around the monitor that you're looking at the shot and discuss. I wouldn't want to work on a movie at either of those two extremes, but they certainly exist ... Every movie has its own unique system and structure, and it's our job to figure that out and create it simultaneously.

Cohen describes a dynamic collaborative procedure that injects great energy into the creative process. Think about how you can 'figure out' the unique system and structure of the organisation 'and create it simultaneously'. How you can explore the different individual perspectives, powers and passions that exist in a team, and harness them for a greater creative outcome, with the same open mindset and willingness to learn from the group. The producer's role here is critical to helping to maintain a creative balance.

Producers rely on the cliffhanger format to keep their audiences hooked. Audiences were left hanging for a whole year to find out if one of the main characters in *Game of Thrones* had really died. In the US it may have begun with the famous promotional hook following the third-season finale of *Dallas*: 'Who shot J.R.?' Cliffhangers used to just come at the end of a season, but with the pace of life speeding up and viewers' attention spans rapidly decreasing there has been a progression to cliffhangers between ad breaks!

We believe the 'innovation race' has become a perpetual serial cliffhanger, and finishing this book will by no means signify the end of the race. The critical question will be: How will we as the main characters in our own drama resolve the dilemmas we find ourselves in? And how will we, simultaneously as the producers, reframe the game? Start to think of yourself as a collaborative producer rather than simply a player or a controlling director, and you might begin to see the unique possibilities open to you and your organisation.

As producers, we will need to rethink the metaphor itself. The way we talk about complex and abstract ideas is suffused with metaphor and this influences the way we reason. One study argues that a metaphor embedded in a text can shape how people think about an issue and influence how they respond to it.[36] Metaphors are not just a way to pretty up a speech — they become the way we perceive and live our lives.[37]

If a good metaphor can change the way we see reality, analysing the metaphors we use may take us beyond our perceived reality and the confines of our current box (or shark tank!). So here is one final paradox to stretch your creative thinking: maybe to win the 'innovation race' we have to go outside the metaphor altogether. In *The Hunting Party* the Australian Aboriginals clearly did not like or understand the premise of the race. They could not see the purpose of the race, and as a result they stepped outside its parameters and changed the narrative. We have shown in this book that the concept of an innovation race is a popular metaphor and has been used effectively to describe our current situation. We've seen that it is no longer a viable option to 'sit out' the race or to be a passive observer. We've argued that everyone is at least a participant (whether willing or unwilling, empowered or manipulated). Finally, we introduced the idea of rising up to become a producer, enabled to write the narrative we need for our collective innovation journey.

But let's keep going right outside this box. Maybe to be truly innovative going forward we need to consider something radically new. Maybe we need a new visionary, a disruptive hero to show us we should not be aspiring simply to run a faster race, and to help us to ask, is there a better metaphor, a new genre that can drive us forward? Maybe we don't need a new season, but a new show!

As master mythologist Joseph Campbell said, 'If you want to change the world, you have to change the metaphor.'

To be continued ...

In closing, we think it fitting to draw back so we can view all of those continents from a more distant, detached perspective. A photograph of the Earth was taken by Voyager 1 on February 14, 1990, which remains the most distant, 'zoomed-out' picture of Earth we have. As the spacecraft journeyed towards the fringes of our solar system, engineers turned it around for one last look at its home planet. Voyager was 16.4 billion kilometres away, and approximately 32 degrees above the eclipse, when it captured this portrait of our world. Caught in the centre of scattered light rays, Earth appears as a tiny point of light, a crescent only 0.12 of a pixel in size. Thinking about that gives us a final, sobering perspective on our 'innovation race', and perhaps the jolt that may prompt us to ask, is there something better?

> Look again at that dot. That's here. That's home. That's us. On it
> everyone you love, everyone you know, everyone you ever heard of,
> every human being who ever was, lived out their lives. The aggregate

of our joy and suffering, thousands of confident religions, ideologies, and economic doctrines, every hunter and forager, every hero and coward, every creator and destroyer of civilization, every king and peasant, every young couple in love, every mother and father, hopeful child, inventor and explorer, every teacher of morals, every corrupt politician, every 'superstar,' every 'supreme leader,' every saint and sinner in the history of our species lived there—on a mote of dust suspended in a sunbeam.

The Earth is a very small stage in a vast cosmic arena... Our posturings, our imagined self-importance, the delusion that we have some privileged position in the Universe, are challenged by this point of pale light. Our planet is a lonely speck in the great enveloping cosmic dark. In our obscurity, in all this vastness, there is no hint that help will come from elsewhere to save us from ourselves...

Like it or not, for the moment the Earth is where we make our stand.

It has been said that astronomy is a humbling and character-building experience. There is perhaps no better demonstration of the folly of human conceits than this distant image of our tiny world. To me, it underscores our responsibility to deal more kindly with one another, and to preserve and cherish the pale blue dot, the only home we've ever known.

Carl Sagan, *Pale Blue Dot: A Vision*
of the Human Future in Space

NOTES

Preface

i. ABC (2016). Shark Alarm. *Four Corners* (Feb 8).

ii. Patel, N. (2015). '90% of startups fail: Here's what you need to know about the 10%. *Forbes.* Retrieved from www.forbes.com/sites/neilpatel/2015/01/16/90-of-startups-will-fail-heres-what-you-need-to-know-about-the-10/#32fd913155e1.

iii. Smith, W. K., and Lewis, M. W. (2011). Toward a theory of paradox: A dynamic equilibrium model of organizing. *Academy of Management Review*, (36)2: 381–403.; Smith, W. K., & Tushman, M. L. (2005). Managing strategic contradictions: A top management model for managing innovation streams. *Organization Science, 16*(5), 522–536.

iv. Fredberg, T. (2014). If I say it's complex, it bloody well will be: CEO strategies for managing paradox. *Journal of Applied Behavioral Science. (50)*2: 171–188; Andriopuloulos, C. & Lewis, M.W. (2009). Exploitation-exploration tensions and organizational ambidexterity: Managing paradoxes of innovation. *Organization Science, (20)*4,: 696–717.

v. Dewey, J. (1922). *Human nature and conduct: An introduction to social psychology.* Amherst, NY: Prometheus Books. p. 306; Perrow, C. (1986). *Complex organizations* (3rd ed.). New York, NY: Random House.; Farjoun, M. (2010). Beyond dualism: Stability and change as duality. *Academy of Management Review*, (35)2: 202–225.; Tushman, M. L. and O'Reilly, C. A. (1996). Ambidextrous organizations: Managing evolutionary and revolutionary change. *California Management Review, (38)*4: 8–30.; Murnighan, J. K., & Conlon, D. (1991). The dynamics of intense work groups: A study of British string quartets. *Administrative Science Quarterly (36):* 165–186.

vi. Ghemawat, P. (1991). *Commitment: The dynamic of strategy.* New York, NY: Free Press.; Leonard-Barton, D. (1992). Core capabilities and core rigidities: A paradox in managing new product development. *Strategic Management Journal, (13):* 111–125.; March, J. G. (1991). Exploration and exploitation in organizational learning. *Organization Science.* (2): 71–87.

vii.   Ghoshal, S., & Moran, P. (1998). Bad for practice: A critique of the transaction cost theory. *Academy of Management Review, (21)*: 13–47. P. 41

viii. Gibson, C., & Birkinshaw, J. (2004). The Antecedents, Consequences, and Mediating Role of Organizational Ambidexterity. *Academy Of Management Journal*, 47(2), 209–226. http://dx.doi.org/10.2307/20159573; Poole, M. S. and Van de Ven, A. H. (1989). Using paradox to build management and organization theories. *Academy of Management Review, (14)*4: 562–578.; Smith, W. K. (2014). 'Dynamic decision making: a model of senior leaders managing strategic paradoxes.' *Academy of Management Journal*, 57(6): 1592–1623. P 34; Farjoun, M. (2010).Beyond dualism: Stability and change as duality. *Academy of Management Review.* ; Adler, P. S., Goldoftas, B., & Levine, E. (1999). Flexibility vs. efficiency? A case study of model changeovers in the Toyota Product System. *Organization Science, (10):* 43–68.

Chapter 1

1.   The Hunting Party (1985). *BFI Film*. Retrieved from http://explore.bfi.org.uk/4ce2b72abe239

2.   Malhotra, D. Ku, G. & Murnighan, J. K. (2008). When winning is everything. *Harvard Business Review*, Retrieved from https://hbr.org/2008/05/when-winning-is-everything.

3.   Malhotra, D. (2009). The desire to win: The effects of competitive arousal on motivation and behaviour. *Organizational Behavior and Human Decision Processes*. Retrieved from https://server1.tepper.cmu.edu/seminars/docs/the%20desire%20to%20win%20-%20obhdp.pdf

4.   Grant, A. & Grant, G. (2011). *Who killed creativity?... And how can we get it back?: Seven essential strategies to make yourself, your team and your organization more innovative.* Brisbane: Jossey Bass.

5.   Almquist, E. Leiman, M., Rigby, D. & Roth, A. (2013). *Taking measure of your innovation performance.* Bain & Company. Retrieved from http://www.bain.com/Images/BAIN_BRIEF_Taking_the_measure_of_your_innovation_performance.pdf

6.   IBM (2010). *Global CEO study: IBM biennial global study series*, 4th edn, Retrieved from www.-03.ibm.com/press/us/en/pressrelease/31670.wss.

7.   Baer, M. (2012). Putting creativity to work: The implementation of creative ideas in organizations. *Academy of Management Journal*, 55(5), 1102–1119

8. Eccles, R.G., Ioannou, I., and Serafeim, G. (2012). The Impact of a Corporate Culture of Sustainability on Corporate Behavior and Performance. *Harvard Business School Working Paper*. Retrieved from http://trippel.sdg.no/wp-content/uploads/2014/09/Eccles-HBR_ The-Impact-of-a-Corporate-Culture-of-Sustainability1.pdf

9. IMD-CSM / Burson-Marsteller (2010). *Corporate purpose impact 2010*. Brussels: Burson-Marsteller EMEA.

10. Helpman, E. (2004). *The mystery of economic growth*. Cambridge, GB: Harvard University Press.

11. Moss Kanter, R. (2011). How great companies do things differently. *Harvard Business Review*. Retrieved from https://hbr.org/2011/11/ how-great-companies-think-differently

12. Ruppel, C.P. & Harrington, S.J. (2000). The relationship of communication, ethical work climate, and trust to commitment and innovation. *Journal of Business Ethics. 25:* 313–328.

13. Carroll, P. (2006). An Introduction to economics with emphasis on innovation. Melbourne, AUS: Thompson.

14. Wiseman, R. (2007). Quickstep: The world is walking faster. *New Scientist Blog*. Retrieved from https://www.newscientist.com/blog/ shortsharpscience/2007/05/quickstep-world-is-walking-faster.html

15. Bettencourt, L. M. A., Lobo, J., Helbing, D., Kuhnert, C., and West, G. B. (2007). Growth, innovation, scaling, and the pace of life in cities. *Proceedings of the National Academy of Science, 104*(17): 7301–7306.; West, G. (2011). *Why cities keep growing, corporations and people always die, and life gets faster.* Interviewed by John Blackman, retrieved from http://edge. org/conversation/geoffrey-west

16. Kim, E. (2015). It's mind boggling how the most valuable internet companies have changed over the past 20 years. *Business Insider.* Retrieved from http://www.businessinsider.com.au/the-5-most-valuable-internet -companies-in-1995-vs-today-2015-6#5-in-1995-webcom-1

17. Meeker, M. (2015). Internet Trends 2015 – Code Conference. *KPCB*. Retrieved from http://www.kpcb.com/blog/2015-internet-trends

18. Christensen, C. M. (1997). *The innovator's dilemma*. Boston, MA: Harvard Business School.

19. Olson, M. S., van Bever, D., & Verry, S. (2008). When growth stalls. *Harvard Business Review*. p 45. Retrieved from https://hbr.org/2008/03/when- growth-stalls

20. ibid.

21. Kalogerakis, K., Luthje, C. and Herstatt, C. (2010). Developing innovations based on analogies: Experience from design and engineering consultants. *Journal of Product Innovation Management*, 27: 418–436.

22. Christensen, C., Raynor, M. E., & McDonald, R. (2015). What is disruptive innovation? *Harvard Business Review*. Retrieved from https://hbr.org/2015/12/what-is-disruptive-innovation

23. Harenstam, F., Thuriaux-Aleman, B. & Eagear, R.(2015). Systematizing breakthrough innovation: Study results. *InnovationManagement.se*. Retrieved from http://www.innovationmanagement.se/2015/05/27/systematizing-breakthrough-innovation-study-results/

24. Andriopuloulos, C. & Lewis, M. W. (2009). Exploitation-exploration tensions and organizational ambidexterity: Managing paradoxes of innovation. *Organization Science,* 20(4): 696–717.; Schulze, P, Heinemann, F., Abedin, A. (2008). Balancing exploitation and exploration. *Academy of Management Proceedings, 1*: 1–6.

25. Marx, K. (1906). *Capital. Vol 1: A critique of political economy*. New York, NY: The Modern Library.

26. Vallely, P. (2011). How Steve Jobs reinvented desire. *Independent*. Retrieved from http://www.independent.co.uk/voices/commentators/paul-vallely-how-steve-jobs-reinvented-desire-2367793.html

27. Ciotti. G. (2013). Why Steve Jobs didn't listen to his customers. *Help Scout*. Retrieved from http://www.helpscout.net/blog/why-steve-jobs-never-listened-to-his-customers/

28. Diamond, J. (1999). Invention is the mother of necessity. *The New York Times Magazine*. Retrieved from https://partners.nytimes.com/library/magazine/millennium/m1/diamond.html

29. Christensen, C. M. (1997). *The innovator's dilemma*. Boston, MA: Harvard Business School.

30. Clemons. R. (2014). Milk buying guide. *Choice*. Retrieved from https://www.choice.com.au/food-and-drink/dairy/milk/buying-guides/milk

31. Schwartz, B. (2005). The paradox of choice. *TED* https://www.ted.com/talks/barry_schwartz_on_the_paradox_of_choice

32. ibid.

33. Vallely, P. (2011). How Steve Jobs reinvented desire. *Independent*. Retrieved from http://www.independent.co.uk/voices/commentators/paul-vallely-how-steve-jobs-reinvented-desire-2367793.html

34. Han, E. (2016). Exploitation in electronics: Too many companies failing to come clean. *The Sydney Morning Herald*. Retrieved from http://www.smh.com.au/technology/technology-news/exploitation-in-electronics-too-many-companies-failing-to-come-clean-20160208-gmohao.html

35. Nimbalker, G., Mawson, J., Cremen, C., Wrinkle, H., & Eriksson, E. (2015). The truth behind the barcode: Australian fashion report. *Baptist World Aid*. Retrieved from http://www.baptistworldaid.org.au/assets/Be-Fair-Section/FashionReport.pdf

36. Sen, P. (2014). Helping the world's poor, via cell phones. *Fortune.* Retrieved from http://fortune.com/2014/07/02/helping-the-worlds-poor-via-cell-phones/

37. Worstall, T. (2013). More people have mobile phones than toilets. *Forbes.* Retrieved from http://www.forbes.com/sites/timworstall/2013/03/23/more-people-have-mobile-phones-than-toilets/

38. Lavin Speakers Bureau (2014). Douglas Merrill: Avoiding innovation for innovation's sake. https://www.youtube.com/watch?v=hP7JMzi6YIo

39. Zax, D. (2013). The religion of innovation. *MIT Technology Review.* Retrieved from https://www.technologyreview.com/s/512621/the-religion-of-innovation/

40. Bhuta, F. (2013). Beyond innovation for innovation's sake. *The Holmes Report.* Retrieved from http://www.holmesreport.com/latest/article/beyond-innovation-for-innovation-s-sake

41. 3M (2015). 3M named as a world's most ethical company for second consecutive year. Retrieved from http://news.3m.com/press-release/company/3m-named-worlds-most-ethical-company-second-consecutive-year

42. Oelwang, J. & Hay, B. (2015). The future of work is 100% human. *The World Post.* Retrieved from http://www.huffingtonpost.com/jean-oelwang/the-future-of-work-is-100_b_6791878.html

43. **Creativity is the front end of innovation:** Amabile, T. M., Burnside, R. M. & Gryskiewicz, S. S. (1999). *User's manual for assessing the climate for creativity: A survey from the center for creative leadership.* Greensboro, NC: Center for Creative Leadership.; Creativity must exist all the way through, not just at the front end: Rickards, T. (2003). Synectics: Reflections of a little-s practitioner. *Creativity and Innovation Management, 12:* 28–31.; **Creativity spawns innovation:** Blau, J. R. & McKinley, W. (1979). Ideas, complexity and innovation. *Administrative Science Quarterly, 24:* 200–219.; **Creativity & innovation together improve market share:** Bharadwaj, S. and Menon, A. (2000). Making innovation happen in organizations: Individual mechanisms, organizational creativity mechanisms or both? *Journal of Product Innovation Management, 17:* 424–434.; Soo, C., Devinney, T., Midgley, D., & Deering, A. (2002). Knowledge management: Philosophies, processes and pitfalls. *California Management Review, 44:* 129–150.

44. Lord Dunsany (1915). *Fifty-one tales.* Retrieved from http://www.fulltextarchive.com/pdfs/Fifty-One-Tales.pdf

Chapter 2

1. Note that much of this content was adapted from a chapter first published in Grant, G. (2015). Can we meaningfully compare creativity across

cultures?. In M. Culpepper & C. Burnett, *Big Questions in Creativity 2015*. Buffalo, NY: ICSC Press.

2. Fuller, T. (2012). Monks lose relevance as Thailand grows richer. *The New York Times*. Retrieved from http://www.nytimes.com/2012/12/19/world/asia/thai-buddhist-monks-struggle-to-stay-relevant.html?_r=0

3. Cameron, A. S. (1999). *Chinese painting techniques.* Toronto, CA: Dover Publications.; Da-Wei, K. (1990). *Chinese brushwork in calligraphy and painting.* New York, NY: Dover Publications.;

4. Bolewski, C. (2008). 'Shan-shiu-hua'- traditional Chinese landscape painting reinterpreted as moving digital visualisation. Conference paper. Retrieved from www.bcs.org/upload/pdf/ewic_eva08_paper4.pdf

5. Artyfactory.com. (n.d.) *Cubism.* Retrieved from http://www.artyfactory.com/art_appreciation/art_movements/cubism.htm

6. Wilbur, K. (2011). *The marriage of sense and soul: Integrating science and religion.* New York, NY: Random House, p. 124–125.

7. Vogt, S. (2007). Expertise in pictorial perception: Eye movement patterns and visual memory in artists and laymen. *Perception. 36*(1): 91–100.; Dingfelder, S. (2010). How artists see. *American Psychological Association.* Retrieved from http://www.apa.org/monitor/2010/02/artists.aspx

8. Chabris, C. & Simons, D. (2011). *The invisible gorilla: How our intuitions deceive us.* New York, NY: Harmony Books.

9. International Work Group on Indigenous Affairs (2005). *Indigenous issues.* Retrieved from http://www.iwgia.org/

10. Arieti, S. (1976). *Creativity: The magic synthesis.* New York, NY: Basic Books.

11. Florida, R. (2002). *The Rise of the Creative Class: And how it's transforming work, leisure, community and everyday life.* New York, NY: Perseus Book Group.

12. Diamond, J. (2012). *The world until yesterday: What can we learn from traditional societies?* London, UK: Viking.

13. McNeil, W. H. (1991). *The rise of the west: A history of the human community.* Chicago: University of Chicago Press.

14. Johnson, S. (2014). *How we got to now: Six innovations that made the modern world.* New York, NY: Penguin.

15. Gorsky (2003), in Hofstede, G. (2003). *Culture's Consequences: Comparing Values, Behaviors, Institutions, and Organizations Across Nations.* Newbury Park, CA: Sage Publications.

16. Ferguson, N. (2011). *Civilisation: The West and the rest.* London, GB: Penguin Books.

17. Acemoglu, D. Robinson, J. A. (2012). *Why nations fail: The origins of power, prosperity and poverty.* New York, NY: Random House.

18. Hall, P.A. (2001). *Varieties of capitalism: The instrumental foundation of comparative advantage.* Oxford: Oxford University Press.

19. Harari, Y. N. (2014). *Sapiens: A brief history of humankind.* London: Harvill Secker.

20. Benedict, R. (1967). *The chrysanthemum and the sword.* Boston, US: Houghton Mifflin Harcourt

21. Weiner, R. P. (2000). *Creativity and beyond: Cultures, values and change.* Albany, NY: State University of New York Press. P. 178).

22. Sternberg R. J. (2006). 'Introduction', in Kaufman J. C and Sternberg RJ (2006) (eds). *The International Handbook of Creativity* pp 1–9. Cambridge, GB: Cambridge University Press.; Kara, H. (2015). Creative research methods in the social sciences.: A practical guide. Bristol, UK: Policy Press.

23. Weiner, E. (2016). *The geography of genius.* New York, NY: Simon & Schuster.

24. Lee, W. (2014). Report: Japanese companies beating US firms in innovation. *The Technology Chronicles.* SFGATE. Retrieved from http://blog.sfgate.com/techchron/2014/11/07/report-japanese-companies-beating-u-s-firms-in-innovation/

25. Kageyama, Y. (2015). Exoskeleton that helps paraplegics walk faces major bureaucratic hurdles in Japan. *Huffington Post.* Retrieved from http://www.huffingtonpost.com/2015/05/13/rewalk-exoskeleton-japan_n_7275796.html

26. Adobe (2012). *Study reveals global creativity gap: Universal concern that creativity is suffering at work and school.* Adobe Systems Incorporated. Retrieved from http://www.adobe.com/aboutadobe/pressroom/pressreleases/pdfs/201204/042312AdobeGlobalCreativityStudy.pdf

27. Lubart, T. I. (2010). Cross cultural perspectives on creativity. In Kaufman, J. C., & Sternberg, R. J. (Eds.) *The Cambridge handbook of creativity.* Cambridge, UK: Cambridge University Press.

28. Westwood & Low (2003). Cited by Lubart, T. I. (2010). Cross cultural perspectives on creativity. In Kaufman, J. C., & Sternberg, R. J. (Eds.) *The Cambridge handbook of creativity.* Cambridge, UK: Cambridge University Press.

29. Lubart, T.I. & Geargsdottir, A. (2004). Creativity: Developmental and cross cultural issues. In Ch 3: Lau, S., Hui, A. N. N., & Ng, G. Y. C. (2004). *Creativity: When East meets West.* Danvers, MA: World Scientific Publishing

30. Pye, L.W. (2000). "Asian values": From dynamos to dominoes? In Harrison, L. E., & Huntingon, S. P. (Eds.) *Culture matters: How values shape human progress.* New York, N.Y.: Basic Books.

31. Webb, in Weiner, R. P. (2000). *Creativity and beyond: Cultures, values and change.* Albany, NY: State University of New York Press.

32. Schumpeter, J. A. (1939). *Business cycles.* New York, NY: McGraw-Hill.

33. Mpofu, E., Myambo, K., Magaji, A. A., Masbego, T-A., & Khaleefa, O. H. (2006). African perspectives on creativity. In Kaufman, J. C., & Sternberg R. J. (Eds.) *The international handbook of creativity.* New York, NY: Cambridge University Press.

34. ibid.

35. Lubart, T. I. (2010). Cross cultural perspectives on creativity. In Kaufman, J. C., & Sternberg, R. J. (Eds.) *The Cambridge handbook of creativity.* Cambridge, UK: Cambridge University Press.

36. Robson, D. (2013). There really are 50 eskimo words for 'snow'. *The Washington Post.* Retrieved from https://www.washingtonpost.com/national/health-science/there-really-are-50-eskimo-words-for-snow/2013/01/14/e0e3f4e0-59a0-11e2-beee-6e38f5215402_story.html

37. De Montaigne, M. (1958). *The complete essays of Montaigne.* Stanford, CA: Stanford University Press.

38. Weiner, R. P. (2000). *Creativity and beyond: Cultures, values and change.* Albany, NY: State University of New York Press.

39. ibid.

40. Okimara & Kagana, in Lau, S., Hui, A. N. N., & Ng, G.Y. C. (Eds.) (2004). *Creativity: When East meets West.* Danvers, MA: World Scientific Publishing.

41. Radjou, N., Prabhu, J., Ahaju, S. & Roberts, K. (2012). *Jugaad innovation: Think frugal, be flexible, generate breakthrough growth.* San Francisco, CA: Jossey Bass.

42. Schomer, K. (2014). *Getting to Mars through 'jugaad'. The Hindu.* Retrieved from http://www.thehindu.com/opinion/op-ed/getting-to-mars-through-jugaad/article6479048.ece

43. Friedman, T. (2005). *The world is flat: A brief history of the twenty-first century.* New York: Farrar, Straus and Giroux.

44. Weiner, R. P. (2000). *Creativity and beyond: Cultures, values and change.* Albany, NY: State University of New York Press. P. 178).

45. Ghemawat, P. (2001). Distance still matters: the hard reality of global expansion. *Harvard Business Review.* 79(8): 137–147

46. O'Brien, B. (2014). Empty your cup. *About Religion.* Retrieved from http://buddhism.about.com/b/2012/08/13/empty-your-cup.htm

47. Gould, D. (2010). *Dana Gould re: reality TV.* Retrieved from https://www.youtube.com/watch?v=KGT9lDjjTRk

Chapter 3

1. Pink, D. (2005). *A whole new mind: Moving from the information age to the conceptual age.* New York, NY: Riverhead Books

2. ABC Nightline (2009). *IDEO Shopping Cart.* Retrieved from https://www.youtube.com/watch?v=M66ZU2PCIcM

3. Brown, T. (2013). How do you build a culture of innovation? *Yale Insights.* Retrieved from http://insights.som.yale.edu/insights/how-do-you-build-culture-innovation

4. ABC Nightline (2009). *IDEO Shopping Cart.* Retrieved from https://www.youtube.com/watch?v=M66ZU2PCIcM

5. Kuang, C. (2016). Microsoft's radical bet on a new type of design thinking. *Co.Design.* Retrieved from http://www.fastcodesign.com/3054927/the-big-idea/microsofts-inspiring-bet-on-a-radical-new-type-of-design-thinking

6. Cushman, D. P. & Sanderson, S. (Eds) (1995). *Communicating organizational change: A management perspective.* Albany: State University of New York Press.

7. Trompenaars, F. & Hampden-Turner, C. (2000). *Riding the waves of culture: understanding cultural diversity in business.* London: Nicholas Brealey Publishing.

8. Cushman, D. P. & Sanderson, S. (Eds) (1995). *Communicating organizational change: A management perspective.* Albany: State University of New York Press.

9. Iacoboni, M. (2009). Imitation, empathy and mirror neurons. *The Annual Review of Pscyhology,* 60: 653–670. Retrieved from http://www.annualreviews.org/doi/abs/10.1146/annurev.psych.60.110707.163604

10. Krznaric, R. (2012). *The Power of Outrospection,* Retrieved from https://www.youtube.com/watch?v=BG46IwVfSu8

11. Kleiner, A. (2001). The dilemma doctors. Strategy + Business. Retrieved from http://www.strategy-business.com/article/17251?gko=444c1

12. The Blog (2014). 19 idiotic (but real) travel complaints. *The Huffington Post.* Retrieved from http://www.huffingtonpost.com/blogdramedy/idiotic-travel-complaints_b_4073107.html?ir=Australia

13. Maddux, W. & Gallinsky, A. D. (2009). Cultural borders and mental barriers: The relationship between living abroad and creativity. *Journal of Personality and Social Psychology,* (96)5: 1047–61. (Excerpt can be retrieved from http://www.tricitypsychology.com/living-abroad-makes-people-more-creative/#ixzz1X7hAxBXS).

14. Shapira, O., & Liberman, N. (2009). An easy way to increase creativity. *Scientific American Global RSS.* Retrieved from http://www.scientificamerican.com/article/an-easy-way-to-increase-c/

15. Lehrer, J. (2010). Why we travel. *The Guardian Observer.* Retrieved from http://www.theguardian.com/travel/2010/mar/14/why-travel-makes-you-smarter

16. Steves, R. (2011). *The value of travel*. TEDxRainier. Retrieved from https://www.youtube.com/watch?v=kYXiegTXsEs

17. Lubart, T. I. (2010). Cross cultural perspectives on creativity. Chapter 14 in Kaufman, J. C., & Sternberg, R. J. (2010). *The Cambridge handbook of creativity*. Cambridge, UK: Cambridge University Press.

18. Lueng Maddux, Galinsky & Chiu 2008, cited in Lubart, T. I. (2010). Cross cultural perspectives on creativity. Chapter 14 in Kaufman, J. C., & Sternberg, R. J. (2010). *The Cambridge handbook of creativity*. Cambridge, UK: Cambridge University Press.

19. Lubart, T. I. (2010). Cross cultural perspectives on creativity. Chapter 14 in Kaufman, J. C., & Sternberg, R. J. (2010). *The Cambridge handbook of creativity*. Cambridge, UK: Cambridge University Press.

20. Newby, J. (2004). Brain switch (interview transcript), *Catalyst*. Retrieved from http://www.abc.net.au/catalyst/stories/s1063853.htm; Esaki, M. (2016). The relationship between creativity, management styles, culture, and language (a case of Japanese and English). Chapter 7 in Dubina, I. N. & Carayannis, E. G. (Eds.) (2016). *Creativity, innovation and entrepreneurship across cultures*. New York, NY: Springer.

21. Kahneman, D. (2011). *Thinking fast and slow*. New York, NY: Farrer, Straus and Giroux

22. Source study: Ghonsooly, B. & Showqi, S. (2012). The effects of foreign language learning on creativity. *English Language Teaching*, *5*(4). Summary article: Simon, Z. (2014). Can learning a new language boost your creativity? *Huffington Post*. Retrieved from http://www.huffingtonpost.com/zach-simon/can-learning-a-new-langua_b_4998795.html

23. ibid.

24. Kokalitcheva, K. (2015). Google's workplace diversity still has a long way to go. *Time*. Retrieved from http://time.com/3904408/google-workplace-diversity/

25. Littleton, C.S. (2005) (ed.). *Gods, goddesses and mythology*. Tarrytown, NY: Marshall Cavendish.

26. Gavetti, G., & Levinthal, D. (2000). Looking forward and looking backward: Cognitive and experiential search. *Administrative Science Quarterly, 45*(1), 113–137.

27. Lajvardi, F. (2015). Spare parts. *TEDx*. Retrieved from https://www.youtube.com/watch?v=YZbkxZgo0qo&list=PLG_Q5swuuw6dZXW2SaY_YVdhgLjyoYSsX&index=1)

28. Anderson, S. (2011). 40 percent of Fortune 500 companies founded by immigrants or their children. *Forbes*. Retrieved from http://www.forbes.com/sites/stuartanderson/2011/06/19/40-percent-of-fortune-500-companies-founded-by-immigrants-or-their-children/#1db4c06b7a22

29. Seigal, A. (2012). The life lessons hidden in reality TV. *New York Times.* Retrieved from http://www.nytimes.com/2012/12/02/magazine/ the-life-lessons-hidden-in-reality-tv.html?hp&_r=2&pagewanted=all&

Chapter 4

1. Gunn, E. (2014). How America's leading science fiction authors are shaping your future. *The Smithsonian.* Retrieved from http://www. smithsonianmag.com/arts-culture/how-americas-leading-science-fiction-authors-are-shaping-your-future-180951169/?no-ist

2. ibid.

3. Klein, G. (2007). Performing a project pre-mortem. *Harvard Business Review.* Retrieved from https://hbr.org/2007/09/performing-a-project-premortem

4. Saeki, N., Fan, X. & Van Dusen, L. (2001). A comparative study of creative thinking of American and Japanese college students. *Journal of Creative Behavior, 35,* 175–192.

5. Kirton, M. J. (2003). *Adaption-Innovation: In the context of diversity & change.* East Sussex, GB: Routledge.

6. Puccio, G. & Gonzales, D. (2004). Nurturing creative thinking: Western approaches and Eastern issues, Ch. 5 in Lau, S., Hui, A. N. N., & Ng, G. Y. C. (Eds.) (2004). *Creativity: When East meets West.* Danvers, MA: World Scientific Publishing.

7. Gebert, D., Boerner, S., & Kearney, E. (2010). Fostering Team Innovation: Why Is It Important to Combine Opposing Action Strategies?. *Organization Science, 21*(3), 593-608. http://dx.doi.org/10.1287/ orsc.1090.0485

8. ibid.

9. Smith, W.K., & Lewis, M.W. (2011). Toward a theory of paradox: A dynamic equilibrium model of organizing. *Academy of Management Review. 36*(2): 381–403.

10. Altshuller, G. (1994). *And suddenly the inventor appeared.* Translated by Lev Shulyak. Worcester, MA: Technical Innovation Center

11. Smith, W. K., & Lewis, M. W. (2011). Toward a theory of paradox: A dynamic equilibrium model of organizing. *Academy of Management Review, 36*(2): 381–403.

12. Mehta, V. (2014). Do opposites really attract? It's complicated. *Psychology Today.* Retrieved from https://www.psychologytoday.com/blog/head-games/201412/do-opposites-really-attract-its-complicated

13. Smith, W. K., & Lewis, M. W. (2011). Toward a theory of paradox: A dynamic equilibrium model of organizing. *Academy of Management Review,* 36(2): 381–403.

14. Tushman, M. L. and O'Reilly, C. A. (1996). Ambidextrous organizations: Managing evolutionary and revolutionary change. *California Management Review. 38*(4): 8–30

15. Lin, H. E., McDonough, E. F., Lin, S.J., & Lin, C.Y.Y. (2013). Managing the exploitation/exploration paradox: The role of a learning capability and innovation ambidexterity. *Journal of Product Innovation Management, 30(2)*: 262–278.

16. Martin, R. (2007). How successful leaders think. *Harvard Business Review,* Retrieved from https://hbr.org/2007/06/how-successful-leaders-think

17. Collins, J. (2001). *Good to great.* New York, NY: HarperCollins. (p 198)

18. Senge, P. (2010). *The fifth discipline: The art and practice of the learning organisation.* New York, NY: Crown Publishing Group.

19. Weiner, R.P. (2012). *Creativity and Beyond: Cultures, Values, and Change.* SUNY Press. (p111)

20. Bateson, G. (1972). *Steps to an ecology of mind.* New York: Ballantine Books. Cited in Farjoun, M. (2010).Beyond dualism: Stability and change as duality. *Academy of Management Review, 35*(2): 202–225.

21. See references from the Preface.

22. Lewis, M. (2000). Exploring paradox: Toward a more comprehensive guide. *Academy of Management Review, 25*(4): 760–776.

23. Kiechel, W. (1982). Corporate strategists under fire. *Fortune.* 106(13): 34–39.; Kiechel, W. (1984). Sniping at strategic planning. *Planning Review.* 8–11; Kaplan, R.S. and Norton, D.P. (2001). *The Strategy-Focused Organization - How Balanced Scorecard Companies Thrive in the New Business Environment.* Boston, MA: Harvard Business School Press.

24. News.com.au. (2014). Mars one Expedition: Is reality TV compatible with science? Retrieved from http://www.news.com.au/technology/science/mars-one-expedition-is-reality-tv-compatible-with-science/story-fnjwlcze-1227125267964

Chapter 5

1. Shaw, J. (2013). Who built the pyramids? *Harvard Magazine.* Retrieved from http://harvardmagazine.com/2003/07/who-built-the-pyramids-html; Associated Press. (2010). Great pyramid tombs unearth 'proof' workers were not slaves. *The Guardian.* Retrieved from http://www.theguardian.com/world/2010/jan/11/great-pyramid-tombs-slaves-egypt

2. Armstrong, K. (1993). *A history of God: The 4,000-year quest of Judaism, Christianity and Islam.* New York, NY: Random House.

3. Shulz, R. & Seidel, M. (2009). *Egypt: The world of the pharaohs.* Cairo: American University in Cairo Press.

4. Weiner, R. P. (2000). *Creativity and beyond: Cultures, values and change.* Albany, NY: State University of New York Press.

5. Wilkinson, T. (2013). *The rise and fall of ancient Egypt.* New York, NY: Random House.

6. Kiger, P. K. (2011). Did Ancient Egypt decline? *National Geographic Blogs.* Retrieved from http://tvblogs.nationalgeographic.com/2011/02/26/why-did-ancient-egypt-decline/

7. BBC, (2016). *Immortal Egypt with Joann Fletcher.* Retrieved from http://www.bbc.co.uk/programmes/b06vsvtx

8. Campbell, J. (1991). *Creative Mythology.* Arkana.

9. ibid.

10. Diamond J. (2012). *The world until yesterday: What can we learn from traditional societies?* London, UK: Viking.

11. Campbell, J. (1991). *The power of myth.* New York, NY: Pan-American.

12. Radjou, N., Prabhu, J., Ahaju, S. & Roberts, K. (2012). *Jugaad innovation: Think frugal, be flexible, generate breakthrough growth.* San Francisco, CA: Jossey Bass.

13. Davis, W. (2012). *Wayfinders.* Western Australia: The University of Western Australia Press.

14. Maslow, A. (1943). A theory of human motivation. *Psychological Review,* 50(4): 370–96. Retrieved from http://psychclassics.yorku.ca/Maslow/motivation.htm

15. Nimbalker, G., Mawson, J., Cremen, C., Wrinkle, H., & Eriksson, E. (2015). The truth behind the barcode: Australian fashion report. *Baptist World Aid.* Retrieved from http://www.baptistworldaid.org.au/assets/Be-Fair-Section/FashionReport.pdf

16. Weisenthal, J. (2013). This pyramid shows how all the world's wealth is distributed and the gigantic gap between rich and poor. *Business Insider.* Retrieved from http://www.businessinsider.com.au/global-wealth-pyramid-2013-10

17. References to Himmelstrand, 1994; Rodney, 1972: and Adedeji, 1993. In Andrews, N. Khalema, N. E., Oriola, T, & Odoom, I. (2013). *Africa yesterday, today and tomorrow: Exploring the multidimensional discourses on 'development'.* Newcastle on Tyne, UK: Cambridge Scholars Publishing.

18. Levitt, S. D. & Dubner, S. J. (2014). *Think like a freak.* New York, NY: Harper Collins.

19. Young, I. M. (2009). Five faces of oppression. Ch. 4 in Henderson, G. & Waterstone, M. (Eds.). *Geographic thought: A praxis approach.* Abingdon, OX: Routledge.

20. Frye, M. (1983). Oppression. In *The politics of reality.* Trumansburg, NY: Crossing.; Young, I. M. (2009). Five faces of Oppression. Ch 4. In Henderson, G. (2009). *Geographic thought: A praxis perspective.* London: Routledge.

21. Haidt, J. (2013). *The righteous mind: Why good people are divided by politics and religion.* New York, NY: Random House

22. Farjoun, M. (2010). Beyond Dualism: Stability and change as a duality. *Academy Of Management Review, 35*(2): 202-225. http://dx.doi.org/10.5465/amr.2010.48463331; Tushman, M. & O'Reilly, C. (1996). The Ambidextrous Organizations: Managing Evolutionary and Revolutionary Change. *California Management Review, 38*(4): 8–30. http://dx.doi.org/10.2307/41165852

23. Freire, P. (2007). *Pedagogy of the oppressed.* New York, NY: Continuum.

24. Maguire, S., Philipps, N. & Hardy, C. (2001). When silence = death, keep talking: The dynamics of trust and control in the Canadian AIDS treatment domain. *Organization Studies, 22*(2): 285–310.

25. Mahbubani, K. (2015). Why Singapore is the world's most successful society. *Huffington Post.* Retrieved from http://www.huffingtonpost.com/kishore-mahbubani/singapore-world-successful-society_b_7934988.html

26. Huffington Post (2013). Singapore named best 'value for money' city for foreign business. *Huffington Post.* Retrieved from http://www.huffingtonpost.com/2013/09/23/singapore-business_n_3976170.html

27. Lu, W. & Chan, M. (2014). 30 most innovative countries. *Bloomberg Business.* Retrieved from http://mobile.bloomberg.com/slideshow/2014–01–22/30-most-innovative-countries.html

28. Singh, K. (2003). *Thinking Hats and Colored Turbans: Creativity Across Cultures.* Prentice Hall.

29. Csikszentmihalyi, M.(Ed) (2006). *A life worth living: Contributions to positive psychology.* New York, NY: Oxford University Press.

30. Arendt, H. (1993). What is Freedom? *Between past and future: Eight exercises in political thought.* New York, NY: Penguin.

31. Lubart, T. I. (2010). Cross cultural perspectives on creativity. Chapter 14 in Kaufman, J. C., & Sternberg, R. J. (2010). *The Cambridge handbook of creativity.* Cambridge, UK: Cambridge University Press

32. Ridley, M. (2015). *The evolution of everything.* New York, NY: Harper.

33. Inglehart, R. (2000). Culture and democracy. Ch 7 In Harrison, L. E., & Huntingon, S. P. *Culture matters: How values shape human progress.* New York, N.Y.: Basic Books. [World Values Survey results were correlated

against scores on freedom through political rights and civil liberties from the Freedom House during the time period 1972 to 1998].

34. Lubart, T.I. & Geargsdottir, A. (2004). Creativity: Developmental and cross cultural issues. In Ch 3: Lau, S., Hui, A. N. N., & Ng, G. Y. C. (2004). *Creativity: When East meets West*. Danvers, MA: World Scientific Publishing

35. Lipset, S. M. (2000). Corruption, culture, and markets. Ch 9 in in Harrison, L. E., & Huntingon, S. P. *Culture matters: How values shape human progress*. New York, N.Y.: Basic Books

36. Ahmed, P. K. (1998). Culture and climate for innovation. *European journal of Innovation Management, 1*(1): 30–43

37. Friere, P. (2007). *Pedagogy of the oppressed*. New York, NY: Bloomsbury.

38. Mandela, N. (1995). *The long walk to freedom*. New York, NY: Little Brown & Co.

39. Lewis, M. (2010). *The big short: Inside the doomsday machine*. New York, NY: W. W. Norton & Company, Inc.

40. Schwarz, B. (2000). Self-determination: The tyranny of freedom. *American Psychologist, 55*(1): 79–88.

41. Schwarz, B. (2004). *The paradox of choice: Why more is less*. New York, NY: Harper Perennial.

42. Schwarz, B. (2004). *The paradox of choice*. TED Talk. Retrieved from http://www.ted.com/talks/barry_schwartz_on_the_paradox_of_choice?language=en

43. Ahmed, P. K. (1998). Culture and climate for innovation. *European Journal of Innovation Management, 1*(1): 30–43

44. Smith, K. (2016). Milennials are being dot.conned by cult-like tech companies. *New York Post*. Retrieved from http://nypost.com/2016/04/03/millennials-are-being-dot-conned-by-cult-like-tech-companies/

45. Conversation with Gerver, R. (2016). Interview.

46. Catmull, E. (2008). How Pixar fosters collective creativity. *Harvard Business Review*. Retrieved from https://hbr.org/2008/09/how-pixar-fosters-collective-creativity

47. Gerver, R. (2016). Interview.

48. Runco, M. (2004). Ch 2 in Lau, S., Hui, A. N. N., & Ng, G. Y. C. (2004). *Creativity: When East meets West*. Danvers, MA: World Scientific Publishing

49. Ferguson, N. (2011). *Civilisation: The West and the rest*. London, GB: Penguin Books.

50. Collins, J. (2001). *Good to great*. New York, NY: HarperCollins.

51. Deutschman, A. (2005). Is your boss a psychopath? *Fast Company* http://www.fastcompany.com/53247/your-boss-psychopath

52. Kreger, R. (2015). Does Donald Trump have narcissistic personality disorder? *Psychology Today.* https://www.psychologytoday.com/blog/stop-walking-eggshells/201510/does-donald-trump-have-narcissistic-personality-disorder

53. Mintzberg, H. (2009). Rebuilding companies as communities. *Harvard Business Review.* Retrieved from https://hbr.org/2009/07/rebuilding-companies-as-communities

54. Ward, V. (2010). *The devil's casino.* Hoboken, NJ: Wiley.

55. Collins, J. C., & Porras, J. I. (1994). Companies need not hire outside CEOs to stimulate fundamental change. *Directorship*, 19(9): 8–10.

56. Bauter, A. (2014). One-on-one with 'Woz': Steve Wozniak talks Steve Jobs. *Charlotte Business Journal* Retrieved from. http://www.bizjournals.com/charlotte/news/2014/07/02/one-on-one-with-woz-steve-wozniak-talks-steve-jobs.htm

57. Goldman, D. (2011). Apple's future: Trying to outlive an icon. *CNN Money.* Retrieved from http://money.cnn.com/2011/10/07/technology/steve_jobs_succession/

58. Brittain L, J. (2015). The leadership gap: What you need, and still don't have, when it comes to leadership talent. *Center for Creative Leadership.* Retrieved from http://media.ccl.org/wp-content/uploads/2015/09/Leadership-Gap-What-You-Need.pdf

59. Caldicott, S. M. (2014). Microsoft CEO Satya Madella's collaboration game: Can he drive innovation growth? *Forbes.* Retrieved from http://www.forbes.com/sites/sarahcaldicott/2014/05/28/microsoft-ceo-satya-nadellas-collaboration-game/

60. Bort, J. (2014). Satya Nadella: This is how I'm really going to change Microsoft's culture. *Business Insider.* Retrieved from http://www.businessinsider.com.au/how-nadella-will-really-change-microsoft-2014-7

61. Perez, J. C. (2014). CEO Nadella promises to shake-up Microsoft's culture: 'Nothing is off the table.'. *PC World.* Retrieved from http://www.pcworld.com/article/2452820/nadella-on-microsofts-culture-change-nothing-is-off-the-table.html

62. Collins, J. (2001). *Good to great.* New York, NY: HarperCollins.

63. Levit & Likna (2001). *How the recession shaped millennial and hiring manager attitudes about millennials' future careers.* USA: Career Advisory Board. (Survey of 1,023 USA adults).

64. Warren, R. (2002). *The purpose driven life.* Grand Rapids, MI: Zondervan.; Seligman, M.E. P. (2006). *Learned optimism: How to change your mind and your life.* New York, NY: Vintage.

65. Diamond J. (2012). *The world until yesterday: What can we learn from traditional societies?* London, UK:Viking.

66. Diamond J. (2012). *The world until yesterday: What can we learn from traditional societies?* London, UK:Viking.; Aldrich, H. E. & Martinez, M. A. (2015). Why aren't entrepreneurs more creative? Conditions affecting creativity and innovation in entrepreneurial activity. Ch. 25 in Shalley, C. E., Hitt, M. A. and Zhou, J. (eds.) *The Oxford handbook of creativity, innovation and entrepreneurship.* Oxford, GB: Oxford University Press.; Christensen, C. M. (1997). *The innovator's dilemma.* Boston, MA: Harvard Business School.

67. Bernstein, S. (2015). Does going public affect innovation? *Journal of Finance, 70*(4): 1365–1403.

68. Edwards, D. (2010). *The lab.* Cambridge, MA: Harvard University Press. P. 17.

69. Kotter, J. (2014). *Accelerate: Building strategic agility for a fast moving world.* Boston, MA: Harvard Business School Publishing.

70. ibid.

71. Westley et al. (2011). Tipping toward sustainability: Emerging pathways of transformation. *Ambio. 40*(7): 762–780. http://www.ncbi.nlm.nih .gov/pmc/articles/PMC3357751/

72. ibid.

73. Gladwell, M (2008). Malcolm Gladwell on culture, cockpit communication and plane crashes. Retrieved from http://blogs.wsj. com/middleseat/2008/12/04/malcolm-gladwell-on-culture-cockpit-communication-and-plane-crashes/

74. Barish, J. (2008). Leadership and innovation. *McKinsey Quarterly.* Retrieved from http://www.mckinsey.com/insights/innovation/ leadership_and_innovation

75. Drucker, P. (1969). *Preparing tomorrow's business leaders today.* Englewood Cliff, NJ: Prentice Hall.

76. Weber, W. (1948). *Essays in sociology.* New York, NY: Routledge.

77. Merton, R. K. (1940). Bureaucratic structure and personality. *Social Forces, 18*(4): 560–568.

78. Koestler, A. (1964). *The act of creation.* London: Hutchinson

79. Kirton, M. (1976). Adaptors and innovators: A description and measure. *Journal of Applied Psychology, 61*(5): 622–629.

80. Farjoun, M. (2010). Beyond dualism: Stability and change as duality. *Academy of Management Review, 35*: 202–225.

81. Turner, S. F. & Fern, M. J. (2012). Examining the stability and variability of routine performances: The effects of experiences and context change. *Journal of Management Studies, 49*(8): 1407–1434.

82. Pink, D. (2015). *Dan Pink on motivating in the workplace.* Retrieved from http://eqsummit.com/dan-pink-on-motivating-the-modern-workplace/

83. Eg Carmeli, Reiter-Palmon, & Ziv (2010); Paulus & Dzindolet (2008). Cited by Shin, Y. & Eom, C. (2014). Team proactivity as a linking mechanism between team creative efficacy, transformational leadership, and risk-taking norms and team creative performance. *The Journal of Creative Behavior,* 48 (2): 89–114.

84. Goncalo, J. A., Vincent, L. C. & Krause, V. (2015). The liberating consequences of creative work: How a creative outlet lifts the physical burden of secrecy. *Journal of Experimental Social Psychology,* 59: 32–39.

85. Stenovec, T. (2015). One reason for Netflix's success – it treats employees like grownups *Huffington Post.* Retrieved from http://www.huffingtonpost.com/2015/02/27/netflix-culture-deck-success_n_6763716.html

86. Weiner, R. P. (2000). *Creativity and beyond: cultures, values and change.* Albany, NY: State University of New York Press.

87. Burns, T., & Stalker, G. (1961). *The management of innovation.* London: Tavistock.

88. Gilson, L. L. & Shalley, C. E. (2004). A little creativity goes a long way: An examination of teams' engagement in creative process. *Journal of Management.* 30(4): 453–470. http://jom.sagepub.com/content/30/4/453.full.pdf

Chapter 6

1. Cable, S. (2014). Travellers break world record. *Daily Mail.* Retrieved from http://www.dailymail.co.uk/travel/travel_news/article-2766380/Travellers-break-world-record-visiting-19-European-countries-just-ONE-DAY-despite-queues-border-crossings-rental-car-nightmares.html

2. Heffernan, M. (2012). *Willful blindness: Why we ignore the obvious at our peril.* New York, NY: Walker & Company.

3. Theroux, P. (2015). Travel writer Paul Theroux's best quotes: 'The basic rules of travelling'. *Traveller.* Retrieved from http://www.traveller.com.au/travel-writer-paul-therouxs-best-quotes-there-are-three-basic-rules-of-travelling-ggx5u1

4. Heffernan, M. (2012). *Willful blindness: Why we ignore the obvious at our peril.* New York, NY: Walker & Company.

5. ibid.

6. Needham, J. (1969). *The grand titration: Science and society in East & West.* New York, NY: Routledge.

7. Poirer, J. (nd). Autonomy and diversity. *Forum of federation: The global network of federalism and developed governance.* Retrieved from http://www.forumfed.org/libdocs/IntConfFed07/Volume_1/IntConfFed07-Vol1-Poirier.htm

8. Lee, B. (2013). The European Union: A failed experiment. *Harvard Business Review.* Retrieved from https://hbr.org/2013/06/the-european-union-a-failed-ex/

9. Rothwell, R. (1994). Towards the fifth-generation innovation process. *International Marketing Review. 11*(1): 7–31.

10. Eurostat (2012). Archive: European population compared with world population. *Statistics Explained.* Retrieved from http://ec.europa.eu/eurostat/statistics-explained/index.php/Archive:European_population_compared_with_world_population

11. Chudzinski, P. (2011). Why the U.S. depends on Europe for building massive, 'multi-local' marketplaces. *Venture Beat.* Retrieved from http://venturebeat.com/2014/09/01/why-the-u-s-depends-on-europe-for-building-massive-multi-local-marketplaces/

12. Diamond, J. (1997). *Guns, germs and steel: The fates of human societies.* New York, NY: W.W. Norton & Company, Inc.

13. Palermo, E. (2014). Who invented the printing press? *LiveScience.* Retrieved from http://www.livescience.com/43639-who-invented-the-printing-press.html

14. Gertler 1995, in Parjanen, S., Harmaakorpi, V., & Frantsi, T. (2010). Collective creativity and brokerage functions in heavily cross-disciplined innovation processes. *Interdisciplinary Journal Of Information, Knowledge, And Management, 5.* Retrieved from http://www.informingscience.org/Publications/713?Source=%2FJournals%2FIJIKM%2FArticles%3FVolume%3D5-2010

15. Simonton, 1984. Cited by Lubart, T. I. (2010). Cross cultural perspectives on creativity. Chapter 14 in Kaufman, J. C., & Sternberg, R. J. (2010). *The Cambridge handbook of creativity.* Cambridge, UK: Cambridge University Press

16. Simonton 1975, 1984. Cited in Chapter 3 Creativity: Developmental and cross cultural issues by Todd I. Lubart and Asta Geargsdottir. In: Lau, S., Hui, A. N. N., & Ng, G. Y. C. (2004). *Creativity: When East meets West.* Danvers, MA: World Scientific Publishing

17. Boschma, R. A. (2005). Proximity and innovation: A critical assessment. *Regional Studies, 39*(1): 61–74.

18. Johnson, S. (2010). *Where good ideas come from: The natural history of innovation.* London, UK: Penguin

19. Henrich, J. (nd). *Why societies vary in their rates of innovation: The evolution of innovation-enhancing institutions.* Retrieved from http://www2.psych .ubc.ca/~henrich/Website/Papers/InventionInnovation05.pdf

20. Lechtenberg, S. (2013). What do skating rinks, ultimate frisbee and the world have in common? A new Freakonomics radio podcast. *Freakonomics.* Retrieved from http://freakonomics.com/2013/11/21/ what-do-skating-rinks-ultimate-frisbee-and-the-world-have-in-common-a-new-freakonomics-radio-podcast/

21. deGrasse Tyson, N. (2015). Appearance on 'The Weekly' with Charlie Pickering. *ABC iview.* Retrieved from http://iview.abc.net.au/ programs/weekly-with-charlie-pickering/LE1409V018S00

22. Weiner, E. (2016). *The geography of genius.* New York, NY: Simon & Schuster.

23. Diamond, J. (1997). *Guns, germs and steel: The fates of human societies.* New York, NY: W.W. Norton & Company, Inc.

24. Dodd, M. (2015). In Manzini, E. & Till, J. eds (2015). *Cultures of resilience: Ideas.* London, UK: Hato Press. P. Retrieved from http://www .culturesofresilience.org/wordpress/?page_id=2

25. Rothwell (1994). An analysis of the Organization for Economic Cooperation and Development (OECD) research data by Jonathan Rothwell of the Brookings Institute.

26. Robert Lucas, Nobel Prize winner – cited by Florida, R. (2002). *The Rise of the Creative Class: And how it's transforming work, leisure, community and everyday life.* New York, NY: Perseus Book Group.

27. Ridley, M. (2015). *The evolution of everything.* New York, NY: Harper.

28. Bettencourt, L. M. A., Lobo, J., Helbing D., Kuhnert, C., & West, G. B. (2007). Growth, innovation, scaling, and the pace of life in cities. *The National Academy of Sciences of the USA.* Retrieved from http://www .pnas.org/content/104/17/7301.full.pdf

29. Lehrer, J. (2010). A physicist solves a city. *New York Times.* Retrieved from http://www.nytimes.com/2010/12/19/magazine/19Urban_West-t .html?_r=0

30. Henrich, J. (nd). *Why societies vary in their rates of innovation: The evolution of innovation-enhancing institutions.* Retrieved from http://www2.psych .ubc.ca/~henrich/Website/Papers/InventionInnovation05.pdf

31. ibid.

32. Johnson, S. (2010). *Where good ideas come from: The natural history of innovation.* London, UK: Penguin; Lehrer, J. (2010). A physicist solves a city. *New York Times.* Retrieved from http://www.nytimes. com/2010/12/19/magazine/19Urban_West-t.html?_r=0; Jacobs, J. (1993). *The death and life of great American cities.* New York, NY: Random House. Bettencourt, Lobo, Helbing, Kuhnert, & West (2007).

33. The World Bank (2014). *Population per sq. km of land*. Retrieved from http://data.worldbank.org/indicator/EN.POP.DNST

34. Bettencourt, L (2014). Mass urbanization could lead to unprecedented creativity – but only if we do it right. *The World Post*. Retrieved from http://www.huffingtonpost.com/luis-bettencourt/mass-urbanization-creativity_b_5670222.html?utm_hp_ref=tw

35. Lehrer, J. (2010). A physicist solves a city. *New York Times*. Retrieved from http://www.nytimes.com/2010/12/19/magazine/19Urban_West-t.html?_r=0

36. Phillips, N. (2015). Your travel leanings may make others ill. *The Sydney Morning Herald*.

37. Westley, F., Olsson, P, Folke, C., Homer-Dixon, T., Vredenburg, H., Loorbach, D., Thompson, J., Milsson, M., Lambin, E., Sendzimir, J., Banerjee, B., Galaz, V., & van der Leeuw, S. (2011) Ambio 2011. Tipping toward sustainability: Emerging pathways of transformation. *Ambio*. Retrieved from http://www.ncbi.nlm.nih.gov/pmc/articles/PMC3357751/

38. Abeyta, L. (2015). Smart phones are equalizing who can access knowledge. *The Huffington Post*. Retrieved from http://www.huffingtonpost.com/lisa-abeyta/smart-phones-are-equalizi_b_7200660.html

39. Rifkin, J. (2015). How the third industrial revolution will create a green economy. *The World Post*. Retrieved from http://www.huffingtonpost.com/jeremy-rifkin/third-industrial-revolution-green-economy_b_8286142.html

40. Reagans & McEvily, (2003). In Parjanen, S., Harmaakorpi, V. and Frantsi, T. (2010). Collective creativity and brokerage functions in heavily cross-disciplined innovation processes. *Interdisciplinary Journal of Information, Knowledge, and Management*. 5: 1–16.

41. Van Norden, R. (2014). Scientists finally catch on to social media. *Scientific American*. Retrieved from http://www.scientificamerican.com/article/scientists-finally-catch-on-to-social-media/

42. Wellman (nd). *Little boxes, glocalization, and networked individualism. Centre for Urban & Community Studies*. Toronto, CA: University of Toronto.

43. ibid.

44. Surowiecki, J. (2005). *The wisdom of crowds*. Toronto, CA: Random House.

45. Lemley, M. A. (2011). The myth of the sole inventor. *Stanley Public Law Working Paper N0. 1856610*. Retrieved from http://papers.ssrn.com/sol3/papers.cfm?abstract_id=1856610

46. Mendoza, J. (2010). 7 incredible scientific inventions held up by petty feuds. *Cracked*. Retrieved from http://www.cracked.com/article_18501_7-incredible-scientific-innovations-held-back-by-petty-feuds.html

47. Oliver, J. (2015). *Last Week Tonight*.

48. Monbiot, G. (2014). The age of loneliness is killing us. *The Guardian*. Retrieved from http://www.theguardian.com/commentisfree/2014/oct/14/age-of-loneliness-killing-us

49. World Health Organization (2007). *Global age-friendly cities: A guide*. Retrieved from http://www.who.int/ageing/publications/Global_age_friendly_cities_Guide_English.pdf

50. Gregoire, C. (2015). Why loneliness is a growing public concern, and what we can do about it. *The Huffington Post*. Retrieved from http://www.huffingtonpost.com/2015/03/21/science-loneliness_n_6864066.html; Song, H, Zmyslinski-Seelig, A., Kim J., Drent, A., Victor, A., Omori, K., Allen, M. (2014). Does Facebook make you lonely?: A meta analysis. *Computers in Human Behavior*, (36): 446 http://www.sciencedaily.com/releases/2014/10/141009163418.htm

51. Bernstein, E. (2014). The transparency trap. *Harvard Business Review*. Retrieved from https://hbr.org/2014/10/the-transparency-trap/ar/1

52. Baschma (2005). In Parjanen, S., Harmaakorpi, V. and Frantsi, T. (2010). Collective creativity and brokerage functions in heavily cross-disciplined innovation processes. *Interdisciplinary Journal of Information, Knowledge, and Management*. 5: 1–16.

53. ibid.

54. Heffernan, M. (2012). *Willful blindness: Why we ignore the obvious at our peril*. New York, NY: Walker & Company.

55. Frey, C.B. (2014). How 21st-century cities can avoid the fate of 20th-century Detroit. *Scientific American*. Retrieved from http://www.scientificamerican.com/article/how-21st-century-cities-can-avoid-the-fate-of-20th-century-detroit/

56. Etounga-Manguelle, D. (2000). *Does Africa need a cultural adjustment program?* Ch 6 In Harrison, L. E., & Huntingon, S. P. *Culture matters: How values shape human progress*. New York, N.Y.: Basic Books.

57. Merton, R. K. (1968). Social Theory and Social Structure. USA: The Free Press. In Lipset, S. M. (2000). Corruption, culture, and markets. Ch 9 in in Harrison, L. E., & Huntingon, S. P. *Culture matters: How values shape human progress*. New York, N.Y.: Basic Books.

58. Ponsford, M. & Glass, N. (2014). Meet the genius behind 3D printing. *CNN*. Retrieved from http://edition.cnn.com/2014/02/13/tech/innovation/the-night-i-invented-3d-printing-chuck-hall/

59. Klaben, G. (2014). Google's 8 innovation principles. *GaryKlaben.com*. Retrieved from http://garyklaben.com/2014/11/26/googles-8-innovation-principles/

60. Insead Knowledge (2014). Global Innovation Index 2014: Switzerland on top for fourth consecutive year. *Forbes*. Retrieved from http://www.forbes.com/sites/insead/2014/07/29/global-innovation-index-2014-switzerland-on-top-for-fourth-consecutive-year/

61. Gregoire, C. (2013). Why Switzerland has some of the happiest, healthiest citizens in the world. *Huffington Post*. Retrieved from http://www.huffingtonpost.com/2013/10/07/switzerland_0_n_4038031.html

62. Cold War Museum (n.d.). Fall of the Soviet Union. Retrieved from http://www.coldwar.org/articles/90s/fall_of_the_soviet_union.asp

63. Lienert, P. & Klayman, B. (2015). Race to define car of the future shifts into high gear. *Reuters*. Retrieved from http://www.reuters.com/article/usj-autos-ces-analysis-idUSKBN0KG2BS20150107

64. Larsson, R., & Finkelstein, S. (1999). Integrating strategic, organizational, and human resource perspectives on mergers and acquisitions: a case survey of synergy realization. *Organization Science, (10)*: 1–26.

65. Florida, R. (2002). *The Rise of the Creative Class: And how it's transforming work, leisure, community and everyday life*. New York, NY: Perseuls Book Group.

66. Distefano, J. & Maznevski, M. L. (2000). Creating value with diverse teams in global management. *Organisational Dynamics*. 29(1): 45–63.

67. Philipps, K. (2014). How diversity makes us smarter. *Scientific American*. Retrieved from http://www.scientificamerican.com/article/how-diversity-makes-us-smarter/?WT.mc_id=SA_SA_20140916'

68. Aldrich, H.E. & Martinez, M. A. (2015). Why aren't entrepreneurs more creative? Conditions affecting creativity and innovation in entrepreneurial activity. Chapter 25 in Shalley, C.F., Hitt, M.A., & Zhou, J. *The Oxford Handbook of Creativity, Innovation, and Entrepreneurship*. Oxford, GB: Oxford University Press.

69. Del Vicario, M., Bessi, A., Zollo, F., Petroni, F., Scala, A., Caldarelli, G., Stanley, H.E. & Quattrociocchi, W. (2016). The spreading of misinformation online. *Proceedings of National Academy of Sciences of the United States of America*. doi:10.1073/pnas.1517441113

70. Hartsell, C. (2014). Stephen Colbert buys TheSarahPalinChannel.com promises his own angry echo chamber. *The Huffington Post*. Retrieved from http://www.huffingtonpost.com/2014/07/30/colbert-buys-thesarahpalinchannel-sarah-palin_n_5633642.html

71. Chowdhry, A. (2014). Apple CEO Tim Cook is 'not satisfied' with employee diversity. *Forbes*. Retrieved from http://www.forbes.com/sites/amitchowdhry/2014/08/13/apple-ceo-tim-cook-is-not-satisfied-with-employee-diversity/ ; Kokalitcheva, K. (2015). Google's workplace diversity still has a long way to go. *Fortune*. Retrieved from http://fortune.com/2015/06/01/google-diversity-demographics/

72. Williams, M. (2015). Driving diversity at Facebook. *Facebook Newsroom.* Retrieved from https://newsroom.fb.com/news/2015/06/driving-diversity-at-facebook/

73. Peck, E. (2015). The stats on women in tech are actually getting worse. *Huffington Post.* Retrieved from http://www.huffingtonpost.com/2015/03/27/women-in-tech_n_6955940.html

74. Aldrich, H.E. & Martinez, M. A. (2015). Why aren't entrepreneurs more creative? Conditions affecting creativity and innovation in entrepreneurial activity. Chapter 25 in Shalley, C.F., Hitt, M.A., & Zhou, J. *The Oxford Handbook of Creativity, Innovation, and Entrepreneurship.* Oxford, GB: Oxford University Press.

75. Rico, R., Molleman, E., Sanchez-Manzanares, M. and Van der Vegt, G. S. (2007). The effects of diversity faultlines and team task autonomy on decision quality and social integration. *Journal of Management, 33:* 111.

76. Philipps, K. (2014). How diversity makes us smarter. *Scientific American.* Retrieved from http://www.scientificamerican.com/article/how-diversity-makes-us-smarter/?WT.mc_id=SA_SA_20140916'

77. Guterl, F. (2014). Diversity in science: Why it is essential for excellence. *Scientific American.* Retrieved from http://www.scientificamerican.com/article/diversity-in-science-why-it-is-essential-for-excellence/?WT.mc_id=SA_SA_20140916

78. Kochan, T., Bezrukova, K., Ely, R., Jackson, S., Joshi, A., Jehn, K., Leonard, J., Levine, D., & Thomas, D. (2003). The effect of diversity on business performance: Report of the diversity research network. *Human Resources Management, 42:* 3–21.

79. O'Brien, K., Reams, J. Casparo, A., Dugmore, A., Faghihimni, M., Fazey, I., Hackman, H., Manuel-Navarette, D., Marks, J., Miller, R., Raivio, K., Romero-Lnkao, P., Virji, H., Vogel, C., & Winiwarter, V. (2013). You say you want a revolution? Transforming education and capacity building in response to global change. *Environmental Science & Policy, 25:* 48–51.

80. Pentland, A. (2012). The new science of building great teams. *Harvard Business Review.* Retrieved from http://hbr.org/2012/04/the-new-science-of-building-great-teams/ar/1

81. Rico, R., Molleman, E., Sanchez-Manzanares, M. and Van der Vegt, G. S. (2007). The effects of diversity faultlines and team task autonomy on decision quality and social integration. *Journal of Management, 33:* 111.

82. Frohnen, B. (2015). Diversity as ideology: Autonomy and recognition. *The Imaginative Conservative.* Retrieved from http://www.theimaginativeconservative.org/2015/05/ideologies-in-conflict-autonomy-and-recognition-diversity.html

83. Craft, K. (2013). The thing that made *The Office* great is the same thing that killed it. *The Atlantic.* Retrieved from http://www.theatlantic.com/ entertainment/archive/2013/05/the-thing-that-made-i-the-office-i- great-is-the-same-thing-that-killed-it/275883/

84. Csikszentmihalyi, M. (1990). *Flow: The psychology of optimal experience.* New York, NY: Harper Collins.

85. Van Hoven, M. (2014). RIP cubicles: Why agencies are gaga over open- office plans. *Digiday.* Retrieved from http://digiday.com/agencies/ open-office-space-pros-cons/ ; Adams, S (2013). New research: workers hate their cubicles. *Forbes.* Retrieved from http://www.forbes.com/ sites/susanadams/2013/11/25/new-research-workers-hate-their- cubicles/ ; Green, S. (2013). Research: Cubicles Are the Absolute Worst. *Harvard Business Review.* Retrieved from https://hbr.org/2013/11/ research-cubicles-are-the-absolute-worst/

86. Sneed, A. (2015). Want to be more creative? Your personality may hold the key. *Fast Company.* Retrieved from http://www.fastcodesign .com/3047983/evidence/want-to-be-more-creative-your-personality- holds-the-key?utm_source=mailchimp&utm_medium=email&utm_ campaign=fast-company-daily-codesign&position=1&partner=newsle tter&campaign_date=06302015

87. Che, J. (2015). 6 desks that will make you happier and more productive at work. *The Huffington Post.* Retrieved from http://www.huffingtonpost. com/2015/05/06/desks-healthier-workplace_n_7162954.html

88. Architect Steven Gale, Architecture by Design.

89. Bradford, H. (2015). This is what your office could look like in 2035. *The Huffington Post.* Retrieved from http://www.huffingtonpost .com/2015/02/11/office-of-the-future_n_6649574.html

90. Kuang, C. (2013). What Google's Cafeterias Can Teach Us About School Lunches. *Fast Company.* Retrieved from http://www.fastcodesign. com/1672319/what-google-s-cafeterias-can-teach-us-about-school- lunches

91. News.com.au (2014). The perks of working at Google: Employees reveal how they lived on campus to save money. Retrieved from http://www. news.com.au/technology/online/the-perks-of-working-at-google- employees-reveal-how-they-lived-on-campus-to-save-money/story- fnjwnhzf-1227055448284

92. Reynolds, E. (2015). A peek behind the curtain at Airbnb. *News.com. au,* Retrieved from http://www.news.com.au/finance/work/at-work/ what-makes-this-company-so-unique/news-story/2336309f443c6c24 2c54e4ed7dec5ac4

93. Subraimanian, C. (2013). Google study gets employees to stop eating so many M&Ms. *Time.* Retrieved from http://newsfeed.time.com/2013/09/03/google-study-gets-employees-to-stop-eating-so-many-mms/

94. Asongu, J.J. (2007). Innovation as an argument for corporate social responsibility. *Journal of Business and Public Policy, 1*(3).

95. Axtell, C. M., Holman, D., Unsworth, K. L., Wall, T. D., Waterson, P. E., & Harrington, E. (2000). Shopfloor *innovation*: Facilitating the suggestion and implementation of ideas. *Journal of Occupational and Organizational Psychology 73*: 265–285.; Amabile, T. M. (1996). *Creativity in context.* Boulder, CO: Westview.; Oldham, G. R., & Gummings, A. (1996). Employee creativity: Personal and contextual factors at work. *Academy of Management Journal (39)*: 607–634.

96. Kleiner, A. (2001). The dilemma doctors. *Strategy + Business.* Retrieved from http://www.strategy*business*.com/article/17251?gko=444c1

97. Senge, P. (1990). *The fifth discipline.* New York, NY: Doubleday.

Chapter 7

1. Dennis, E. E. & Smyder, R. W. (1998). *Media and democracy.* New Brunswick, NJ: Transaction Publishers.

2. Karau, S. J. & Williams, K. D. (1993). Social loafing: A meta-analytic review and theoretical integration. *Journal of Personality and Social Psychology, 65*: 681–706

3. Dunbar, K. (1997). How scientists think: On-line creativity and conceptual change in science. In T. B. Ward, S. M. Smith, & J. Vaid (Eds.), *Creative thought: An investigation of conceptual structures and processes* (pp. 461–493). Washington, DC: American Psychological Association. ; West, M. A. (2002). Sparkling fountains or stagnant ponds: An interactive model of creativity and innovation implementation in work groups. *Applied Pscyhology: An International Review, 51*: 355–387

4. Macgowan, M. J. (1997). A Measure of Engagement for Social Group Work, *Journal of Social Service Research, 23*(2): 17–37

5. Hofstede, G. (1984). *Culture's consequences.* Beverly Hills: Sage Publications.

6. Franzoi, S. (2011). *Psychology, a discovery experience.* South-Western: Cengage Learning.

7. Ghoshal, S., & Moran, P. (1996). Bad for practice: A critique of the transaction cost theory. *Academy of Management Review, 21*: 13–47.

8. Axelrod R (2006). *The Evolution of Cooperation: Revised Edition.* Basic books.

9. Stout, L. (2011). *Cultivating conscience: How good laws make good people.* Princeton, NJ: Princeton University Press.

10. Ghoshal, S., & Moran, P. (1996). Bad for practice: A critique of the transaction cost theory. *Academy of Management Review, 21*: 13–47.

11. Hansen, N. (1992). Competition, trust, and reciprocity in the development of innovative regional milieu. *The Journal of the RSAI. 71*(2): 95–105.

12. Ghoshal, S., & Moran, P. (1996). Bad for practice: A critique of the transaction cost theory. *Academy of Management Review, 21*: 13–47.

13. Hardin, G. (1968). The tragedy of the commons. *Nature 162*: 1243–1248.

14. Decety, J., Jackson, P. L., Sommerville, J. A., Chaminade, T., & Meltzoff, A. N. (2004). The neural bases of cooperation and competition: an fMRI investigation. *NeuroImage, 23*(2): 744–751.

15. Shallice, T. (1998). *From neuropsychology to mental structure.* Cambridge, UK: Cambridge University Press.

16. Flavell, J. H. (1999). Cognitive development: Children's knowledge about the mind. *Annual Review of Psychology*, 50:21–45.

17. Shallice, T. (1998). *From neuropsychology to mental structure.* Cambridge, UK: Cambridge University Press.

18. Bachelard, M. (2013). Paradise on the brink of catastrophe. *Sydney Morning Herald.* Retrieved from http://www.smh.com.au/world/paradise-on-the-brink-of-catastrophe-20130504-2izj0

19. ibid.

20. Haidt, J. (2013). *The righteous mind: Why good people are divided by politics and religion.* New York, NY: Random House

21. Ridley, M. (1996). *The origins of virtue.* New York, NY: Penguin.

22. Game theory is "the study of mathematical models of conflict and cooperation between intelligent rational decision-makers." Background: Jackson M: A Brief Introduction to the Basics of Game Theory, (2011) Stanford University

23. Ridley, M. (1996). *The origins of virtue.* New York, NY: Penguin.

24. Bowen, J. R. (1986). On the political construction of tradition: Gotong royong in Indonesia. *The Journal of Asian Studies. 45*(3):545–561.

25. Ruppel, C.P. & Harrington, S.J. (2000). The relationship of communication, ethical work climate, and trust to commitment and innovation. *Journal of Business Ethics. 25*(4): 313–328.

26. Rothwell, J. T. (2010). Trust in diverse, integrated cities: A revisionist perspective. *Social Science Research Network.* Retrieved from http://papers.ssrn.com/sol3/papers.cfm?abstract_id=1358647

27. Maguire, S., Philipps, N. & Hardy, C. (2001). When silence = death, keep talking: The dynamics of trust and control in the Canadian AIDS treatment domain. *Organization Studies, 22*(2): 285–310.

28. Miles, R. E. (2007). Innovation and leadership values. *California Management Review, 50(1): 192-201.*

29. Gittins, R. (2011). Trust makes the world go around, honestly. *The Sydney Morning Herald.* Retrieved from http://www.smh.com.au/federal-politics/political-opinion/trust-makes-the-world-go-around-honestly-20110719-1hn4y

30. Penenberg, a. L. (2011). Digital oxytocin: How trust keeps Facebook, Twitter humming. *Fast Company.* Retrieved from http://www.fastcompany.com/1767125/digital-oxytocin-how-trust-keeps-facebook-twitter-humming

31. Ridley, M. (1996). *The origins of virtue.* New York, NY: Penguin.

32. Zak, P.J., & Knack, S. (1998). Trust and growth. *Social Science Research Network.* Retrieved from http://papers.ssrn.com/sol3/papers.cfm?abstract_id=136961 ; Zak, P.J.(2013). *The moral molecule.* New York, NY: Penguin.

33. Harford, T. (2007). *The undercover economist.* New York, NY: Random House.

34. Gittins, R. (2011). Trust makes the world go around, honestly. *Sydney Morning Herald.* Retrieved from http://www.smh.com.au/federal-politics/political-opinion/trust-makes-the-world-go-around-honestly-20110719-1hn4y.html

35. Haidt, J. (2013). *The righteous mind: Why good people are divided by politics and religion.* New York, NY: Vintage Books.

36. Ridley, M. (1996). *The origins of virtue.* New York, NY: Penguin.

37. Dubina, I. N. & Carayannis, E. G. (Eds.) (2016). *Creativity, innovation and entrepreneurship across cultures.* New York, NY: Springer.

38. Blomström, M., Corbett, J., Hayashi, F. & Kashyap, A. (Eds.) (2003). *Structural impediments to growth in Japan.* Chicago, CH: The University of Chicago Press.

39. Lee, C. R., Levine, T. R. & Cambra, R. (2009). Resisting compliance in the multicultural classroom. *Communication Education. 46(1)*:29–43.

40. Xu, F. (2016). Group creativity and individual creativity: A case study of the differences between Japanese and Chinese creativity. Chapter 5 in Dubina, I. N. & Carayannis, E. G. (Eds.) (2016). *Creativity, innovation and entrepreneurship across cultures.* New York, NY: Springer.

41. Singelis, T. M., Triandis, H. C., Bhawuk, D. P. S., & Gelfand, M. J. (1995). Horizontal and vertical dimensions of individualism and collectivism: A theoretical and measurement refinement. *Cross-Cultural Research, (29)*: 240–275. Retrieved from http://cmaps.cmappers.net/rid=1K9FD7G2V-1S9P23Y-TT1/Orientacion%20Cultural%20-%20Escala.pdf

42. Gorodnichenko, Y. & Roland, G. (2011). Individualism, innovation, and long-run growth. *PNAS, 108*(4): 21316–21319.

43. Axelrod R (2006). *The Evolution of Cooperation: Revised Edition.* Basic Books.

44. Based on Matt Ridley's research, Ridley, M. (1996). *The origins of virtue.* New York, NY: Penguin

45. Blakely, E.J. (2012). Survival lessons from an ancient failed city. *Citylab.* Retrieved from http://www.citylab.com/design/2012/08/survival-lessons-ancient-failed-city/2800/

46. Thomas, L. (2009). What's behind Japan's love affair with robots? *Time.* Retrieved from http://content.time.com/time/world/article/0,8599,1913913,00.html#ixzz0j5ZxitJX

47. Baer, M. (2012). Putting creativity to work: The implementation of creative ideas in organizations. *Academy of Management Journal. 55*(5): 1102–1119

48. Vroom, V. H. (1964). *Work and motivation.* Oxford, GB: Wiley.

49. Tiessen, J. H. (1998). Individualism, collectivism, and entrepreneurship: A framework for international comparative research. *Journal of Business Venturing, 12*(5): 367–384. Retrieved from http://www.sciencedirect.com/science/article/pii/S0883902697811998

50. News.com.au (2015). What does it take to be a genius? Retrieved from http://www.news.com.au/lifestyle/health/what-does-it-take-to-be-a-genius/story-fniym874-1227242190269

51. Goleman, D. (1998). *Working with emotional intelligence.* New York, NY: Bantam Books.

52. Harford, T. (2007). *The undercover economist.* New York, NY: Random House.

53. Senge, P. (1990). *The fifth discipline.* New York, NY: Doubleday. p. 24.

54. Right Management. (2012). *Employee engagement.* Retrieved from http://www.rightmanagement.com.au/thought-leadership/research/employee-engagement-benchmark-study.pdf

55. Senge, P. (1990). *The fifth discipline.* New York, NY: Doubleday. p. 24.

56. Rose, F. (1994). The civil war inside Sony. *Wired.* Retrieved from http://archive.wired.com/wired/archive/11.02/sony_pr.html

57. Hansen, M. T. (2009). *Collaboration: How leaders avoid the traps, create unity and reap big results.* Boston, MA: Harvard Business School Publishing.

58. Ridley, M. (1996). *The origins of virtue.* New York, NY: Penguin.

59. Harari, Y. N. (2014). *Sapiens: A brief history of humankind.* London: Harvill Secker.

60. Ridley, M. (1996). *The origins of virtue.* New York, NY: Penguin.

61. Breen, B. (2004). The 6 myths of creativity. *Fast Company.* Retrieved from http://www.fastcompany.com/51559/6-myths-creativity

62. Dougherty, D. (2006). Organizing for innovation in the 21st century. In S. Clegg, C. Hardy, T. Lawrence, & W. R. Nord (Eds.), *The Sage handbook of organization studies* (2nd ed.): 598–616. London: Sage. ; Schumpeter, J. A. 1942. *Capitalism, socialism, and democracy.* New York: Harper & Row.

63. Longbottom, J. (n.d.) Collaboration among mutually dependent players is required to achieve large scale change in a ground transport system. *Texas A&M University.* Retrieved from https://faculty.washington.edu/jbs/itrans/longbottom.htm

64. Murnighan. J. K.. & Conlon, D. E. (1991). The dynamics of intense work groups: A study of British string quartets. *Administrative Science Quarterly.* 36: 165–186.

65. Lewis, M. (2000). Exploring paradox: Toward a more comprehensive guide *Academy of Management Review. 23*: 750–776.

66. Longbottom, J. (n.d.) Collaboration among mutually dependent players is required to achieve large scale change in a ground transport system. *Texas A&M University.* Retrieved from https://faculty.washington.edu/jbs/itrans/longbottom.htm

67. Malone, T. (2009). All together now (or, can collective intelligence save the planet?). *MIT Sloan.* Retrieved from http://sloanreview.mit.edu/article/can-collective-intelligence-save-the-planet/

68. Puccio, G.J., Mance, M. & Murdock, M. C. (2011). *Creative Leadership.* Los Angeles, CA: Sage.

69. Grivas, C. & Puccio, G. (2012). *The innovative team.* San Francisco, CA: Jossey Bass.; Osborne, A. (1979). *Applied imagination: Principles and procedures for creative thinking.* Charles Scribner's Sons.

70. Hill, L. (2015). How to manage for collective creativity. *TEDx.* Retrieved from http://www.ted.com/talks/linda_hill_how_to_manage_for_collective_creativity/transcript?language=en

71. Moore, J. (1993). Predators and prey: A new ecology of competition. *Harvard Business Review.* Retrieved from https://hbr.org/1993/05/predators-and-prey-a-new-ecology-of-competition/ar/1

72. Lin, Lin, H.E., McDonough, E.H, Lin, S.J., & Lin, C. Y. Y. (2013). Managing the exploitation/exploration paradox: The role of a learning capability and innovation ambidexterity. *Journal of Productive Innovation Management, 30*(2): 262–278.

73. Keeley, L. (2015). Business ecosystems come of age. *Deloitte University Press,* Retrieved from http://d27n205l7rookf.cloudfront.net/wp-content/uploads/2015/04/DUP_1048-Business-ecosystems-come-of-age_MASTER_FINAL.pdf

Chapter 8

1. Silver, N. (2012). *The signal and the noise: Why so many predictions fail – but some don't.* New York, NY: Penguin. Loc. 212.

2. McCoy, S. (2015). The American dream is suffering, but Americans are satisfied: 15 charts. *The Atlantic*. Retrieved from http://www.theatlantic. com/politics/archive/2015/07/american-dream-suffering/397475/

3. World Economic Forum (2011). The Global Competitiveness Report 2011–2012, table 5

4. Lazonick, W. (2010). Innovative business models and varieties of capitalism: Financialization of the U.S. corporation. *Business History Review*, 84(04), 675-702. http://dx.doi.org/10.1017/s0007680500001987

5. Cowen, T. (2011). *The great stagnation: How America ate all the low-hanging fruit of modern history, got sick, and will (eventually) feel better.* New York, NY: Dutton.

6. Pisano, G. P., & Shih, W. C. (2012). Does America Really Need Manufacturing? *Harvard Business Review* 90(3).

7. Wessner, C. & Wolff, A. W. (Eds) (2012). Rising to the challenge: US innovation policy of the global economy. *National Research Council (US) Committee on Comparative National Innovation Policies: Best Practice for the 21st Century*. Washington, DC: National Academies Press.

8. Vest, C. (2011). Universities and the U.S. innovation system. Building the 21st Century: U.S. - China Cooperation on Science, Technology, and Innovation. Wessner, C. (ed)., Washington, DC: The National Academies Press.

9. Ostrom, E. (2005). *Understanding institutional diversity*. Ewing, N. J.: Princeton University Press.

10. Bettencourt, L. M. A., Lobo, J., Helbing, D., Kuhnert, C., and West, G. B. (2007). Growth, innovation, scaling, and the pace of life in cities. *Proceedings of the National Academy of Science*, 104(17): 7301–7306.; Johnson, B. (n.d.) Great horse manure crisis of 1894. *Historic UK*. Retrieved from http:// www.historic-uk.com/HistoryUK/HistoryofBritain/Great-Horse-Manure-Crisis-of-1894/

11. Johnson, S. (2014). How we got to now with Steven Johnson. *PBS*. Retrieved from https://www.youtube.com/watch?v=keKPrLYxYgA

12. Greene, D. (1997). Renewing Tocqueville's American tour. *The New York Times*. Retrieved from http://www.nytimes. com/1997/04/20/nyregion/renewing-tocqueville-s-american-tour. html?pagewanted=all&src=pm

13. Keller, J. (2015). What makes Americans so optimistic? *The Atlantic*. Retrieved from http://www.theatlantic.com/politics/archive/2015/03/ the-american-ethic-and-the-spirit-of-optimism/388538/

14. Gao, G. (2015). How do Americans stand out from the rest of the world? *Pew Research Center*. Retrieved from http://www.pewresearch.org/fact-

tank/2015/03/12/how-do-americans-stand-out-from-the-rest-of-the-world/

15. Keller, J. (2015). What makes Americans so optimistic? *The Atlantic*. Retrieved from http://www.theatlantic.com/politics/archive/2015/03/the-american-ethic-and-the-spirit-of-optimism/388538/

16. Sreeharsha,V. (2013).The world's 10 most innovative companies in South America. *Fast Company*. Retrieved from http://www.fastcompany.com/most-innovative-companies/2013/industry/south-america ; Weiss, J. (2014). The world's 10 most innovative companies in South America. *Fast Company*. Retrieved from http://www.fastcompany.com/3026319/most-innovative-companies-2014/the-worlds-top-10-most-innovative-companies-in-south-america

17. Adams, T., Anderson, L., Turner, M., & Armstrong, J. (2011). Coping through a disaster: Lessons from Hurricane Katrina. *Journal of Homeland Security and Emergency Management, 8*(1): 1–11.

18. Tierney, K.J., Lindell, M.K., & Perry, R.W. (2001). *Facing the unexpected: Disaster preparedness and responses in the United States*. Washington, DC: John Henry Press.; Bourque, L.B., Russell, L.A., & Goltz, J.D. (1993). Human behavior during and immediately after the earthquake. In P. Bolton (Ed.), *The Loma Prieta, California, Earthquake of October 17, 1989 – Public Response* (pp.3–22). Washington, DC: U.S. Geological Survey Professional Paper 1553-B.

19. Lazarus, R.S. & Folkman, S. (1984). *Stress, appraisal, and coping*. New York, NY: Springer.

20. Carver, M.F., Scheier, J.K., & Weintraub, J.K. (1989). Assessing coping strategies: A theoretically based approach. *Journal of Personality and Social Psychology, 26*(2): 267–283.

21. Oxford Dictionary. Retrieved from http://www.oxforddictionaries.com/definition/english/optimism

22. Merriam-Webster Dictionary. Retrieved from http://www.merriam-webster.com/dictionary/optimism

23. Aspinwall, L. G. & Staudinger, U. M. (Eds) (2003). *A psychology of human strengths: Fundamental questions and future directions for a positive psychology*. Washington, DC: American Psychological Association. p 12.

24. ibid.

25. Carver, C. S., & Scheier, M. E (1990). Principles of self-regulation: Action and emotion. In E. T. Higgins & R. M. Sorrentino (Eds.), *Handbook of motivation and cognition, Volume 2*. (pp. 3–52). New York, NY: Guilford Press.

26. Aspinwall, L. G., Richter, L., & Hoffman, R. R. (2001). Understanding how optimism "works": An examination of optimists' adaptive moderation of belief and behavior. In E. C. Chang (Ed.), *Optimism and*

pessimism: Theory, research, and practice (pp. 217–238). Washington, DC: American Psychological Association.

27. Eg Staudinger, U. M., Marsiske, M., & Baltes, P. B. (1995). Resilience and reserve capacity in later adulthood: Potentials and limits of development across the life span. In D. Cicchetti & D. Cohen (Eds.), *Developmental psychopathology* (Vol. 2: Risk, disorder, and adaptation, pp. 801–847). New York: Wiley

28. Marshall, G. N., Lang, E. L. (1990). Optimism, self-mastery and symptoms of depression in women professionals. *Journal of Personality and Social Psychology, 59*(1): 132–139.

29. Webber, R. (2010). Make your own luck: Five principles for making the most of life's twists and turns. *Psychology Today.* Retrieved from https://www.psychologytoday.com/articles/201005/make-your-own-luck

30. World Health Organization (n.d.). Depression. *WHO Media Centre.* Retrieved from http://www.who.int/mediacentre/factsheets/fs369/en/

31. Adams, T., Anderson, L., Turner, M., & Armstrong, J. (2011). Coping through a disaster: Lessons from Hurricane Katrina. *Journal of Homeland Security and Emergency Management, 8*(1): 1–11.

32. Manzini, E. & Till, J. eds (2015). *Cultures of resilience: Ideas.* London, UK: Hato Press. Retrieved from http://www.culturesofresilience.org/wordpress/?page_id=2

33. Poole, M. S. & Van de Ven, A. H. (1989). Using paradox to build management and organization theories. *Academy of Management Review. 14*(4): 562–578.

34. Acemoglu, D. Robinson, J. A. (2012). *Why nations fail: The origins of power, prosperity and poverty.* New York, NY: Random House.

35. University of London (n.d.). Cultures of resilience *UAS.* Retrieved from *http://*www.culturesofresilience.org/wordpress/?page_id=2

36. The Bible. See the book of Job, particularly Job 1:1-3 and Job 42: 10-12-13.

37. Jung, C. G. (2010). *Answers to Job* (English version). Princeton University Press. Original: Antwort auf Hiob Carl Gustav Jung (1952).

38. *Road traffic deaths.* (2016). *World Health Organization.* Retrieved 5 May 2016, from http://www.who.int/gho/road_safety/mortality/en/

39. WHO (2013). Road safety: Estimated road traffic death rate (per 100,000 population), 2010. Retrieved from http://gamapserver.who.int/gho/interactive_charts/road_safety/road_traffic_deaths2/atlas.html

40. Tedeschi, R. G., Park, C. L., & Calhoun, L. G. (1998). *Posttraumatic growth: Positive transformations in the aftermath of crisis.* Mahwah, NJ: Lawrence Erlbaum Associates Publishers.; Kaufman, S. B. & Gregoire, C. (2015).

Wired to create: Unravelling the mysteries of the creative mind. New York, NY: Perigee Random House LLC.

41. Haidt, J. (2006). *The happiness hypothesis: Finding modern truth in ancient wisdom.* New York, NY: Basic Books. p. 200

42. Melnick, M. (2011). Study: Religious folks have a sunnier outlook. *Time.* Retrieved from http://healthland.time.com/2011/11/11/study-religious-folks-have-a-sunnier-outlook/

43. Hawking, S. (1994). *Black holes and baby universes and other essays.* New York, NY: Bantam Books.

44. Bénabou, R., & Tirole (2006). Incentives and prosocial behaviour. *Journal of Political Economy, 112*(4): 848–887.; Bénabou, R., & Tirole (2011). Laws and norms. *National Bureau of Economic Research Working Paper 17579.* Cambridge, MA: 2011

45. Bénabou, R., Ticchi, D. & Vindigni, A. (2013). Forbidden fruits: The political economy of science, religion and growth. *Princeton University.* Retrieved from http://www.princeton.edu/~rbenabou/papers/Religion%20December%201i_snd1.pdf

46. ibid.

47. Western Reserve University (2016). The conflict between science and religion lies in our brain, researchers say. *Phys Org.* Retrieved from http://phys.org/news/2016-03-conflict-science-religion-lies-brains.html#jCp

48. Keen, S. (1994). *Hymns to an unknown God: Awakening the spirit in everyday life.* New York, NY: Bantam Books.

49. Haidt, J. (2013). *The righteous mind: Why good people are divided by politics and religion.* New York, NY: Random House p313

50. Dawkins, R. (2006). *The Selfish Gene* (30th Anniversary edition) 2006.; Axelrod R (2006). The Evolution of Cooperation: Revised Edition Basic Books. Foreword by Richard Dawkins.

51. Seligman, M. E. P. (2006). *Learned optimism: How to change your mind and your life.* New York, NY: Vintage.; Peterson, C., Maier, S. P., Seligman, M. E. P. (1995). *Learned helplessness: Theory for the age of personal control.* Oxford, GB: Oxford University Press.

52. Seligman, M. E. P. (1972). Learned helplessness. *Annual Review of Medicine, 23*(1): 407–412.

53. Bénabou, R., Ticchi, D. & Vindigni, A. (2013). Forbidden fruits: The political economy of science, religion and growth. *Princeton University.* Retrieved from http://www.princeton.edu/~rbenabou/papers/Religion%20December%201i_snd1.pdf

54. Swift, R. (1990). Fundamentalism: Reaching for certainty. *New Internationalist. Issue 210.* Retrieved from http://newint.org/features/1990/08/05/keynote/

55. Heath, C., Dunning, D. & Suls, J./ M. (2005). Ignorance is bliss. *The Guardian.* Retrieved from http://www.theguardian.com/money/2005/dec/03/workandcareers.careers

56. Dye, L. (n.d.). Study: Self-images often erroneously inflated. *ABC News.* Retrieved from http://abcnews.go.com/Technology/DyeHard/story?id=1291826

57. ibid.

58. ibid.

59. Grabher, G. and Stark, D. (1997). Organizing diversity: Evolutionary theory, network analysis and postsocialism, *Regional Studies 31*, 533–544.

60. Feldman & Pentland (2003). Reconceptualizing organizational routines as a source of flexibility and change *Administrative Science Quarterly, 48* (1): 94–118

61. Gilbert, J. (2013). Paraguayan landfill orchestra makes sweet music from rubbish. *The Guardian.* Retrieved from http://theguardian.com/world/2013/apr/26/paraguayan-landfill-orchestra-music
Retrieved from http://www.theguardian.com/world/2013/apr/26/paraguayan-landfill-orchestra-music.

62. Schumpeter, J. A. (1942). *Capitalism, socialism, and democracy.* New York: Harper & Row.

63. Weick, K. E., Sutcliffe, K. M. & Obstfeld, D. (2005). Organizing and the process of sensemaking. *Organization Science. 16*(4):409–421.

64. Lotto, B. (n.d.). Illusions. *Lotto Labs.* Retrieved from http://www.lottolab.org/articles/illusionsoflight.asp

65. Gonzales, L. (2004). *Deep survival: Who lives, who dies, and why.* New York, NY: W.W. Norton & Company.'

66. Wilson, M. (2015). Why Samsung design stinks: Blame Steve Jobs syndrome. *Fast Company.* Retrieved from http://www.fastcodesign.com/3042408/why-samsung-design-stinks

67. Turner, S. F. & Fern, M. J. (2012). Examining the stability and variability of routine performances: The effects of experiences and context change. *Journal of Management Studies. 49*(8): 1407–1434.

68. Eg. Collins & Porras (1994). *Built to last: Successful habits of visionary companies.* March (1991). Exploration and exploitation in organisational learning. *Organization Science. 2*(1): 71–87.; Leventhal and March (1993). The myopia of learning. *Strategic Management Journal. 14*(S2): 95–112.; Foster, R. N., & Kaplan, S. (2001). *Creative destruction.* New

Jersey, Financial Times Prentice Hall.; Peters, T. J., & Waterman Jr., R. H. (1982). How the best-run companies turn so-so performers into big winners. *Management Review,* 71(11): 8–16.; Devins, G. & Kahr, C. (2010). Structuring ambidextrous organisations: Exploitation and exploration as a key from long-term success. in Stadtler, L, Schmitt, A. Kalrner, P. & Straub, T. (2012), *More than bricks in the wall: Organizational perspectives for sustainable success.* Wiesbaden, GER: Gabler Verlag.

69. Tushman, M. L. & O'Reilly, C. A. (1996). Ambidextrous organizations: managing evolutionary and revolutionary change. *California Management Review, 38*(4):8–30.

70. Kirton (1976). Adaptors and innovators: A description and measure. *Journal of Applied Psychology. 61*(5): 622–629.

71. O'Brien, K., Reams, J. Casparo, A., Dugmore, A., Faghihimni, M., Fazey, I., Hackman, H., Manuel-Navarette, D., Marks, J., Miller, R., Raivio, K., Romero-Lnkao, P., Virji, H., Vogel, C. & Winiwarter, V. (2013). You say you want a revolution? Transforming education and capacity building in response to global change. *Environmental Science & Policy 28*:48–51.

Chapter 9

1. Bromwich, D.H.; Nicolas, J.P.; Monaghan, A.J.; Lazzara, M.A.; Keller, L.M.; Weidner, G.A.; Wilson, A.B. (2013). Central West Antarctica among the most rapidly warming regions on Earth. *Nature Geoscience. 6:* 139–145.

2. Norris, P. (2010). *Watching earth from space: How surveillance helps us – and harms us.* Chichester, UK: Praxis Publishing.

3. Kida, T. E. (2006). *Don't believe everything you think: The 6 basic mistakes we make in thinking.* New York, NY: Prometheus Books.

4. Fowler, J. W. (1981). *Stages of faith.* New York, NY: Harper & Row.

5. Note that the labels for the purposes of making a link to innovation are our labels, not Fowler's

6. Del Vicario, M., Bessi, A., Zollo, F., Petroni, F., Scala, A., Caldarelli, G., Stanley, H.E. & Quattrociocchi, W. (2016). The spreading of misinformation online. *Proceedings of National Academy of Sciences of the United States of America*

7. ibid.

8. Stallen, M. Smidts, A. & Sanfey, A. (2013). Peer influence: Neural mechanisms underlying in-group conformity. *Frontiers in Human Science, 7:* 50. Retrieved from http://www.ncbi.nlm.nih.gov/pmc/articles/PMC3591747/

9. The Situationist Staff (2008). Solomon Asch's conformity experiment…Today. *The Situationist.* Retrieved from https://

thesituationist.wordpress.com/2008/06/11/solomon-aschs-conformity-experiment-today/

10. Heffernan, M. (2012). *Wilful blindness: Why we ignore the obvious at our peril.* New York, NY: Walker & Company.

11. Kenyon, G. (2016). The man who studies the spread of ignorance. *BBC.* Retrieved from http://www.bbc.com/future/story/20160105-the-man-who-studies-the-spread-of-ignorance

12. Macwilliams, M. (2016). The weird trait that predicts whether you're a trump supporter. *Political Science.*http://www.politico.com/magazine/story/2016/01/donald-trump-2016-authoritarian-213533

13. Lakoff, G. (2016). Why Trump? *The Huffington Post.* Retrieved from http://www.huffingtonpost.com/george-lakoff/why-trump_1_b_9372450.html

14. Edwards-Levy, A. (2016). The difference between Clinton and Trump supporters in one chart. *The Huffington Post.* Retrieved from http://www.huffingtonpost.com.au/entry/clinton-trump-optimism_us_56fd4151e4b0daf53aeef005?section=australia&utm_hp_ref=politics

15. Konnikova, M. (2016). *The confidence game: Why we fall for it… every time.* New York, NY: Viking.

16. Viser, M. (2015). For presidential hopefuls, simpler language resonates. *Boston Globe.* Retrieved from https://www.bostonglobe.com/news/politics/2015/10/20/donald-trump-and-ben-carson-speak-grade-school-level-that-today-voters-can-quickly-grasp/LUCBY6uwQAxiLvvXbVTSUN/story.html

17. Česká inovace' (n.d). Retrieved from http://www.ceskainovace.cz/en/

18. Friere, P. (2007). *Pedagogy of the oppressed.* New York, NY: Continuum.

19. Ferguson, N. (2011). *The 6 killer apps of prosperity.* TED Talk. Retrieved from https://www.ted.com/talks/niall_ferguson_the_6_killer_apps_of_prosperity?language=en

20. Withnall, A. (2014) North Korean defector says she believed Kim Jong-il was a god who could read her mind http://www.independent.co.uk/news/north-korean-defector-says-she-believed-kim-jong-il-was-a-god-who-could-read-her-mind-9251983.html

21. Davis, W. (2012). *Wayfinders.* Western Australia, AUS: The University of Western Australia Press.

22. Haidt, J. (2013). *The righteous mind: Why good people are divided by politics and religion.* New York, NY: Random House p313

23. Kohlberg, L. (1981). *Essays on Moral Development, Vol. I: The Philosophy of Moral Development.* San Francisco, CA: Harper & Row

24. Vallely P: (2011) How Steve Jobs reinvented desire. *The Independent.* Retrieved from http://www.independent.co.uk/voices/commentators/paul-vallely-how-steve-jobs-reinvented-desire-2367793.html

25. Baptist World Aid (2015). *The Australian Fashion Report 2015*. Retrieved from http://www.baptistworldaid.org.au/assets/Be-Fair-Section/FashionReport.pdf

26. Ethisphere (2015). World's Most Ethical Companies® Honorees. Retrieved from http://worldsmostethicalcompanies.ethisphere.com/honorees/

27. Keen, S. (1994). *Hymns to an unknown God: Awakening the spirit in everyday life*. New York, NY: Bantam Books.

28. Riley, A. (2013). *Secrets of the superbrands*. London, GB: BBC.

29. Lakoff, G. (2004). *Don't think of an elephant!: Know your values and frame the debate*. White River Junction, VR: Chelsea Green Publishing.

30. Orr, R. (2016). *Virtual reality bites back*. The University of Melbourne. Retrieved from https://pursuit.unimelb.edu.au/articles/virtual-reality-bites-back

31. Armstrong, K. (1993). *A history of God: The 4,000-year quest of Judaism, Christianity and Islam*. New York, NY: Random House.

32. Davis, W. (2012). *Wayfinders*. Western Australia, AUS: The University of Western Australia Press.

33. Fowler, J. W. (1981). *Stages of faith*. New York, NY: Harper & Row.

34. Klein, K. J. & Sorra, J. S. (1996). The challenge of innovation implementation, *The Academy of Management Review, 21*(4): 1055–1080.

35. Gioia, D. A., Patvardhan, S. D., Hamilton, A. L., & Corley, K. G. (2013). Organizational identity formation and change. *The Academy of Management Annals, 7*(1): 123–193.

36. E.g. Hofstede, G., Neuijen, B., Ohayv, D. V. & Sanders, G. (1990). Measuring organizational cultures: A qualitative and quantitative study across twenty cases. *Administrative Science Quarterly, 35*(2): 286–316.

37. Tushman, M. L. & O'Reilly, C. A. (1997). *Winning through innovation: A practical guide to leading organizational change and renewal*. Boston, MA: Harvard Business School Press.

38. Ekvall, G. (1996). Organizational climate for creativity and innovation. *European Journal of Work and Organizational Psychology. 5*(1): 105–123.

39. Keen, S. (1994). *Hymns to an unknown God: Awakening the spirit in everyday life*. New York, NY: Bantam Books.

40. ibid.

Chapter 10

1. Brown, K., O'Neill, S. & Fabricius, C. (2013). Social science understandings of transformation. *UNESCO World Social Science Report*. Paris, FRA: UNESCO Publishing.

2. Mackay, J. & Sisodia, R. (2014). *Conscious capitalism: Liberating the heroic spirit of business.* New York, NY: Harvard Business Review Press.

3. Meadows, D. Randers, J. & Meadows, D. (2004). *Limits to Growth: The 30-Year Update.* Vermont: Chelsea Green Publishing Company.

4. McCloskey, D. (2010). *Bourgeois dignity: Why economics can't explain the modern world.* Chicago: University of Chicago Press.

5. Reich, R. (2012). *Beyond outrage: What has gone wrong with our economy and our democracy, and how to fix it.* New York, NY: Random Books.

6. Florida, *R.,* Mellander, C. & King, K. (2015). *The Global Creativity Index 2015.* Toronto, CA: Martin Prosperity Institute. p. 8.

7. ibid.

8. ibid.

9. Frey, C.B. (2014). How 21st-century cities can avoid the fate of 20th-century Detroit. *Scientific American.* Retrieved from http://www.scientificamerican.com/article/how-21st-century-cities-can-avoid-the-fate-of-20th-century-detroit/. Also: http://www.scientificamerican.com/article/will-automation-take-our-jobs/

10. Davis, W. (2012). *Wayfinders.* Western Australia, AUS: The University of Western Australia Press.

11. Diamond, J. (2012). *The world until yesterday: What can we learn from traditional societies?* London, UK: Viking.

12. Sachs (2000). Notes on a new sociology of economic development. Ch 3 in Harrison, L. E. & Huntington, S. P. (Eds.) (2000), *Culture matters: How values shape human progress.* New York, NY: Basic Books. (p.30)

13. Rosling, H. (2010). *200 countries, 200 years, 4 minutes: The joy of stats.* [Video file]. Retrieved from https://www.youtube.com/watch?v=jbkSRLYSojo

14. Rifkin, J. (2015). *The zero marginal cost society: The internet of things, the collaborative commons, and the eclipse of capitalism.* New York, NY: St. Martin's Press.

15. Liu, M. M., Zhang, J. A. and Hu, B. (2006). Domestic VCs Versus Foreign VCs: A Close Look at the Chinese Venture Capital Industry. *International Journal of Technology Management, 34* (1–2), 161–84.; Wright, M., Pruthi S., & Lockett, A. (2005). International Venture Capital Research: From Cross-Country Comparisons to Crossing Countries. *International Journal of Management Reviews, 7* (3), 135–65.

16. Al Abdullah, Queen Rania (2015). What good is technological progress without moral progress? *Huffington Post,* Retrieved from http://www.huffingtonpost.com/rania-al-abdullah/what-good-is-technological-progress-without-moral-progress_b_7217068.html

17. Diamandis, P. & Kotler, S. (2012). *Abundance*. New York: Free Press.

18. Miles, K. (2015). We need the liberal arts more than ever in today's digital world, Fareed Zakaria says. *The World Post*. Retrieved from http://www.huffingtonpost.com/2015/04/20/digital-liberal-arts-zakaria_n_7048496.html

19. Malone, T (2009). All together now (or, can collective intelligence save the planet?). *MIT Sloan Management Review*. Retrieved from http://sloanreview.mit.edu/article/can-collective-intelligence-save-the-planet

20. Malone, T (2004). *The future of work: How the new order of business will shape your organization, your management style, and your life*. Cambridge, MA: Harvard Business School Press.

21. Diamandis, P., & Kotler, S. (2012). *Abundance*. New York, NY: Free Press.

22. Schwab, K. (2016). *The fourth industrial revolution*. Geneva, Switzerland: World Economic Forum.

23. Buluswar, S. Friedman, Z., Mehta, P., Mitra, S., & Sathre, R. (2014). *50 breakthroughs: Critical scientific and technological advances needed for sustainable global development*. Berkeley, CA: Institute for Transformative Technologies, Lawrence Berkeley National Lab.

24. Diamandis, P., & Kotler, S. (2012). *Abundance*. New York: Free Press.

25. Abeyta, L. (2015). Smart phones are equalising who can access knowledge. *The Huffington Post*. Retrieved from http://www.huffingtonpost.com/lisa-abeyta/smart-phones-are-equalizi_b_7200660.html

26. Tucker, E. (2015). Using data to improve how we serve the world's poor. *Huffington Post*. Retrieved from http://www.huffingtonpost.com/emily-tucker/using-data-to-improve-how_b_7117908.html

27. Tweedie, N. (2013). Bill Gates interview: I have no use for money. This is God's work. *The Telegraph*. Retrieved from http://www.telegraph.co.uk/technology/bill-gates/9812672/Bill-Gates-interview-I-have-no-use-for-money.-This-is-Gods-work.html

28. Whitney, L. (2014). Bill and Melinda Gates top Forbes list as most philanthropic Americans. *Cnet*. Retrieved from http://www.cnet.com/au/news/bill-and-melinda-gates-top-forbes-list-as-most-philanthropic-americans/

29. Bort, J. (2015). Bill Gates talks about the heartbreaking moment that turned him to philanthropy. *Business Insider*. Retrieved from http://www.businessinsider.com.au/why-bill-gates-became-a-philanthropist-2015-1

30. Wadhwa, V. (2013). Corruption in business and the importance of ethics. *Wall Street Journal*. Retrieved from http://wadhwa.com/2013/06/29/wall-street-journal-corruption-in-business-and-the-importance-of-ethics/

31. Gruber, H. E. (1989). Creativity and human survival, In D. Wallace and H.E. Gruber (Eds.). *Creative people at work*. New York, NY: Oxford University Press.
32. Mahony, A. (2014). The day the Pintupi Nine entered the modern world. *BBC News*. Retrieved from http://www.bbc.com/news/magazine-30500591
33. ABC (2003). *One Red Blood*. ABC Broadcasting Corporation.
34. Benioff, M. (2016). Businesses are the greatest platforms for change. *Huff Post World Economic Forum*. Retrieved from http://www.huffingtonpost.com/marc-benioff/businesses-are-the-greate_b_8993240.html
35. Holk Henriksen, B. & Lassenius, F. (2014). *The mind of a leader I: The complete transcripts*. UK: Andrews UK Limited.
36. Thibodeau, P. H., & Boroditsky, L. (2011). Metaphors we think with: The role of metaphor in Reasoning. *Creative Commons*. Retrieved from http://lera.ucsd.edu/papers/crime-metaphors.pdf
37. Inglis-Arkell, E.(2013). This study shows how a good metaphor can change the world. *IO9*. Retrieved from http://io9.gizmodo.com/this-study-shows-how-a-good-metaphor-can-change-the-wor-1482482320

INDEX

MORE WAYS TO GET INNOVATIVE

Andrew and Gaia Grant and their team at Tirian International have designed a series of interactive learning and development programs that help to develop creative thinking and innovation for building a culture that supports growth. A selection of the programs on offer includes:

Keynote

The Innovation Race: Who wins, who loses, who gets eliminated – and why we need to change the game

Why have some great countries, cultures and companies charged ahead at the forefront of innovation, while others have struggled to survive? Who are the most innovative cultures in the world and why? And what does this mean for organisations today and for the race to survive and thrive?

Through drawing out fascinating insights from different cultures around the world this keynote presentation reveals principles we can all use to improve the way we think about innovation and ultimately change the game. Fast-paced entertainment and humor are blended with deep social and anthropological research, with profound implications for facing contemporary challenges. Along the way participants discover the enduring cultural traits that foster true creative thinking and innovation. They identify how organisational culture can shape creative and innovative thinking – and in turn how creative thinking can shape organisational culture for ultimate success.

Focus Session 1: How to survive the innovation race and stay ahead

Tools for creating a competitive advantage

This session provides clues for building a solid culture of innovation through identifying the roadblocks, detours and fast forward strategies to stay ahead of the game. Parallels are drawn with organisation survival and success, identifying the traits of ordinary and extra-ordinary organisations.

Focus Session 2: How to create a sustainable culture for innovation

Tools for sustainable innovation

How often do we stop to think about how and why we innovate? Are we in danger of innovating for the sake of innovating? And what does all this mean for contemporary organisations? This session challenges the typical assumption that innovation is about designing bigger, better, and faster products and services – and suggests, instead, that it should be about creative culture change. By turning the standard 'success' paradigm upside down, this session examines the real meaning of progress, and demonstrate how it is possible to transform an organisation at the most fundamental levels in a socially responsible way.

Simulation

The *Amazing* Innovation Race

An engaging around-the-world race challenge with multiple case studies to explore the roots and future of how to create a culture that supports innovation (uses gamification to explore culture change paradoxes and principles and including the unique 'polar positioning' tool).

Workshops

PDI (Purpose Driven Innovation) Program Suite

PDI MODULE 1: Clarifying and Prioritising Values (DIAGNOSTIC TOOL)

A diagnostic tool for identifying the effectiveness of current values, and re-prioritizing values for future sustainability and success.

Participants will walk away with a clearer understanding of current and desired values PLUS a new values prioritisation template

PDI MODULE 2: Aligning Vision, Mission and Values for Purpose-Driven Innovation (STRATEGIC PLAN)

A diagnostic tool for identifying the blocks to creative thinking and innovation in individuals, teams, organizations and cultures.

Participants will walk away with a more aligned vision and mission according to their newly prioritised values PLUS a strategy for implementing a purpose-driven mission

PDI MODULE 3: Leading a culture for innovation (CULTURE CHANGE PLAN)

An interactive workshop that helps leaders reflect on their own leadership style, and how this impacts their culture. Assessing the current state and action plans for transitioning to a desired state. In the process leaders learn how to change a culture to learn what sort of climate fosters or impedes innovation. (Uses the unique 'polar positioning' tool.)

Participants will walk away with a model for culture change that will support creative thinking and innovation PLUS the application of a diagnostic tool to help them assess their own culture and know how to target proactive change processes.

CSI (Creative Scene Investigation) Program Suite

CSI MODULE 1: CSI Who Killed Creativity? (DIAGNOSTIC TOOL)

A diagnostic tool for identifying the blocks to creative thinking and innovation in individuals, teams, organisations and cultures (Simulation board game).

Participants will walk away with an understanding of why creativity has difficulty flourishing in a typical work environment PLUS learn the traits of a creative mindset and an innovative work environment.

CSI MODULE 2: The 7 Creative Thinking Strategies
(PRACTICAL STRATEGIES)

How to rescue creative thinking and problem solving — 7 enabling design thinking strategies for creative thinking success (workshop with real workplace case studies).

Participants will walk away with practical tools for coming up with workable ideas and implementable solutions faster PLUS one or more business issues solved using the tools.

CSI MODULE 3: Innovative Team Actions
(TEAM PROFILING)

Identifying individual strengths within a team to ensure a team is able to innovate together to maximise potential (workshop with profiling).

Participants will walk away with an efficient high performing team able to maximise individual strengths and collaborate effectively to come up with innovative new ideas and solutions PLUS one or more practical new business applications ready for implementation.

CSI MODULE 4: Innovative Organization Applications
(INNOVATION MODEL)

A model for systematising innovation in the organisation (workshop with real workplace case studies).

Participants will walk away with a blueprint for organisational innovation that is responsive to customer needs PLUS one or more innovation models for the organisation ready for execution.

CSI MODULE 5: Organization Implementation
(INNOVATION PROCESS)

'The Chocolate Factory' simulation provides the opportunity to practice creative thinking tools and examine how customer centric innovation can be systematized through the organization (simulation).

Participants will walk away with an understanding of innovative process redesign PLUS a recommended solution for an improvement to a practical workplace challenge.

Assessment
Innovation Climate Indicator (ICI)

An organisational assessment that measures preparedness for change and readiness for growth. Identifies the paradoxical positions that indicate whether an organization is prepared for innovation and growth, and where they can focus for development.

Visit www.the-innovation-race.com for more information

Connect
with WILEY ▶▶▶

WILEY

Browse and purchase the full range of Wiley publications on our official website.

www.wiley.com

Check out the Wiley blog for news, articles and information from Wiley and our authors.

www.wileybizaus.com

Join the conversation on Twitter and keep up to date on the latest news and events in business.

@WileyBizAus

Sign up for Wiley newsletters to learn about our latest publications, upcoming events and conferences, and discounts available to our customers.

www.wiley.com/email

Wiley titles are also produced in e-book formats. Available from all good retailers.

Learn more with practical advice from our experts